I0815436

FORTY-THREE WAYS OF LOOKING AT HEMINGWAY

BOOKS BY JEFFREY MEYERS

BIOGRAPHY

A Fever at the Core: The Idealist in Politics

Married to Genius

Katherine Mansfield

Hemingway

Manic Power: Robert Lowell and His Circle

D. H. Lawrence

Joseph Conrad

Edgar Allan Poe: His Life and Legacy

Scott Fitzgerald

Edmund Wilson

Robert Frost

Privileged Moments: Encounters with Writers

Orwell: Wintry Conscience of a Generation

Somerset Maugham

Samuel Johnson: The Struggle

The Genius and the Goddess: Arthur Miller and Marilyn Monroe

Remembering Iris Murdoch: Letters and Interviews, with a Memoir

Robert Lowell in Love

Resurrections: Authors, Heroes—and a Spy

Parallel Lives: From Freud and Mann to Arbus and Plath

CRITICISM

Hemingway: The Critical Heritage

Hemingway: Life into Art

ART

Painting and the Novel

The Enemy: A Biography of Wyndham Lewis

Impressionist Quartet: The Intimate Genius of Manet and Morisot, Degas and Cassatt

Modigliani

The Mystery of the Real: Letters of the Canadian Artist Alex Colville and Biographer Jeffrey Meyers. Edited, with Four Essays, by Jeffrey Meyers

FILM

Bogart: A Life in Hollywood

Gary Cooper: American Hero

Inherited Risk: Errol and Sean Flynn in Hollywood and Vietnam

John Huston: Courage and Art

FORTY-THREE WAYS OF LOOKING AT HEMINGWAY

JEFFREY MEYERS

Louisiana State University Press ||| Baton Rouge

Published with the assistance of the V. Ray Cardozier Fund

Published by Louisiana State University Press
lsupress.org

Copyright © 2025 by Jeffrey Meyers
All rights reserved. Except in the case of brief quotations used in articles or reviews, no part of this publication may be reproduced or transmitted in any format or by any means without written permission of Louisiana State University Press.

Manufactured in the United States of America
First printing

Designer: Barbara Neely Bourgoyne
Typeface: Whitman
Printer and binder: Sheridan Books

Cover photograph: Hemingway's author photo from the first edition of *For Whom the Bell Tolls*, taken by Lloyd Arnold in 1939. Library of Congress Prints and Photographs Division.

Earlier versions of these chapters have appeared in *American Notes & Queries*, *Antioch Review*, *The Article* (London), *Chronicles*, *Commonweal*, *Hemingway Review*, *London Magazine*, *Michigan Quarterly Review*, *New Criterion*, *Notes on Contemporary Literature*, *Papers on Language & Literature*, *Salmagundi*, *Sewanee Review*, *Style*, *Times Literary Supplement*, *Virginia Quarterly Review* and *Wall Street Journal*.

LIBRARY OF CONGRESS CATALOGING-IN-PUBLICATION DATA
Names: Meyers, Jeffrey author
Title: Forty-three ways of looking at Hemingway / Jeffrey Meyers.
Description: Baton Rouge : Louisiana State University Press, [2025] |
Includes bibliographical references and index
Identifiers: LCCN 2025018363 (print) | LCCN 2025018364 (ebook) | ISBN 978-0-8071-8509-4 (cloth) | ISBN 978-0-8071-8568-1 (epub) | ISBN 978-0-8071-8569-8 (pdf)
Subjects: LCSH: Hemingway, Ernest, 1899–1961 | Hemingway, Ernest, 1899–1961—Criticism and interpretation | LCGFT: Biographies
Classification: LCC PS3515.E37 Z741776 2025 (print) | LCC PS3515.E37 (ebook)
LC record available at https://lccn.loc.gov/2025018363
LC ebook record available at https://lccn.loc.gov/2025018364

CONTENTS

PREFACE

The multifaceted, cubist and comprehensive perspective, *Forty-Three Ways of Looking at Hemingway*, like Wallace Stevens' "Thirteen Ways of Looking at a Blackbird," has never before been used to illustrate the complexity of his character, the range of his interests and the brilliance of his work. Through the eyes of his biographer, this authoritative book uses sources in Italian, Spanish, French and German. It reveals his reading of literature and history, his transformation of friends into fiction, his personal battles and mythic stature, his persona and ever-growing legend. This work analyzes his name and background, early work, friendships, relations with artists, connections to contemporary writers, description of historical figures and events, war reporting, military experience, life in Cuba, links with Hollywood, wives and lovers as well as the novels that influenced *The Sun Also Rises* and the background of "The Short Happy Life of Francis Macomber." It also considers Hemingway's feasts, humor, quarrels, self-condemnation, Nobel Prize, unwritten works, family tragedies, suicide and achievements.

Ernest disliked his effete name—Oscar Wilde's *The Importance of Being Earnest* was first performed in 1895, four years before he was born—and sometimes referred to himself as the tougher "Oinutz." He then transformed himself from a midwestern puritan into a Continental sophisticate. The right age and with an uncanny instinct for being in the right place at the right time, he volunteered in the Great War, was an expatriate in Paris and reported the Greco-Turkish War in the early 1920s. He met Mussolini in 1923 and compared the gangsters in Chicago to those in fascist Italy with its "lead pipe government, where everybody who squeals gets bumped off." He hunted big game in Africa, went deep-sea fishing in the Caribbean, owned a grand house in Key West during the Depression, and was a journalist at the front in the Spanish

Civil War in the late 1930s. He reported the Sino-Japanese War and World War II in the 1940s, and continued to exhibit his public persona and enhance his legend throughout the 1950s.

Hemingway was one of the great stylistic innovators of the twentieth century. His striking descriptive passages and sharply chiseled images of the landscape and weather in Paris, San Sebastián, Pamplona, Burguete in the Pyrenees and Madrid in *The Sun Also Rises* vividly evoke what D. H. Lawrence called "the spirit of place." A handsome and vigorous young man, living among the sexually free expatriates, Hemingway was often tempted, especially by Duff Twysden, the model for Brett Ashley in that novel. In their quarrel about the seductive femme fatale, he insulted and punched his sometime friend Harold Loeb, Duff's lover and the model for Robert Cohn in the novel. *The Sun Also Rises*, like his best fiction, had exotic settings, wounded but appealing characters, strong sexual undercurrents and a tragic resolution. It portrayed a group of young, attractive, well-off people, mostly with no need to work, in glamorous France and Spain. But Brett Ashley and all the others have been fatally wounded by the war and are miserably unhappy.

Immensely attractive as boy and man, Hemingway first nourished friends and, when subjected to excessive strain, broke with his closest companions. After he became successful, hardened and embittered, he quarreled not only with Harold Loeb but also with many old friends: Scott Fitzgerald, Gertrude Stein, Robert McAlmon, Sherwood Anderson, John Dos Passos and Ford Madox Ford. By contrast, Hemingway needed to fall in love with many different women in order to fire his imagination. He felt the excitement of four marriages and a few love affairs, and had a new wife for every big book. He was inspired by falling in love, by sexual excitement and clandestine affairs as well as by the intense pain and corrosive guilt of his betrayals.

The crucial event of his teenage life—the wounding on the Italian front while serving with the Red Cross in July 1918—inspired his dominant subjects: killing and death. Going off to war often rescued Hemingway from emotional crises, and in the course of his life he took part in five different conflicts. He was interested in and excited by extremes of experience and the dangers that tested his personal courage. War, he believed, "is the best subject of all. It groups the maximum of material and speeds up the action and brings out all sorts of stuff that normally you have to wait a lifetime to get." War proved his valor and revealed the quality he most valued: grace under pressure. He believed it was essential to acquire sophisticated inside knowledge and that suffering was essential to art. Always attracted to violence, he took dangerous risks and was often injured when seeking the vital experience he would use in his fiction. The greater the struggle, he felt, the greater the achievement.

Hemingway was aware of the dangers of megalomania, but knew that his swaggering Byronic persona (later imitated by Norman Mailer and other tough-guy writers) attracted many readers to his work. As early as October 1918, he adopted a Romantic attitude and anticipated his own tragic fate: "how much better to die in the happy period of undisillusioned youth, to go out in a blaze of light, than to have your body worn out and old and illusions shattered."

Hemingway changed my life and influenced my values. He propelled me to visit Italy in my teens, live in Spain for four years, see dozens of bullfights, interview the matadors Antonio Ordóñez and Luis Miguel Dominguín, take two safaris to East Africa, work on a yacht in the Caribbean and write in the Rocky Mountains. Reading his unpublished letters and manuscripts, meeting his family and friends, and exploring his life have made him more intriguing than ever. He remains for me and many others the most attractive and important figure in modern American literature.

I agree with Tom Stoppard who said, "An author I love unconditionally is Ernest Hemingway. I've revered him all my life—passionately, when I was a young man." When Hemingway died, the distinguished critic and novelist Lionel Trilling observed: "Except Lawrence's thirty-one years ago, no writer's death has moved me as much—who would suppose how much he has haunted me? How much he existed in my mind—as a reproach? He was the only writer of our time I envied."

FORTY-THREE WAYS OF LOOKING AT HEMINGWAY

ONE

ERNEST

Born in 1899, at the very end of the Victorian era, Hemingway was named after his maternal grandfather and always hated his Christian name (there is no Saint Ernest). He considered it bourgeois, expressionless and unimaginative, and associated it with the naive, even foolish hero of Oscar Wilde's *The Importance of Being Earnest* (1895). In Wilde's play Gwendolen, addicted to the very name of Ernest, marries Jack Worthing, whose real name (it turns out) is Ernest. In 1897, two years before Hemingway was born, Wilde, the antithesis of earnest, was released from prison for homosexual offenses.

Hemingway hated not only his first name, but also the whole tradition of moral earnestness, the dominant characteristic of the Victorian age and object of Wilde's sparkling and rather precious satire. Its major prophets were the Anglican church, the dissident low-church Evangelical and high-church Oxford Movements, the hortatory writings of Thomas Carlyle and the muscular Christianity of Thomas Arnold, headmaster of Rugby school and father of the poet Matthew Arnold. As Walter Houghton wrote in *The Victorian Frame of Mind*: "The prophets of earnestness were attacking a casual, easy-going, superficial, or frivolous attitude, whether in intellectual or in moral life; and demanding that men should think and men should live with a high and serious purpose. . . . The importance of being earnest was first recognized about 1830—on the threshold of the Victorian era . . . [when] people had begun to feel a danger or an evil in not being earnest." The Victorians particularly disliked any mockery of grave or sacred subjects.

Longfellow's "A Psalm of Life" (1838) marked the beginning of this moral tradition by announcing, "Life is real! Life is earnest!" and Samuel Butler drove the final nails into its coffin. In *The Way of All Flesh* (1903) the father of Ernest Pontifex (like Hemingway's mother) believed "The word 'earnest' was just beginning to come into fashion, and he thought the possession of such a name might . . . have a permanent effect upon the boy's character, and influence him for good during the more critical periods of his life." At about the same time Butler was composing this posthumously published time bomb of a novel, he also blasted the literary entombment, in massive but all-too-discreet biographies, of eminent Victorians and praised readers who were sickened by such works. Echoing Genesis 6:9, he wrote: "the word [earnestness] has for some time been discarded entirely by all reputable people. Truly, if there is one who cannot find himself in the same room with the life and letters of an earnest person without being made instantly unwell, the same is a just man and perfect in all his ways."

Hemingway's unfortunate name came at the fag end of this moral tradition. Writers like E. T. A. Hoffmann and W. E. Henley had hidden Ernst and Ernest beneath their initials; and Hemingway's father, Clarence, who had an equally effete name, was called the more manly "Ed." So Hemingway gave himself—and all his friends, wives and children—facetious and familiar nicknames and everyone in his circle had to surrender his real name. He was Wemedge, Taty, Stein, Hemingstein, and even Ernie Hemorrhoid (the poor man's Ernie Pyle). Agnes von Kurowsky, the nurse he fell in love with during World War I in Italy, was one of the few allowed to call him Ernie (she could call him whatever she liked). He was first called Papa by his three sons; and Jack (nicknamed Bumby) announced, with more French charm than grammar, "*la vie est beau avec Papa*." In the early 1930s, when Hemingway's public persona was first displayed in *Death in the Afternoon* and *Green Hills of Africa*, he finally became, even to his older friends, the patriarchal Papa.

Hemingway's whole boisterous life was a reaction against his parents' religion, moral and even musical values. Early on, he renounced the church choir and the cello. He rebelled against suburban Oak Park and the Congregational church, against provinciality, respectability, conformity, sobriety, monogamy and fidelity—though he could not escape a guilty conscience. All four of his marriages ended badly. On July 24, 1920, soon after he returned wounded and traumatized from the Great War, his moralistic mother attempted to snatch her wayward son from the hellfire that surely awaited him. She castigated him for his idleness, hedonism, parasitism, selfishness, wantonness, irreligion and corruption. Grace told him that unless you "come to yourself; cease your lazy loafing and pleasure seeking, stop trying to graft a living off anybody and everybody; spending all your earnings lavishly and wastefully on luxuries for yourself; stop trading on your handsome face to fool little gullible girls, and neglecting your duties to God and your Savior . . . there is nothing before you but moral bankruptcy." In "Soldier's Home" (1925), the best account of Hemingway's postwar feelings, the hero is made instantly unwell by his mother's sentimental and stifling emotions: "'Don't you love your mother, dear boy?' 'No. . . . I don't love anybody.' . . . 'I'm your mother,' she said. 'I held you next to my heart when you were a tiny baby.' Krebs felt sick and vaguely nauseated." Hemingway shocked John Dos Passos by exclaiming that he hated his mother.

When Hemingway's early book *in our time* (1924) arrived in Oak Park, his father refused to tolerate such filth in his house, and destroyed all his rare and now precious copies. Hemingway, refusing to mend his ways, later wrote blasphemous stories that horrified his parents. In "Today is Friday" (1926) three Roman soldiers callously discuss the crucifixion in modern slang. In "A Clean, Well-Lighted Place" (1933) he portrayed his loss of religious faith by parodying the Lord's Prayer: "Our nada who art in nada, nada be thy name." It took Hemingway several decades to work off the effects of his sententious, good-goody first name. In the end, he made Hemingwaves and no one was less earnest than Ernest.

TWO

MILAN EXPLOSION

The explosion, suppression of vital information, gruesome details and Hemingway's account of the accident have striking parallels to the collapse of modern buildings a century later: negligence, sudden destruction, many fatalities, body fragments and lost victims.

The Second Battle of the Piave in the mountains north of Venice took place from June 15 to 23, 1918. After initial setbacks the Italians, with the help of their Allies, decisively defeated the Austro-Hungarian army. This turning point of the war overshadowed one of the worst industrial accidents in Italian history. On Friday June 7, 1918, at 1:50 p.m. the Sutter & Thèvenot munitions factory, in the village of Castellazzo di Bollate ten miles northwest of Milan, was suddenly shaken by a devastating explosion that killed more than sixty workers. Hemingway, then a nineteen-year-old with some experience as a journalist, had a newsman's luck. He arrived on that very day by train from Paris to Milan, and was immediately sent to the scene as a Red Cross ambulance driver. This experience of death and destruction made a deep impression on him.

During the four long years of World War I the Italian government constructed many factories to produce bombs and grenades for the infantry fighting at the front. The Italian army recruited the Swiss company Sutter which, under license from the French company Thèvenot, built a production plant in the Lombardy countryside. It was suitably distant from urban centers, hidden by vegetation, and close to both the Milan railway line and the nearby military depot. The factory began production on the site of an old furnace in Castellazzo on November 6, 1916. By June 1918, when the demand for munitions was most intense, the factory had expanded to forty buildings. Most of the 1,500 employees were women.

The blast occurred in the shipping department, where the maximum concentration of explosive material was stacked in wooden crates. It scattered the remains of the dead, and no one knew the fate of many workers or the exact number of fatalities. It is not clear if the company took responsibility for the explosion or if the families of the victims received compensation. In January 1919, after a second explosion which this time caused no casualties, the factory was dismantled at the request of the Municipal Council. (Sutter still exists and has new modern headquarters near Freiburg, Germany, which kindly "focuses on the well-being of people.")

The first bulletin from Reuters in Rome on June 10, which misspelled Castellazzo and mistakenly said was in the province of Bollate, was reprinted as far away as Australia and New Zealand. Heavily censored by the Italian government, which demanded propagandistic support for the war, the report minimized the fatalities and listed only thirty-five killed and one hundred injured. It claimed the damage was slight and, ignoring the possibility of sabotage, said the cause was accidental. Despite the great tragedy, news of the event was suppressed. Even the *Corriere della Sera* (Evening Courier) in Milan minimized the disaster in order to maintain support for the war.

On June 9, 1918 *L'Avanti* ("Forward") in Rome repeated that the explosion took place on June 7 and that there were only thirty-five victims, though at least fifty-nine were dead. The *Corriere della Sera* of June 10 described the funerals in Bollate. There were twenty-one coffins containing entire bodies and ten coffins containing the fragments of other victims. More than 15,000 people, including delegations from the Italian and American armies, were present at the funerals, which proceeded from the village to the Bollate cemetery. The brief news reports stated that since only the shipping area was destroyed, the factory resumed production the next day. Sabotage was suspected, but on June 11 the newspapers hastily reported that no such evidence was found. It's surprising that the conservative *Corriere della Sera* wrote more about the possibility of sabotage than the socialist *L'Avanti*, especially since Mussolini, a socialist at that time, was on the staff.

Martina Salvante wrote, "The outbreak of the war and its prolonged duration led to insatiable demands for workforce and munitions." By the end of the conflict, there were nearly 2,000 factories and 903,000 workers, 22 percent of them female. As unskilled women progressively replaced the men called to arms, "military law was implemented in the factories." Though the working class had opposed Italy's entry into the war, all categories of workers were placed under the strict disciplinary surveillance. "Workers were not allowed to strike, resign or change their workplace without permission of the military authorities." The Italian government "aimed at repressing 'defeatism' through the introduction of severe punishments against those who would 'dishearten public morale,' arouse workers in the wake of the Russian revolution or call for peace."

In 1917, a year before the explosion, Luca Comario's realistic photographs of the Sutter factory revealed the horrific working conditions. Since the men had been drafted to fight in the trenches, most of the victims were women between the ages of fifteen and twenty, whose smaller hands were needed for detailed work. Many of the young women stood barefoot on the crowded cement floor, wearing ragged dresses and with no protective clothing or safety goggles. The brick gunpowder factory was hot, dark, dusty and filthy, with very little ventilation coming from the small high windows. The foreman was neatly dressed in a suit, tie and high collar. Many fathers, brothers and husbands had been killed or wounded in the war. The women, left with no money and no protection, received low wages and were subjected to sexual predators, high risks, toxic chemicals and industrial slavery. Many families reported that workers had not returned home after the explosion and their bodies were never found.

Despite the enormity of the disaster, this incident disappeared from collective memory, and the story of the victims and injured was forgotten for nearly a hundred years. After World War I fascist propaganda prohibited all talk about the faults of the government. But in 2010 a record left by the local parish priest Don Ambrogio Rocca was rediscovered and gave a reliable account of the forgotten tragedy. The priest wrote that the explosion was heard at a distance of 30 kilometers and broke the glass in all the kindergartens, schools, houses, churches and factories in the neighboring villages. From 2:30 p.m. until 9:00 p.m. there was a continuous stream of Red Cross emergency vehicles and private cars that came from Milan to help the victims. Eighty-two women and thirteen men were rushed to hospital in Milan. The makeshift mortuary in the village was a scene of real carnage. At 10:00 p.m. the parish priest, who had seen a severed head in the fields, stared at his young dead parishioners and wrote that no human pen could describe his grief on that terrible day.

A few days before Hemingway was sent to the battlefront, he had his first traumatic exposure to the war dead. He drove to the scene in a Red Cross truck, saw the civilian casualties, and had to carry mutilated corpses and human fragments detached from the barbed-wire fence around the factory. In "A Natural History of the Dead" (1932), an eyewitness, documentary short story, he stresses in a fiercely ironic style the catalog of horrors and describes the *un*natural dead: "Arriving where the munitions plant had been, some of us were put to patrolling around those large stocks of munitions which for some reason had not exploded, while others were put at extinguishing a fire which had gotten into the grass of an adjacent field, which task being concluded, we were ordered to search the immediate vicinity and surrounding fields for bodies. We found and carried to an improvised mortuary a good number of these and, I admit, frankly, the shock it was to find that these dead were women rather than men."

Hemingway does not connect the explosion to Sutter & Thèvenot, but bitterly emphasizes the grisly details that were deliberately excluded from contemporary newspaper accounts. He added material from his later war experience in Italy and Turkey, and created a verbal equivalent of Goya's etchings *Disasters of War*, which portrayed men dying like animals from bullets, shells and disease.

THREE

GANGSTERS

Hemingway believed that insults could be crushed and arguments settled, gangland fashion, with menacing threats or physical force. His friends agreed that he could be violent when crossed and angered. His sidekick Toby Bruce said he "could be as mean as a striped-assed ape"; the photographer Robert Capa stated, "Papa can be more severe than God on a rough day when the whole human race is misbehaving"; and General Buck Lanham insisted, "When Hemingway was nasty he qualified as The King of All Nasties." The huge and powerful Hemingway was always dangerous. When the timid, weak-eyed James Joyce got into drunken arguments with strangers he could scarcely see, he'd summon his strongman and bodyguard, and declare, "Deal with him, Hemingway! Deal with him!"

The thin-skinned, quick-tempered Hemingway was easily provoked. When Don Wright, one of the bachelor tenants in their Chicago flat, was having an affair with his friend's wife, Hemingway wanted to punch him. When his satire of Chard Powers Smith in his story "Mr. and Mrs. Elliott" provoked an abusive letter, Hemingway threatened to hit him. When Arthur Moss, the editor of the *Boulevardier*, had to cut obscenities from his essay, Hemingway threatened to knock his block off. After a drunken Polish engineer on a ship to Europe called him a "capitalist, bourgeois pig," Hemingway challenged him to a duel on deck with pistols, but the engineer failed to appear. Women were not immune from his fury. When his fourth wife, Mary, called him a son of a bitch, he warned her, "Most people would be running if they called me that." He carried out his threats in physical combat with Harold Loeb, who aroused his jealousy by having an affair with Duff Twysden in Spain; with Robert McAlmon, who called him a fairy; with Max Eastman, who said he had no hair on his chest; and with Wallace Stevens, who publicly insulted him and made his sister cry. But he never went a few rounds with his archenemy, Gertrude Stein.

Hemingway grew up in the genteel suburb of Oak Park. But during his teenage and young adult years Chicago had a worldwide—and to him exciting—reputation for violence, corruption and crime. In 1910, for example, the city had 7,500 legal saloons, and 192 houses of prostitution with 189 madames and 1,012 inmates. The average age of a prostitute was twenty-three, and her professional life lasted for about five years. One gang boss earned as much as $50,000 a month for eight years. The mobster Johnny Torrio had a saloon on the first floor of his Four Deuces club, offices and a horse-betting room on the second floor, a gambling den on the third floor, and a two-dollar whorehouse on the top floor. According to Herbert Asbury's *The Gangs of Chicago*, Torrio "bought and sold women, conferred with the managers of his brothels and gambling dens, issued instructions to his rum-runners and bootleggers, arranged for the corruption of police and city officials, and sent his 750 gunmen out to slaughter rival gangsters." He gave liberally to political campaign funds, and bribed attorneys and judges, prohibition and law enforcement agents, county officials and politicians. The corruption unleashed rampant crime in the city. Bandits who didn't even bother to wear masks robbed banks all over Chicago. Robbers who failed to survive were awarded lavish gangland funerals with oceans of flowers and long processions of limousines.

Alphonse "Scarface" Capone, the most notorious Chicago gangster, was born in 1899, the same year as Hemingway. He made money by corrupting labor unions, pimps and prostitution, gambling and extortion, racketeering and bootlegging. (Saul Bellow's father was a small-time Chicago bootlegger.) Capone ruled by leaden clubs and tommy guns, and held power by constant gang wars and frequently massacring his enemies. But he also had a Gatsby-like obsession with expensive haberdashery. His biographer Laurence Bergreen writes that "in 1927 and 1928 he had bought himself twenty-three suits and three topcoats," which cost $3,715. "The shirts, which went for $18 to $30, he bought literally by the dozen, as he did the neckties, the collars and the handkerchiefs."

Though Capone had an ironclad alibi, he was supposed to have organized the St. Valentine's Day massacre. On February 14, 1929 seven men, Asbury writes, "waiting at the garage for a truckload of booze . . . were disarmed and lined up against the wall by three gangsters wearing police uniforms. Then two other men, in plain clothing, stepped forward and raked the line with machine-guns." *Some Like It Hot* (1959) parodied this scene when Jack Lemmon and Tony Curtis accidentally witness George Raft's gangland massacre and have to disguise themselves as women to escape retribution. (Underground garages are always sinister in gangster movies.) When Capone was convicted of carrying a concealed weapon, he "continued to transact his business from the Eastern Penitentiary [in Philadelphia]. He was given a private cell, allowed to make long-distance calls, and to use the Warden's office for conferences with his lawyers."

Like the great masculine writers—Joseph Conrad, André Malraux and George Orwell—Hemingway did not go to college but learned from practical experience in the real world, from reporting gang wars in Kansas City and Chicago and international wars in Europe. As Herman Melville said, "A whale ship was my Yale College and my Harvard." The young Hemingway first worked, from October 1917 through April 1918, as a journalist on the *Kansas City Star*. He then served in World War I with the Red Cross and was seriously wounded in Italy. After returning from Europe he spent more than a year in Chicago in the early 1920s working on the *Co-operative Commonwealth* magazine. At a time when gangsters flourished during Prohibition (1920–33), he published many articles about crime in Chicago in the *Toronto Star Weekly*.

Hemingway's time in Kansas City was his first break from the conventional values of his family in Oak Park and from the church's tedious preaching about personal cleanliness, filial obedience, sobriety, piety and chastity. In Missouri he developed a lifelong fascination with prostitutes and horror of venereal disease. He declared, "I never thought Chicago was a tough place," but allowed, in a characteristic understatement, that Kansas City "was a little rough."

All discussions of his time in Kansas City, beginning with Charles Fenton's *The Apprenticeship of Ernest Hemingway* (1954), emphasize how he learned to write clearly and concisely from the *Star*'s style sheet. But the gangsters he wrote about were even more important. Just as Upton Sinclair's *The Jungle* (1906) had exposed the exploitation of immigrant workers (one of whom gets ground up and packaged after falling into a machine) in the Chicago meatpacking industry, so the vividly morbid newspaper articles by Hemingway and other reporters exposed the unchecked crime in those midwestern cities.

Hemingway's exact, crisp and violent "Battle of Raid Squads," published in Kansas City on January 6, 1918, described the danger of trigger-happy officials, as well as of the real gangsters, in urban battles:

> John M. Tully and Albert Raithel, revenue officers from St. Louis, may die, and two city detectives narrowly escaped injury as a result of a revolver battle yesterday through a case of mistaken identity. Tully and Raithel had gone to raid a house at 2743 Mercier Street, reported to be a rendezvous for drug users. Edward Kritser and Paul Conrad, city detectives, arrived a few minutes later on the same mission. Each party of officers mistook the other for drug peddlers.
>
> Tully was shot in the right leg, left arm and lower abdomen. Raithel was wounded in the abdomen and left wrist. Both will recover. The two detectives were uninjured, but both had bullet holes through their clothing.

In "At the End of the Ambulance Run," which appeared in the *Star* on January 20, 1918, Hemingway revealed his taste for gory details and use of inside information (which he later called "the true gen"), and described the different ways of inflicting damage in different parts of the city: "It's razor wounds in the African belt and slugging in the wet [liquor] block. In Little Italy they prefer the sawed-off shotgun. We can almost tell what part of the city a man is from just by seeing how they did him up."

Two years later, in his postwar *Toronto Star* stories about Chicago, the seasoned veteran continued to concentrate on violent gangsters. In "Rum-Running" (June 5, 1920), he reported the unrestrained liquor smuggling during Prohibition: "Canadian whiskey can be bought by the case from bootleggers in almost all of the Michigan border towns for one hundred and twenty dollars a case." "Wild West: Chicago" (November 6, 1920) compared the escalating murders in Chicago—eerily similar to those in that city today—to the lawless shootouts on the old frontier: "in the city of Chicago during the present year from January to November there have been one hundred and fifty killings. . . . By including the police bag, it would be pretty safe to say they kill somebody every day in Chicago. . . . So there is murder, drink and gambling in the new Wild West just as in the old."

The professional murderers in Chicago were so highly regarded, Hemingway explained in "Plain and Fancy Killings, $400 Up" (December 11, 1920), that "Gunmen from the United States are being imported to do killings in Ireland" during the war of independence. "The price for a simple killing, such as a marked policeman or member of the 'Black and Tans,' is four hundred dollars."

Finally, in "Ballot Bullets" (May 28, 1921)—whose title would be echoed in the Humphrey Bogart and Edward G. Robinson movie *Bullets or Ballots* (1936)—Hemingway connected politics with violent death and narrated the incident from the victim's point of view, as he would later do when describing the wounded lion in "The Short Happy Life of Francis Macomber":

> Anthony D'Andrea, pale and spectacled, defeated candidate for alderman in the 19th Ward, Chicago, stepped out of the closed car in front of his residence and, holding an automatic pistol in his hand, backed gingerly up the steps.
>
> Reaching back with his left hand to press the door bell, he was blinded by two red jets of flame from the window of the next apartment, heard a terrific roar and felt himself clouted sickeningly in the body with the shock of the slugs from the sawed-off shotgun. . . . It's all part of the unfinished story of the gunmen's political war that is raging in Chicago at present.

Hemingway expressed his fascination with gangsters in his fiction, and evoked the atmosphere of Kansas City during the last year of the war in two minor short stories and an interchapter of *In Our Time*. In "A Pursuit Race" (1927), a staggered bike race, an advance man for a burlesque show breaks down with drink and drugs. Hemingway wrote that "It was very cold in Kansas City" and that the hopeless anti-hero "did not like Kansas City," but "knew there were good cures in Kansas City" for drug addicts.

The ironically titled "God Rest You Merry, Gentlemen" (1933) begins with a far-fetched comparison, "In those days . . . Kansas City was very like Constantinople," and also mentions the Woolf Brothers' saloon and the city hospital. In this Christmas Day story, an incompetent doctor is unable to deal with a religious fanatic's attempt to castrate himself. Hemingway may have been thinking of the two most famous castrati. The third-century theologian

Origen, slavishly following Matthew 19:12—"there be eunuchs, which made themselves eunuchs for the kingdom of heaven's sake"—castrated himself for the love of God. Abelard, the medieval French philosopher, was castrated by the uncle of Héloïse for secretly marrying her. In *The Sun Also Rises*, Jake Barnes' penis is shot off in the war. In this Christmas story the would-be castrator amputates his own penis. But both mutilated men still have sexual feelings.

Interchapter VIII, based on an incident that took place in Kansas City on November 19, 1917, subtly connects urban violence with war and is related to Hemingway's news story of the gunfight between revenue agents and detectives. In this taut vignette a policeman, Jimmy Boyle, kills two Hungarians who have robbed a cigar store at two o'clock in the morning. His partner, Drevitts, fears there will be trouble, but he is reassured by the murderer, who insists there will be no difficulty because the victims were crooks and "wops." Since all "wops" are crooks, their deaths don't matter. Boyle claims "he can tell wops a mile off." His false identification, which reflects the racial hostility between Irish and Italian immigrants, will be accepted in court to justify the deaths of the Hungarians.

On April 15, 1921, Hemingway wrote to his father from Chicago: "They hanged Cardinella and Cosmano and some other Wop killer today. . . . Cardinella is a good man to swing I guess. Passed the County Jail this morning and there was a big crowd standing outside waiting for the event." Sam Cardinella—the forty-one-year-old mobster, extortionist and leader of the Black Hand gang—was executed for murdering a saloonkeeper. When Cardinella refused to walk to the gallows, he was strapped to a chair, carried to the scaffold and hanged in his chair. When the jailers took his body to an ambulance (not a hearse) hired by his family, they found medical equipment, a nurse and a doctor who hoped to revive the corpse.

Hemingway's version, interchapter XV from *In Our Time*, takes place in the corridor of the county jail. One of the condemned men wraps a blanket around his head in an infantile attempt to escape reality. The guards carry Cardinella, accompanied by two priests who mutter meaningless words—another instance of unreality. The terrified prisoner loses control of his sphincter muscle and the disgusted guards, one of them wearing an incongruous derby hat, strap him into a chair. The agile priest skips back onto the scaffolding just before the drop falls. Hemingway realistically described the callousness of the guards, the futility of the priests and the cowardice of the prisoner, who responds to the injunction to "Be a man" by emptying his bowels before he is "jerked to Jesus."

Hemingway's influential story "The Killers" (1927) is based on the comical-sinister gangsters of Al Capone's Chicago. Max and Al turn up in a diner, converted from a saloon during Prohibition, to murder a heavyweight boxer. Ole Andreson had agreed to throw a fight but betrayed the gamblers who backed his opponent. The suspense builds up as time passes, threats are made, motives are slowly revealed and Ole fails to appear for dinner at his customary time. In the story, which reads like a screenplay, the killers, passively awaiting the arrival of their victim, taunt and intimidate the workers in the diner with a series of insults that require immediate assent:

> "You're a pretty bright boy, aren't you?"
> "Sure," said George.
> "Well, you're not," said the other little man. "Is he, Al?"
> "He's dumb."

The gangsters convey their indifferent, immoral but highly professional attitude—"We're killing him for a friend. Just to oblige a friend"—which astonishes Nick Adams but is passively accepted by the victim. The two main events in the story, the prizefight and the murder, are left out. The theme, Nick's discovery of evil and death, is also conveyed obliquely when he goes to warn Ole. The boxer stoically, if not heroically, confronts his fate and rolls over toward the wall: "There isn't anything I can do about it. . . . I'm through with all that running around."

Nick moves from fear to compassion to disillusionment and realizes things are not what they appear to be: the clock is twenty minutes fast, the lunchroom serves dinner, the corrupt-honest fighter is strangely indifferent, Mrs. Hirsch is actually Mrs. Bell and Ole's friends are much more frightened than he is. The men in the diner are confused and obedient, Andreson is fatalistic and resigned. The gangsters boldly announce their intention to defy the law and murder the boxer, but do not hunt him down in his boardinghouse. Though the murderers don't kill Ole, they merely delay the inevitable and will surely come back to finish the job. The boxer, tired of running, awaits his inexorable fate and doesn't take his last chance to escape. "The Killers" portrays Hemingway's recurrent theme of The Undefeated and suggests that pity can be earned only by men who never demand it.

One film critic maintained that gangsters did not "know how they were supposed to behave. So Hollywood taught them." But Hemingway taught Hollywood. The gangsters of Kansas City and Chicago not only sparked his lifelong taste for violence, they also inspired his portrayal of the criminals that was adopted by movies in the 1930s. The menacing wisecracks, the sense of immediate experience and sharp cinematic scenes influenced the portrayal of underworld characters in films like Robinson's *Little Caesar* (1930) and James Cagney's *Public Enemy* (1931).

Hemingway, who emphasized the dramatic and visual aspects of gangsters, actually created the natty dress and unrestrained violence of stereotyped movie mobsters. One of the murderers in "The Killers" "wore a derby hat and a black overcoat buttoned across the chest. His face was small and white and he had tight lips. He wore a silk muffler and gloves. . . . [They] ate with their gloves on . . . [and] were dressed like twins. Both wore overcoats too tight for them. . . . The cut-off barrels of the shotgun made a slight bulge under the waist." This precise description clearly foreshadows Bogart's smart attire in all his gangster roles from the early 1930s to "Gloves" Donahue in *All Through the Night* (1942). As Bogart says in *Across the Pacific* of the Japanese villains who are trying to hide their weapons, "tight clothes don't go with guns."

Emphasizing the theatrical element, Hemingway compares one of the killers, giving orders to his captives, to a member of a vaudeville team and to "a photographer arranging for a group picture." The murderer tells George, "Ever go to the movies? . . . You ought to go to the movies more. The movies are fine for a bright boy like you." The detective in Hemingway's "The Gambler, the Nun, and the Radio" warns the wounded Mexican about confusing art and life: "Listen. This isn't Chicago. You're not a gangster. You don't have to act like a moving picture. It's all right to tell who shot you."

Hemingway's first-hand experience with gangsters encouraged his propensity to violence and attraction to violent themes in his fiction. His portrayal of criminals in a skeptical, stoical and belligerently masculine style, with speech and gestures cut down to a minimum, tapped into the Hollywood consciousness that recreated his laconic gangsters and doomed tough guys. There was a volatile connection throughout his life between the gangsters he wrote about while still in his impressionable teens, his passion for danger in war, boxing, bullfighting and big-game hunting, and his brain-splashed suicide.

FOUR

CHARLES SWEENY

In September 1922, reporting the Greco-Turkish War in Constantinople, Hemingway met the adventurous soldier of fortune Charles Sweeny, who weaved in and out of his life for the next forty years. Sweeny (1882–1963) was born in San Francisco, the second oldest of twelve children, son of a mining engineer who'd made a great fortune excavating gold and silver in Idaho. Both parents came from an Irish-Catholic background, and sent him to the Jesuit Gonzaga prep school in Spokane, Washington. After a year at Notre Dame University in Indiana, he attended West Point but—like Edgar Allan Poe and James McNeill Whistler—was expelled. He was later readmitted, but resigned after another half year.

Though Sweeny's military record is often unclear or nonexistent, he apparently fought in eleven wars in eight countries, and moved up (and sometimes down) in rank from private to brigadier general. In his twenties he joined revolutions against corrupt and murderous dictators: Porfirio Díaz in Mexico in 1906, Cipriano Castro in Venezuela in 1907 and José Zelaya in Nicaragua in 1910. These revolutions were crushed, Sweeny barely escaped with his life, and the dictators were later overthrown and replaced by equally brutal despots. In 1911 Sweeny married a Belgian woman, Eva Vons, and they had four children.

When World War I broke out, he joined the French Foreign Legion. In the spring of 1915 he won the Croix de Guerre for capturing a German machine-gun crew. In September 1915 he was wounded by a machine-gun bullet in his right lung and liver, and was awarded the French Legion of Honor. The photo of Sweeny and his nurse in the French hospital foreshadows the one of Hemingway and his nurse in the Milan hospital in 1918. Sweeny became a lieutenant colonel in the U.S. Army from 1917 to 1919. Like most officers blind to the reality of combat, he used suicidal tactics and sustained heavy casualties when leading troops in the fierce battles of Champagne and the Argonne Forest. When he ordered his men to charge two lines of German trenches and his lieutenant said the enemy machine guns made the attack impossible, Sweeny flew into a rage and shouted, "I'll not have my orders debated." Within twenty-five yards the machine-gun fire cut down the entire first wave. In the Argonne he commanded his soldiers to charge down a slope into mustard gas and a rain of shrapnel, and once again all his men were wiped out. In April 1917 he accompanied Marshal Joseph Joffre on a propaganda trip that helped persuade America to enter the war that month. He commanded a group of the newly invented tanks in the Nivelle offensive that spring, and sustained a minor bullet wound shortly before the Armistice of November 1918.

Though Sweeny offered no details of his action in the Polish-Russian War of 1920, he supposedly organized guerrilla forces to fight the Bolsheviks and served under the French General Maxime Weygand in the Battle of Warsaw. Posing as a war correspondent, Sweeny was a French Intelligence agent in the Greco-Turkish War of 1919–22. After the Turkish victory, he became a military advisor to the future president Kemal Ataturk, and tried to discredit accounts of the Turkish massacre of a million Armenians.

Hemingway arrived toward the end of the war, after the defeat, the retreat and the evacuation of the Greek army from Smyrna, after the fire and the massacre that followed the Turkish occupation of the city. Sweeny helped the young war correspondent obtain information for his dispatches from Turkey and cared for him during his attacks of malaria. Though Hemingway sympathized with the Greeks, he was tremendously impressed by Sweeny, who was seventeen years older. He thought he had a brilliant military mind, and became his close lifelong friend.

In the Rif War of 1921–26 Moroccan tribesmen led by Abd el-Krim rose against Spanish and French colonial rule. In 1925 Sweeny recruited—his specialty—American pilots to fight for the French. He did not think the Arabs were capable of self-rule and declared, "We are going to Morocco believing we can sustain the civilizing work the French have done under the Protectorate." This "civilizing work" included bombing Chefchaouen, a defenseless civilian city of 7,000, which foreshadowed the Nazi bombing of the Spanish city of Guernica in 1937. After his initial victories, Abd el-Krim surrendered to the French, was exiled on the Indian Ocean island of Réunion, escaped to Egypt and died (the same year as Sweeny) in 1963.

Hemingway and Sweeny met again during the Spanish Civil War when Sweeny, advisor to the Loyalists, exhibited his expertise. During the battle of Teruel, east of Madrid, the Loyalists captured the town after a bitter struggle. But they were unable to sustain the attack and a counteroffensive retook the city. Hemingway wrote that Sweeny "made the plans for the Teruel offensive. Rather he corrected them and showed everything that was wrong with the Russian staff work and every goddamned thing came out exactly as he said it would including how we lost the town and why because of not doing one thing which should have been done when it was taken."

In World War II Sweeny again spied for and delivered reports to French Intelligence. Before America entered the war in December 1941 Sweeny became a Group Captain (equivalent of an army colonel) in the RAF, where he again recruited American pilots to fight against Germany and enraged the FBI for violating neutrality. His Eagle Squadron once again sustained high casualties. Of the 244 Americans, 140 were either killed in action or shot down and taken prisoner. He also served obscurely with Wild Bill Donovan's guerrilla campaigns in North Africa and Europe. Sweeny fought courageously from war to war, but fighting and losing foreign wars had no future. He often refused to take orders and quarreled with his superiors. After World War I he could not submit to military discipline and never became a career officer in any army.

Sweeny's *Moment of Truth: A Realistic Examination of Our War Situation* (1943) praised Hemingway's bullfighting book *Death in the Afternoon* (1932) and took his title from the moment the matador kills the bull: "Its Rabelaisian presentation did not have the good fortune to please our neo-Puritan public. The sword represents force, the red cloth deception. These are the man's weapons to counterbalance the bull's advantages in speed and strength and ferocity. . . . America, today, is also face to face with that 'Moment of Truth.'" But he was less successful as a writer than as a soldier, and unwisely rejected Hemingway's introduction, which would have greatly increased the prestige and sales of his book. In October 1942 Sweeny wrote dismissively to their mutual editor Max Perkins: "The first part is very brilliant. The rest did not impress me. I disagree with his judgment both military and political.'" Sweeny's strategic conclusions were unconvincing and mistaken. He predicted a stalemate between Germany and Russia, and said the decisive battle would take place in Siberia—7,000 miles from the European war—when American troops in Alaska crossed the Bering Strait.

Hemingway thanked Sweeny for advice with his 1,000-page anthology *Men at War* (1942), but didn't include him in the book. Sweeny's biographers Charley Roberts and Charles Hess write that during the war in July 1944, Scribner's "were shocked and appalled by Sweeny's harsh denunciations against Roosevelt [whom he blamed for Pearl Harbor] and the Allies and immediately decided to cancel his contract." The *Ring in Our Nose* remained unpublished. Sweeny had served under Philippe Pétain in the Rif War, and in October 1945 Hemingway told Perkins: "Charley sent me his Pétain pamphlet. It has much excellent sense in it but it also ignores many unpleasant things about the Marechal. Charley admired him so much he deliberately closed his eyes to much." Sweeny's privately printed work defended the World War I hero of Verdun and head of the Vichy government, who had collaborated with the Nazis during the Occupation of France. In 1945 Pétain was convicted of treason. After many pleas for mercy, his death sentence was commuted to life in prison, he was exiled on a small French island in the Atlantic and died there in 1951.

Hemingway often praised Sweeny's military genius (and gave Teruel as his only example), but often disagreed with and criticized him on crucial issues. Sweeny used suicidal trench-warfare tactics in World War I; defended French colonialism and bombed defenseless cities in the Rif War; made several mistaken predictions in *Moment of Truth*; and was completely wrong in predicting that Japan would not attack America. On December 11, 1941, four days after Pearl Harbor, Hemingway told Perkins that Sweeny would never moderate his views: "Don't take Charley Sweeny seriously when he baits you about the Civil War: when he is angry he always says such wild unjust things. He . . . was completely and fatally wrong about the war with Japan when we argued it in Washington as events have proved."

Sweeny had a quick temper and a sharp tongue; was self-confident, impulsive and dogmatic; rebellious, competitive and domineering; aggressive, argumentative and abusive. Hemingway had some of these traits and, rather surprisingly, meekly submitted to Sweeny and tolerated his constant ranting. The two friends had a lot in common. Both were six-feet, one-inch tall, though

Hemingway was heavier. Both always dominated women, and were experienced correspondents and cosmopolitan travelers. They took many risks, were brave under fire and involved in many wars: Hemingway in Italy, Turkey, Spain, China and France. Both had been wounded in combat and decorated for bravery. They created myths about themselves, and Hemingway exaggerated his exploits: in battle in World War I, hunting German submarines in the Caribbean, leading men in France, killing Germans and helping to liberate Paris, as well as collecting huge trophies as a big-game hunter and deep-sea fisherman. Their feats were widely publicized in newspapers and magazines; and both men aroused the suspicion of the FBI.

Sweeny's first biographer, Donald McCormick, states in *One Man's Wars* (1972) that Hemingway "saw in Sweeny the kind of man he wished to be, a tough, battle-scarred man of action, a war hero and a romantic soldier of fortune following whichever side captured his imagination and sympathy, an extrovert who enjoyed life and could hold his own with women." Sweeny was one of his few "intelligent friends," and became Hemingway's military mentor along with his other heroes: Eric Dorman-Smith in World War I, Gustavo Durán in the Spanish Civil War and Charles Lanham in World War II. In Paris in the 1920s they were athletic and spiritual friends. They watched the six-day bike races until Sweeny discovered they were fixed and refused to go. After Hemingway had married Pauline Pfeiffer and became a temporary Catholic the two ex-choirboys went to Sunday mass together in Saint-Sulpice.

Hemingway portrayed, analyzed, admired and eviscerated Sweeny's character in letters to mutual friends and in his posthumous novel. He wrote Gertrude Stein that he was skeptical about Sweeny's heroics for obscure and sometimes hopeless causes, especially since he'd already won France's highest medal: "[Sweeny] off to fight the Riffs. Awfully sweet thing to do. But if you've got the legion of Honor already what's it all about?" In a 1930 letter to the artist Waldo Peirce, he emphasized and then dismissed Sweeny's mythmaking: "He's a damned good Bird—Even if he's only done 1/8 things he's supposed to have done he's a hell of a citizen—I'm damned fond of him."

In a 1943 letter to Perkins he praised Sweeny's stern attitude toward women: "That's one thing you have to hand to Charley Sweeny. He doesn't take nothing from them. If they start to make any trouble with Charley he gives them that old tone of command." In 1946 Hemingway again expressed approval in a letter to Sweeny's recent rival Charles Lanham: "Charley Sweeny, very old pal and soldier in various armies. . . . We were together in Near East and in Spain and he is one of [my] very oldest friends."

In 1940 Sweeny was pleased to receive an inscribed copy of Hemingway's Spanish War novel *For Whom the Bell Tolls*: "For Charley with the same affection and the same admiration as always. Ernest." In 1952 he was delighted by Sweeny's response to *The Old Man and the Sea*: "I was surprised and pleased. It is magnificent." In *The Garden of Eden* (1986) Hemingway portrayed Sweeny in Madrid as Colonel John Boyle, whose name suggested his hot temperament and was linked to the name of the hero David Bourne. Boyle spoke outrageously, and "was wearing a dark blue suit of a cloth that looked stiff but cool and a blue shirt and black tie. . . . [He] had deep blue eyes, sandy hair and a tanned face that looked as though it had been carved out of flint by a tired sculptor who had broken his chisel on it." He barks orders to the Spanish waiter as if he were commanding a regiment and criticizes the restaurant: "Bring a cold bottle. You don't need to ice it. Bring it immediately. . . . No anchovies? What sort of *fonda* is this?"

Hemingway's fascinating letter to Perkins, his final *tout comprendre c'est tout pardonner* judgment, gives the most complete account of his exasperating friend. Hemingway was one of the very few people who could sympathize with and restrain the impulsive Sweeny: "He can't get along with *anybody* in action. He can with me because I love him and understand him and will take anything from him knowing he doesn't mean what he says when he is angry. But he is *always* angry when things are bad. He has one of the most brilliant military brains I have ever known and the French General Staff trust and respect him." Sweeny wanted to kill men the way Hemingway killed animals: "every time Charley gets angry he wants somebody shot. Well I agree and they are [to be] shot. Only I wouldn't shoot them and afterwards it would be o.k."

In Madrid, Sweeny argued fiercely and abusively about the Spanish War, "Sweeny calling me all sorts of names, continually insulting me, harping on my lack of military education, my abysmal ignorance, my lack of this, my lack of that, bawling me out in front of everybody and everyone there thought we must be bitter enemies. Then at three a.m. they all were very surprised when Charley said, 'You old bastard. You're getting a little sense after all.' . . . He's really absolutely goddamned insufferable sometimes but I know he won't shoot me and I'm about the only white man alive that can get along with him all the time." He could maintain their friendship only by accepting Sweeny's dismissal of Hemingway's extensive experience and ignoring Sweeny's insults and overweening egoism about his role in Spain: "the minute he got into it he acted as though all the rest of us were simply criminal lunatics and the minute the war started was when he entered. And the war stopped when he left."

Hemingway didn't name any of his sons after himself, but Sweeny named his grandson Ernest Hemingway O'Hare. Hemingway often wrote about Sweeny, but in a 1929 conversation in Paris with the poet Allen Tate, Sweeny gave a rare description of the writer. Tate and Sweeny "talked about war, safaris, the rise of Hitler, women—the usual subjects of conversation between intelligent men." Sweeny self-reflectively said that Hemingway, who often rejected his wild assertions, "although from Oak Park Illinois, was a Mediterranean type, extroverted, suspicious, unloyal and violent."

Estranged from his wife, Sweeny spent the last 16 years of his life in Salt Lake City with Dorothy Bamberger Allen, the Jewish, wealthy, childless widow of a professional soldier. Five feet tall and weighing less than 100 pounds, she had red hair and intense blue eyes, and was crazy about the cats that swarmed around her luxurious mansion. Her father, like Sweeny's, was a mining tycoon, and she had a vast estate served by two maids, a cook, butler, chauffeur and gardener, as well as a guest house, large swimming pool and seven-car garage.

In February 1959 Hemingway wrote his editor denying the serious effects of his friend's illness: "Just had a telephone from Charley Sweeny from Salt Lake. He had another stroke after visiting here. But waited to let me know until he was well enough to call. Says he is fine. Strokes don't mean anything any more. This one paralyzed him slightly on one side." In July 1961 Sweeny traveled from Salt Lake to Ketchum, Idaho, to attend Hemingway's funeral and was an honorary pallbearer.

Like Hemingway, Sweeny loved France and devoted a great deal of his life to that country. His wife and children had been brought up in France. He was wounded when fighting in the French Foreign Legion, fought for France against the Moroccans in the Rif War, worked for French Intelligence and recruited American pilots to join the French in World War II. After that war, when he believed that Britain was provoking a conflict between America and Russia while also trying to demolish France, he came to a tragic conclusion about all his mistakes, losses and disasters: "Why have I lived? Why have I fought? Why have I suffered?"

Sweeny was pro-Turk and anti-Armenian, pro-French colonial in the Rif War, violently anti-Roosevelt and pro-Pétain. Despite their very different political views, Sweeny's irascibility and abusive personality, and his unwillingness to tolerate any contradiction of his views, Hemingway always deferred to his charismatic hero and remained his lifelong friend.

FIVE

FRIDTJOF NANSEN

The Norwegian Fridtjof Nansen (1861–1930) seemed exactly the sort of brilliantly talented man whom Hemingway would admire. He was a pioneer skier across the ice of Greenland, Arctic explorer of the highest latitude then known to man, author of *Farthest North*, professor of zoology and oceanography, diplomat negotiating the separation of Norway from Sweden, ambassador to Great Britain, savior of half a million prisoners of war, rescuer of famine-stricken postwar Russia, League of Nations high commissioner for refugees in Greece and Turkey. In 1924 Hemingway told a friend that he was having a "swell time" reading Nansen's book. Yet in the first italicized flashback of his greatest story, "The Snows of Kilimanjaro" (1936), Hemingway blamed Nansen for the death of the postwar Greek refugees in Eastern Thrace. What caused Hemingway's bitter hostility to Nansen's humanitarian efforts?

On August 18, 1922 the Turkish general Mustapha Kemal attacked the Greek army that had occupied Anatolia after the Great War. Within a month, a series of Turkish victories had pushed the Greeks westward from Ankara to Smyrna (modern Izmir) on the Mediterranean coast and forced them out of Turkey. As a result of the Greek defeat, a million destitute and broken-spirited refugees from Anatolia, Smyrna and Eastern Thrace had been driven on foot to seek safety across the Greek frontier. The Greek government had no food or shelter for these hordes of exiles who had lost almost everything, and as winter approached disease broke out in the overcrowded refugee camps. At the same time and under the same desperate conditions, the Turks in Greece were flooding eastward toward their Anatolian homeland.

In the midst of this chaos, the Greek prime minister Eleutherios Venizelos officially asked Nansen to negotiate with the Turks for an immediate exchange of the Greek and Turkish populations. After witnessing the grim situation in Thrace in October 1922, Nansen was deeply moved and wrote a friend: "Life seems so very sad. . . . The roads were simply one continuous series of wagons, people and cattle. I have never known what it meant to see a whole people on foot before. . . . They do not know where they are going and will find no shelter where they come—oh, misery."

Hemingway, who'd been on the scene at exactly the same moment, wrote a powerful vignette in *in our time* (1924) that was derived from, but infinitely superior to, his *Toronto Star* article of October 20, 1922, "A Silent Ghastly Procession Wends Way from Thrace." From Madame Marie's lice-ridden hotel in Adrianople, near the Greek and Bulgarian frontier, he vividly reported the hopeless flight of the Greek refugees. The wretched procession trudged toward and across the bridge from the Moslem minarets on the Turkish side of the Maritza River to the squalid Greek sanctuary at Karagatch: "Minarets stuck up in the rain out of Adrianople across the mud flats. The carts were jammed for thirty miles along the Karagatch road. Water buffalo and cattle were hauling carts through the mud. No end and no beginning. Just carts loaded with everything they owned. The old men and women, soaked through, walked along keeping the cattle moving."

Hemingway also used his experience in Asia Minor in the flashbacks of Harry's adventures in war in "The Snows of Kilimanjaro." The first one takes place on October 18, 1922, the date Hemingway left the Greek frontier for Sofia and Paris: "He saw a railway station at Karagatch and . . . the headlight of the Simplon-Orient cutting the dark now and he was leaving Thrace then after the retreat. . . . [He was] looking out the window and seeing snow on the mountains in Bulgaria and Nansen's Secretary [Philip Noel-Baker] asking the old man if it were snow and the old man looking at it and saying, No, that's not snow. It's too early for snow. . . . But it was the snow all right and [Nansen] sent them on into it when he evolved exchange of populations. And it was snow they tramped along in until they died that winter." In this passage, to achieve a more forceful literary effect, Hemingway changes the October "mud" into "snow" in the Rhodope mountains of Bulgaria to match the snow on Mount Kilimanjaro and on Nansen's famous Arctic expeditions. Nansen knew snow as well as any man alive. But in this flashback Hemingway writes, with devastating irony and wit, that Nansen was fatally mistaken about, almost indifferent to, the snow that would soon kill thousands of refugees in the Thracian winter.

Nansen's laudatory biographer Roland Huntford, discussing the exchange of populations, rather surprisingly admitted that his hero was at fault: "Nansen had been used as the originator of a proposal which, though wholly expedient, brought moral condemnation in its train. . . . As in the case of the Russian famine, Nansen was criticized for the way he carried out relief. 'The Americans and other charitable organisations all consider him unpractical and anxious to obtain credit for work for which they supply money,' the British Embassy in Athens reported. . . . When it came to practical details, Nansen was found wanting." The young Hemingway, an astute foreign correspondent, was right to criticize the egoistic Nansen for failing to provide protection, medicine, food and shelter for the Greek refugees, many of whom were slaughtered or died of disease, starvation and exhaustion. In 1922, ironically enough, Nansen—with many deaths on his conscience—was awarded the Nobel Peace Prize.

SIX

EXECUTING MINISTERS

Hemingway forged his innovative style when he was young. The stark, intense and dramatic account of an execution in *in our time* (1924), one of the best things he ever wrote, conveys sympathy for the victims while narrating their death with apparent objectivity. He was not in Athens when the ministers were executed on November 28, 1922 and relied on newspaper reports for the facts behind his description. But he heightens reality by imagining the wet weather, the traditional hour of dawn and the shuttered hospital. The hard rain, dead leaves and degradation of one victim all accentuate the injustice and cruelty of the tragic event:

> They shot the six cabinet ministers at half-past six in the morning against the wall of a hospital. There were pools of water in the courtyard. There were wet dead leaves on the paving of the courtyard. It rained hard. All the shutters of the hospital were nailed shut. One of the ministers was sick with typhoid. Two soldiers carried him downstairs and out into the rain. They tried to hold him up against the wall but he sat down in a puddle of water. The other five stood quietly against the wall. Finally the officer told the soldiers it was no good trying to make him stand up. When they fired the first volley he was sitting down in the water with his head on his knees.

Ironically, the ministers are shot against the wall of a closed hospital whose shutters, conclusively nailed shut, echo the Crucifixion. The pools of water suggest the blood that flowed from the bullet wounds. The wet dead leaves in the courtyard, emphasized by the rhetorical parallels, "There were pools. . . . There were dead leaves," foreshadow the inevitable fate of the men. One minister, sick but imprisoned, suffers a humiliating death. Carried downstairs and propped up like a dummy against the wall, he slithers helplessly into the puddle while his silent and impotent colleagues watch him. The officer's remark, "it was no good," casts doubt on the ethics of the execution. During the first volley—there must always be a second gunshot to make sure of death—the dead man "was sitting down in the water with his head on his knees," crumpled up like the broken-down man in Picasso's *Old Guitarist*. His undignified death recalls the saying of the Mexican revolutionary Emiliano Zapata, "better to die on your feet than live on your knees." The firing squad evokes the horrific images of innocent victims in Francisco Goya's *Third of May 1808* and Edouard Manet's *Execution of Maximilian* (1869).

Hemingway intensifies the effect of this episode by eliminating all the essential information that readers would expect to find in a news story. He does not explain who the ministers were, why they were shot, who shot them, when they were killed, where they were killed and what happened after their execution. C. M. Woodhouse's *Modern Greece* (1998) provides the historical background that Hemingway deliberately left out. In October 1920, the prime minister Eleftherios Venizelos ordered the troops in the Greek city of Smyrna, on the west coast of Turkey, to advance against Mustafa Kemal's army. On October 25 King Alexander died of a monkey bite and was succeeded by King Constantine. Woodhouse writes, "The army in Anatolia, inadequately equipped and led by inexperienced officers appointed for their loyalty [to the new king], marched on to its destruction."

The Greek offensive to conquer the Turks, who'd been defeated in the Great War, began on June 15, 1921 and after a series of victories reached the River Sakaria in August. It was the final obstacle between the Greeks and Ankara, the Turkish capital, and the line on which Kemal chose to fight. In August, he counterattacked and won a brilliant victory. Constantine, leading his troops, broke off his assault, and throughout August and September the Greeks were driven 330 miles back to Smyrna. In three months Turkey regained all the territory it had lost in the war.

Woodhouse adds, "While Constantine desperately shuffled prime ministers and commanders-in-chief, the Turks mounted an overwhelming offensive against Smyrna. It began at the end of August 1922 and ended in complete victory within ten days. Smyrna was sacked and looted; every Greek inhabitant who could escape took to the sea; the Greek government ordered the demobilization of the army and resigned; Constantine abdicated and retired to Sicily, where he died four months later." After the withdrawal of the Greek troops from Turkey, the military junta who had seized power in Greece needed scapegoats. In what Woodhouse calls "one of the most lamentable and uncharacteristic acts of modern Greek history," five senior, pro-Constantine ex-ministers and one general (not *six* cabinet ministers) were put on trial for their lives before a military court of eleven officers.

In October 1922 Hemingway reported the Greco-Turkish War and in November he was at the Lausanne Conference, which ratified the territorial acquisitions after the Turkish victory. The war was over before he arrived in Turkey and he never reached Anatolia or Smyrna. But his powerful short story "On the Quai at Smyrna" (1930) vividly describes the retreat and evacuation of the Greek army from that city, which enabled the Turks to burn down the Greek quarter and massacre the civilians. When the fleeing Greeks couldn't take their mules with them, they broke their legs and pushed them into the water. In another brilliant vignette of *in our time*, "Minarets stuck up in the rain out of Adrianople," Hemingway described the horrific conditions of the refugees. They were forced to leave Turkish territory after the defeat in Anatolia and driven on foot to seek safety across the Greek frontier.

In a dispatch to the *Toronto Daily Star* on November 3, 1922, three weeks before the execution, Hemingway explained what he'd deleted in the vignette:

> When Constantine came into power all the officers of the army in the field were suddenly scrapped, from the commander-in-chief down to platoon commanders. Many of these officers had been promoted from the ranks, were good soldiers and splendid leaders. They were removed and their places filled with new officers of Constantine's party, most of whom had spent [World War I] in Switzerland or Germany and had never heard a shot fired. That caused a complete breakdown of the army. . . . Artillery officers who had no experience at all took over the command of batteries and massacred their own infantry. . . . That is the story of the Greek army's betrayal by King Constantine who was responsible for the Greek defeat.

Constantine had fled and could not be captured. But the junta arrested almost all the politicians who had briefly served in consecutive governments during the Asia Minor campaign. These men were held responsible for the military defeat and tried for high treason. The popular Venizelos had initiated the disaster but was not in office when it occurred, so Constantine's ministers were blamed for the catastrophe. The accused included three former prime ministers and only one soldier, the white-haired and goateed General Georgios Hatzianestis, Commander-in-Chief of the Greek army in Asia Minor.

Despite Greece's promises to the Allies, the trial from November 13 to 27, 1922 was not fair. The accused were denied access to important documents, a long written defense by Dimitrios Gounaris was not admitted and his plea for medical postponement was rejected. Though Gounaris was sick during the trial and the mentally ill General believed his legs were made of glass and easily shattered, neither illness nor madness saved them. All six once-powerful defendants were sentenced to death, and there was no appeal. The British government called the trial judicial murder, and the *New York Times* compared it to Robespierre's slaughter during the French Reign of Terror.

The tall, thin Prince Andrew, brother of King Constantine, had been commander of the Second Corps in Asia Minor. He was first sentenced to death and then, after pressure from his blood relations in the royal families of Europe, banished from Greece for life. The prince and his family, including the one-year-old future Duke of Edinburgh who was carried in a wooden vegetable crate, were evacuated on a British cruiser and sailed from Corfu to Brindisi on December 4.

One eyewitness foreign reporter, who signed himself S.S.P., described (in the *Current History Review* of April 1923) the execution that was hastily carried out, before protests could mount, at 11 a.m. on the day after the sentence. "Gounaris was in a clinic suffering from typhoid when the sentence was issued, but at 7 a.m. three trucks full of policemen called on the hospital and transported him to the Averoff prison trembling with fever and wrapped in a blanket." At the prison in northern Athens, named for the Greek benefactor who paid for it, "Gounaris, white-pale from his sickness and staggering, had to be supported." The army was eager to shoot him before he died.

Like a character in a Greek tragedy, "Nikolaos Stratos, in parting from his son, was heard to say, 'You will have my curse if you ever interfere in politics.'"

Two of the old victims polished their monocles as if to see more clearly, and calmly or nervously puffed their last cigarette. One officer, degrading the General, declared "You are unworthy to wear the military insignia" and tore off his medals. The number five kept recurring as the five standing men were placed in a straight line five meters from each other, and the five-man firing squad stood five meters from the prisoners. They all refused to be blindfolded when faced with death. The commander raised his naked sword and shouted, "Attention! Take aim! Fire!" A sixth soldier fired shots through the heads of the dead men. As the reporter followed the truck carrying away the corpses, he saw through the flapping back curtains "the white-haired head of Protopapadakis moving to-and-fro with the jerks of the camion," as if he were still alive.

In 2010, eighty-eight years later, the Greek courts reversed the convictions and ruled that the victims had been incompetent but not treasonous: "They had been scapegoats to appease public anger at the humiliation that the Greeks had suffered. They had no desire to see Greek forces defeated, and had been in reality just victims of circumstances they were unable to control."

SEVEN

BRETT ASHLEY

> And worse I may be yet: the worst is not
> So long as we can say, "This is the worst."
>
> —*King Lear*

An obscure reference in *The Sun Also Rises* to Brett Ashley's experience as a V.A.D., ignored by readers and critics, provides the crucial clue to her tragic character. Hemingway does not describe her years as a civilian nurse for the British army in a Voluntary Aid Detachment. But her exposure to the horrors of war explains why she wants to forget her ruined life and lose herself in drink and sex. The alcoholic and nymphomaniac is a noncombatant casualty of World War I.

Most young V.A.D. women, after twenty years of sheltered genteel life, had never been intimate with a man outside their family, never seen a naked man and never had sexual intercourse. But suddenly changed from having servants to becoming one, they were thrown into close contact with many severely wounded and emotionally wrecked young soldiers. Agatha Christie, another V.A.D., wrote in her posthumously published *Autobiography* (1977), "our early cases came in straight from the trenches with field dressings on, and their heads full of lice. . . . It was a shock to us all."

The V.A.D. wore a demure but attractive uniform: dark blue dress down to her ankles, high stiff collar, long white headscarf, and white starched apron with straps crossed at the back and red cross on her chest. Vera Brittain's *Testament of Youth* (1933) noted the difference between the Florence Nightingale ideal of the nurse and the rough reality of their life: "In a surgical ward the nurses hardly occupy the silent-footed, gliding role which they always do in story-books and on the stage." Bound by strict rules, they were "allowed to run only in cases of haemorrhage or fire."

Most volunteers, like Brett Ashley, came from the middle and upper classes, and were not used to the hardships and severe discipline of military hospitals. Though they lacked the experience and advanced skills of trained nurses, they were often snobbishly critical of their middle-aged, salaried superiors. Brittain emphasized the intense hostility between the two kinds of nurses. The volunteers drove some of the professionals "almost frantic with jealousy and suspicion, which grew in intensity as the V.A.D.s increased in competence. . . . The longer a V.A.D. had performed the responsible work that fell to her on active service, the more resolutely her Ward-Sister appeared to relegate her to the most menial and elementary tasks."

The V.A.D.s endured harsh living conditions, worked long, exhausting hours and had a nervous horror of making potentially fatal mistakes. They suffered from septic infections and the delicately abbreviated "d. and v." (diarrhea and vomiting), and were exposed to malaria, influenza and tuberculosis. The volunteers could hear the explosions of big guns, not only from behind the lines in France, but even across the Channel from the south coast of England. Their well-marked hospital ships were attacked by German submarines, their hospitals in France shelled by artillery. While sacrificially serving, many women heard that their brothers, friends and fiancés had been killed.

The V.A.D.s' work ranged from disgusting duties and dealing with crazy patients to repairing wounds and assisting at operations. There was the endless routine of emptying bed-pans and urinals, cleaning up vomit and blood, inserting suppositories and scrubbing floors while rats ran around them in the dark—all this amid the penetrating odor of suppurating injuries. A paralytic patient drove Vera Brittain half-insane by screaming like an animal all through the night. She was also "chased up and down the hut by a stark naked six-foot-four New Zealander in the fighting stage of delirium . . . his fury exploding in a torrent" of vile and abusive language.

All the V.A.D.s saw grotesquely mutilated men and the slaughterhouse of gangrenous wounds with the bones laid bare. Agatha Christie had to carry an amputated leg down to the cellar and throw it into the furnace. Brittain recalled with a shudder, "I had seen men without faces, without eyes, without limbs, men almost disembowelled, men with hideous truncated stumps of bodies. . . . Stopping haemorrhages, replacing intestines and draining and re-inserting innumerable rubber tubes in that foetid stench was a regular baptism of blood and pus." Worst of all were the mustard gas victims. Their skin was burned from their bodies as if they had been flayed alive and they gasped for breath with corrupted lungs. One patient, rolling his eyes and choking in continuous paroxysms, died of convulsions. Most repulsive to look at were the abdominal operations, made even worse by the heat and ether in the room. The sight of bloody wounds made many women faint, and Christie had to turn her "eyes away from the original incision with the knife."

The V.A.D.s also had to deal with their patients' psychological problems as well as their own. As Wilfred Owen wrote in the preface to his *Poems*, "My subject is War, and the pity of War. The Poetry is in the pity." The wounded soldiers needed emotional as well as physical comfort, with tender hair-stroking at bedtime and hand-holding in the dark. (There's a poignant moment in *The English Patient* film when a wounded soldier begs for a kiss and his wish is granted by the Canadian nurse.) In order to protect themselves and work efficiently, the volunteers had to harden their hearts against the suffering patients and "force all the warmth out of themselves before they could be really good nurses." Ironically, Brittain also had to treat German prisoners of war, who had recently attempted to kill her brother. The English first tried to kill the Germans, then tried to save them. More hopeless than the British soldiers, the prisoners bore their wounds with stoical fortitude and waited phlegmatically to die.

Brittain had to watch many mutilated bodies bleeding to death, and witness the waste of legions of men dead before they had a real chance to live. All the deaths seemed meaningless, and most survivors felt guilty about being alive. The severely wounded men were bribed with medals and paid with pensions for their lost youth and ruined lives. Like the injured soldiers, Brittain was plagued by gruesome memories of fear and guilt long after the war was over. Both victims and volunteers found it difficult to readjust to civilian life. These V.A.D. patients were very different from the photograph of the smiling, healthy-looking young Hemingway recovering from his leg wounds in the Red Cross hospital in Milan in July 1918. His leg was healing, he was in love with his nurse and he seems happy rather than traumatized.

The real Duff Twysden (1892–1938) was significantly different from Hemingway's dramatically heightened Brett Ashley. Born Mary Duff Smurthwaite in Richmond, Yorkshire, the daughter of a wine-shop owner, she was not, despite her title, an aristocrat. Her parents were divorced; she was educated in Paris and fluent in French; and was tall and thin (not voluptuous). In 1915 she was divorced from Edward Byrom, who cited a co-respondent. Two years later she married Sir Roger Twysden, 10th baronet and a commander in the Royal Navy. Duff divorced Roger in 1926. His family was given custody of their son Anthony (1918–1946), who died prematurely, possibly related to service in World War II.

In 1928 she married her third husband, the amateur American painter Clinton King (1901–1979), who was nine years younger than Duff. He was heir to a Texas candy fortune but his family, suspecting that Duff was after his money, cut off his funds. During their ten-year happy marriage, they lived modestly from 1930 to 1932 in Chapala, Mexico, where D. H. Lawrence wrote *The Plumed Serpent*. In 1933 they moved to Santa Fe, New Mexico, where she may have gone to treat her neglected tubercular lesions. Mary Duff Sterling Smurthwaite Byrom Twysden King died there at the age of forty-six.

Hemingway was attracted to women older than he when he was young: the Milan nurse Agnes von Kurowsky, his first wife Hadley Richardson, Duff Twysden and his second wife Pauline Pfieffer; and to much younger women when he was old: Jigee Viertel, Adriana Ivancich and Valerie Danby-Smith. He met Duff in Paris in 1925. She was not a great beauty, but her title, and her androgynous short hair, boyish looks and manly dress appealed to him. She was (unlike Hadley) chic, witty, sexy, reckless, self-destructive, exciting and a great drinking companion. Though he felt constrained by his marriage, Hemingway lusted after her.

In *The Sun Also Rises* Brett Ashley's traumatic experience as a V.A.D. has transformed the bright young woman into a wounded spirit. Hemingway slowly reveals her complex character, and she first appears in chapter 3 with a group of homosexuals, outsiders like herself who make no sexual demands on her. Jake Barnes rages against the homosexuals, who are sexually active but don't want women. He wants women but, with his genitals injured in the war, he is impotent. He also attacks Jews because Robert Cohn has had a brief affair with Brett. When Cohn first sees Brett, Hemingway wittily alludes to Moses after wandering for forty years in the wilderness: "He looked a great deal as his compatriot must have looked when he saw the promised land. . . . She was built with curves like the hull of a racing yacht, and you missed none of it with that wool jersey." But Brett, who loves only Jake, is "afraid of so many things." As self-punishment for her fear and guilt as a wartime nurse, she "only wanted what she couldn't have."

In chapter 5 Jake tells Cohn the essential facts about the tragic background of the thirty-four-year-old Brett. "She was a V.A.D. in a hospital I was in during the war." She has seen Jake's wound and is also wounded. While she was a volunteer, "her own true love had just kicked off with the dysentery," a degrading rather than heroic death. On the rebound, she has married Ashley, who became shell-shocked and half-crazy. Much later and with bitter understatement, Hemingway reveals that "Ashley, chap she got the title from, was a sailor, you know. Ninth baronet. When he came home he wouldn't sleep in a bed. Always made Brett sleep on the floor. Finally, when he got really bad, he used to tell her he'd kill her. Always slept with a loaded service revolver. Brett used to take the shells out when he'd gone to sleep. She hasn't had an absolutely happy life." Hemingway adds that "Her name's Lady Ashley. Brett's her own name." She's "in the stud book," *Burke's Peerage*, but will lose the title when she divorces Ashley. "She's a drunk" and is going to marry Mike Campbell, who's also a drunk and a bankrupt.

Meanwhile, in a subtle and rarely noticed scene in chapter 7, Brett and Jake enjoy some sort of rare sexual pleasure: "Then later [she says]: 'Do you feel better, darling? Is the head any better?' . . . 'Couldn't we live together, Brett? Couldn't we just live together?'" But her sexual desire is too great and she replies, "I don't think so. I'd just *tromper* [deceive] you with everybody. You couldn't stand it." Jake must pay a cruel price for her love and his devotion. He's forced to witness Brett's liaisons with a diverse group of lovers: the infatuated American Jew Robert Cohn in San Sebastián, her Scottish Presbyterian fiancé Mike Campbell in Paris, and the teenaged Spanish Catholic bullfighter Pedro Romero in Madrid. All her love affairs end badly.

Like many V.A.D.s, unable to reconcile the horrors of war with the existence of God, Brett has lost her religious belief. She wants to hear Jake go to Catholic confession and talk about her, but she has no hat and is refused admission to the church. In Pamplona she egoistically behaves as if the fiesta were being staged in her honor. A group of drunken Spaniards dance wildly around her and worship her as a pagan goddess. Cohn bitterly calls her a Circe who turns men into swine. Without restraint, always acting impulsively and doing exactly what she wants to do, Brett pursues sex without love while Jake pursues love without sex. He tries to escape from the decadence of Paris to the outdoor freedom of Spain. He sees the running of the bulls in Pamplona, fishes in the Pyrenees and swims in San Sebastián. But like Brett, he cannot cure his war wounds.

Unlike most Englishwomen Brett, familiar with blood and death, is fascinated by the savage and cathartic spectacle of the *corrida*. She wants to see Pedro Romero get dressed in his satin matador's *traje de luces* (skin-tight so the bull's horns won't catch the silk cloth) and says he must use a shoehorn to slide into it. Always unconstrained and free, she falls in love with the nineteen-year-old Romero—half her age—right after she sees him kill the bulls. Against his better judgment and at the cost of his valued friendship with the hotel owner Montoya, Jake helps Brett start her affair with Romero and distract him at the height of the bullfighting season. Caught in a masochistic trap, Jake pimps for Brett and observes the symbolic debris in the café while she makes love with the matador. But Jake's awkward role allows him, at least, to participate vicariously in her liaison. Hemingway doesn't describe Brett's love scenes with Romero, but powerfully suggests the psychological and moral effects of their relations.

Brett goes off with Romero, as she had with Cohn before Pamplona, then forces him to leave her as suddenly as she'd left Cohn. She then summons Jake for emotional support and makes her confession to *him*. Romero, who'd learned English as a waiter in Gibraltar, wants to marry her. But in her first moral act, she has made the *gran rifiuto* before she damages his career. She tells Jake she was not "going to be one of these bitches that ruins children. . . . It makes one feel rather good deciding not to be a bitch. . . . It's sort of what we have instead of God." But she doesn't love Jake enough to make the same kind of sexual renunciation for him.

The careless Brett, fatally damaged by her experience as a V.A.D., leaves a trail of broken hearts and emotional misery behind her. Jake and Brett come together at the end of the novel, as they did at the beginning, but remain in the same paralyzed state. With no redemptive savior and no hope for the future, Brett remains an alcoholic, tragically unfulfilled, miserable about her wrecked marriage to Ashley and her doomed love for Jake. She finally decides to return to the hopeless Mike Campbell and confesses, "He's so damned nice and he's so awful. He's my sort of thing."

EIGHT

SCOTT FITZGERALD

Two of the greatest American novels—*The Great Gatsby* (1925) and *The Sun Also Rises* (1926)—were published in consecutive years by two close friends living an expatriate life in postwar Paris. In that bitter, disillusioned period they created strikingly similar characters, scenes and ideas. Both novels represented a breakthrough in style and subject for the young writers, and both concern the hero's doomed pursuit of a woman. Fitzgerald's Gatsby is murdered as a result of his infatuation with Daisy; Hemingway's Jake Barnes, impotent yet in love with the promiscuous Brett Ashley, ends up in a physical and emotional impasse. Read together, the two novels illuminate each other and reveal, despite their personal and artistic differences, their tragic view of life. The fate of these fictional heroes suggests the bleak self-projection of their authors. Fitzgerald, like Gatsby, was a romantic who loved not wisely but too well; Hemingway, equally romantic, could not sustain his love for one woman but was inspired by the pursuit of love. Throughout his life Fitzgerald sought Hemingway's approval, but instead received harsh criticism. Though their friendship foundered early on, each remained an important influence on the other. Both lives ended badly and much too soon.

Fitzgerald, three years older than Hemingway, had gone to Princeton. But in college he concentrated on writing musicals for the Triangle Club, failed his courses and never graduated. In his early twenties he achieved instant success with *This Side of Paradise* (1920) and *The Beautiful and the Damned* (1922), but these popular novels and his lucrative stories for the *Saturday Evening Post* were, as he knew, superficial. He first met Hemingway in Paris in April 1925, two weeks after *Gatsby* was published and at the high point of his career. Hemingway envied Fitzgerald's literary fame, material success and luxurious way of life, a vivid contrast to his own obscurity and rather pinched existence. But they had very different personalities: Hemingway was absolutely sure of himself while Fitzgerald, despite his impressive achievements, was full of self-doubt.

Fitzgerald introduced Hemingway to Scribner's and helped him toward recognition, and Hemingway became both his artistic rival and heroic ideal. He had masculine strength, capacity for drink, athletic prowess and experience in battle which Fitzgerald, with his "non-combatant's shell-shock," sadly lacked. Six inches taller and forty pounds heavier than Fitzgerald, he was a literary version of the bloodied football heroes Fitzgerald had worshiped at Princeton. Many of their expatriate friends—including John Dos Passos, Archibald MacLeish and Gerald Murphy—had gone to Harvard or Yale. Hemingway—like Conrad, Kipling and Orwell—had not been to college and was educated by violent experience in the real world. Hemingway was admired for his strengths, Fitzgerald was loved despite his weaknesses.

The two authors had parallel but contrasting lives. Fitzgerald was born into a midwestern Irish-Catholic family in St. Paul, Minnesota, in 1896. His father, who "came from tired old stock with very little left of vitality and mental energy," was a small, ineffectual man, a failure as a furniture-store owner and a soap salesman. Fitzgerald's mother, whom he disliked, was strong and domineering. He had a delicate, almost feminine beauty, was of middle height, physically frail and unathletic. A dispensable second lieutenant, he had stateside war service on a general's staff. After his literary success, he married the gorgeous and wild Zelda Sayre in 1920 and moved to Paris to work on *Gatsby*, set in Long Island and Manhattan. Their daughter Scottie was born in 1921. His style was romantic, lyrical and lush, his heroine both exalted and condemned. An alcoholic who frequently humiliated himself when drunk, he adored his fellow expatriate Gerald Murphy, the wealthy, amateur painter, a model for Dick Diver in *Tender Is the Night* (1934).

Hemingway was born into a midwestern Protestant family in Oak Park, a wealthy suburb of Chicago, in 1899. His father, a doctor and great outdoorsman, was dominated by his wife, whom Hemingway hated and blamed for his father's suicide in 1928. After high school, Hemingway worked as a reporter in Kansas City and approached fiction through journalism. Handsome and physically powerful, he was a good skier, boxer, hunter and fisherman. In 1918, while still a teenager, he served as a Red Cross volunteer on the Italian front, where he was badly wounded by shrapnel in his legs yet managed to rescue a fallen comrade. Three years later he married Hadley Richardson, a good sport, jolly hiker and notable contrast to the stunning Zelda. Hemingway moved to Paris in 1922, worked as a foreign correspondent for the *Toronto Star*, and covered international conferences and wars as far away as Constantinople. He also began to publish with highbrow magazines and little presses. *The Sun Also Rises*, set in Paris and Spain, has a terse, compressed and laconic style, and an attractive but damaged and drunken heroine. He was a heavy drinker who could hold his liquor. Fitzgerald had idolized Gerald Murphy, Hemingway found him idle and superficial.

Generous, helpful and dreamy, cautious and averse to risks, Fitzgerald led a glamorous life. He disliked the French, never went to Spain and never learned a foreign language. Zelda developed a disastrous obsession with ballet and had a series of mental breakdowns. She was committed in an insane asylum in 1936 and died there in a fire twelve years later. Fitzgerald went into a sharp decline after the disappointing reception of his most ambitious novel, *Tender Is the Night*, and lacerated himself in the "The Crack-Up" (1936). In the late 1930s he worked unsuccessfully as a screenwriter in Hollywood and had a lasting love affair with the English journalist Sheilah Graham. In the low, dishonest decade of the 1930s, he had no interest in politics. He wound up poor and after a self-destructive life had a fatal heart attack, aged forty-four, in 1940.

By contrast, Hemingway was competitive, selfish and realistic, tough, short-tempered and dangerous. He liked violent situations in sport and war, which tested his physical courage and moral values, took many risks and suffered frequent injuries. He loved bullfights in Spain; learned Italian, French, Spanish and German; lived in Cuba and traveled in Africa and Asia. He avoided Hollywood, and reported the Loyalists' battles in the Spanish Civil War. After the great success of *A Farewell to Arms* (1929) and *For Whom the Bell Tolls* (1940), his work declined, but he won the Nobel Prize in 1954. He ended up rich, but fell into a deep depression and killed himself, aged sixty-one, in 1961. His posthumous masterpiece, *A Moveable Feast* (1964) was scathing about Fitzgerald and other expatriates of the 1920s.

Fitzgerald and Hemingway knew each other intimately and were extremely perceptive about one another's virtues and faults. Fitzgerald saw that Hemingway, oppressed by his mother's influence, was "still rebelling against having been made to take cello lessons when growing up." Helping him leave Liveright for the more prestigious Scribner's, Fitzgerald took the role of an older sophisticate who guided his charming but naive friend toward the promised land. He told his editor Max Perkins, "To hear him talk you'd think Liveright had broken up his home and robbed him of millions—but that's because he knows nothing of publishing, except in the cuckoo magazines, is very young and feels helpless so far away. You won't be able to help liking him—he's one of the nicest fellows I ever knew." Eager to sign the contract, Hemingway confirmed that his literary experience did not include receiving money from publishers.

Hemingway, who rarely praised contemporaries and rivals, called *Gatsby* "an absolutely first-rate book." Fitzgerald's novel reveals a new and confident mastery of his material, a mysterious hero and idealized heroine, a complex plot with adultery, crime and murder, class conflicts and incisive social satire, an opulent setting and lavish parties, a Keatsian ability to evoke a romantic atmosphere, the loss of impossible dreams and illusions, and a silken style that seems as fresh today as it did almost a century ago.

Instead of cultivating the snobbery and remoteness of the rich, Gatsby recklessly throws open his doors to all the riff-raff, so he can attract the unattainable Daisy. She wants her little daughter to become exactly like her own flawed self, and remembers thinking when the baby was born: "I hope she'll be a fool—that's the best thing a girl can be in this world, a beautiful little fool." She has no maternal feelings and merely exhibits her daughter as a precious toy in her wealthy hermetic world. Gatsby does not buy his beautiful shirts to wear, but to throw onto his bed to impress Daisy. His grand gesture appeals to her materialistic character and makes her sob with joy.

Daisy is perennially bored and wants to drive into Manhattan in the blazing heat. Like the neurasthenic heroine in "The Waste Land" who pleads, "What shall I do now? What shall I do . . . / What shall we do tomorrow? / What shall we ever do?" Daisy asks, "What'll we do with ourselves this afternoon, and the day after that, and the next thirty years?"—a great vacuous leap in time. Daisy's husband, Tom Buchanan, sees through Gatsby's lies about his background and wealth, but she is deceived by him. The irony, which Gatsby doesn't see, is that Daisy is shallow, narcissistic and mercenary—completely unworthy of his sacrificial quest. Gatsby gets everything he ever wanted—except Daisy. Tom, though brutal, rotten and adulterous, manages to keep her.

The imagery and sense of loss in *The Great Gatsby* influenced the conclusion of *A Farewell to Arms*. The narrator Nick Carraway says, when he leaves Gatsby's mansion as Gatsby and Daisy seem to recapture but are really about to lose their dreams:

> Then I went out of the room and down the marble steps *into the rain, leaving* them there together.

Hemingway boldly appropriated this and used it as the last sentence in *A Farewell to Arms*:

> After a while *I went out* and *left* the hospital and walked back to the hotel *in the rain*.

The plot and mood of Fitzgerald's novel also influenced two other works of art. The dead Gatsby floating face down in the swimming pool inspired the dead Joe Gillis floating face down in the pool in Billy Wilder's film *Sunset Boulevard* (1950). In *Gatsby* and Nabokov's *Lolita* (1955) vulgar women, Myrtle Wilson and Charlotte Haze, have been rejected by their lovers. They rush madly into the street, are hit by a car and instantly killed. Myrtle's death frees Tom from his entanglement with her and allows him to recapture and escape with Daisy. Charlotte's death allows Humbert to capture and escape with Lolita.

Fitzgerald had heard about Hemingway before they met, and Nick Carraway is a composite of the first name of Hemingway's hero Nick Adams and an echo of his own three-syllable last name ending in "way." In his most artistically refined novel, Fitzgerald contrasts midwestern and East Coast values with Nick Carraway as the moral center and the polo player Tom Buchanan as Gatsby's masculine rival. In *The Sun Also Rises* Hemingway contrasts American and expatriate values with Jake Barnes as the unsteady moral center and the bullfighter Pedro Romero as his masculine rival.

There is heavy drinking in both novels: during Prohibition in America (Gatsby is a bootlegger) and in the more bibulous France and Spain. Barnes tells Robert Cohn, who wants to travel to South America, "You can't get away from yourself by moving from one place to another." In *Gatsby* the characters move frantically from Long Island to Manhattan and the fatal car accident takes place on the way back. In *The Sun Also Rises* Barnes shifts uneasily from Paris to Spain to see the running of the bulls in Pamplona, fish in the Pyrenees, swim in San Sebastián and rescue Brett in Madrid.

In both novels the heroes of the Lost Generation face formidable problems. Jay Gatsby has lower-class origins, degrading poverty, criminal activities, fantastic dreams and futile gestures. He's exposed and victimized by Tom Buchanan and murdered by Wilson, who mistakenly thinks that Gatsby, not Daisy, has killed his wife Myrtle in the car accident. Barnes has suffered a war wound that made him impotent, leads a decadent life and is hopelessly in love with Brett Ashley. Brett's great love has been killed in the war, she's had a bad marriage to a shell-shocked husband, is an alcoholic and nymphomaniac, and has a disastrous affair with Pedro Romero. Both Gatsby and Barnes are in love with an unworthy and unattainable woman, and the novels end with shattered illusions.

Brett, "built with curves like the hull of a racing yacht," is a much more interesting and substantial character than the deliberately vague and wraith-like Daisy. Brett was a British nurse during the war and, like Barnes, "only wanted what she couldn't have." In Pamplona, all the celebrants worship her and dance around her. "Never able to help anything," she craves sexual satisfaction, is deeply attached to Barnes but sleeps with her fiancé Mike Campbell, the infatuated Robert Cohn and the teenaged Pedro Romero. Barnes, who pursues love without sex, is sadly reunited with Brett after she renounces Romero.

Brett's lovers give Barnes the "rotten habit of picturing the bedroom scenes of [his] friends." Gatsby is horrified to think of Daisy's bedroom scenes with Tom, and wants her to deny the past and say she never loved her husband. Barnes believes that "you paid in some way for everything that was any good." Gatsby pays with money and death, Barnes pays with wounds and pain. Corrupted by pimping for Brett with Romero, Barnes is despised by an old Spanish friend and when he leaves Pamplona, Montoya avoids him. In contrast to Daisy, who sacrifices Gatsby and remains with Tom, the lovesick Brett makes a moral choice. She gives up Romero before she ruins his career and tells Barnes, "you know it makes one feel rather good deciding not to be a bitch."

Just as Hemingway borrowed from *Gatsby*, so Fitzgerald lifted two passages from *The Sun Also Rises*. In a witty exchange in that novel, a friend asks the dissolute Mike Campbell, "How did you go bankrupt?" and he responds: "Two ways. Gradually, then suddenly." In "The Crack-Up" Fitzgerald writes that his second kind of nervous breakdown happened gradually, "almost without you knowing it but is realized suddenly." In *The Sun Also Rises*, when Cohn fatuously says, "I'd rather play football again with what I know about handling myself, now," Barnes calls him "a case of arrested development." Later on, when walking down Fifth Avenue in New York, Fitzgerald tells Hemingway, almost verbatim, "if only I could play foot-ball again with everything I know about it now." Forgetting the source, Hemingway quoted this as a typically foolish remark. But in *Across the River and into the Trees* the failed hero Richard Cantwell quite seriously thinks the very same thing about war: "I wish I could fight it again . . . Knowing what I know now." This remark is foolish when Cohn and Fitzgerald say it, but it's all right for Cantwell.

The rich themes in *Gatsby* reverberate through *The Sun Also Rises*. Originally rejected by Daisy because he had no money, Gatsby has devoted most of his adult life to winning her back. "'Can't repeat the past?' he cried incredulously. 'Why of course you can!'" Barnes and Brett, more realistically, want to escape from rather than repeat the tragic past. Both novels are social satires. Carraway's declaration to Gatsby, "They're a rotten crowd. . . . You're worth the whole damn bunch put together," is echoed by the solid Bill Gorton's condemnation of expatriates: "You drink yourself to death. You become obsessed with sex. You spend all your time talking not working."

Carraway calls Tom and Daisy careless people who "smashed up things and creatures and then retreated back into their . . . vast carelessness . . . and let other people clean up the mess they had made." The careless Brett also leaves a trail of broken hearts and emotional misery behind her. At the conclusion of the novels, Gatsby's dream of the green light across the water that led him to Daisy is extinguished. Barnes and Brett are together, as at the beginning, but remain in the same impotent state and with no hope for the future.

Hemingway admired Fitzgerald in the mid-1920s, became more critical as he knew him better in the late 1920s and cruelly attacked him in the 1930s. The first fissure in their friendship occurred early on when Fitzgerald advised him to cut the first two chapters of *The Sun Also Rises*, which described the background of the characters and afforded a more leisurely approach to the novel. Though Max Perkins wanted to keep them, Hemingway cut them and later resented his submission to Fitzgerald's judgment. The first chapter now begins with a misleading emphasis on the odious Robert Cohn, who seems to be the main character but is actually much less important than Jake Barnes and Brett Ashley.

A more volatile incident, which Hemingway never forgave, took place in June 1929 when Fitzgerald lost track of the time in Hemingway's boxing match with the Canadian writer Morley Callaghan. After Callaghan knocked Hemingway down, Fitzgerald woke up and screamed: "Oh, my God! I let the round go four minutes." "'All right, Scott,' Ernest said savagely. 'If you want to see me getting the shit knocked out of me, just say so. Only don't say you made a mistake.'" "He thinks I did it on purpose. Why would I do it on purpose?" He must have had an unconscious desire to let Callaghan express his hostility and provide vicarious punishment.

Fitzgerald remained faithful to Zelda during her breakdowns; Hemingway discarded three wives and gave the fourth one a rough time. Fitzgerald shrewdly prophesied that Hemingway needed the emotional anguish of a divorce and excitement of a new wife to create a major work. He told Callaghan, "I have a theory that Ernest needs a new woman for each big book. There was one for the stories and *The Sun Also Rises*. Now there's Pauline. *A Farewell to Arms* is a big book. If there's another big book I think we'll find Ernest has another wife." Sure enough, Martha Gellhorn, his companion in the Spanish Civil War, became his third wife when he was writing *For Whom the Bell Tolls*.

Fitzgerald obliquely alludes to Hemingway in his sad self-exposure and evisceration in "The Crack-Up," a three-part essay that appeared in *Esquire* in February, March and April 1936. This public catharsis, when he was blocked as a writer, confirmed Hemingway's criticism of Fitzgerald's weaknesses and was more severe than anything Hemingway ever wrote about him. Like Hemingway, Fitzgerald believes that "life was something you dominated if you were any good," and then admits that life has dominated him and he's cracked up. Contrasting his tame military service to Hemingway's war wounds, he foolishly equates two very different tests of manhood: "not being big enough (or good enough) to play football in college, and not getting overseas during the war."

The insecure Fitzgerald lists four men who served as his external conscience, though the man Hemingway called a guided missile without a guide rarely took their advice. The brilliant writer Edmund Wilson was his moral conscience. The bright, athletic and popular Charles "Sap" Donahoe, his friend at prep school and Princeton, was his moral conscience. The acerbic Hemingway, who maintained high standards when Fitzgerald sold out for money, was his artistic conscience. Gerald Murphy, who lived a hedonistic life on the French Riviera, was his social conscience.

Hemingway always learned a great deal from expert teachers: fishing and shooting from his father; military tactics from the World War I hero Chink Dorman-Smith; journalism from the experienced and respected Lincoln Steffens; politics from observing Georges Clemenceau and Lloyd George; writing from Leo Tolstoy, Rudyard Kipling, Stephen Crane and T. E. Lawrence; art from the Spaniards Pablo Picasso and Joan Miró; big-game hunting in Africa from Philip Percival.

In a letter to Perkins, Fitzgerald contrasted his own laborious writing to Hemingway's deceptively effortless ease: "everything I have ever attained has been through long and persistent struggle while it is Ernest who has a touch of genius that enables him to bring off extraordinary things with facility." He confessed that he'd always wanted to have a nourishing connection to Hemingway, "had always longed to absorb into himself some of the qualities that made Ernest attractive, and to lean on him like a sturdy crutch in times of psychological distress." His last wish, however, was never granted, and he always got more abuse than comfort from his caustic friend. In 1936 he admitted that he could never face Hemingway after their positions had been disastrously reversed: "I talk with the authority of failure—Ernest with the authority of success. We could never sit across the table again." Yet in another tragic prophecy, he saw himself and his friend as two sides of the same manic-depressive personality: "He is quite as nervously broken down as I am but it manifests itself in different ways. His inclination is toward megalomania and mine toward melancholy."

Though Fitzgerald had mocked Hemingway's incongruous cello playing in Oak Park, his hometown taught his friend to look down on the Irish, who were usually servants. In *A Moveable Feast* he even criticized Fitzgerald's attractive but effeminate appearance: "He looked like a boy with a face between handsome and pretty. . . . [He had] a delicate long-lipped Irish mouth that, on a girl, would have been the mouth of a beauty. . . . The mouth worried you until you knew him and then it worried you more," because it suggested a kind of androgynous decadence. Satirizing Fitzgerald's hermetic, rich, faithful, snobbish and alcoholic milieu, he wrote that his idea of heaven was "a beautiful vacuum filled with wealthy monogamists, all powerful and members of the best families all drinking themselves to death."

Hemingway despised Fitzgerald's worship of youth, sexual naivete, self-pity, attraction to money and lack of dedication to his art. His worst qualities were his inability to hold his liquor and the compulsion to debase himself in public. Putting the knife in, he said Fitzgerald never achieved maturity and "jumped straight from youth to senility" without going through manhood. He bluntly told Fitzgerald that his egoistic self-absorption prevented him from getting valuable material, and advised him to pay attention to people and learn from what they said: "A long time ago you stopped listening except to the answers to your own questions. . . . That is where it all comes from. Seeing, listening. You see well enough. But you stop listening."

No friend did more for Hemingway than Fitzgerald. Apart from placing him with Scribner's, he gave him money when he needed it, lent the family his Riviera villa when their little son John was sick, and personally rushed from Delaware to the Philadelphia railroad station when Hemingway suddenly needed cash to get to Chicago after his father's suicide. But Hemingway, who valued his independence and disliked obligations, often quarreled with friends who'd helped him. There's a striking contrast between telling Fitzgerald in 1927, "I get maudlin about how damned swell you are. . . . You are the best damn friend I have," and the end of something two years later when his drunken best friend went out of control. In a murderous letter Hemingway told Perkins, "Last time he was in Paris he got us kicked out of one apt. and in trouble all the time. (Insulted the landlord—pee-ed on the front porch—tried to break down the door at 3–4 and 5 a.m.). . . . I am very fond of Scott but I'll beat him up before I'll let him come and get us ousted from this place—as a matter of fact I'm afraid I'd kill him."

The stoic condemned Fitzgerald's pitiful self-exposure in "The Crack-Up" and told Perkins, "He seems to almost take a pride in his shamelessness of defeat. . . . He had a marvelous talent and the thing is to use it—not whine in public." He felt that Fitzgerald's self-autopsy and premature funeral sermon gave him the right to publicly criticize him in "The Snows of Kilimanjaro," which appeared in *Esquire* in August 1936—only three months after Fitzgerald's essays. In "Snows" Harry, the failed writer, bitterly thinks: "He remembered poor Scott Fitzgerald and his romantic awe of [the rich]. . . . He thought they were a special glamorous race and when he found they weren't it wrecked him just as much as any other thing that wrecked him." Hemingway knew that the self-destructive Fitzgerald had not been wrecked by the rich, whom he'd satirized in *The Great Gatsby*.

Fitzgerald, especially vulnerable the year Zelda became insane, was so disturbed by this story that he attempted suicide, but vomited from an overdose of morphine, an episode that proved not only his weakness but also Hemingway's power to wound. Though Hemingway changed Fitzgerald's name to "Julian" when the story appeared in a book, the damage was done. It's difficult to see how this attack could possibly have helped Fitzgerald, but it allowed him to absorb some of Hemingway's own guilt about selling out to the rich. Despite rough treatment by the taskmaster, Fitzgerald continued to admire Hemingway. He felt his criticism was valid and that his friend was really trying to help him.

Hemingway's posthumous time bomb, *A Moveable Feast*, cruelly retaliated for Fitzgerald's extraordinary generosity and kindness. He portrayed Fitzgerald as rude to all foreigners, childish and gauche, wasteful and irresponsible, quarrelsome and irritating. Completely unreliable, he misses the train to take him and Hemingway to retrieve his automobile in Lyon and does not have a top on his car to protect them from the rain. A ludicrous and self-indulgent hypochondriac, he interferes with Hemingway's writing, and most improbably—since a negative judgment would be devastating—humiliates himself by asking Hemingway to decide if his penis is too small. As Zelda became increasingly frigid, she attacked his sexual capacity and made him doubt his ability to satisfy her.

The sexually exciting Zelda was Hemingway's *bête noire* and he told Fitzgerald, with his usual sensitivity and tact, "I thought Zelda was crazy the first time I met her and you complicated it even more by being in love with her." He blamed Zelda for trying to destroy her husband and wrote to Perkins, "I think 90 per cent of all the trouble he has comes from her." In *A Moveable Feast* he wrote that "Zelda was jealous of Scott's work. . . . As soon as he was working well Zelda would begin complaining about how bored she was and get him off on another drunken party." Most grievously, he condemned Fitzgerald for allowing her to cuckold him with the dashing French aviator Edouard Jozan. By contrast, three of Hemingway's wives adored him. Only Martha Gellhorn put her own interests first.

Hemingway satirized Zelda, a model for Margot Macomber, in his great story "The Short Happy Life of Francis Macomber," whose hero has the same first name as Francis Scott Fitzgerald. Like Zelda, Margot is a great beauty and has a nasty character. The white hunter, experienced with wealthy female clients, calls her kind of woman "the hardest in the world; the hardest, the cruelest, the most predatory and the most attractive and their men have softened or gone to pieces nervously as they have hardened."

Also like Zelda, who slept with the French aviator, Margot sleeps with the red-faced white hunter Robert Wilson. (He has the same surname as the garage-man George Wilson who murders Gatsby, an ironic tribute to both authors' mutual friend Edmund Wilson.) In a bitter exchange after Macomber discovers her adultery, he feebly complains about her past and present behavior, and she mocks him with cutting endearments:

> "You think that I'll take anything."
> "I know you will, sweet."
> "There wasn't going to be any of that. You promised there wouldn't be."
> "Well, there is now," she said sweetly.

Zelda tried to destroy Fitzgerald; Margot actually murders Macomber when he recovers his self-esteem by killing the charging buffalo and now has the courage to leave her.

In "The Short Happy Life" Hemingway lifted another moment of crucial transformation from *The Great Gatsby*. Both Gatsby and Macomber reach an emotional peak and experience a euphoric moment. When Daisy (partly modeled on Zelda) weeps and expresses her love for Gatsby on her first visit to his mansion,

> there was a change in Gatsby that was simply confounding. He literally glowed; without a word or gesture of exaltation a new well-being radiated from him.

Similarly, after redeeming himself by shooting the buffalo, Macomber

> instead of fear had a feeling of definite elation. Macomber felt a wild unreasonable happiness that he had never known before.

At the end of his life, Hemingway had fulfilled Fitzgerald's prophesies and become tragically like his old friend. He too had been dazzled by the rich, turned into a celebrity and created a legend that made his life better known than his work. He too was blocked as a writer, had failed in marriage, escaped into alcoholism and cracked up. Ill-equipped to deal with depression, he finally put a shotgun in his mouth and killed himself. Fitzgerald, though apparently weaker, endured poverty and neglect in the 1930s—he sold only forty copies of his books in the last year of his life—but published his best novel, *Tender Is the Night*, in 1934.

NINE

D. H. LAWRENCE

In April 1927, while composing *Lady Chatterley's Lover* (1928), Lawrence praised the characters, compression and intensity of Hemingway's *In Our Time* (1925): "The sketches are short, sharp, vivid, and most of them excellent. . . . These few sketches are enough to create the man and all his history: we need to know no more." Lawrence also perceived that the stories in *In Our Time* foreshadowed the theme of *The Sun Also Rises*: "Avoid one thing only: getting connected up. Don't get connected up. If you get held by anything, break it." Though I've written biographies of Hemingway and Lawrence, I had not noticed until recently the striking similarities that reveal Lawrence was influenced by *The Sun Also Rises* (1926) while writing his last novel.

The first sentence of Lawrence's work—"Ours is essentially a tragic age, so we refuse to take it tragically"—applies with equal force to Hemingway's novel. Both Jake Barnes and Clifford Chatterley have been injured and destroyed by the war. Barnes, hit in the groin, appears outwardly normal but is sexually impotent. Clifford, paralyzed below the waist, is confined to a mechanical wheelchair. Like Jake, the naked and despairing Connie stares at her own sad reflection. Jake undresses and says,

> *I looked at myself in the mirror*. . . . It was a rotten way to be wounded. . . . I put on my pajamas and got into bed. . . . I was thinking about Brett. . . . Then all of a sudden I started to cry.

In a similar scene, Connie

> *looked at herself naked in the huge mirror.* . . . And she thought as she had thought so often: what a frail, easily hurt, rather pathetic thing a naked human body is: somehow a little unfinished, incomplete! . . . She slipped into her nightdress, and went to bed, where she sobbed bitterly.

Like Jake, who's literally incomplete without his sexual organ, Connie realizes how vulnerable, pathetic and incomplete she is without love and the fulfillment of motherhood. Both characters cry as they confront their useless bodies and their longing for a sexual life.

Both Hemingway and Lawrence satirize homosexuals whose transgressive lives reflect and infuriate the sexually dysfunctional characters. Jake exclaims, "They always made me angry. I know they are supposed to be amusing, and you should be tolerant, but I wanted to swing on one, any one, anything to shatter that superior, simpering composure." Lawrence's apparently manly General Tommy Dukes rejects heterosexual relations and conventional marriage, and declares, "I neither marry nor run after women. . . . My-husband-my wife sort of love? No my fine fellow, I don't believe in it at all!" The homosexual painter Duncan Forbes, a peculiar man, agrees to acknowledge paternity of Connie's child in order to absolve Mellors, avoid scandal and facilitate her divorce. Connie's feisty, sensual father asks her:

> "Well I'm damned! Poor Duncan! And what's he going to get out of it?"
> "I don't know. But he might rather like it, even."
> "He might, might he? Well he's a funny man, if he does. Why you've never even had an affair with him, have you?"
> "No! But he doesn't really want it. He only loves me to be near him, but not to touch him."
> "My God, what a generation!"

Though both Jake and Clifford are sexually incapacitated, they manage to get some sexual gratification. In a brief moment in *The Sun Also Rises*, which is usually overlooked, Brett asks Jake, after a discreet interval in the novel, "Do you feel better, darling? Is the head better?" "It's better." "Lie quiet." In *Lady Chatterley*, Ivy Bolton clings to Clifford and gives him the sympathy and physical pleasure that Connie fails to provide: "Clifford became like a child with Mrs. Bolton. . . . When she sponged his great blond body . . . she would lightly kiss his body, anywhere, half in mockery. . . . Then he would put his hand into her bosom and feel her breasts, and kiss them in exaltation, the exaltation of perversity, of being a child when he was a man." Though Clifford's torso is still attractively masculine, Lawrence portrays his sexual exaltation with Ivy Bolton as childishly regressive and perverse in order to contrast it to Connie's relations with Mellors.

Both Lady Ashley, age thirty-four, and Lady Chatterley, age twenty-seven, received their titles from their baronet husbands. Both Ashley and Chatterley (whose names sound similar) have been severely damaged by the war. Mike Campbell tells Jake that Brett's soon-to-be-divorced husband is shell-shocked, violent and crazy. Brett and Connie (before she meets Mellors) are sexually liberated but physically dissatisfied and deeply unhappy; Jake and Clifford are emotionally drained and passive. Jake and the alcoholic and promiscuous Brett Ashley love each other. But he is forced to observe her disastrous sexual encounters with a diverse group: Mike Campbell, Robert Cohn and Pedro Romero. In the end, after sacrificially forcing the teenaged Romero to leave her, Brett summons Jake and counts on him for emotional, if not sexual, support. Neither Brett nor Jake is psychologically or physically fit for marriage.

Clifford represses his feelings for Connie and wants to use her mainly as a broodmare to produce a male heir who will inherit his title, vast estate and prosperous coal mines. He encourages her to find a suitable upper-class stud, but disapproves of the lower-class Mellors who had served under him in the war. Hemingway's novel ends tragically, Lawrence's—despite formidable obstacles—happily. Brett, with no redemptive savior, remains alcoholic, tragically unfulfilled, and miserable about her wrecked marriage and doomed passion for an impotent lover. Mellors and Connie have transcended class barriers and he gives her everything that Clifford has failed to provide. They have ecstatic sexual relations and plan to marry; she's secure in her love, the prospect of a child and the promise of future happiness.

Three dominant themes in *The Sun Also Rises* recur in *Lady Chatterley's Lover*. The regenerative power of nature is portrayed when the characters fish in the mountain steams of Burguete and raise pheasants in the secluded woods. Jake and Clifford suffer tragic sexual wounds that cannot be healed. And after the war these traumatized soldiers cannot adjust to civilian society.

Hemingway's famous epigraph from Gertrude Stein, "You are all a lost generation," which refers to men who have lost their youth in the war and have not found a new life, is echoed in Lawrence's recurrent references to Connie's tragic "generation."

TEN

LUIS DE GÓNGORA

Hemingway owned three works by the poet and satirist of the Spanish Golden Age, Francisco de Quevedo (1580–1645), and mentions Quevedo three times in *For Whom the Bell Tolls*. An old man's dialect was "like reading Quevedo"; Pilar's storytelling is "better than Quevedo"; and Robert Jordan imagines that when he returns to teach Spanish in America, he and his students will have "valuable informal discussions about Quevedo." In November 1952 he wrote Edmund Wilson, "If you really want to learn the language you can skip a lot and start in with Quevedo." Four months later he told Bernard Berenson, "Quevedo I feel I know better than my brother."

These persistent but culturally decorative and thematically superficial references have led scholars to list Quevedo among Hemingway's "favorite Spanish artists" [*sic*]; to mention Quevedo as an example of the old cliché, the typically "Spanish preoccupation with death"; to call him "the classical Spanish writer most obsessed by mortality" (how can you measure this?); and, though *capea*, or bull-baiting, is real and takes place outdoors in village squares, to compare "the mob brutality and taste for blood of the capea" to "the hallucinatory, infernal atmosphere of death reminiscent of Quevedo's prose" [*sic*].

Quevedo's older contemporary and Spain's greatest poet, Luis de Góngora (1561–1627)—a close contemporary of John Donne, who provided the title of *For Whom the Bell Tolls*—is not mentioned by Hemingway or his critics. But he had a more significant influence on Hemingway than Quevedo ever did. Hemingway would have been attracted to Góngora's sexual innuendos and scatological humor; his descriptions of passionate encounters, hunting scenes, bravery in war, bloody battlefields; his lyrical passages on "beautiful Andalusian horses, the flight of hawks, the color of red and white wine mixed, a river winding through fields, the rising sun dispelling mists, pools of water on the seashore sparkling in the sunlight."

Góngora's most famous, beautiful and intensely chromatic poem is "Mientras por competir con tu cabello" (While trying to rival your hair):

Now while to match your hair bright gold must know
it seeks in vain to mirror the sun's rays,
and while amid the fields with envious gaze
the lily regards the whiteness of your brow;

and while on each red lip attend more eyes
than wait on the carnation, as if intent
on plucking it, and while your graceful neck
outdoes bright crystal with disdainful ease,

enjoy them all, neck, hair, lip, and brow,
before the gold and lily of your heyday,
the red carnation, crystal brightly gleaming,

are changed to silver and withered violet,
and you and they together must revert
to earth, to smoke, to dust, to shadow, to nothing.

The poem's theme of loss suggests Hemingway's tragic heroines: Brett Ashley, an alcoholic nymphomaniac; Catherine Barkley, dead in childbirth; Maria, raped in her youth. In the octave of the sonnet, the lady's golden hair is compared to the sun, her white brow to the lily, her red lips to the carnation, her graceful neck to bright crystal. In the sestet, "neck, hair, lip, and brow" (their order changed) degenerate to silver-gray and withered violet, "to earth, to smoke, to dust, to shadow, to nothing" ("en tierra, en humo, en polvo, en sombra, en nada"). The poem warns not of old age, but of extinction, and ends with "a cry of anguish at the prospect of annihilation."

For Hemingway, the crucial word is Góngora's authoritative *nada*. In one of his most intense and compassionate stories, "A Clean, Well-Lighted Place"

(1933), "nothing" is mentioned six times, "*nada*" repeated twenty-two times. The war, the destruction of idealism and the loss of God have inevitably led to the concept of *nada*: no tangible thing, but a palpable and overwhelming sensation of nothingness. As Wallace Stevens observed in "The Snow Man," the listener, "nothing himself, beholds / Nothing that is not there and the nothing that is."

In Hemingway's story, the old man in the café has lost his wife and sought annihilation; he has tried to hang himself and failed. At the beginning, the two meanings of *nada* are suggested by the younger and the older waiters. The older one knows the old man "was in despair . . . about nothing." The younger one merely asks, "How do you know it was nothing?" At the end, the older waiter sympathizes "with all those who need a light for the night." And the insomniac old man confirms that he feared "a nothing that he knew too well. It all was a nothing and a man was nothing too. . . . He knew it was all *nada*." His savage parody of the Lord's Prayer—"Our nada who art in nada, nada be thy name . . ."—expresses a desperate but illusory hope for some shred of comfort in this world, if not in the next. Góngora's concept of *nada*, of the horror at the end of human existence, must be confronted, if not overcome.

ELEVEN

FRANCISCO GOYA

After his combat experience in World War I, Hemingway sought visual analogues that would inspire his writing and found them most significantly in Francisco Goya's stark images of suffering. In "A Natural History of the Dead" he wanted to equal the clarity and intensity that Goya had achieved in *The Disasters of War* (published thirty-five years after his death in 1863). Hemingway's story first appeared inside the text of his bullfighting book *Death in the Afternoon* (1932) and was reprinted, without the irritating interruptions of the Author and Old Lady, as a separate story in *Winner Take Nothing* (1933). This unusual story is a perfect example of how Hemingway transformed Goya's visual qualities in his own verbal art. His favorite Spanish painter was closer to him, in defiant and combative temperament, than any other artist.

Though Goya painted royal portraits in brilliant colors, he is also famous for his satiric etchings in black and white. He even advocated limiting the palette in order to intensify his visual effects and wrote, "in art there is no need for color; I see only light and shade. Give me a crayon, and I will *paint* your portrait." Following Goya's emphasis on chiaroscuro in *Death in the Afternoon*, Hemingway praised the artist's qualities as a way of heightening the significance of his own work: "Goya did not believe in costume but he did believe in blacks and grays, in dust and in light, in high places rising from the plains, in the country around Madrid, in movement, in his own cojones, in painting, in etching, and in what he had seen, felt, touched, handled, smelled, enjoyed, drunk, mounted, suffered, spewed-up, lain-with, suspected, observed, loved, hated, lusted, feared, detested, admired, loathed, and destroyed. Naturally no painter has been able to paint all that but he tried." His allusion to the movement, spectacle and drama in Goya's thirty-three etchings in *La Tauromaquia* (The Art of Bullfighting, 1816), like his use of the Spanish "cojones" for "balls," made this alien subject more culturally acceptable to American readers. His powerful catalog of active verbs, so different from his normally austere style, suggests his desire to live fully both the macho and the artistic life. In a vertiginous passage he celebrated the artist's portrayal of the arid high plateau of Castile, his sexual energy (in "cojones," "mounted," "lain-with" and "lusted"), his direct appeal to four of the five senses ("seen, felt . . . smelled . . . drunk") and his intense passions.

Edmund Wilson was characteristically perceptive in his review, the first on Hemingway, of the small-press pamphlet *in our time*, with eighteen short untitled interchapters, in the *Dial* of 1924. Noting the writer's affinity with the Spanish painter, Wilson wrote: "His bull-fight sketches have the dry sharpness and elegance of the bull-fight lithographs [i.e., etchings] of Goya. And, like Goya, he is concerned first of all with making a fine picture." Goya and Hemingway convey the most intense emotions, one in razor-sharp lines, the other in diamond-cut prose.

Hemingway paid tribute to Goya by using names closely connected to the artist. Goya painted frescoes in the cathedral of Nuestra Señora de Pilar in Zaragoza, where the Virgin Mary was said to have appeared atop a pillar (*pilar*), and the aged artist's country house outside Madrid was called "La Quinta del Sordo" (the deaf man's villa). Hemingway named his boat the *Pilar*, and Pilar and El Sordo appear as characters in the guerrilla band in *For Whom the Bell Tolls* (1940).

Though Hemingway did not mention Goya's most striking and notorious picture (with her fringe of pubic hair), the *Naked Maja*, he admired his realistic and symbolic paintings of cruelty and repression. Goya's *Inquisition* and *Procession of Flagellants* portray the perverse connection between religion and torture. In *Saturn Devouring One of His Sons* a gigantic, shaggy, wide-eyed, open-mouthed, ravenous, demonic god, clutching his helpless victim, has gnawed an arm and head off the bloody torso and is feasting on the torn flesh of the remaining arm stump. Hemingway saw in this painting a convincing illustration of a malevolent and destructive world without God. There are also specific parallels between the works of Goya and Hemingway. Goya's *Third of May 1808*, in which a firing squad executes a Christ figure, is similar to Hemingway's description of the executions of Greek politicians in interchapter V of *In Our Time*—"They shot the six cabinet ministers at half-past six in the morning against the wall of a hospital"—and his portrayal of Santiago as a Christ figure, splayed out cruciform on the strand, at the end of *The Old Man and the Sea* (1952).

Hemingway collected Goya's etchings, which are now owned by his daughter-in-law. Carlos Baker stated that when Hemingway was writing *Across the River and Into the Trees* (1950) he was inspired by Spanish painters: "the Goya and the El Greco had been taken down from the walls and leaned against chairs in the bedroom so that they would be the first objects his eyes would see when he awoke at dawn." In that novel Colonel Cantwell interprets the character of a fiercely ugly man, based on Sinclair Lewis, by recalling how Goya had portrayed such feral types in his satiric portraits: "He had a strange face like an over-enlarged, disappointed weasel or ferret. . . . I was looking at him as at a drawing by Goya. Faces are pictures too." By contrast, he idealized his young Irish secretary, Valerie Danby-Smith, by comparing her to Goya's portraits of his supposed mistress, the Duchess of Alba.

Goya remained Hemingway's key to Spanish culture. In his biography *Papa Hemingway*, Aaron Hotchner depicts their tour of the Prado museum in Madrid in the 1950s and Hemingway's interpretation of Goya's *The Family of Carlos IV*. Salvador de Madariaga writes that the "half-witted" Carlos had "mental powers of the most touching modesty." In Goya's painting the king's sister is a wide-eyed old witch with a black patch covering her skin cancer. But the younger generation is quite attractive and the children are charming. On the shadowy left side Goya, like Velázquez in *Las Meninas*, portrays himself contemplating this masterpiece on a gigantic canvas. Though Goya risked dungeons and chains, he felt that Carlos was too ignorant, egoistic and complacent to realize he was being satirized. Hotchner recreates Hemingway's conversation by repeating his "movement," "*cojones*" and "*felt*" from *Death in the Afternoon*: "Is it not a masterpiece of loathing? Look how he has painted his spittle into every face. Can you imagine that he had such genius that he could fulfill this commission and please the King, who, because of his fatuousness, could not see how Goya had stamped him for all the world to see. Goya believed in movement, in his own *cojones*, and in everything he ever experienced and *felt*. You don't look at Goya if you want neutrality."

The Disasters of War, which had the greatest impact on Hemingway, and "A Natural History of the Dead" have strikingly similar content. Goya portrays the Napoleonic wars in Spain, Hemingway describes the Italian front in World War I. Goya's title applies with equal force to Hemingway's story, Hemingway's title also applies to Goya's etchings. He found Goya's terse, bitter and ironic titles, with only a few words for each etching, analogous to his own compact prose. Both accounts were created by eyewitness observers, by deeply damaged survivors who forced spectators and readers to confront these horrors.

In *Disasters* Goya portrays many atrocities that Hemingway also describes in his story: women fighting and dying, dead horses, pillaging the dead, mass burials, rotting corpses, dead women, mutilated bodies, piles of corpses, cartloads for the cemeteries and the death of truth. The most ghastly etching, "Great deeds—against the dead!," portrays a decapitated man with amputated arms hanging upside down with his legs over the branch of a dead tree. His severed arms and staring head hang next to him. Compared to such tortures the firing squad is merciful. The emotional impact of Goya's "I saw it," the furious impotence of "And it can't be helped" and the concept of Nada in "Nothing" influenced Hemingway's depiction of war. Both suffer with those who suffered. Both men, as André Malraux observed of Goya, want "to tear the mask of deception from the world's face."

Like the brilliant interchapters in Hemingway's first book of stories, *In Our Time*, "A Natural History of the Dead" illuminates the themes of *Death in the Afternoon*. (The story was not reprinted verbatim. "Shits the bed full" in *Death* was softened to "fills the sheets as full as any diaper" in *Winner Take Nothing*.) Hemingway's shocking account of the dead and wounded in battle illustrates his comparison between bullfighting and war. He tries to justify the *corrida* by suggesting that war is much worse: a weak argument in an excellent story. "A Natural History of the Dead" is also an *Un*-natural History of the Living. Hemingway's clinical description forces his audience to recognize the brutal facts of modern warfare.

"A Natural History of the Dead" has two distinct but subtly related parts: an objective and clinical narrative of atrocities in war and a personal conflict with characters and plot expressed in dramatic dialogue. The second part hinges on what the word "humane" means to each character. The story first argues, as in an essay, that our belief in God is gone and our attempt to replace religion with humanism is futile. The story then shows, in a different literary mode and with a bleak conclusion, the impossibility of humane behavior in modern warfare.

Hemingway (who names only one of the titles, I identify the others) parodies the "charming" style, preachy tone, and close observation of animals and birds in several far-flung and highly respected natural histories: the Reverend Gilbert White's *The Natural History of Selborne* (1789), which provides Hemingway's title, Mungo Park's *Travels in the Interior of Africa* (1799), Bishop Edward Stanley's *A Familiar History of Birds* (1848) and W. H. Hudson's *Idle Days in Patagonia* (1893). These books express the Christian "argument from design," which asserts that the perfection of the world proves the existence of a benign God. Mungo Park rhetorically asks, "Can that Being who planted, watered and brought to perfection in this obscure part of the world . . . look with unconcern upon the situation and suffering of creatures formed after his own image?" The equally inspired Edward Stanley, Bishop of Norwich, also asks, "can any branch of Natural History be studied without increasing [our] faith, love and hope?"

Hemingway demolishes their naive belief that one achieves moral uplift from observing nature—even in the menacing African jungle—and their faith in the essential goodness of man. He begins by recalling the atrocities he'd seen during the Greco-Turkish War in 1922. Driven out of that town and wanting to prevent the Turks from seizing their valuable beasts of burden, the Greeks "broke the legs of all their baggage animals and pushed them off the quay into the shallow water to drown." Hemingway comments that only Goya could do justice to this cruelty of cracked legs, slow drowning and bloated carcasses floating to the surface: "The numbers of broken-legged mules and horses drowning in the shallow water called for a Goya to depict them." He then abruptly changes his tone and jokingly contradicts himself: "Although, speaking literally, one can hardly say that they called for a Goya since there has only been one Goya, long dead."

Hemingway's next exemplary atrocity describes the explosion of a munitions factory in the Lombard landscape outside Milan, toward the end of the war in June 1918. In a letter of September 26, 1920, D. H. Lawrence had noted that "powder factories always explode in Italy." Hemingway is shocked by the unusual sight of dead factory women rather than dead military men, and by the short hair that makes them look like men until he realizes they are actually women. Fascinated by gruesome photographs of mutilated bodies, Hemingway took and collected pictures of bloated corpses after the disastrous hurricane in the Florida Keys in 1935.

Hemingway adopts the naturalists' accurate observational style for his satiric purpose. He seems to relish the chromatic and voluminous changes in the Italian victims of the Austrian offensive in June 1918. These corpses take on the appearance of three different races: "The color change in Caucasian races is from white to yellow, to yellow-green, to black. . . . The dead grow larger each day until sometimes they become quite too big for their uniforms, filling these until they seem blown tight enough to burst." The use of the adverb "quite" is quite effective. He's also struck by the amount of paper that is scattered about from the pulled-out pockets of the dead.

Hemingway interrupts his ghastly account to take another shot at the intrepid but deluded traveler Mungo Park and to disprove his optimistic belief that man is "formed in [God's] own image." Everything Hemingway had learned from participating in and reporting wars denied this concept. He insists that in a world without God men die like animals from bullets, shells, tear gas and disease. The Spanish influenza epidemic of 1918, which killed more people than the war, also helps destroy the now "extinct phenomenon" known as humanism, which emphasizes the value of human beings and human life.

He continues his parodic mode by rewriting the famous lines from Andrew Marvell's seductive love poem "To His Coy Mistress" (1681). If the mistress rejects her lover's overtures, Marvell writes, only death awaits her: "then worms shall try / That long-preserved virginity, / And your quaint honour turned to dust, / And into ashes all my lust." Hemingway's caustic version of the poem condemns the writings of the self-appointed humanists: "worms will try that long preserved sterility, with their quaint pamphlets gone to bust and into foot-notes all their lust." He also mocks academic pedantry by putting footnote 2 at the bottom of the page, but leaving out note 1.

He then moves from Marvell's worms to an industrious half-pint of maggots that are disturbing the dead and "working where their mouths have been." After describing the beauty of the mountains in war and of blood on the snow, Hemingway mentions the death of a German general during the Italian retreat from Caporetto in October 1917. Following the trajectory of the bullet through the skull, he writes that the general had a sniper's bullet hole in his forehead "you couldn't put your little finger in and a hole in back you could put your fist in."

The story then suddenly shifts to a dressing station in the mountains. A hopelessly wounded man, "his brains disturbed by a piece of broken steel

. . . all held together by membranes," is brought in by the stretcher-bearers and shown to the doctor. In the chiaroscuro atmosphere the doctor "looked at the man twice; once in daylight, once with a flashlight. That too would have made a good etching for Goya, the visit with the flashlight." But there is nothing to be done about "it," rather than "him." The bearers want to put the barely breathing moribundus with the wounded; the doctor wants him placed with the dead.

An artillery officer suggests putting the man out of his misery with an overdose of morphine. The doctor, unwilling to waste the precious drug on a terminal case, tells the officer to "shoot him yourself" and accuses the officer of rubbing onions in his own eyes to simulate the effects of tear gas and safely removing himself from the front line. The officer, furious at this insult, exclaims (though Hemingway had declared that humanists were extinct), "I will shoot the poor fellow. . . . I am a humane man. I will not let him suffer." The doctor, changing his mind, threatens to report him if he shoots the dying man; the officer accuses him of being inhuman; and the doctor defends himself by stating, "my business is to care for the wounded, not to kill them. That is for gentlemen of the artillery."

When the officer, returning the insult, tells the doctor to fuck himself, his mother and his sister, the doctor loses control, explodes with rage and retaliates by throwing iodine in the eyes of the tear-gassed officer. He then trips and kicks the officer and, replacing his forceps and needle with a weapon, picks up his pistol. As the officer threatens to kill him as soon as he regains his sight and the bearer announces the death of the wounded man, the doctor says they have fought about nothing and begins to treat the blinded man's eyes. In an ironic twist, the doctor who would not kill the man dying in agony throws iodine in the eyes of an officer who'd rubbed onions into his own eyes, and then heals him in a humane fashion. The self-proclaimed humane officer, who recommends a fatal dose of morphine but doesn't shoot the wounded man, threatens to kill the doctor who has blinded him. This effective episode, which reverses the roles of doctor and officer and plays on the different meanings of "humane," completes Hemingway's destruction of the humanist argument that he'd attacked in the first part of the story.

The title in the frontispiece of Goya's *Caprichos*, "the sleep of reason produces monsters," suggests that when people do not think rationally and critically, the dark side of human nature takes over in the guise of religion or nationalism, and monstrous bloodshed breaks out. In "Variations on Goya" (1943), written during World War II, Aldous Huxley noted, "the longer Goya lived, the more frightful did his world seem. . . . All he shows us is war's disasters and squalors, without any of the glory or even picturesqueness." Goya and Hemingway do not portray the consolation of courage or celebration of victory—only danger and death, bullets and blood. There are no battles, only the cruel aftermath; no heroes, only victims in that slaughter of the innocents.

In Goya and Hemingway it is not enough to kill a man: death has to be delivered in the most horribly conspicuous way. The destruction of the civilian population belies the comforting assumption that European society is civilized. As Dostoyevsky proclaimed in *The Brothers Karamazov* (1880): "If God is dead, everything is permitted." Fred Licht wrote that Goya's vision reveals "a gratuitous demolition of all that had once been pleasurable or meaningful in life, a realization of the stark anarchy that reigns in the outside world as mindlessly as it does in the interior world of irrational lusts and fears." Following Goya and countering the Panglossian arguments of the naturalist observers, Hemingway suggests that God does not exist. If there is no God, man is left with Nada and with the devastating concept, in Wallace Stevens' words, of the "Nothing that is not there and the nothing that is." Hemingway recognized in Goya a kindred spirit and fellow artist who had faced the evil in man as honestly as he had.

TWELVE

PAUL CÉZANNE

We dance round in a ring and suppose,
But the Secret sits in the middle and knows.

—Robert Frost, "The Secret Sits"

In 1921 Joachim Gasquet recorded that his friend Paul Cézanne wanted to "treat nature by the cylinder, the sphere and the cone." This concept was hardly new. In his book on the seventeenth-century Italian architect Francesco Borromini, Anthony Blunt quoted Galileo's *The Assayer* (1623), which foreshadowed Cézanne by three centuries: "the great book of nature . . . is written in the language of mathematics, and its characters are triangles, circles and other geometric figures without which it is humanly impossible to understand a single word of it." But when we look at nature—at the shifting sky, the turbulent sea or a blooming flower—we do not in fact see these rigid geometrical forms. Yet Cézanne's remark was influential and frequently quoted.

The Cézanne exhibitions at the Paris Salon d'Automne in 1906 (the year of his death) and again in 1908, and his pictures in the Post-Impressionist exhibitions at the London Grafton Gallery in 1910 and 1912, made it fashionable and sophisticated to admire him as the rising star of art. He had a powerful impact on Cubism, which began in 1910 and shifted modern art toward abstraction. Picasso, who worshipped Cézanne, called him "the father of us all, a sort of God of painting . . . my one and only master." Alex Danchev, the biographer of Cézanne, affirmed that for Picasso, he was the great progenitor and "protector: mother, father, grandfather and spiritual advisor." Rainer Maria Rilke expressed his adoration in his *Letters on Cézanne*, written in 1907, and Roger

Fry admired him in *Cézanne: A Study of His Development* (1927). In the "Introduction to [His Own] Paintings" (1929), the contentious D. H. Lawrence also praised him for both personal and aesthetic reasons as "the most interesting figure in modern art, and the only really interesting figure . . . and that, not so much because of his achievement as because of his struggle." Repeating the geometrical comparison and emphasizing the cubes, he also mocked the trendy critics: "With Cézanne, landscape 'crystallized,' to use one of the favorite terms of the critics, and it has gone on crystallizing into cubes, cones, pyramids, and so forth ever since."

Gertrude Stein and her brother Leo began collecting Cézanne as early as 1904. She owned four works by him, including the famous portrait of his wife Hortense. In *Lectures in America* (1935) Stein sounded off about Cézanne with typically pretentious obfuscation that could mean almost anything: "Finished or unfinished it always was what it looked like, the very essence of an oil painting because everything was always there, really there." By contrast, she also condemned her hometown, Oakland, California, because "there was no *there* there."

In "The Transatlantic Interview" (1946), her most famous pronouncement on this subject, Stein repeated what she had often told Hemingway during their extensive conversations in the 1920s: "everything I have done has been influenced by Flaubert and Cézanne, and this gave me a new feeling about composition. . . . Cézanne conceived the idea that in composition one thing was as important as another thing. Each part is as important as the whole, and that impressed me enormously." Despite her assertion, which does not logically derive from Cézanne, elements in a work of art have varying degrees of importance, but are not equally important.

Hemingway was also fond of making statements that were as cunningly misleading, deliberately provocative and manifestly untrue as those of Cézanne and Stein. In *Green Hills of Africa* (1935) he claimed that "all modern American literature comes from one book by Mark Twain called *Huckleberry Finn*," a statement he knew was false. The whole genteel tradition from James and Wharton to Fitzgerald and Cheever, and the whole realist tradition of Dreiser and Norris, did not derive from Twain's comic, picaresque book. In his great leg-pull, the highly acclaimed *The Old Man and the Sea* (1952), Hemingway expressed his contempt for *Life* magazine, the reading public, the critics and religion by writing an ironic and mock-profound fable that gave readers exactly what they wanted and could understand. The novella offered moral uplift, transparent symbolism and a pretense of culture. It was universally admired, and earned him a Pulitzer Prize and a considerable fortune.

In *A Moveable Feast*, where he discussed his secret connection to Cézanne, Hemingway also made several other dubious statements. He declared that Wyndham Lewis had the eyes of an "unsuccessful rapist." In fact, Lewis was a handsome ladies' man and charismatic seducer. When attacking Lewis, Hemingway had no way of knowing about his sexual life by looking into his eyes. Similarly, Scott Fitzgerald would never have humiliated himself, and risked devastating confirmation of Zelda's charge that his sexual organ was inadequate, by exposing himself to Hemingway. It should therefore be clear that *A Moveable Feast* is a memoir of his youth in the 1920s, enhanced thirty years later by the imagination of a novelist. Not everything in it is true.

Instead of believing everything Hemingway claimed about Cézanne, it would be far more useful—for the first time—to maintain a skeptical attitude and carefully examine what he actually said. In August 1924 the young Hemingway, starting his literary career, was still trying to please his influential mentor Gertrude Stein, though his chaste and concise style was very different from her own. Following her advice but not her example, he deferentially wrote, "I'm trying to do the country like Cézanne and having a hell of a time and sometimes getting it a little bit." Eight years later, he wrote his painter-friend Henry Strater, "A man can be a hell of a serious artist and not have to make his living by it—see Flaubert, Cézanne and Co." It is extraordinary that from all the examples of writers and artists he could have chosen, he cited precisely the two influences that Stein had previously mentioned.

In "On Writing" (1925), originally the ending of his story "Big Two-Hearted River," Hemingway was still seeking the approval of Stein—who bore a remarkable physical and psychological resemblance to his mother—and repeated the Cézanne trope: "He could see the Cézanne. The portrait [of Hortense] at Gertrude Stein's. She'd know it if he ever got things right. The two good ones at the Luxembourg [museum], the ones he'd seen every day at the loan exhibit at Bernheim's" gallery. Contrasting "tricks" and "the real thing" and using both methods, Hemingway insisted that the inspiration had to come from "inside," not outside, himself. He emphasized his point by moving into the "picture" as well as into the "stream": "He wanted to write like Cézanne painted. Cézanne started with all the tricks. Then he broke the whole thing down and built the real thing. . . . You had to do it from inside yourself. . . . Nick, seeing how Cézanne would do the stretch of river and the swamp, stood up and stepped down into the stream. . . . He waded across the stream, moving in the picture."

Hemingway gave the fullest account of this idea in the posthumously published *A Moveable Feast* (1964). Speaking of the Musée du Luxembourg, he claimed, with considerable exaggeration, "I went there nearly every day for the Cézannes." In a crucial passage he added, "I was learning something from the painting of Cézanne that made writing simple true sentences far from enough to make the stories have the dimensions that I was trying to put in them. I was learning very much from him but I was not articulate enough to explain it to anyone. Besides it was a secret." He had always been frank and forthcoming about the craft of writing in *Death in the Afternoon* and in his long interviews with George Plimpton and Lillian Ross. Now, he twice vaguely stated that he "was learning something" from Cézanne in order to add the depth and "dimensions" he needed to strengthen his stories. But he said he was "not articulate enough" to reveal the dark secret about Cézanne.

In a later chapter of *A Moveable Feast* he repeated, "I learned to understand Cézanne much better and to see truly how he made landscapes when I was hungry. I used to wonder if he were hungry too when he painted. . . . It was one of those unsound but illuminating thoughts." Since hunger usually distracts from rather than intensifies concentration, this idea, as Hemingway romanticized his young manhood in Paris, was fanciful. Anyway, Hemingway never had to go hungry or catch pigeons for dinner. The flat over the sawmill—like catching pigeons for food and writing in the room where Paul Verlaine died—was a myth-making fiction. Either there never was a sawmill or it no longer functioned. No sane writer, with a wife who liked to sleep late and an infant who needed to sleep during the day, would ever choose to live above the endless and intolerably screeching noise made by machines cutting thick logs. With Hadley's trust fund, he could easily afford better quarters, just as he could afford a French nursemaid for the baby, ski trips to Austria in the winters and bullfighting tours to Spain in the summers. In *A Moveable Feast* he placed himself in the tradition of the impoverished writer, who went all the way back to François Villon in the Middle Ages and to nineteenth-century novels and operas about impoverished bohemians struggling to survive in Parisian garrets.

Connecting Cézanne and hunger once again, Hemingway also told Lillian Ross, who exaggerated his characteristic exaggerations, "I learned how to make a landscape from Mr. Paul Cézanne by walking through the Luxembourg Museum a thousand times with an empty gut." A rough estimate of Hemingway's time in Paris reveals that his Homeric boast was clearly impossible. He lived in Paris from 1922 to 1928, and during that time returned to North America for six months. The movable beast worked as a foreign correspondent for the *Toronto Star* in 1922 and 1923, traveling from Spain to Turkey for about half that time. From 1924 to 1928 he spent about half the year vacationing in Austria and Spain. So he was away from Paris for about four of his seven years. In order to visit the museum a thousand times, he would have had to go there every single day when he was leading an unusually busy athletic, social and writing life in Paris. This exaggeration casts doubt on many of his dubious claims.

Hemingway also imitated his Paris friend James Joyce, who was pleased to boast about the catnip he'd hidden in *Ulysses*: "I've put in so many enigmas and puzzles that it will keep the professors busy for centuries arguing over what I meant, and that's the only way of insuring one's immortality." Like panting hounds pursuing the scent of an elusive fox, Hemingway's critics have made desperate attempts—with vague parallels and far-fetched analogies—when trying to decipher his secret. But they offered no substantial evidence to support their contentions.

Hemingway could also have learned from many other painters. If he'd substituted Matisse for Cézanne, there would have been myriad articles trying to figure out that enigmatic connection. Emily Watts, whose 1971 book started the modish critical trend of connecting Hemingway to Cézanne, undermined her argument with many telltale qualifications: *perhaps*, *can be associated with*, *seems to have known*, *could very well have* (twice), *is entirely possible*, *is possible to assume*. She admitted Hemingway's difficulty in trying to emulate Cézanne, whose techniques had been used by his contemporaries and by modern painters for a century before Hemingway's death. Watts confessed, "A writer is working under a severe handicap if and when he might attempt to imitate the type of complex color modulation or color orchestration used by painters from Cézanne to the present."

Watts' always vague and all-too-general statements contained no precise meaning. Using but not explaining his work in *A Moveable Feast*, she claimed that "Hemingway sought the *dimensions* which were present in the paintings of Cézanne"; that the painter "helped Hemingway develop [undefined] techniques by which he could indicate 'the shape of the country'"; and that "Hemingway was able to flatten [why?] and foreshorten [how?] the landscape much as Cézanne did." When she tried to give specific examples, she retreated to tautology and did not explain her assertion: "Hemingway's specific reference to 'the rocks we have to climb over' indicates his own tactile response to the volumes of those large gray rocks in the shadowy forest of Fontainebleau. Cézanne had formed these volumes primarily by color which, at least for Hemingway, had become something tactile, something which it was necessary 'to climb over.'"

In 1984 Kenneth Johnston quoted Patrick Heron on Cézanne using white or leaving parts of the canvas bare. Dutifully following the trail of Emily Watts, he weakly added, "Hemingway's theory of 'omission' has seldom been better stated." But there is a big difference between the white or bare patch on Cézanne's canvas that shows nothing and its direct opposite: Hemingway's iceberg that is most solidly there both above and below the surface. Johnston tried to argue, with the telltale *may also be*, that in "the oblique rendering of more than meets the eye; the repetition of line, color and motif; the fusion of simplicity and complexity; the union of abstraction and reality; the elimination of non-essential details—the 'secret' of Cézanne may also be discovered in Hemingway's landscape." All this generally applies to many painters and many writers, but not specifically to Cézanne and Hemingway. In his short article, only six pages later, Johnston repeated the previous quotation almost verbatim. As Byron said of Coleridge, "I wish you would explain your explanation."

In 1999 Theodore Gaillard also moved unsteadily toward deciphering the secret, and he too indulged in far-fetched and unconvincing comparisons. In Cézanne's *Still Life with Apples* (1893–94), he wrote, "we first look obliquely across the open mouth of the centrally positioned blue-gray glazed ginger jar but, almost eerily, down the throat of the nearer green vase to its left. . . . And *so it is* with Hemingway in 'The Short Happy Life of Francis Macomber.'" But there is nothing eerie about the mouth of a jar and it is *not* at all this way with Hemingway. Gaillard also maintained that, following Cézanne, Hemingway's mastery "manifests itself in the meticulous placement and repetition of key words and images"—though Cézanne's picture has no "key words." Finally, this critic stated that "the patterns of Cézanne's artistic life *seemed* to reflect *much of the same* confining verticality faced by Ole Andreson" in "The Killers." But Hemingway surely did not have to *learn* from Cézanne how to describe Andreson lying *horizontally* in bed in a small room. Time and again, critics have tried and failed to make the analogy between the techniques of a painter and a writer.

Between Johnston and Gaillard, Meyly Hageman boldly attempted to unravel the great mystery, but got no closer than anyone else. She said, "The 'secret' Hemingway discovered, then, from studying *Ferme* consists of at least three visual devices: to reduce art forms into geometric planes that create tensions when placed at angles with one another; to contain this tension by using overlapping dynamic and static planes; and to omit distracting surface details that invite literary translation so that spatial forms remain pure." But Hemingway would never want to write nor would anyone ever want to read this sort of mechanical, geometrical and overlapping fiction.

In his life of Cézanne, Alex Danchev noted the critics' problem when trying to define the greatness of the painter: "admirers of Cézanne's art have always been extravagant in their admiration, but have always had difficulty explaining themselves." Danchev weakly concluded that "Hemingway's secret remains secret." When I wrote to him and asked him to explain it, he did not reply. But Hemingway left an important clue to that mystery. He revived the idea of the secret in a little-known passage about the Parisian painter Jules Pascin in *Islands in the Stream* (1970): "He was small and very tough and very strange. He used to wear a derby hat most of the time. . . . He always acted as though he knew a great secret, as though he had just heard it and it amused him. . . . You could always tell he knew it and it amused him very much." Like the sly Hemingway (keeping the professors busy), Pascin "acted as though he knew a great secret" which, also like Hemingway, always "amused him very much."

Many authors have been inspired by specific paintings and used them in their fiction. But no other writers, before Hemingway imitated Stein, had claimed to *learn* how to write from looking at paintings. He pretentiously maintained that he had learned to give more depth and dimension to his prose by using the pictorial techniques that Stein told him *she* had learned from Cézanne. Hemingway deliberately misled his critics by claiming that Cézanne had influenced his work. Though many critics, blindly following each other, have invented ingenious explanations to justify Hemingway's claim, there is no convincing evidence of his debt to Cézanne.

Hemingway's real secret in *A Moveable Feast* was his attempt to hide the powerful influence of Stein by insisting that *he* was the one who had learned from Cézanne. At one stroke he amused himself by eliminating Stein and deluding the professors. He'd bitterly quarreled with Stein after her attack in *The Autobiography of Alice B. Toklas* (1933), fiercely counterattacked her in his memoir and did not want to acknowledge her impact on his work. We can now see (to paraphrase Hemingway) that all of Cézanne's influence on Hemingway comes from one talk by Gertrude Stein called "Transatlantic Interview."

THIRTEEN

VINCENT VAN GOGH

Hemingway was familiar with Van Gogh's life and locales. He visited Arles, where Van Gogh painted *The Night Café* in September 1888, and knew that masterpiece. Writing to Ezra Pound on May 2, 1924, he catered to the poet's anti-Semitism and reported that Lincoln Steffens' "Bloomsbury Jewine treats him like Gauguin treated Van Gogh." He added, mixing irony with reverential language, "I made a pilgrimage to Van Gogh's whorehouse in Arles and other shrines."

In a burst of genius between episodes of insanity, Van Gogh spent three nights in a row painting *The Night Café* and slept in the daytime. He gave an elaborate description of the grim setting, dissipated homeless people and hellish theme. "I shall probably make a start today," he wrote, "on the interior of the café where I live—at night, by gaslight. It is what they call a 'night café' (they are fairly common here), which stays open all night. 'Night owls' can take refuge there if they haven't enough money to pay for lodgings or are too drunk to be taken in anywhere." He then explained, "little sleeping hooligans [are] in the empty dreary room. . . . The white clothes of the landlord, on vigil in a corner of this furnace, turn lemon-yellow, or pale luminous green." Defining his intentions, he stated, "The café is a place where one can ruin one's self, run mad or commit a crime. So I have tried to express as it were the powers of darkness in a low drink shop . . . and all this is an atmosphere like a devil's [oven], of pale sulphur."

The vertiginous café, painted with jagged brush strokes, thick impasto and clashing colors, seems charged with electric current. The blood-red walls, sea-green ceiling and bilious-yellow floor convey a morbid aura. Three drunk and drowsing men (one near the stove) and a courting couple—the woman in a red shawl, the man in a straw hat—huddle separately near the edge of the frame. The time is ten minutes after midnight, but no one seems inclined to depart. The bored and idle waiter, dressed in white and with hands in his pockets, has not cleared the bottles and glasses on three tables. Their wooden chairs with cane seats stand, where departed clients have left them, at odd angles. With a blurred face and cut off at the knees, the waiter seems strangely suspended between the billiards and the adjacent table. The opening through the rear wall behind the bar, which has a bright bouquet of flowers bisecting a row of dark bottles, leads to emptiness. The sharply slanted wood-plank floor resembles the deck of a pitching ship and everything threatens to slide down toward the viewer. This extremely well-lighted place has four gas lamps, surrounded by swirling yellow halos that illuminate the drinkers' misery. The billiard table, casting an ominous shadow, looks like an operating table, a mortuary slab (with pockets draining the blood) or a coffin.

Hemingway's "A Clean, Well-Lighted Place" (1933) is the fictional equivalent of Van Gogh's powerful painting. In his story the order, peace, security, solace and refuge of the Spanish café are opposed to the deafness, isolation, fear, despair and suicide of the old man, who is extremely reluctant to leave despite the late hour. The young waiter, who wants to get home and sleep with his wife, is worried that the old man will stay all night. In contrast, "'I am of those who like to stay late at the café,' the older waiter said. 'With all those who do not want to go to bed. With all those who need a light for the night.'" The sympathy between the old waiter and the old man alleviates the theme of nada, despair and emptiness.

The shocking parody of the Lord's Prayer—"Our nada who art in nada"—brings not comfort but wretchedness: "It was all a nothing and a man was nothing too. It was only that and light was all it needed and a certain cleanness and order. . . . He knew it was all nada y pues nada y nada y pues nada." The concept of nada is not a tangible thing, but a palpable and overwhelming sensation of nothingness. Hemingway's story describes the absence suggested by nothing as well as the menacing presence of nothingness.

Hemingway expresses his theme, inspired by Van Gogh, through a series of polarities: light and shadow, sleep and insomnia, confidence and despair, courage and fear, dignity and degradation, faith and skepticism. Hemingway's story, like Van Gogh's painting, has a brightly lit but dreary Mediterranean night café where drunks, seeking refuge, confront nothingness. Hemingway's old man tried to commit suicide; Van Gogh and Hemingway actually killed themselves.

FOURTEEN

PABLO PICASSO

Our perceptions are subjective, and accounts of any event are colored by the narrator's memory and attitudes. Fascinated by our own stories and favorite jokes, we also have a keen interest in stories about the Famous and the Great. For a biographer, anecdotes are interesting not only for what happened and when, but also for who told them and why. Like popular tales that change in the telling, anecdotes about famous people alter with time. Initially the story is told by the participants themselves or by eyewitnesses; then the friends or descendants take over; finally the journalists and biographers come along to collect and reshape it. Little is known of the precise relationship between Picasso and Hemingway. They were friends in Paris in two postwar periods and two high points of Hemingway's life, first in the early 1920s, then in 1944. What did they think of each other, and were they really friends? Two anecdotes crop up in several versions whenever writers consider these questions.

Hemingway first met Picasso through Gertrude Stein in March 1922. He was twenty-three, just married and getting started as writer; Picasso was eighteen years older and a famous artist. Stein had bought pictures from Picasso and helped promote his career, and she was then telling Hemingway how to write. Both men also knew the wealthy, arty and stylish American expatriates Gerald and Sara Murphy, who lived in France and entertained lavishly. In the summer of 1925, in Antibes on the French Riviera, Hemingway spent June and Picasso July with the Murphys, who thought it safer to separate the two gigantic egos.

In *A Moveable Feast*, written in the late 1950s and posthumously published in 1964, Hemingway bitterly regretted some personal choices, looked back on these happy, intensely productive years and blamed the Murphys for leading him astray. He satirized them (without naming them) as "pilot fish" who led prosperous parasites to their artistic prey: "They never wasted their time nor their charm on something that was not sure. Why should they? Picasso was sure and of course had been before they had ever heard of painting." Conscious of his present fame and wealth, and now equal as a celebrity, he co-opted Picasso in his denunciation of the rich. According to Hemingway, Picasso protected himself by pretending to accept social invitations from well-off patrons: "Much later Picasso told me that he always promised the rich to come when they asked him because it made them so happy and then something would happen and he would be unable to appear." In fact, both Hemingway and Picasso eagerly accepted the Murphys' generous hospitality. They were not only rich, they also loved books and art and knew how to have a good time. Biographers aren't the only ones who rewrite history.

The young Hemingway often saw Picasso at Stein's salon, where he learned about art and developed his connoisseur's eye by looking at Picasso's work and discussing it with him. In the Twenties, despite his limited means, Hemingway bought important pictures by Juan Gris, Joan Miró, Paul Klee and André Masson. One early story about his personal relations with Picasso, in which the painter read his poetry aloud, has survived in three variants. Influenced by his friend Max Jacob, who used "the data of the unconscious: liberated words, free association of ideas, day and night dreams, hallucinations," Picasso wrote a good deal of predictably obscure "poetry," with private content and vague structure.

In May 1949, twenty-five years after the event, Stein's companion, Alice Toklas, echoing Stein and patronizing Picasso, wrote a friend: "the trouble with Picasso was that he allowed himself to be flattered into believing he was a poet too. Gertrude and he had quite a scene but she told it in *Everybody's Autobiography*." In that book, published in 1937, Stein described an evening in Picasso's flat: "We all went over to listen all evening to Pablo Picasso's poetry. . . . The poems were in French and Spanish and first he read a French one and then a Spanish one that he turned into French and then he read on and on and then he looked at me and I drew a long breath and I said it is very interesting. . . . Pablo went on reading and he looked up and said to Thornton Wilder did you follow and Thornton said yes and might he look at it and Picasso passed it to him. Thornton said yes he was not nervous he said yes yes it is very interesting."

In her typically repetitive and self-aggrandizing account, Stein makes it plain that it was not interesting at all. Picasso couldn't decide which language to write in and read on far too long. It was a social occasion with a penalty attached—you had to listen to the host drone on. When he looked to Stein for approval she was politely noncommittal. Picasso naturally wondered if the Americans had understood his strange poems. The playwright Thornton Wilder cagily repeated exactly what Stein had said.

According to a story that passed from Hemingway's first wife, Hadley, to her son Jack, the "scene" that Toklas mentioned did not take place at Picasso's flat, but at Stein's, when Hemingway, not Wilder, was present. Jack Hemingway described the scene to his mother's biographers. Bernice Kert's version appeared in print in 1983: "One evening when Picasso was at Stein's he read some of his poetry to the hushed group, none of whom dared say anything when he was finished. There was a long silence. Hadley noticed how he was fidgeting. Still no comments from the other guests. Finally Gertrude said, 'Pablo, go home and paint.'"

Jack told Gioia Diliberto a second version as he warmed to the story and provided a few more details. This account made Picasso "insist" on reading, supplied a motive for his poetic endeavors, and brought Hemingway into the story as a silent, neutral witness: "Hadley told her son, Jack, that one night when she and Ernest were at 27 rue de Fleurus, Picasso, who was also a guest, insisted on reading a poem he'd written. 'Picasso thought that if he applied the same energies to poetry as he did to painting then he could be a great poet as well.' . . . After Picasso read the poem aloud, the Hemingways stared at Stein, waiting for her verdict. Finally Stein spoke. 'Pablo,' she said gravely, 'go home and paint.'"

In Jack's first version, Picasso fidgeted; in the second, the Hemingways, who probably could not grasp the meaning of the poems, stared. In both versions Picasso's attempt at poetry is interpreted as a challenge to Stein's status as a "great" writer, and her response is hardly tactful. The point of this *violon d'Ingres* anecdote was that Stein, who thought she owned those she patronized, resented Picasso's intrusion on her territory and rather rudely put him down. Today we read Picasso's poetry for revelation of his character, rather than its value as poetry, but Stein did not see any value in it at all. Hadley, more tactful than Stein, did not describe his undoubtedly angry reaction to her remark and the "scene" that followed. Picasso was not put off by Stein's reaction and continued to write poetry. But it provided a valuable lesson to the young Hemingway, who wisely remained silent. In future he would learn to guard his work and not risk public humiliation by Stein.

Hemingway and Picasso at first admired Stein and then quarreled with her. In September 1951, five years after her death, Hemingway, alluding to gay painters in Stein's circle like the Russian Pavel Tchelitchev, patronized his patron of thirty years before. As in *A Moveable Feast*, he asserted that Picasso shared his view. He wrote Edmund Wilson that during "her patriotic homo-sexual phase, [Stein] lost her judgement on painting completely and judged pictures by the sexual habits of those who painted them. Picasso and I used to laugh about it but we always agreed how fond we were of her no matter what she did."

When they met twenty years later, in 1944, both men were internationally celebrated. Picasso, aged sixty-three, had been famous since *Les Demoiselles d'Avignon* in 1907, Hemingway, aged forty-five, since *The Sun Also Rises* in 1926. The two titanic personalities were still handsome and charismatic, competitive and ambitious. The English writer Gerald Brenan recalled that "when Hemingway was in the room, it seemed that there was not sufficient air left for anyone else," and Picasso had the same capacity to dominate. Hemingway knew Spanish and shared Picasso's passion for the bullfight. He'd reported the Spanish Civil War from the Loyalist side and wrote his novel about the Spanish War, *For Whom the Bell Tolls* (1940), while Picasso was painting *Guernica* (1937) to condemn the Nazi bombing of the Basque capital.

In their private lives both were ruthless with women, whom they used up and discarded, though Hemingway had a puritanical streak that made him feel guilty. Picasso painted each of his two wives and five long-term mistresses and each one was associated with a different phase of his artistic career. Scott Fitzgerald shrewdly observed a similar pattern in Hemingway: "I have a theory that Ernest needs a new woman for each big book." Most important of all, both Hemingway and Picasso created new styles of art that spawned many imitators. As Fitzgerald wrote his daughter in 1940: "You asked me whether I thought that in the Arts it was greater to originate a new form or to perfect it. The best answer is the one Picasso made rather bitterly to Gertrude Stein: 'You do something first and then someone else comes along and does it pretty.'"

As a war correspondent with the American army in Normandy from June to December 1944, Hemingway participated in combat as if he were an infantry officer and then reported what he had actually experienced. Contrary to the Geneva Convention, he carried weapons, and on August 3 threw a grenade down a cellar where German troops were hiding. He deliberately exposed himself to danger and had two serious accidents. He did intelligence work, made judicial decisions about prisoners, led partisans and conducted counterespionage missions. He entered Paris with the first Allied troops and liberated his old watering hole, the Hotel Ritz.

Just after Paris was liberated on August 25, 1944, an intensely emotional and historical moment, Hemingway went to Picasso's studio, near the Pont Neuf. There are three versions of this well-recorded visit. In the most reliable and objective account, published in 1964, Françoise Gilot, Picasso's wartime mistress, recalled:

> One of the first effects of the Liberation was the arrival of Hemingway at the Rue des Grands-Augustins. . . . [The concierge] had no idea who Hemingway was but she had been used to having many of Pablo's friends and admirers leave gifts for him when they called in his absence. . . . When she told Hemingway that Pablo was not there and Hemingway said he'd like to leave a message for him, she asked him—so she told us later—"Wouldn't you perhaps like to leave a gift for Monsieur?" Hemingway said he hadn't thought about it before but perhaps it was a good idea. He went out to his jeep and brought back a case of hand grenades. He set it down inside her *loge* and marked it "To Picasso from Hemingway." As soon as the concierge deciphered the other markings on the case, she ran out of the *loge* and refused to go back until someone took the case away.

Hemingway's grenades were left over from the battle for Paris and he'd use more of them during the invasion of Germany. His mock-offering served to emphasize the difference between Hemingway's military and Picasso's civilian status, and had the additional advantage of frightening the concierge, who'd cheekily suggested he leave a gift. She had an interest in soliciting gifts and hoped to share in the spoils. The grenades were obviously of no use to Picasso and no joke to the concierge, who'd just endured four years of the German occupation. Instead of bringing something useful—food, fuel or cigarettes—the war-crazed Hemingway (who had nothing else in his jeep), gave symbolic grenades to the explosive painter who'd blown up traditional art. The joke was in bad taste, and revealed Hemingway's tendency to hunt trophies and take risks.

Peter Viertel, the American writer and friend of Hemingway, heard the story from Picasso himself. He reported that when the bullfighter Luis Miguel Dominguín introduced him to the painter, "Picasso briefly related how Papa had come to visit him during the liberation of Paris and had offered him a hand grenade for his protection. 'What do I want a hand grenade for?' Picasso said he told Papa. 'I'm a painter!' He laughed, amused in retrospect by Hemingway's bellicose attitude." In this slightly embellished version, published in 1992, Hemingway, instead of leaving a case of grenades, personally hands one to Picasso "for his protection." Picasso, commenting on the incident, is amused rather than angered by Hemingway's bizarre behavior.

Another variant of this incident, told to the author by James Lord, appeared in 1988 in a hostile book on Picasso by Arianna Stassinopoulos Huffington. According to Lord, Picasso scorned Hemingway and, to free himself from his long standing obligation to his old patron, used Hemingway as a stick to beat Stein. Speaking of the two American writers, Picasso supposedly said:

> "To listen to her, the whole world would think that she created me piece by piece. But if you want to see what she really understands about painting, all you have to do is look at the trash she likes at the moment. She says the same about Hemingway. Actually, those two were made for each other. I've never been able to stand him, never. He never really understood bullfighting, not as a Spaniard understands it. He was a charlatan, Hemingway. I've always known it, but Gertrude never knew it." . . .
>
> The torrent of abuse was still gathering force, demolishing Hemingway on the way. "He came to see me after the Liberation and he gave me a piece of an SS uniform with SS embroidered on it, and he told me that he had killed the man himself. It was a lie. Maybe he had killed plenty of wild animals, but he never killed a man. If he had killed one, he wouldn't have needed to pass around souvenirs. He was a charlatan and that's why Gertrude liked him."

Luis Miguel Dominguín, angry that Hemingway had favored his rival Antonio Ordóñez in his *Dangerous Summer* (1959), gave Picasso the idea that Hemingway didn't really understand bullfighting, but Picasso may have also resented Hemingway's appropriation of his own artistic theme. In this version of Hemingway's visit, he didn't give Picasso grenades, but a fragment of an SS uniform, which belonged to the fanatical Nazi military elite rather than to the regular German army. Picasso could not have known if Hemingway had actually killed a German soldier (in fact, he had), and his logic about this matter ("he wouldn't have needed to pass around souvenirs") was weak. Even weaker was his reasoning that Stein never knew he was a charlatan but she liked him *because* he was a charlatan. James Lord, trying to show that he was closer to Picasso than Hemingway, recycled a half-remembered story, substituting a scrap of uniform for grenades. This malicious anecdote, which reports Picasso attacking Hemingway and Stein, discredits Lord rather than Hemingway.

In the postwar years Picasso's life in Nazi-occupied Paris, like Hemingway's role in the liberation of Paris, took on a symbolic character, and both were among the most popular figures in France. Though Gilot didn't mention it, Hemingway soon returned to Picasso's studio and dined with him in a restaurant. In these self-conscious, semipublic and still competitive, though disappointingly insubstantial meetings, the great complacently consorted with the great. (This is not unusual. When Joyce met Proust they found they had nothing to say to each other.) In 1976 Mary Welsh, who'd reported the incident for *Time* magazine and married Hemingway in 1946, wrote in her memoir: "Another evening we went to the studio of M. Picasso. . . . He welcomed Ernest with open arms and while Picasso's girl, Françoise Gilot, a slim, dark, quiet girl with serpentine movements, and I kept ourselves behind them, Picasso showed Ernest the big, chilly studio and much of the work he'd done in the past four years. '*Les boches* left me alone,' P.P. said. 'They disliked my work, but they did not punish me for it.'" As they left the studio, Hemingway told Mary, who disliked Picasso's paintings: "He's pioneering. Don't condemn them just because you don't understand them. You may grow up to them." Françoise Gilot may have omitted this return visit because she didn't want to appear as a self-effacing nonentity, in awe of Picasso.

Soon after the visit to the studio, Hemingway compromised his principles by taking Picasso to a black-market restaurant in order to provide a worthy feast for his eminent friend. Mary wrote that "Picasso's face . . . showed a dozen reactions of amusement, concern, delight at Ernest's accounts of his adventures with the U.S. Army in France, and they reminisced rather solemnly together about the early days in Paris. . . . When Ernest asked Picasso if he would consider doing a bust of me, a portrait from the waist up, nude, Picasso's enormous black radar eyes turned onto me, shrouded in my uniform, for a moment, smiled and said, '*Bien sûr*. Have her come to the studio.'" Hemingway then left Paris to rejoin the army and, Mary added, "without him to prod me, I kept postponing my return to Picasso's studio. It seemed so presumptuous of me."

Though Hemingway knew Picasso's native language, they seemed (perhaps for Mary's sake) to be speaking in French. Hemingway deliberately exaggerated his adventures to entertain Picasso. As he wrote of the French writer Blaise Cendrars, "when he was lying, he was more interesting than many men telling a story truly." Mary, unfortunately, did not bother to record the rather solemn memories of their early days in Paris, which probably included some savage swipes at Stein. She was none too keen to take up Hemingway's suggestion (it's not clear if he'd consulted her about this beforehand) to pose half-naked in the cold studio of the notoriously lecherous Picasso, whose pictures she disliked. Hemingway admired Picasso's latest paintings, but didn't buy any.

Mary's account was substantiated by letters Hemingway wrote to his son Patrick in November 1944 and to Sara Murphy in May 1945. Echoing Picasso's "*Les boches* left me alone," he wrote Patrick that the austerities of the occupation had actually stimulated the artists and that there were "lots of fine new *very* fine pictures by Picasso and other good painters. Under Krauts painters had nothing to do but stay home and paint. Worked out quite well. Made fine pictures." Still infatuated with Mary and emphasizing what a great model she would be, he told Sara that lack of time (Mary's excuse) rather than lack of interest or undue modesty on Mary's part prevented her from posing for her portrait: "Was out a couple of times with Picasso. His stuff painted while the krauts were there is very good. Wonderful. I call Welsh my pocket Rubens and he was going to paint her but we didn't have time. Maybe next year."

Though Picasso never painted Mary, he did satisfy another of Hemingway's wishes by illustrating his works. In March 1947 Hemingway wrote his editor Max Perkins that "if I can get to Europe think I might be able to get Picasso to do at least one of the books. He can illustrate beautifully you know and is a good friend of mine." Picasso did twenty-eight black-and-white drawings for the 1959 German translation of Hemingway's story "The Undefeated," about an old wounded matador attempting a comeback. He also illustrated the Italian serialization, in *Tempo* in 1966, of Hemingway's authoritative bullfighting book, *Death in the Afternoon*, which he evidently admired.

In his autobiography *The Sorcerer's Apprentice* (1999), the art historian John Richardson purports to give an eyewitness account of an event that took place during a *corrida* at Nîmes in the summer of 1959: "As the band struck up the 'Marseillaise,' we all stood. Suddenly Picasso laughed and pointed down at Hemingway. The author of *Death in the Afternoon* was standing rigidly to attention, his right hand up to his peaked cap in a military salute. When Hemingway looked around and saw that nobody else was saluting . . . he withdrew his hand and ever so slowly repositioned it in his pocket." The point of the anecdote was to show Richardson's intimacy with Picasso and the artist's mockery of his absurdly naive old friend. The incident, however, is completely out of character. Hemingway, having attended hundreds of bullfights in France and Spain while many people in the audience scrutinized his behavior, would surely know how to act when the national anthem was played. In fact, he was not even present at the *corrida* to which Richardson refers. In *The Dangerous Summer*, Hemingway's account of the bullfights of 1959, he wrote: "I love Nîmes but did not feel like leaving Madrid, where we had just arrived, to make such a long trip to see bulls with altered horns fought, so decided to stay in Madrid."

Hemingway's letters and Mary's memoir suggest that he regarded Picasso as his "good friend." Yet Picasso, according to James Lord and John Richardson, was quite hostile to Hemingway. Lord and Richardson, who made their careers by attaching themselves to great artists and writing personal books about them, had their own particular motives, and wished to portray themselves as confidants of the great. They succumbed to the temptation to enliven their accounts by embroidering and even inventing stories about famous people. These distortions cluster around subjects like Hemingway and Picasso, who were legends in their lifetimes. We do not know exactly what their friendship was like, but it seems to have involved some jockeying for position. Hemingway never lost his respect for Picasso's work. Though Picasso was cagier about his feelings, and may have found Hemingway's boisterous arrival in Paris in the vanguard of the victorious Army a bit hard to take, he kept up professional and private relations with him. When they first knew each other, the differences in age and status would have prevented intimacy; later on, they were pleased to acknowledge each other's celebrity.

FIFTEEN

JOAN MIRÓ

Hemingway met the Catalan painter Joan Miró (1893–1983) through Gertrude Stein in the early 1920s. The tall solid Hemingway and the short thin Miró both boxed in Paris, and the painter sometimes kept time when the writer was in the ring. In 1922 Miró completed *The Farm* and showed it to several dealers, but no one bought it. He then hung it in a Montparnasse café that allowed artists to display their work to attract customers, but it also failed to sell. In October 1925 Hemingway's friend Evan Shipman, habitué of bar and racetrack, saw the painting and wanted to buy it. In *Cahiers d'art* (1934) Hemingway described how he acquired *The Farm* (1922) for the equivalent of $250 as a birthday present for his first wife, Hadley:

> If Miró was to have a dealer he had to let *The Farm* go with his other pictures. But Shipman, who found him the dealer, made the dealer put a price on it and agree to sell it to him. This was probably the only good business move that Shipman ever did in his life. But doing a good business move must have made him uncomfortable because he came to me the same day and said, "Hem, you should have *The Farm*. I do not love anything as much as you care for that picture and you ought to have it." . . . So we rolled dice to decide and I won and made the first payment. We agreed to pay five thousand francs for *The Farm*.

Hemingway made the down payment and the picture stayed with the dealer. When the final payment was due, he, Shipman and John Dos Passos had to borrow the money from friends in bars and restaurants. Hemingway added that as they took the large 4-by-4½ foot picture home "in the open taxi, the wind caught the big canvas as though it were a sail and we made the taxi driver crawl along. At home we hung it and everyone looked at it and was very happy. I would not trade it for any picture in the world. Miró came in and looked at it and said: 'I am very content that you have *The Farm*.'"

Miró painted the picture in his native town, Montroig, near Tarragona in northeast Spain, in Barcelona and in his Paris studio. He even brought some grass from his town to Paris as a concrete symbol. Jacques Dupin writes, "this work is grounded in the earth of Montroig that molded him, and is bathed in the transparency of its light and air." *The Farm* is one of Miró's last realistic paintings. It portrays in precise intense detail the manifold activities of the farmyard at his country house. It is illuminated by the high-hanging sun, echoed in the round black disk below the tree, and colored by the ocher of the earth and cobalt of the sky. The water tank and the trickling brook in the right foreground are also blue; the large wheel of the cart and spout of the watering can are bright red.

The picture is dominated by the gnarled spikey-branched eucalyptus tree that shoots out small explosions of leaves. This central tree separates the family house with cracks and lichens in its facade, and the farmhouse and yard, fenced with chicken wire and teeming with life: hens, a rabbit, rooster and pigeon. The tiled and curving foot-printed path runs past a barking dog to the wife wearing a pleated skirt and washing clothes in a tub near the water tank. Her naked infant is seated and spread-eagled on the ground behind her. Miró balances the two houses, agricultural implements and domestic animals on both sides of the tree: two A-shaped ladders, a donkey in the cellar of the house and a circling mule threshing wheat in the background, a dog and goat as well as a tiny green lizard and curly snail in the right foreground. He also portrays the essential farm implements: plow, axe, buckets and pails. In the background luxuriant foliage erupts in front of sharp mountain peaks. There are no shadows: everything seems cut with a knife.

The Farm conveys the impression of stark vitality and, like *Death in the Afternoon*, captures the essence of Spain. Hemingway, who loved and lived with the picture for thirty years, said: "No one could look at it and not know it had been painted by a great painter. . . . It has in it all that you feel about Spain when you are there and all that you feel when you are away and cannot go there. No one else has been able to paint these two very opposing things."

He moved the painting to Hadley's new flat in Paris when they separated in 1926. In 1934 he asked her if he could borrow the painting for five years, and never returned it. His fourth wife, Mary, inherited it and later gave it to the National Gallery in Washington. Critics agree that *The Farm*, the masterwork of Miró's entire career, is at the heart of his poetic work. Miró himself regarded *The Farm* as the foundation and key to all his art. In 2012 a less important Miró, *Blue Star*, sold at Sotheby's for $36.62 million. Hemingway knew other Parisian artists and also owned works by Braque, Gris, Masson and Klee. Masson told me that Hemingway had good taste and a sound knowledge of modern painting.

In July 1929, after watching the bullfights in Pamplona, Hemingway visited his old friend in Montroig and wrote Shipman, "He has a lovely place there." Miró said that his recent plans for marriage "would have been a great mistake." Using a boxing metaphor, Hemingway added, "it was called off just as the gong was about to ring. Now he is going to marry a fine girl this fall. From Palma de Mallorca. We saw her pictures and she looks lovely." In October 1929 Miró married his distant cousin Pilar.

In chapter 20 of *Death in the Afternoon* (1932), Hemingway gave a lyrical (and grim) description of the landscape, vistas, wine and food of the farm that had inspired *The Farm*:

> [We sat] in the heavy twilight at Miró's; vines as far as you can see, cut by the hedges and the road; the railroad and the sea with pebbly beach and tall papyrus grass. There were earthen jars for the different years of wine, twelve feet high, set side by side in a dark room; a tower on the house to climb to in the evening to see the vines, the villages and the mountains, and to listen and hear how quiet it was.
>
> In front of the barn a woman held a duck whose throat she had cut and stroked him gently while a little girl held up a cup to catch the blood for making gravy. The duck seemed very contented and when they put him down (the blood all in the cup) he waddled twice and found that he was dead. We ate him later, stuffed and roasted; and many other dishes, with the wine of that year.

SIXTEEN

WALDO PEIRCE

The artist Waldo Peirce (1884–1970) was more like Hemingway than any other friend. Both men were tall, strong and bearded; good athletes, powerful swimmers and expert fishermen; heavy drinkers, aggressive and sometimes violent. They played football: Hemingway in high school, Peirce in college. Both drove ambulances as volunteers in World War I and earned medals for bravery. They were postwar expatriates in Paris, spent years in Spain, and were fluent in French and Spanish. Each had four wives and several children, and married the next wife soon after divorcing the previous one. Peirce painted three portraits of Hemingway as well as bullfights in Pamplona and fishing in the Caribbean. Though Hemingway often criticized his friends and broke with them, he never quarreled with the talkative and ebullient Peirce, and had a rare lifelong friendship with him.

Peirce was born in Bangor, Maine, the son of a powerful lumber baron. Educated at Andover and Harvard, he was a classmate of Hemingway's future editor Max Perkins, for whom he started to write an autobiography. At six feet, two inches tall, the bawdy, witty, lusty, cigar-smoking Peirce was even taller and stronger than Hemingway. The biographer of the romantic revolutionary John Reed, another Harvard classmate, described Peirce's most daring feat. In Boston, Reed persuaded his wealthy friend

> to give up reservations on the *Mauretania* and join him. Together they boarded the S.S. *Bostonian* on July 9 [1910], with Waldo already grumbling over the venture. His fears were justified. A British vessel carrying 648 steers, the freighter was a wretched hulk with a dank forecastle,

> an unbearable stench of cattle and unpleasant officers. After a noon meal that featured worms in the soup, Waldo left his wallet and watch on Reed's bunk and dove overboard to make a ten-mile swim back to shore. Nobody saw him go, and when he was found to be missing, nobody except Jack believed anyone would try to swim so far. Because he held Peirce's effects, Reed was, by the end of his first day at sea, scheduled to face murder charges in England.

Eleven days later at a Board of Trade inquiry in Manchester, Peirce—who'd been picked up by lobster fishermen and had caught a fast liner—"bustled into the room, all smiles and hearty shouts," and saved Reed from prison. Peirce later recalled the mythic appeal of his adventure: "Everybody likes the story. Likes the idea. Jumping overboard. Getting away from it all. Starting new. Everybody wants to do that. So the story sticks. They imagine themselves me. Imagine themselves doing it."

Like Hemingway, Peirce had a colorful life. After art training at the Académie Julian in Paris, he studied from 1912 to 1914 under Ignacio Zuloaga in Segovia. Though Zuloaga was a better draftsman and more accomplished painter than Peirce, Hemingway criticized the traditional artist's influence and sharply remarked, "The only trouble was that Waldo couldn't take painting Zuloagas seriously and Zuloaga could." Peirce later criticized his teacher and called him, with a hint of his own character, "a great masculine simple soul, rhinoceros-skinned to any subtlety of thought or paint." When Peirce discovered Goya he spent a lot of time copying the greater artist.

After the war broke out, Waldo returned to Paris and joined the American Ambulance Field Service. He won a Croix de Guerre for conspicuous bravery when transporting the wounded in the battle of Verdun, and described an artillery bombardment and infantry attack in his memoir "Christmas Eve 1915": "From one mountain slope to another roared all the lungs of war. For five days and five nights—scraps of days, the shortest of the year, nights interminable—the air was shredded with shrieking shells—intermittent lulls for slaughter in attack and after the bombardment, then again the roar of counter-attack." Toward the end of the war he was assigned to the Army Intelligence Service and sent to work in Madrid.

In 1921 Peirce rented an old fortress in Tunis and used it as his studio. He lived as an expatriate in Paris in the 1920s, and met Hemingway at the

Café du Dôme in about 1926. In April 1927, the year after Hemingway's novel was published, Peirce wrote his mother that he knew its real-life models: "Did you read *The Sun Also Rises* by Ernest Hemingway? A good novel of the Latin Quarter and the derelicts of the war—that lost generation—they are real people—friends or acquaintances of mine. The heroine of the book Duff Twysden has just moved into my place in Cagnes [on the Riviera]. She's broke and deserted. She came here to be married to the Mike of the book but another lady removed the perfidious spouse a day before the ceremony. The novel is brutal and triste, if you like, but true." Peirce described Hemingway, who was committed to his art, as "a sturdy youth, and serious contrast to the general populo of Paris that I see."

Hemingway had been going to the *feria* and bullfights in Pamplona, northern Spain, since 1923, and in July 1927 Peirce went with him. He didn't have the same *afición* for the *corrida* as Hemingway and was upset by the disemboweling of the *picador*'s horses (who became padded in 1928). But he watched the spectacle, painted the bullfights that Hemingway wrote about and told his mother about their adventures: "Hemingway fights bulls on occasion and I stand every morning on the top outside gallery of the coliseum [bullring]—whence we could watch the running [through the streets], then go down to see the entry into the ring. . . . Hemingway got in with the cow the last day—who isn't dangerous, but he wasn't keen on the sudden appearance of the steer from behind. . . . Hemingway left last night for San Sebastian to meet his new wife [Pauline]. He doesn't want people to know about his second marriage as he had another wife [Hadley] here last year and the Spanish are not as [tolerant] with divorce as we are."

He later recalled his failure to record Hemingway's bravery: "One day Ernest got in the ring with a cow. I was supposed to take pictures of him, but put in my camera a previously used film backwards and didn't get a single thing. Ernest performed prodigies of courage in the ring, but could have killed me when he discovered my stupidity." In October 1929, however, Peirce took a grim photo of a man's intact arm taken from the belly of a shark. He also recorded his friend's passion for fishing in the mountains: "Whenever we went riding in a car and drove over a stream, Ernest insisted upon getting out of the car to see if there were any trout swimming around."

In a letter to Hemingway of June 1929 Peirce described, in his most perverse and lubricious style, an imaginary monstrous fish they could include in a fishing book they planned but never wrote. Punning on vernal equinox, he wrote:

> Balls like a Bull, wings like a bat, shits like a sawmill, half man and half woman, three hind quarters, self-sufficient androgynous hermoaphrodizzycal son of a bitch, a Jacal with seventy-three arseholes which he scratches on the sand on the venereal equinox by fair weather only and one hundred and eighty-seven cocks with which he buggers himself to death in the rutting season, which is very often, causing few of these comparatively unknown monsters to attain full growth owing to aforesaid pernicious habit.

Peirce had to shave off his massive beard during the war in order to wear a gas mask. When he cut it again in 1920 Hemingway asked Perkins: "How does he look without the beard? It's a loss to the world." In 1920 George Bellows painted a fine portrait of the still-bearded Peirce (now in the de Young Museum in San Francisco). Hemingway liked to recall a heroic encounter that took place in a bar when two drunken sailors made fun of Peirce's beloved beard. He then picked up one in each hand and banged their heads together. Hemingway, who exaggerated stories of Peirce's great strength, claimed that his friend was "as fast and as strong as a bear and damned impressive when he was angry." Peirce modestly responded, "looking strong is more impressive than being strong, so what the devil, if Ernest has a good story let him stick to it."

Beginning in 1928, Peirce visited Hemingway for several fishing trips out of Key West and had many wet drinks in the Dry Tortugas. He painted the rowdy *Silver Slipper* dance hall, with a sign over the door, "No vulgar dancing," adjacent to Sloppy Joe's, Hemingway's favorite Key West bar. In *Death in the Gulf Stream* (1932), Peirce sits in the stern of a small boat, steering it with a pole. Bill Smith, Hemingway's boyhood friend, stands in the bow pulling mightily on a rope attached to a harpoon in a shark. In the center of the boat Hemingway, armed with a machine gun, shoots the huge shark in the belly.

Peirce said, "I always make sketches and then I go to it without inhibition. . . . I like to paint the man in his true authentic milieu." His loosely painted pictures have soft forms, intense colors and elaborate decorations. But his work is not, as some claim, like the art of Matisse and Renoir. His hastily executed second-rate work, with sentimental pictures of children and flowers, resembles the illustrations of popular magazines. His witty titles include *Breakfast on the Beach*: a mother nursing her child; and *On Again Off Again*: a mother persuading her child to use the potty. He turned out hundreds of pictures and gave away many he could not sell.

Peirce painted several portraits of his friend. *Hemingway as "Kid Balzac"* (1929) did not look at all like the flabby French novelist nor much like Hemingway himself. Against a cloudy and green-sea background, the chest-length, full-face subject, in an open-collared white shirt, has a pillar-like neck, helmet of dark hair, thick eyebrows, red-blotched face, drooping mustache, strong chin, tight lips and severe look. Peirce's ink-on-paper portrait (1928), superior to the oil painting, captures Hemingway's appearance and brooding character. In a head-and-shoulders three-quarter view, Hemingway wears the same white shirt and reveals a hint of chest hair. He has a dark mane, shadow circling his firm jaw, straggly mustache and eyebrows, asymmetrical eyes and pensive expression.

Peirce's painting of Hemingway fishing appeared on the October 18, 1937 cover of *Time* magazine to coincide with the review of his novel *To Have and Have Not*. Against a sharply divided blue sea and cloudy background, Hemingway in profile has broad shoulders, thick eyebrows, small eyes, half-open mouth and indented chin. Wearing a long-billed striped cap and striped shirt, clutching the fishing rod and winding the reel, he's crouched over while struggling to land a huge catch.

In February 1940 Hemingway wrote Perkins about Peirce's unusual tolerance when their irascible and arrogant friend, Charles Sweeny, interfered with his art: "Waldo gets along with him by takeing what no human would take. Ask Waldo about the time he was painting Charley's portrait and Charley finally started painting it himself. Boy I'd like to have that confidence." In his posthumous novel *Islands in the Stream* (1970), the Hemingway character, remembering the old days in Paris, tells his sons that he's an old, old friend of Picasso, Braque, Miró, Masson and Pascin. His son then adds: "And of Waldo Peirce." But there's an awkward contrast between these major artists—Hemingway owned works by Miró, Gris, Masson and Klee—and the inferior work of his old pal Waldo.

Hemingway and Peirce watched prizefights in New York in October 1928 and went to a Harvard football game in October 1931. Hemingway wrote many chummy, comradely, man-to-man letters to Peirce about bulls, fishing, guns and drink. He claimed he'd been poor in Paris, and noted his current money problems, accidents and illnesses, the birth of his sons Patrick and Gregory, the difficulty of writing and raising money to buy ambulances for the Loyalists in the Spanish Civil War. He wrote about his wives and the scars of divorce, frequently summoned Peirce to Key West, and confirmed his friendship and high regard for his art.

Hemingway felt there was no one he could really talk to while isolated in Key West (the southernmost point in America) and in January 1929, with great emotion, told Peirce how much he missed his old friends: "I am lonesome to see some of youse guys. . . . I am in need of society and want you down whenever you can come. . . . Miss you like hell down here." He said if he had a daughter he would name her Pilar, but without a daughter gave his boat that name. Always generous with money, in February 1929 he said he was supporting his recently widowed mother, two sisters, one brother, one ex-wife, one current wife and two sons, and amusingly announced: "I have to work or thousands starve."

In December 1929 his six-year-old son accidentally poked his finger in Hemingway's one good eye, cut the pupil with his nail and gave Hemingway "a hell of a time." Still suffering three years later, he referred to the half-blind James Joyce and told Peirce: "My bloody eyes are bad (not trying to pull a Joyce on the boys but they give me bad trouble reading and writing and I am dictating this to Pauline)." When he finally lured Archibald MacLeish to fish in Key West, the rather proper poet and stiff government official was not, like the roisterous Peirce, a good companion. He reported that "Archie has become, between ourselves righteous, fussy, and a bloody bore. Strange mixture of puerility and senility."

Peirce had an extremely complicated married life. He met his first wife, Dorothy Rice—a wealthy socialite, artist, aviator and motorcyclist—after both had studied with Zuloaga and were painting in Madrid, and they were married from 1913 to 1917. He said that the colorful bohemian Dorothy "paints her lips a bit and puts shoe black on her eyes, wears earrings like bracelets, looks like a gypsy." In 1918 his French lover, Gabrielle, died of influenza in Biarritz and shattered Peirce. He and his second wife, the American actress and painter Ivy Troutman (1883–1979), met in Paris and were married from 1920 to 1930. He met his third wife, another wealthy artist, Alzira Boehm (1908–2010), at a Matisse show in New York. She was Jewish and twenty-four years younger than Peirce, and they were married from 1930 to 1945. They had twin sons, Mike and Bill, in 1930, and a daughter, Anna Gabrielle, in 1934.

Hemingway's most interesting letters concern Alzira and their twins. In May 1930, while settling his divorce with Ivy in Paris, Peirce sent his pregnant future wife, twenty-two years old but looking much younger, to Key West to await his delayed arrival. Hemingway, as when he hid Pauline in Spain, was torn between his Oak Park puritanism and European bohemianism. With considerable embarrassment, he told Peirce that Alzira was causing an intolerable scandal among the respectable folk in town:

> What's simple as hell in Paris is as complicated as same in U.S.A. If you're planning to stay somewhere and have a baby, K.W. is too small a place now that you know or anyway are known by so many local merchants. . . . She's had and has a hell of a difficult show with having to go to the Dr. who is also director of the bank in as small a town as this. . . . If you think you could come here where you're as widely known as say the Eiffel Tower and live with her alone with her looking about 16 and things the way they are without getting into a jam you're crazy. . . . Guys like you and me that live and have lived around and don't give a damn what people say about anything so long as the law ain't invoked are one thing and merchants that have to live on in a town and have people say to them "so your swell friends just turned out to be a bunch of scandalous bastards" are another.

The worldly and sophisticated Hemingway claimed he didn't care about what other people thought. But he *was* terribly worried, in this nervous and contorted letter, about Alzira creating a scandal, getting into a jam and earning the disapproval of the conventional *merchants*! Peirce heeded his warnings, and Alzira had their twins in a more congenial locale.

Hemingway and Peirce had very different ideas about how to bring up children. The writer strongly felt that work, even fishing, should come before paternal duties. In July 1928, before the twins were born, Peirce punned on "wedlock" and wrote Hemingway, "having no offspring I have only the machinery of life, that is of holy bedlock to contend with, without the major consolation, penalty or reward as you like. . . . Children should be had if at all when you and the girl are young, park em with the grandparents afterwards, who are of the age to care for and enjoy them, then look em over on return from Mesopotamia." But when his offspring were born two years later, conditions had changed and his feelings were quite different. At forty-six and no longer young, he became completely domesticated, was deeply attached to them, did not leave them with grandparents and did not take long trips without them. In November 1931 Hemingway urged him to free himself from degrading household chores: "Now that you know you have twinmaking *cojones* for gods sake layoff of domestic life and come down to Key West." By contrast to Peirce, in 1933 Hemingway and Pauline left their two children with nursemaids and went on a three-month African safari.

In February 1936 Peirce's visits to Key West with his five-year-old twins provoked Hemingway's most furious and hilarious letters about him. He wrote John Dos Passos (whose future wife had been seriously courted by Peirce) that the artist was foolishly besotted by his offspring: "with absolutely nothing wrong with the kids nor to worry about them he worries all day and all night and literally, actually, thinks nor ever talks of anything else. . . . I am prejudiced against them as a full time occupation for a man—and old Waldo is certainly damned nice."

In a letter that February to Sara Murphy, whose exceptionally well-bred boy had died tragically in 1935, Hemingway insisted that Peirce's wild children had to be disciplined and tamed: "Waldo is here with his kids like untrained hyenas and him as domesticated as a cow. Lives only for the children and with the time he puts in on them they should have good manners and be well trained but instead they never obey, destroy everything. . . . They have a nurse and a housekeeper too, but he is only really happy when trying to paint with one setting fire to his beard and the other rubbing mashed potato into his canvases." Peirce seemed to encourage and enjoy their outrageous behavior. When one twin hit him over the head with a beer bottle, he smiled tolerantly and said, "Well, pretty soon they'll be in school."

Peirce's marriage to Alzira ended during World War II just as his marriage to Ivy had ended in World War I. In 1946 he married his fourth wife, the artist Ellen Larsen (1920–2001), and had two more children, Jonathan in 1941 and Karen in 1948. He settled down and remained with her until his death in 1970. Each marriage to wealthy-artist wives had lasted longer than the previous one: five, ten, fifteen and twenty-four years.

Hemingway kept in touch with his old friend and knew that Peirce was living in the dry climate of Tucson, Arizona, to alleviate Ellen's asthma. When Hemingway drove from Idaho to Key West in 1959, they met there, for the last time, two years before his death. Hemingway's fourth wife, Mary, who adopted his inflated view of Peirce's art, gushed that he "seemed a flowing fountain of volubility, a cigar-ash dropper with an entrancing childish delight in ideas, jokes, words, and a true modesty about his excellent work and an overwhelming generosity. An enchanting man." Hemingway once asked his young son Jack, "Who's the greatest man you know?" expecting him to say "Papa." Instead, Jack answered "Waldo." Always faithful to the burly and bearded Peirce, Hemingway overrated his work, overlooked his faults and admired his character: "As a painter I think he is one of the very finest in America. As a friend he is loyal, understanding, generous and the best company anybody ever had."

SEVENTEEN

HENRY STRATER

The painter Henry (Mike) Strater (1896–1987) was born in Louisville, Kentucky, where his father and uncles had founded the prosperous Strater Brothers Tobacco Company that manufactured snuff, chewing and smoking tobacco. During the Depression, Hemingway wrote Strater, "I hope the snuff racket is holding up well." Strater, given the incongruous middle name of "Hyacinth," was educated at the Lawrenceville School and Princeton University, where he was a friend of Scott Fitzgerald. He was the model for the rebellious and philosophical Burne Holiday in Fitzgerald's first novel, *This Side of Paradise* (1920): "Broad-browed and strong-chinned," with fine gray eyes, "he gave an immediate impression of bigness and security." Strater's first wife, Margaret Connor (1895–1972), was born in Philadelphia and educated at Vassar. They met when she was studying sculpture at the Philadelphia Museum of Art, married in 1920, had three sons and a daughter, born between 1921 and 1931. Margaret suffered from chronic asthma and sinus problems; they divorced in 1942.

Hemingway's artist-friends Strater and Waldo Peirce (1884–1970)—tall, strong and athletic—had parallel careers and a great deal in common. (Strater's photo appears in the Cambridge edition of Hemingway's *Letters, 1932–1934*, after page 200.) Peirce was born in Maine; Strater lived in Maine from 1926. He paid for the land and helped design the Ogunquit Museum of American Art, which opened in 1953. Both men came from wealthy families who enabled them to paint without financial pressure. They went to elite prep schools and Ivy League colleges, and drove ambulances in World War I, where Peirce won the Croix de Guerre and Strater was wounded. They studied art in Spain and France (Strater's teacher was Edouard Vuillard). Both met Hemingway in Paris, told him about the bullfights, painted three portraits of him and fished with him in the Caribbean. Peirce had four wives and five children; Strater had three wives and eight children. Most of their wives were artists, and none of Strater's wives liked him to paint nudes. The marriages of both men broke up during wartime. Late in life they spent winters in Arizona; Peirce lived to eighty-six, Strater to ninety-one.

Hemingway had recently returned from reporting the Greco-Turkish War and had not yet published any fiction when he met Strater, who had a painting in the 1922 Paris Salon, at Ezra Pound's flat in January 1923. Strater complained that he'd been drinking weak tea, Hemingway offered him whisky from his hip flask. Strater told him he boxed, they both weighed 195 pounds, and the next day in his studio they fought a few rounds and sealed their friendship. Just as competitive in drinking, skiing and fishing as in boxing, Hemingway liked to win everything and couldn't believe that a man with the effete middle name could hold his own in a fight. They visited Pound in Rapallo on the Italian Riviera, in February 1923, and Hemingway was so eager to knock out Strater that he stopped sleeping with his wife to conserve his vital energy. Strater sprained his ankle and couldn't box, but they managed to play tennis.

They discussed writing and painting, and the concise Hemingway criticized "the freedom with which writers like Faulkner and Bob McAlmon expressed themselves: 'it just comes out of them as though they were evacuating their bowels.'" His only criticism of Strater's work, when thinking of Cézanne, was "why don't you artists make mountains look like mountains?" Hemingway liked Strater and called him an all-right nice guy.

Strater had lived in Spain and aroused Hemingway's interest in bullfights before he had seen one. Strater drew a map of Spain with his favorite places, told him about the best restaurant in Madrid and the pension where the matadors lived. In September 1923 Hemingway wrote Pound that he'd been working on a long story about Strater and his wife Maggie. He abandoned that story, but wrote another one, also unfinished, with "Strater's voice telling of a Spanish bullfight where the first two matadors were both gored badly; the last matador, a young kid, had to kill all five bulls. On the fifth bull he kept missing with the sword: 'He tried five times and the crowd was quiet because it was a good bull and it looked like him or the bull [would die] and then he finally made it. He sat down in the sand and puked and they held a cape over him while the crowd hollered and threw things down into the bull ring.'"

In Rapallo, Strater painted two portraits of Hemingway. In the first, a profile against a bluish-grey background, Hemingway wears a blue tie and heavy brown overcoat. He has thick dark hair touching his collar, wide forehead, firm nose, full mustache and tight mouth, and looks down with a thoughtful expression. Strater recalled: "The first portrait, the profile, he said made him 'look too literary, like H. G. Wells.' He always rather resented that part of himself, the perfectionist artist, which made him a great writer. He wanted to be a real tough guy. His coloring was very handsome, dark hair and pink-and-white complexion; but the fair skin bothered him, so midway in the second portrait I said 'O.K., I'll paint you the way you look boxing.'" The young Hemingway didn't look at all like the fifty-seven-year-old Wells. But Hemingway believed that writers were slightly effeminate and had to project a virile image. Strater's "pink-and-white complexion" bothered him and he wanted it changed into a boxer's look.

The second, close-up, full-face, head-and-shoulders portrait shows Hemingway's head tilted slightly to the right. Against a rust-colored background, he wears a white tunic and has thick hair, large dark eyes, square nose, red lips, partly open mouth and strong jaw, and looks appropriately tough. Pleased with the second portrait, he told his sister that Strater is "miles ahead of all the rest of the pigmenters." He also said, "Mike spoils many paintings, but he has enough money so it does not matter." He used a woodcut of the boxer portrait as the frontispiece of his second book, *in our time* (1924). Strater recalled that Hemingway "begged me for years to give him the boxer portrait and I said, 'I'll leave it to you in my will.' I would have but he predeceased me." The first two portraits are now in the Smithsonian Institution in Washington, D.C.

In 1925 Strater created large colored decorative initials, with fine drawings inside and next to them, for Pound's *XVI Cantos*. Three years later Hemingway told Pound, "I haven't seen any of his painting for a long time but I thought some was pretty good." Hemingway was deeply tanned when Strater painted his third portrait in Key West in 1930. In a three-quarter view facing right he wears an open-collar green shirt against a dark background. He has wavy brown hair, broad forehead, curved eyebrows, red cheeks, strong nose, full dark mustache and pillar-like neck, and has a severe expression. More vivid and incisive, it reveals Hemingway's brooding character. Strater added, "with his usual verve, he took away my brush after I had signed, and added his own name." In May 1930 Strater wrote, "The portrait of you didn't look so good later, so I spent four or five days on it, and now it is right."

Hemingway discussed Strater's marriage problems—and his own. In August 1923 Strater had an affair with a woman in Paris. But he and Maggie were reconciled, went on a second honeymoon and, Hemingway skeptically remarked, "patched up for a year." In March 1924 Hemingway said Strater had mistakenly left expatriate life in Paris for a puritanical-and-Prohibition existence in America. Quoting Luke 23:34, he told patriarchal Pound, "Father forgive them for they know not what they do." In Rapallo, Hemingway had told Strater about the trunk filled with his precious early manuscripts that Hadley had lost—and had never been found—in the Gare de Lyon in December 1922: "'You know, Mike, if you had had those manuscripts in your trunk, you would not have left them to go and get something to read.' In other words, I was a fellow artist and if he had given them to me I would never have left them in an exposed position. He was very upset because it showed how little she valued what he was doing." Hemingway never forgave Hadley's carelessness and indifference. Three years later, when he was having an affair with Pauline Pfeiffer and his marriage was breaking up, he wrote Strater from Valencia mentioning the consolation of the *corridas*: "Everything is all shot to hell in every direction but in the meantime there are eight fights here starting tomorrow." Strater was sympathetic and gave him sexual carte blanche by assuring him that "all men of genius are immoral."

Hemingway kept in touch with Strater. In November 1928 they watched boxing matches in Madison Square Garden in New York and the Princeton-Yale football game in Princeton. In December 1928, when Hemingway's father killed himself and he needed money to get home to Oak Park, he phoned Strater for help. He saw the artist in New York in February 1930, often begged him to come down to Key West, and took the expert fisherman on many trips between 1929 and 1937. Pauline's rich Uncle Gus Pfeiffer had offered to pay $25,000 for Hemingway's safari to East Africa, and he generously invited Strater, Archibald MacLeish and Charles Thompson, who owned a hardware store in Key West, to be his guests.

Wildly enthusiastic about the expedition, Hemingway referred to the Yale elite society Skull and Bones and told MacLeish, who'd been a member, "Mike and Charles can go—yr the last man tapped for Bones—[African] Buffalo bones—Lion bones." Hemingway, claiming expertise, added, "Don't let Mike tell you anything about guns. Every thing he has written me about guns is utter nonsense." Fancifully combining allusions to bullfighting and sailing—kites flown behind a boat helped attract fish—he told Strater, "May take a sword and muleta [cape] for buffalo and you carry a kite for us to climb the string for elephants."

As Hemingway tried to coordinate the lives of his three potential companions, his plans for the eagerly awaited safari became plagued with problems. In June 1932 he postponed the trip and gave several unconvincing excuses. He explained that his recurrent eye problems would interfere with his shooting, he wanted to hunt and fish in Wyoming that fall, and he had many good stories to write. MacLeish could not go that year and the delay would help Thompson's business. A presidential election would be held in November; he didn't like to leave the country during the uncertain Depression, and felt guilty about taking a luxurious holiday when so many people were unemployed and suffering hardship.

In June 1932 he informed MacLeish in telegraphic style: "Am going to call off Africa until next June on a chance you can go—It's better for Charles—If it's ok with Mike—Hope it will be—Must write him and hate to—I wrote Uncle Gus—My god damned conscience says not to go now—Too long away the way things are going." He also told Strater: "Hate like a bastard to postpone Africa—But the way things are going in the country I would feel like a heel to be hunting in Africa with the country in such a hell of a shape." MacLeish was actually delighted and said, "I hope to thunder you do put off that African trip. I never liked the idea of it anyhow."

Strater, by contrast, was furious but forced to agree. He had made his own elaborate plans and the delay damaged their friendship. Hemingway knew he'd postponed for mainly selfish reasons, and for several months he tried—humbly and most unusually—to make peace with Strater. In July he sent a series of emotional bulletins to his two friends, and apologetically told the artist: "I wrote Archie there was a chance of postponement when got a very blue and dismal letter from him. . . . It must have been a hell of a jolt to you and I feel like hell about it—It is my damned fault." Six days later he wrote to MacLeish that it had been difficult to make all the arrangements and the trip was definitely postponed. Strater was angry, but (since he had no choice) had to accept the delay: "Not going to Africa until next June or end of June—Mike seemed very upset that you told him this before I did—But I couldn't tell him until I heard from Charles. . . . Trip was still on until he agreed to postponement."

Seven days later, after Strater had refused to go on the Wyoming hunting trip, Hemingway feared the artist was holding a grudge: "hope you arent pooping on it on acct of my delaying Africa or not writing or writing anything that makes you sore." On July 31 he complained to MacLeish that Strater was unreasonably angry and that he himself was now the injured party: "Mike is on his very high horse now and wont come—He says he's not sore but he is or was very sore about Africa—It is Africa or nothing with old Mike and bugger Wyoming . . . and he is really being very snotty to me. . . . After all I postponed trip for your, for Charles and for my benefit and trip to be made whenever best for majority"—but not best for Strater.

In October, still troubled and desperate to maintain the friendship, he apologized again, admitted it was all his fault and felt guilty about it: "I wish I could talk to you and I could explain the African postponement so it would take the hurt out of your feelings. . . . I know you still feel hurt and sore. . . . I did bitch your plans and have and do feel goddamned bad about it and feel worse about it all the time." In February 1933 he again complained to MacLeish that though he'd tried to appease Strater, he refused to go fishing in Cuba "to snoot me probably because I delayed the Africa trip."

In late November 1933 Hemingway, Thompson and Pauline finally sailed from Marseilles to Mombasa, Kenya, for their three-month safari. In June that year Strater, not mentioning his anger, gave a reasonable excuse for not joining them. Maggie's deteriorating health was caused by "babies + operations + metropolis." He had to stay home to take care of her and "build her up unless I wanted to have a permanent invalid on my hands." Strater later added, "I was going, and then my wife got pregnant. I wasn't going to go off and leave a pregnant wife. So I didn't go, and Ernest's nose was out of joint that I'd placed my wife ahead of him. . . . It was a big blow to him when I refused to go with him. That was when our friendship ended"—though they had two more fierce quarrels before it finally terminated.

Hemingway loved to lead a group of male friends on hunting and fishing adventures, but they were often unwilling to be led. MacLeish later explained that the real reason for his two African refusals began in the islands off the

Florida coast in the Gulf of Mexico just before the postponement. He discreetly said, "Ernest and I and Mike Strater and Pauline's Uncle Gus took a trip across to the Dry Tortugas in the spring of 1932 and got caught in a northerner [windstorm]. We were marooned for three days. As a result we saw a little too much of each other."

In April of that year, in a rare admission of blame, Hemingway confessed his faults and told MacLeish: "I know I am bossy and irritating son of a bitch in action when I get crabby. And as you justly said no one takes offense quicker nor as I say more unjustly." Both men had quarreled with Hemingway on that fishing trip. They refused his Africa invitation, fearing that his fierce competitiveness would turn the safari into a grim struggle for superiority. Hemingway's lesser kudu would always be greater their greater kudu.

Their battle continued in April 1935 when Hemingway became resentful about the artist's refusal. Strater recalled: "Hemingway was a fine sportsman, but in this case too competitive. He was very alive and more fun to be with than anybody I ever knew, but he could be a real S.O.B. In 1935 he was an S.O.B. because I had refused to go with him to Africa." Sailing with Strater and John Dos Passos in Bimini in the Bahamas, the sport-fishing capital of the world, the accident-prone Hemingway shot himself in both legs while holding a pistol and trying to land a huge fish. Then, after Strater had hooked a giant twelve-foot marlin, the wounded Hemingway, pretending to keep the marlin from being mutilated, cried "sharks." He fired tommy-gun bullets past his friend's head and into the voracious sharks. Attracted by the blood, the sharks devoured half the marlin and left only 500 pounds. A photo showed them standing next to the skeletal half-eaten fish that Hemingway had helped to destroy. Strater later added: "The truth is that Ernest was overcome with jealousy because I had the world's record marlin hooked and had brought it up in record time. Hemingway didn't want me to be the one to catch the first big fish. In fact the fish was never in danger from the sharks because I had already bought it to gaff with no damage whatsoever."

Hemingway again offended Strater when a photo of him next to a giant fish in Bimini appeared in *Time* magazine on October 18, 1937. Strater explained, "I caught a tremendous big fish in Bimini. It was a great feat and I was very much the local hero. But Hemingway stood in front of me every time the fish was photographed. He'd stand between the camera and fish so he would be visible and I would not." Hemingway got credit for catching Strater's fish and enraged his friend by refusing to tell the truth. The artist said, "I was curious whether Hemingway would write in a denial in *Time*. Nooooooo."

Hemingway had always been solicitous about Maggie's poor health. But in August 1942, when the Straters divorced and he was having problems with his second ill-fated marriage, he expressed resentment about the artist placing his wife ahead of himself and asked a mutual friend: "What do you know about Mike Strater getting married? . . . If Maggie Strater should be triumphed over after all these years, there is hope for our side in the great unending battle between men and women." Soon after his divorce Strater married Janet Meacham, who'd been a model in a department store. They had one son, and divorced in 1946. In 1951 he married Lois Thompson, who worked as a waitress in an Ogunquit restaurant. They had three children (bringing his total to eight) and divorced in 1967.

At the beginning of their careers the young Hemingway and Strater shared a passion for boxing and Spain, an admiration for Pound, a professional interest in writing and painting. Strater's portraits enhanced Hemingway's reputation and increased his fame. But the writer's intense competitiveness led to a battle of egos and three bitter quarrels. Eager to preserve the friendship, Hemingway was unusually guilt-ridden and apologetic. They discussed their marriage problems and the artist was attracted to the writer's charismatic character. Despite all their conflicts, when Hemingway died Strater forgave and praised him: "he was not easy to get along with at times; but he had such overpowering charm and aliveness that one was always glad to see him again."

EIGHTEEN

ALFRED FLECHTHEIM

Alfred Flechtheim, the German collector, art dealer and publisher, was a shadowy but significant figure in Hemingway's life. Hemingway knew him at the peak of his prestige, influence and fame, but lost contact when Flechtheim was overwhelmed by disasters that resembled a Greek tragedy. Flechtheim was born in Münster in northwest Germany in 1878, the son of a wealthy Jewish family who—like the Buddenbrooks in Thomas Mann's novel—had been grain merchants for several generations. He began work in his father's business, but was soon drawn to modern paintings. "There is something crazy about art," he declared. "It's a passion stronger than gambling, alcohol and women."

In 1910 Flechtheim married the Jewish heiress Betty Goldschmidt, and during their honeymoon in Paris he spent a large part of her substantial dowry on Cubist art. They had no children, but their elegant home was lined with bookcases and filled with contemporary paintings and Oceanic sculpture. In 1913 he opened his first gallery in Düsseldorf on the Rhine—followed after the war by others in Berlin, Frankfurt, Cologne and Vienna. He invited many celebrities from the world of theater and film to his famous costume parties in the main gallery. His friend, the German heavyweight champion Max Schmeling, loyally affirmed, "if I were a painter, I would want Flechtheim to represent me."

In the Düsseldorf catalog of 1987, *Alfred Flechtheim: Sammler. Kunsthändler. Verleger*, Wilmont Haacke wrote that Flechtheim "was impulsive and explosive, bold and productive, quick-witted and amusing, always trustworthy and ready to help, a true brother and pal." The art dealer Daniel-Henry Kahnweiler, his former partner and fellow German-Jewish exile, fondly recalled his friend's impressive personality: "He was startlingly colorful and won everyone over by his sense of humor, his jokes and his derisive wit, his vitality and daring. . . . He was the dynamic businessman, permanently chewing on a huge cigar, both cunning and effusive, and revealing above all his great passion for modern art." The influential Greco-French art critic Christian Zervos described him, in a barrage of adjectives, as "nervous, agitated, lively, shrewd, joyful, despairing, sensual, unfair, enthusiastic, chatty, theatrical."

In his essay on the Weimar art world of the 1920s, Malcolm Gee writes that Flechtheim "stood not just for French-influenced taste, but for a cosmopolitan awareness, intelligence and sense of style." His gallery "was a meeting point for a cross-section of Berlin society, from the world of high finance to that of sport and entertainment." He exhibited works by Impressionist and Post-Impressionist artists—Manet, Renoir, Cézanne, Van Gogh and Seurat—before they became fashionable and expensive. He also represented many of the best contemporary painters: Picasso, Braque and Gris in France; Klee, Beckmann and Grosz in Germany. His ugly face fascinated artists. As a patron of the arts he helped many of them by commissioning his own portraits and was painted by Paul Klee, Jules Pascin, Otto Dix and many others.

Klee's weird linear sketch of Flechtheim, with overlapping planes, is idiosyncratically colored in red, blue, beige, gray and yellow. His profile has curlicue hair, eyes on a tilted axis, cigar-like pointed nose, jutting prognathous jaw and wide-open mouth that seems to be screaming. In Pascin's blurred frontal portrait (1927), Flechtheim is seated on a wooden chair with legs crossed and hands on his lap. He wears a matador's "suit of lights," as he sometimes did at his costume parties. His slim figure is dressed in a black bicorn hat, tight brown jacket, thick shoulder pads, knee breeches, red tie, white stockings and black slippers. A heavy greenish-brown cape, draped over his left arm, falls to the floor. His eyebrows are arched, his nose thin, his face long, his expression contemplative and sad.

Dix's brilliant but cruel portrait (1926), completed after their quarrel, has strong anti-Semitic overtones. Standing and gazing to the left, Flechtheim has hunched shoulders and compressed neck. His lined face looks like a cross between a great ape and a primitive statue. He has dark hair, heavy-lidded eyes, yellowish skin, thick red underlip, protruding ears and gigantic hooked nose. Frank Whitford observes that "with his left hand firmly on the frame of a painting by Braque and his [spidery] right hand supporting his weight on an erotic drawing by Picasso, the dealer has been made to personify the acquisitiveness and even greed on which his trade depends. Almost thirty years after painting this picture, Dix admitted that it made Flechtheim look avaricious and grasping."

In a positive contrast to Dix, George Grosz—who had a successful career in exile—remembered Flechtheim with great affection and called his old companion and dealer "a veritable mirror of civilization." Grosz's biographer Kay Flavell notes that Flechtheim was "one of the few friends who had turned up at the railway station to say farewell to Grosz and his wife in January 1933. He had also firmly supported Grosz's determination to leave Germany and make a completely new start elsewhere. The cause of Flechtheim's death, Grosz suggested, was the strain of living 'in a vacuum,' the inevitable accompaniment of exile."

As in Russia before the revolution of 1917, there was a flowering of great art in Weimar Germany before the old order disintegrated and the Nazi dictatorship took power. The magazine *Der Querschnitt* (Cross-Section), published by Flechtheim, promoted the very best work in Germany and was the first to bring out Hemingway's work in that country. In a 1934 Stanley-and-Livingstone encounter in the wilds of Africa, Hemingway was astonished to meet a man who was unfamiliar with *The Sun Also Rises* and *A Farewell to Arms*, but had read his youthful *jeux d'esprit* in Germany. The stranger said:

> "Hemingway is a name I have heard. Where? Where have I heard it? Oh, yes. The *Dichter*. You know Hemingway the poet?"
> "Where did you read him?"
> "In the *Querschnitt*."
> "That is me," I said, very pleased. The *Querschnitt* was a German magazine I had written some rather obscene poems for, and published a long story in, years before I could sell anything in America.

At that time "Undefeated" had been rejected by the *Dial* and he had not published any stories in America or England, but he had recently sold his first trade book, *In Our Time* (1925), to Liveright.

In his study of Hemingway and the little magazines, Nicholas Joost describes the avant-garde *Querschnitt*—published from 1921 to 1935—as "an even more sophisticated if also more raffish monthly than *The Dial*. It was similar to the American journal in its cosmopolitan taste, its espousal of the vanguard and its practice of publishing contemporary art." The editor, Hermann (known as Hans) von Wedderkop, was "dubbed 'Mr. Awfully Nice' because his spoken English apparently was confined to those two words." But "awfully nice" was probably his favorite phrase rather than the absolute limit of his English. *Der Querschnitt* published caricatures, nude drawings and photos of boxers, skiers in snowball fights and swimmers splashing in a stream. The urbane, sophisticated and satirical magazine continued to appear during the horrendous German inflation of the 1920s, and in the middle of that decade reached an impressive circulation of 14,000.

In Paris in the early 1920s, Wedderkop met the young American pianist and composer George Antheil in Sylvia Beach's Shakespeare and Company bookstore. Under the mistaken impression that Antheil was a literary man, Wedderkop asked him to become his Paris representative. With the help of Ford Madox Ford and Ezra Pound, Antheil acquired five poems from James Joyce's *Chamber Music* (originally published in 1907) and an essay by Pound.

In 1924–25 *Der Querschnitt* also published in English four caustic and violent, atheistic and deliberately obscene poems by Hemingway and his story "Undefeated," translated into German as "*Stierkampf*" (Bullfight). The slight but shocking poems were "The Earnest Liberal's Lament," punning on his hated first name, which cites three kinds of sexual transgressions and echoes Hamlet's "That I was ever born to set things right"; "The Lady Poets With Foot Notes," which mocked Edna Millay, Amy Lowell and others; "The Soul of Spain with McAlmon and Bird the Publishers," proprietors of the Paris small press Contact Editions and Three Mountains Press that brought out Hemingway's first two books. Part I of this poem repeats "fart" and "shit"; Part II, about bullfighting, includes photos taken by Hemingway during the running of the bulls at the feria in Pamplona.

The fourth poem, "The Age Demanded," which echoed Pound's "Hugh Selwyn Mauberley," was a bitter and retaliatory postwar satire:

The age demanded that we sing
And cut away our tongue.

The age demanded that we flow
And hammered in the bung.

The age demanded that we dance
and jammed us into iron pants.

And in the end the age was handed
the sort of shit that it demanded.

In "Undefeated" an old wounded matador attempts a comeback at a night fight in Madrid. After being gored, he finally kills the bull on the sixth try and is rushed to the hospital. When asked, "What do you keep on doing it for?" he stoically replies, "I was going good. . . . I didn't have any luck. That was all."

Hemingway couldn't resist calling the title "Der Queer Shit" and referring to "Wedderschnitt, editor of the Querkopf." (Later on, mentioning his German translator, he said, "she may have made errors but was always Horschitz.") But he was well pleased with his handsome first appearance in Germany and in April 1925 wrote, "*Der Querschnitt* have translated the bull fight story into German and Picasso is illustrating it for them. The '*Schnitt* is also publishing a book of my dirty poems to be illustrated by Pascin." In November 1924 Eugene Jolas, friend of Joyce and editor of the Paris little magazine *transition*, failed to see the humorous and provocative aspects of Hemingway's juvenilia. In an "Open Letter to Ernest Hemingway" he warned that "the young author was much admired, but that he was on the wrong tack with the poems he was publishing in *Der Querschnitt*."

Hemingway was amused to be earning good money in this unseemly fashion. Ignoring Jolas' paternalistic advice, in April 1925 he told a friend that "Wedderkop publishes my complete obscene works faster than I can write them. In Germany I am known as the junge amerikanische Heine"—a follower of the great German satiric poet. Delighted by his scandalous reputation, he also wrote, "Wedderkop and Flechtheim are in town. Flechtheim claims I'm Germany's only lyric poet. Appears greatly happy that people all over the world write in and cancel their subscriptions every time a poem is published. Says he wants one for every number. . . . Wants me to write a Stierkampf book with him. He is an old aficionado. Drawings by Gris and Picasso photographs." Flechtheim paid an advance for the bullfight book that became *Death in the Afternoon* (1932). It was finally published by Rowohlt in 1957.

In *A Moveable Feast* Hemingway recalled that Sylvia Beach handed him a serendipitous payment from the magazine:

"This came while I was out," she said. It was a letter and it felt as though it had money in it. "Wedderkop," Sylvia said.

"It must be from *Der Querschnitt*. Did you see Wedderkop?"

"No. But he was here with George [Antheil]. He'll see you. Don't worry. Perhaps he wanted to pay you first."

"It's six hundred francs. He says there will be more."

"I'm awfully glad you reminded me to look. Dear Mr. Awfully Nice."

"It's damned funny that Germany is the only place I can sell anything. To him and the *Frankfurter Zeitung*."

Six hundred francs, or $24, was half of what he'd earned from writing in 1925.

Hemingway and Flechtheim, both defiant and larger-than-life personalities, shared a strong interest in war, boxing and bullfighting as well as in literature and art. In November 1927 Hemingway mentioned his second wife and announced, "Pauline and I are going for a week and see the Six Days [bike race], Flechtheim, Rowohlt my German publisher and drink a little beer." The *Dichter* got a warm reception when they met again in Berlin. Referring to the German heavy cavalry, he noted that Flechtheim "was the only Jew who had been an officer in an Uhlan regiment in the war." (Photos of Flechtheim in his Uhlan uniform appear in the Düsseldorf catalog.) On April 1, 1928 Hemingway contributed an unrecorded poem to a special issue of *Der Querschnitt* that celebrated his publisher's fiftieth birthday. The magazine reprinted "The Age Demanded" but ruined the meter and meaning by leaving out "iron" in the sixth line. He added a brief tribute after the last line of his poem: "the sort of shit that it demanded. / (But not by Flechtheim)."

Hemingway tended to resent people who helped him and repaid generosity with hostility, and Flechtheim was no exception. Though the magnanimous publisher was not his sole supply of income and was not a homosexual, in October 1928 Hemingway claimed, "my only source of jack [was] the money paid by the noble citizen and prominent jewish bugger and great art dealer Alfie Flechtheim, who was featuring my obscene poems throughout the fatherland." He also declared that Wedderkop, employed by a Jew, "hates Kikes worse than we do." Hemingway's anti-Semitism was nasty though didn't go beyond words. But it would prove life-threatening in Germany and would soon drive the helpless dealer into exile.

In his poem "The Soul of Spain" Hemingway parodies Gertrude Stein's stuttering repetitions, takes a swipe at the *Dial* for rejecting his work and honoring Proust instead of Pound, and uncannily foreshadows the title of the painting he bought from Flechtheim: "The Dial does a monument to Proust. / We have done a monument to Ezra. / A monument is a monument." In September 1929 he returned to Berlin for beer and bike races, and with the money from his latest novel, *A Farewell to Arms*, acquired Paul Klee's *The Monument in Arbeit* (Under Construction, 1929).

The subject of this picture has a massive, powerful and rounded-rectangular head, with a thatch of hair, strong brow, thick wavy eyebrows, large round black eyes, small mouth and firm jaw. Two tiny laborers, carrying shoulder baskets of construction material—like Egyptians building the pyramids—climb up fragile ladders to the tall triangular scaffolding. Hemingway immediately identified with the formidable giant, who actually looks like him. The tiny figures build the monument as he builds his work and creates his image. He could also have seen them as his family and followers, parasites and critics, swarming over his great figure. Each of Hemingway's three sons inherited an important picture. Gregory, the youngest, desperate for immediate payment in cash, impulsively sold the Klee to a Madison Avenue dealer for much less than he could have earned at auction. Flechtheim and Hemingway bought paintings they loved; the Germans and Gregory cared only about their commercial value.

In *Islands in the Stream* (1970) Thomas Hudson describes the weird colors in Hemingway's painting:

> Across the room, above the bookcase, was Paul Klee's *Monument in Arbeit*. He didn't love it as he loved [Juan Gris'] *Guitar Player* but he loved to look at it and he remembered how corrupt it had seemed when he first bought it in Berlin. The color was as indecent as the plates in his father's medical books that showed the different types of chancres and venereal ulcers, and how frightened of it his wife had been until she learned to accept its corruption and only see it as a painting. He knew no more about it now than when he first saw it in Flechtheim's Gallery in the house by the river [Spree] that wonderful cold fall in Berlin.

The corruption in the painting represents the corruption in Hudson's (and in Hemingway's) third marriage.

Hemingway left Paris and returned to America in 1928, and never saw Flechtheim again. But Flechtheim's great wealth and prestige did not protect him, and he was one of the first prominent Jews to be persecuted by the Nazi regime. In 1933 Storm Troopers invaded his gallery and broke up his auction. The Nazis also seized the contents of his galleries and stole his personal art collection. Later that year he fled to Paris and then to London. In January 1934 he organized a Klee exhibition at the Mayor Gallery on Cork Street in London. Meanwhile, his former employee Curt Valentin sold Flechtheim's stolen art in New York to raise money for the Nazis.

Two friends described Flechtheim in Paris in July 1933. The German diarist, diplomat and patron of the arts, Count Harry Kessler, reported that Flechtheim believed, against all evidence, that modern art might still be able to survive in Germany: "He told me what is happening in the Berlin art world. Diametrically opposed trends exist among the Nazis. One supports modern art, the other wants to exterminate it. . . . He thinks that there is a bitter running fight between antagonistic trends and personalities within the Party, Göring and Goebbels. These internal quarrels and the inevitable dreadful economic emergency will destroy them. The crash, in his view, will come in autumn." Hopelessly optimistic about Nazi art policy, Flechtheim was psychologically unprepared for the disastrous events that soon destroyed him. A woman friend, who failed to understand the terror of a persecuted exile, recalled, "what horrifies me the most is the senseless fear that has taken hold of Flechtheim. In a completely empty restaurant, he looks left and right, even during the most harmless conversations, to make sure no one is listening to us." After escaping from Germany, he was still afraid he'd be captured and dragged back to a concentration camp.

In August 1935 Flechtheim, in a poignant letter, pleaded with Alfred Barr, the director of the Museum of Modern Art in New York: "I lost all my money and all my pictures. The only things I didn't lose are my name, my experience, my knowledge of nearly every French modern picture, my connections in Europe." He asked Barr to buy "nearly the only thing I saved," *Standing Youth* by the German sculptor Wilhelm Lehmbruck. Abby Rockefeller bought the statue for the museum in 1936.

The Nazi exhibition of "Degenerate Art," beginning in Munich from July to November 1937, attracted a million viewers and provided an excellent opportunity to attack both modern art and the Jews, and to condemn both as immoral and corrupt. The exhibition claimed that the 650 works of art, some originally sold by Flechtheim and confiscated from German museums, lacked artistic technique, destroyed natural beauty and insulted German ideals. Only six of the 112 artists were Jewish. But the "*Kunst*" poster advertising the exhibition, like Otto Dix's portrait, used and distorted Flechtheim's pronounced Semitic features and transformed them into an exaggerated African mask. Some exhibitions featured a life-size photo of Flechtheim expensively dressed and smoking a capitalistic cigar that matched his hooked nose.

In London in March 1937 Flechtheim, who had diabetes, first slipped on an icy street, then punctured his leg on a rusty nail, got blood poisoning and had his leg amputated. He died penniless and was buried in the Jewish cemetery in Golders Green, North London. Ivor Churchill, younger son of the Duke of Marlborough, published an appreciation in the *Times*: "When he survived the amputation of a leg, hopes were high for his recovery, but a sudden relapse cut short the gallant and protracted fight which he had waged." To complete the tragedy, Betty Flechtheim rashly returned to Germany in 1941. About to be deported to a concentration camp, she poisoned herself and died a slow death from an overdose of veronal. The injustice to Flechtheim continues today. Sixteen of his works sold by the Nazis in New York are now in the Museum of Modern Art, but a United States court ruled that time had expired on the family's claims. His descendants are still trying unsuccessfully to seek restitution from German museums.

Flechtheim shared the terrible fate of several Jewish German and Austrian writers who never adjusted to the vacuum of life in exile. Joseph Roth drank himself to death in Paris in 1939, Ernst Toller hanged himself in New York in 1940, Walter Benjamin poisoned himself in Spain in 1940, Stefan Zweig poisoned himself and his wife in Brazil in 1942. Despite Flechtheim's knowledge of French and English, his extraordinary experience, expertise and connections in the international art world, he never regained his old powers. Devastated emotionally and financially, he was a broken man who'd lost the will to live. He ended up maimed, in misery, pain and despair. As Robert Lowell wrote in his elegy of Ford Madox Ford, he was a good man and he "died in want."

NINETEEN

WALLACE STEVENS

Hemingway, thin-skinned and quick-tempered, was famous for brawling. In the mid-1930s he punched a vase of flowers in Sylvia Beach's bookshop after reading Wyndham Lewis' criticism in "The Dumb Ox" and wrestled with Max Eastman in Scribner's offices in retaliation for "Bull in the Afternoon." His most notorious fight took place with Wallace Stevens (who weighed 225 pounds but was twenty years older than Hemingway) after the poet reduced Hemingway's sister to tears by insulting the novelist, "by telling her forcefully what a sap I was, no man." Hemingway pursued the poet, "knocked all of him down several times and gave him a good beating" before Stevens broke his hand in two places by hitting the novelist in the jaw. Stevens emerged from the fray with a black eye and bruised face, and was seen the next day wearing dark glasses to conceal the damage.

Though Hemingway gleefully revealed the story to Sara Murphy, he warned her that Stevens was extremely anxious about protecting his reputation as a Hartford business executive: "you mustn't tell this to anybody . . . because he is very worried about his respectable insurance standing and I promised not to tell any body and the official story is that he fell down a stairs." Hemingway added that his wife Pauline, who hated his fights, was delighted, and that he eventually shook hands and made it up with Stevens. The poet apparently held no grudge and in his letters later praised Hemingway's poetry.

The fight took place on February 19, 1936 and influenced one of Hemingway's best stories, "The Short Happy Life of Francis Macomber," which he completed on April 19. Macomber compounds his cowardly flight from a lion by breaking the code of gentlemanly behavior and asking the hunter Wilson:

> "It doesn't have to go any further, does it? I mean, no one will hear about it, will they?"
> "You mean will I tell it at the Mathaiga Club?" Wilson looked at him now coldly. He had not expected this. So he's a bloody four-letter man as well as a bloody coward he thought. . . . "It's supposed to be bad form to ask us not to talk."

Macomber's lapse from the code of courage brings out the predatory nature of his wife Margot (partly based on Pauline), who is delighted by the revelation that her husband is "no man" and by the opportunity to humiliate him by sleeping with Wilson. When Macomber redeems his honor by killing the charging buffalo, he wrests the sexual power from Margot and makes it up with Wilson. But Margot exacts revenge on both men. When she sarcastically remarks, "I didn't know you were allowed to shoot [animals] from cars," Wilson responds, "Wouldn't mention it to anyone though. It's illegal if that's what you mean." . . . "What would happen if they heard about it in Nairobi?" "I'd lose my license for one thing. Other unpleasantnesses. . . . I'd be out of business." When the elated and sexually restored Macomber goes after the wounded buffalo, Margot fears he will leave her and shoots him in the head from the car. At the end of the story the balance of power shifts to Wilson, who repeats, "There will be a certain amount of unpleasantness" in Nairobi, and now "has something on her" as she once had on Macomber and on him.

Hemingway's use of his fight with Stevens—his transformation of reality into fiction—reaffirms his belief that violence tests one's moral code, and reveals the close connection of physical courage and moral strength in both his life and art. Hemingway beat Stevens who had insulted his manhood, as Margot did Macomber's. He despised the poet who exhibited bad form by worrying more about his reputation than his physical prowess, and exposed his corruption by asking Hemingway not to tell anyone about his shameful behavior, as Macomber did by asking Wilson to keep silent about his cowardice.

Though Hemingway kept his promise to say nothing publicly about the fight, he retained his moral stranglehold on Stevens by telling the story to Sara Murphy and hinting at it to John Dos Passos. In a similar fashion, Margot threatened to expose the moral faults of Macomber and Wilson, and Wilson revenged himself by threatening to expose her murder of Macomber. Stevens' shameful request "not to tell anybody" became a dominant theme of the story and binds all the characters in a net of corruption.

TWENTY

ISAAC BABEL

The subject of Babel's and Hemingway's stories is "War, and the pity of War." Both writers have, as John Berryman observed of Babel, "an obsessive concern with compression and explosion, a kinesthetic ferocity of control, a readiness to wrench language in order to gain nervous immediacy." Their tales of cruelty are structured by concision, intensity, violence and resolution.

Isaac Babel was born into a Jewish family in Odessa, a Crimean port on the Black Sea, in 1894. Short and stocky, he studied finance in Kiev, moved illegally to St. Petersburg in 1916 and became a protégé of Maxim Gorky, who published his first stories. After the Russian Revolution of 1917 Babel served for a time in the Cheka, the Soviet secret police, and in 1918–19 went on grain-extorting expeditions to feed the people in Moscow. From June to September 1920—the most crucial months of his life—he was a journalist attached to General Semyon Budenny's Cossack Red Cavalry, who fought on horseback with swords and rifles. He wrote battle reports, interrogated prisoners and treated the wounded.

He published *Odessa Stories* (1923) about Russian gangsters who were very like the Chicago gangsters that Hemingway portrayed in "The Killers" (1927). Babel achieved great fame and favor with his *Red Cavalry* stories in 1926, joined the Russian elite, traveled abroad and had a *dacha* in a writers' colony near Moscow. But in the 1930s he was mostly silent. He had a dangerous affair with the wife of Genrikh Yagoda, ruthless head of the secret police. When Yagoda fell from power, Babel, guilty by association, was arrested and was shot in January 1940. Babel's last futile words were, "Let me finish my work." All his manuscripts were seized and destroyed, and his existence was completely obliterated until his official exoneration in 1954.

Hemingway—five years younger than Babel—owned and admired his *Red Cavalry* (1929) and his *Collected Stories* (1955). In January 1936 he told his Russian translator Ivan Kashkin, "Isaac Babel I know ever since his first stories were translated in French [in the late 1920s] and the *Red Cavalry* came out. I like his writing very much. He has marvelous stuff and he writes very well." Later that year, during the Spanish Civil War, he told Babel's close friend, the Soviet writer Ilya Ehrenberg, "I have been criticized for writing too concisely, but I find that Babel's style is even more concise than mine." Babel did not influence Hemingway, who had formed his own style in *In Our Time* (1925) and *The Sun Also Rises* (1926) before he read the Russian writer, but their technique and portrayal of war are strikingly similar.

Babel and Hemingway were not soldiers but war correspondents. Both exaggerated their heroic exploits and created myths about themselves. Babel claimed to have served in the Czar's army on the Romanian front in World War I and then to have fought with the northern army against the White Russian General Nikolai Yudenich. Hemingway claimed to have fought on the side of the Italian Arditi in World War I and to have killed a lot of "Krauts" in World War II.

In 1920 (two years after Hemingway was wounded while serving with the Red Cross on the Italian front) and during their brief months of victory, the Red Cavalry invaded Poland in an attempt to impose Communism on that country. Poland had been partitioned, occupied and oppressed by Russia, Prussia and Austro-Hungary since 1795, and did not achieve independence until 1918, when these three powers were defeated in World War I. The historian Norman Davies wrote: "For the Bolsheviks, in the full flush of their revolutionary enthusiasm, the advance to the West was an ideological necessity to ensure the survival of their Revolution in Russia" and carry it to industrial Germany. "In June the arrival of Budenny's 'Red Cavalry' army drove the Poles out of Ukraine. . . . Within six weeks, the Red Army stood at the gates of Warsaw. . . . The Polish Army then delivered a shattering blow which no one had expected to succeed. [Jozef] Pilsudski's flank attack from the south split the Soviet advance, severed communications" and destroyed their armies.

Babel described himself as a man with spectacles on his nose and autumn in his heart. Though his heart was not yet frozen, he was heading toward the winter of war. Lionel Trilling observed that the values of Jews and Cossacks were absolutely antithetical, and that Babel was completely out of place in the Red Cavalry: "The Jew conceived his own ideal character to consist in his being intellectual, pacific, humane. The Cossack was physical, violent, without mind or manners." Mounted Cossacks were often used by the Czars to slaughter Jews, their traditional enemies, during government-incited pogroms. Babel contrasted not only Cossacks and Jews, but also the well-fed, bons vivants Russian Jews from Odessa to the vulnerable and terrified Polish Jews, who were frequently massacred by invading armies: "the image of southern Jews flares up in my memory—jovial, potbellied, sparkling like cheap wine. There is no comparison between them and the bitter aloofness of these long bony backs, these tragic yellow beards."

Babel achieves stunning effects by using surrealistic imagery in realistic stories: "Blue roads flowed past me like streams of milk spurting from many breasts," or by startling similes: "the moon hung above the yard like a cheap earring," "evening flew up to the sky like a flock of birds." Some of his sentences, in English translation, have perfect poetic meter: "The frozen, basalt Venice stood transfixed." Stephen Crane famously wrote that "the red sun was pasted in the sky like a wafer"; Babel surpasses this with "the orange sun rolled down the sky like a lopped-off head." His narcotic morning that "seeped out of us like chloroform seeping over a hospital table," recalls T. S. Eliot's "Love Song of J. Alfred Prufrock, "when the evening is spread out against the sky / Like a patient etherized upon a table."

Like Hemingway, Babel creates a vivid and disturbing ambience, a kind of lyrical horror, using sharp contrasts and many simple sentences with monosyllabic words:

> Darkness thickened around us. The cavalry transport crawled heavily along the Brody high road. Simple stars rolled through the Milky Ways in the sky, and distant villages burned in the cool depths of the night. ("Afonka Bida")

> On the plain, flat as a board, the brigades were regrouping. The sun rolled through the crimson dust. Wounded men sat in ditches, eating. Nurses lay on the grass and sang in hushed voices. Afonka's scouts roamed over the field, looking for dead soldiers and ammunition. ("Dolgushov's Death")

His account of a village on fire ends with a surprising simile: "The earth smoked beneath his feet, a blue ring of flame flew out of the chimney and melted away, the abandoned calf began wailing. The fire was as bright as a holy day" ("Prishchepa").

Interchapter II in Hemingway's *In Our Time*, based on his dispatch from Thrace during the Greco-Turkish War in October 1922, has the bare, direct, elemental effect of Babel's war stories: "Minarets stuck up in the rain out of Adrianople across the mud flats. The carts were jammed for thirty miles along the Karagatch road. Water buffalo and cattle were hauling carts through the mud. . . . The Maritza was running yellow almost up to the bridge."

Interchapter V, also seen by an objective eyewitness, begins with sudden dramatic intensity: "They shot the six cabinet ministers at half-past six in the morning against the wall of a hospital. There were pools of water in the courtyard. There were wet dead leaves on the paving of the courtyard. It rained hard." Like a momentous news story, the first sentence states the theme and the rest of the paragraph describes the execution. The anxious repetition of "There were" and "courtyard," powerfully reinforced by the symbolic closed hospital, the pools of water that collect the blood and the dead leaves that surround the dead men suggest the inevitability of death.

Interchapter VI takes place outside a church (rather than outside a hospital), which provides precarious safety but not sanctuary. As in the previous passage, Hemingway does not reveal who and where Nick is, why he is fighting and whether he will survive his terrible wound: "Nick sat against the wall of the church where they had dragged him to be clear of the machine-gun fire in the street. Both legs stuck out awkwardly. He had been hit in the spine."

Babel's recurrent word is "slaughtered" and his war stories are also filled with ghoulish images of death. His "vague odor of corruption," his "fire of silent and intoxicating revenge," made Frank O'Connor wonder if he was "a real writer or a dangerous lunatic." The title of his finest story, "Crossing into Poland," suggests crossing a river as well as an advance to Warsaw. The disasters of war include violence and cruelty, grief and loss. The narrator travels across a lyrical landscape of peaceful streams and roaring rivers, with the sun like a chopped off head and trails of the moon reflected in the water. But he finds the blood of slaughtered horses, a pregnant woman and a man apparently asleep amidst the intolerable filth in a Jewish house that has been looted by retreating Polish soldiers.

The narrator also falls asleep and has a nightmare in which his commander's eyes are shot out, and wakes to discover that the man is not asleep but has actually been murdered. His nightmare echoes this grim reality just as the victim, his throat cut and face cleft in two by a sword, recalls the slaughtered horses. The woman tells the narrator that in the final moments of his life, the dead man had offered to sacrifice himself and maintain a shred of dignity. He begged to be killed outside the house to prevent his pregnant daughter from witnessing his murder, to deflect the soldiers' violence from her and to preserve through her the life of the next generation.

The Poles killed him because they could kill Jews with impunity. His daughter's sudden cry, an elemental reaction to the domestic bloodshed, recalls Greek tragedy: "And now I should wish to know," she asks, "I should wish to know where in the whole world you could find another father like my father?" Though the story is only a page-and-a-half long, Babel characteristically and effectively repeats many words: sun, moon, asleep, filth, commander, eyes, pregnant woman, I should wish to know and father. The daughter has kept her dead father in the ruined house. She's too frightened to go outside during the war, it's impossible to bury him under these brutal conditions and she's too traumatized by his horrific death. Her final, grateful, loving, memorable words are her version of the Kaddish, the prayer recited by mourners for the dead.

In Babel's "My First Goose," an initiation story, the writer and educated outsider is embedded with the crude and illiterate Cossacks. Their gigantic commander is introduced in the first paragraph with two striking similes: when he stands up he divides "the hut in two like a banner splitting the sky" and his "long legs looked like two girls wedged to their shoulders in riding boots." In stark contrast, the narrator, a law graduate from the University of St. Petersburg, is scorned as an incongruous intellectual and "powder puff" in an army where "you get hacked to pieces just for wearing glasses!"

When he is ordered to lodge with the Cossacks, they greet him with a burst of farts, throw his suitcase into the street and force him to retrieve his tattered possessions and precious manuscripts on his knees. He asks the half-blind mistress of the house for food, but she rudely refuses to feed him. Humiliated and furious, he performs a violent act by catching a goose and treating it the same way the Cossacks deal with weaklings like himself. He "forced it to the ground, its head cracking beneath [his] boot, cracking and bleeding. Its white neck lay stretched out in the dung, and the wings folded down over the slaughtered bird." He then spears it with a saber and orders the now-cowering woman to roast it for him. After creating a brutal bloodbath, if only with a goose, he's accepted by the Cossacks and joins them in a close, comradely fashion: "Six of us slept there warming each other, our legs tangled, under the holes in the roof which let in the stars." A woman appears in his dream, not a fine lady nor a farmyard peasant, but he can't respond to her and his heart, still "crimson with murder, screeched and bled." Babel's stories describe the scars of wartime barbarity on his own emotional life.

In "Dolgushov's Death" the narrator fails a crucial test during a fierce battle against the Poles. The wounded are carted way, but the soldier Dolgushov knows he's finished: "His stomach was torn open, his intestines spilling to his knees, and we could see his heart beating." He begs for a bullet so he won't be captured and tortured by the Poles. But the narrator is unable to commit this merciful act and the dying man condemns him by screaming, "Running away? . . . Then run, you bastard!" As the dying Franz Kafka said to his doctor, "If you don't kill me, you are a murderer."

The Cossack Afonka then appears and shoots Dolgushov. The narrator feebly confesses, "*I* couldn't have done that," and Afonka threatens to shoot him just as he shot the dying man: "You spectacled idiots have as much pity for us as a cat has for a mouse!" He's only prevented from murdering the narrator by the intervention of another soldier, Grishchuk. As the narrator regrets his own moral cowardice and the loss of Afonka's esteem, Grishchuk offers comradely comfort by urging the narrator to share his savior's food and eat a wrinkled apple with him.

"Salt," like "Crossing into Poland," describes the effect of war on civilians. When a Cavalry transport train unexpectedly stops en route to Berdichev in the Russian Ukraine (where Joseph Conrad was born), women selling contraband salt and despised as "capitalists" swarm around it. Some women are allowed into the railroad cars, others are refused. One woman, holding a baby and trying to return to her husband, begs to be admitted. The soldiers say she'll be raped like the others: "Once we're done with her, she won't be wanting that husband of hers no more!" But their leader Balmashov persuades them to leave the mother alone and, in a sudden change of heart, the soldiers now swear, "no one will touch you in the corner, so you can travel untouched to your husband."

Then Balmashov, unable to sleep, has a sudden revelation. He takes the baby from the mother, rips off its swaddling rags and discovers instead of an infant a heavy sack of salt. Just as the sleeping man in "Crossing into Poland" was not sleeping, so this baby is not a baby. The woman justifies her smuggling and begs for her life. But Balmashov, after delivering a propaganda harangue about the enemies of the Revolution, throws her off the moving train. She survives the traumatic fall but, enforcing the severe Party line, he shoots her as she tries to run away and "wiped that blot off the face of the working land." General Budenny never forgave Babel for his brutal depiction of the Cossacks in *Red Cavalry*, and his hostility became especially dangerous when Babel was later accused of political crimes.

Babel is concise and brutal; Hemingway, in the superb opening paragraph of "In Another Country" (1927), uses repetition and rhythmic prose to suggest menace:

> In the fall the war was always there, but we did not go to it any more. It was cold in the fall in Milan and the dark came very early. Then the electric lights came on, and it was pleasant along the streets looking in the windows. There was much game outside the shops, and the snow powdered in the fur of the foxes and the wind blew their tails. The deer hung stiff and heavy and empty, and small birds blew in the wind and the wind turned their feathers. It was a cold fall and the wind came down from the mountains.

The soldiers, as if they had a choice, did not go to the endless war any more because they were either wounded or had deserted. The liquid "l" sound—in fall, always, cold, fall, Milan, early, electric, lights, pleasant, along and looking—ligate the concise sentences and lighten the harsh subject. The hanging game and stiff deer, emptied of their intestines, recall the wounded and dead soldiers in war. The wind that blows the tails of foxes, predators of game, also blows the fragile birds that are at risk in winter. The last sentence identifies the source of the wind and reprises the themes of the paragraph with: cold, fall and wind.

Hemingway begins "A Natural History of the Dead" (1932) by recalling the atrocities he'd seen in Smyrna during the Greco-Turkish War. Driven out of that town and wanting to prevent the Turks from seizing their valuable beasts of burden, the Greeks "broke the legs of all their baggage animals and pushed them off the quay into the shallow water to drown." Hemingway describes the cruelty of cracked legs, slow sinking animals and bloated carcasses floating to the surface: "The numbers of broken-legged mules and horses drowning in the shallow water called for a Goya to depict them." He conveys two powerful impressions: cruelty to animals rather than to men; cruelty by Greeks rather than by Turks, who massacred the Greek civilians as soon as they captured the city.

Hemingway also shocks the reader by coldly describing the morbid, chromatic and voluminous changes in the Italian victims of the Austrian offensive in June 1918. These corpses take on the appearance of three different races: "The color change in Caucasian races is from white to yellow, to yellow-green, to black. . . . The dead grow larger each day until sometimes they become quite too big for their uniforms, filling these until they seem blown tight enough to burst." The adverb "quite," rhyming with "tight," is a darkly comic touch.

He also notes an industrious half-pint of maggots that are disturbing the dead and "working where their mouths have been." After describing the beauty of the mountains in war and of blood on the snow, Hemingway mentions the death of a German general during the Italian retreat from Caporetto in October 1917. Following the trajectory of the bullet through the skull, he writes that the general had a sniper's bullet hole in his forehead "you couldn't put your little finger in and a hole in back you could put your fist in." Like Babel, he combines scenic splendor with close-up horrors of death.

The story then shifts from the battlefield to a dressing station in the mountains and, like "Dolgushov's Death," portrays the moral dilemma of whether to shoot a hopelessly wounded man who begs for a quick death. The victim with shattered brains is brought in and shown to the doctor, but nothing can be done about "it." The bearers want to put the moribundus with the wounded; the doctor wants to place him with the dead.

An artillery officer suggests putting the man out of his misery with an overdose of morphine. The doctor, unwilling to waste the precious drug on a terminal case, tells the officer to "shoot him yourself." In an ironic twist, the doctor who would not kill the man dying in agony throws iodine in the eyes of an officer who'd rubbed onions into his own eyes, and then heals him in a humane fashion. The self-proclaimed humane officer, who recommends injecting a fatal dose of morphine but doesn't shoot the wounded man, threatens to kill the doctor who has blinded him. Like Babel, Hemingway portrays the moral anguish of such conflicts.

Both writers employ effective repetition; emphasize lingering pain, gratuitous cruelty and morbid details; adopt an ironic viewpoint, stoical attitude and poetic rhythm; exalt personal courage; always note the weather; and describe the natural landscape—the rivers and the stars. Ford Madox Ford's description of Hemingway's style applies equally to Babel's: "it has the effect of a brook-bottom into which you look down through the flowing water. The words form a tessellation, each in order beside the other."

TWENTY-ONE

ANDRÉ MALRAUX

Bear, like the Turk, no rival near the throne.

—Alexander Pope

Hemingway and Malraux, the outstanding modern examples of the artist in action, had hostile and combative relations. They respected each other's great novels, but loathed many of their rival's personal characteristics and saw through their painfully constructed facade of lies. Malraux criticized Hemingway's machismo, boastfulness and apparent simple-mindedness. Hemingway condemned Malraux's dandyism, pomposity and tedious philosophical monologues. Malraux was fascinated by his own torrential disquisitions. His facial tics, which magnetized many, irritated Hemingway. Since Hemingway spoke French and Malraux had no English, they always talked to each other in the language of Malraux, who had an unfair advantage in their face-to-face confrontations. Hemingway tried hard to understand the voluble Malraux, but didn't think the necessary concentration was worth the effort. The two writers were both vulnerable and aggressive, egoistic and abrasive. Sensing formidable rivals, they watched each other jealously, and attacked each other in verbal and printed combats that lasted for three decades. It was typical of Hemingway to challenge a threatening competitor and of Malraux to retaliate with caustic comments.

They had, apart from nationality and inherited religion, some notable differences. Hemingway was a good athlete; the awkward Malraux had no interest in sports. Hemingway lived simply and rejected a hedonistic way of life; Malraux liked luxurious living and expensive restaurants. Scrupulous about money, Hemingway (though cheated by his lawyer) left a sizeable fortune; Malraux, living well above his income, left a pile of debts. Hemingway could be quite funny; Malraux was always serious. Hemingway distrusted abstractions and had no philosophical pretensions; Malraux, fond of the Metaphysical and always in quest of the Absolute, loved them. When famous, Hemingway protected his privacy by retreating to the remote fastness of Cuba; Malraux increased his fame and power by becoming a government minister. More politically perceptive than Malraux, Hemingway never accepted Communist propaganda, nor adhered to the party line, nor condoned Stalin's atrocities, purge trials and gulags. He made André Marty, the French Communist commissar, the murderous villain of *For Whom the Bell Tolls*. Hemingway remained firmly on the liberal left; Malraux, enchanted by and advisor to de Gaulle, moved to the conservative right.

But their similarities were striking and significant. They were close contemporaries: Hemingway was born in 1899, Malraux in 1901. Both rebelled against their middle-class childhoods in Oak Park and Dunkirk. They did not go to universities but were educated by violent experience. Handsome, charismatic and photogenic, they filled a space with their impressive presence. They lived on their first wives' trust funds to jump start their literary careers and, with notable talent and ambition, were known as writers before they'd published anything. Both were cat lovers and serious collectors of art, though Malraux stole some of his precious objects. They attracted a cadre of flatterers and parasites. Both drank heavily and destructively in the last decades of their lives. Both suffered severe depressions and nervous breakdowns, though Malraux handled mental illness much better than Hemingway.

Hemingway and Malraux glorified male comradeship and the bonds of the virile fraternity, but had touchy temperaments and frequently severed relations with close friends. Both were committed to fight for the underdog and against injustice: Hemingway in "Who Murdered the Vets?" (1935) and with the Spanish Loyalists; Malraux in Indochina and China as well as in Spain. Obsessed with death, they constantly confirmed their personal courage by taking risks and drinking the aphrodisiac of danger. Both believed, as Malraux wrote, "a man is what he does." They wanted to leave a scar on the map of world history and were themselves deeply scarred. Experts in generating publicity and legends (even, in Hemingway's case, accounts of his own death), they burnished their literary reputations with daring Byronic exploits. Malraux's biographer Olivier Todd observed: "They have a physical and intellectual need to see history at first hand to write about it. War is one of their powerful literary drugs; they have great admiration for physical courage and are themselves brave. This admiration leads to exhibitionism. . . . Spain satisfies both writers' appetite for bravery, blood and death."

Attractive to women but not great womanizers, they were more interested in long-term unions than numerous conquests. Absorbed in their writing, they were contentious husbands and difficult fathers. Hemingway had three divorces and four marriages. Malraux was married twice: to Clara Goldschmidt and to Madeleine Malraux (widow of his half-brother), and had two common-law marriages: to Josette Clotis (mother of his two sons) and Louise de Vilmorin, succeeded after death by her young niece Sophie de Vilmorin. They each had three children. Hemingway's son was nicknamed Bumby; Malraux's son was called Bimbo. Both men, while married, brought their lovers to Spain and intensified their sex life with the excitement of war. Clara, Josette and Hemingway's third wife, Martha Gellhorn, were openly unfaithful.

The families of Hemingway and Malraux acted out modern versions of a Greek tragedy. Hemingway killed himself, and his father, brother and sister also committed suicide. Malraux survived every danger while his family disintegrated around him. His father died by suicide. Josette Clotis, in a freak accident in 1944, jumped off a moving train, fell under the wheels and was killed. His two half-brothers, Roland and Claude, worked for the Resistance, were arrested by the Gestapo and killed that year. His two sons, Gauthier and Vincent, died in a car crash in 1961. Malraux lamented, "almost all those I have loved have been killed in accidents."

Both creators of fiction were mythomaniacs. Hemingway exaggerated his World War I wounds and medals, heightened the number of "probable" and "definite" Germans he killed in World War II, and claimed to have been the first man to enter Paris and to liberate the wine cellars of the Ritz Hotel. Malraux, inter alia, awarded himself a doctoral degree from the School of Oriental Languages and claimed to have been a revolutionary leader in Canton. In *The Royal Way* (1930) he insisted, "every adventurer is born a mythomaniac." In his mind, as in Hemingway's, possibilities became certainties. More forthright than Hemingway, Malraux stated, "what is true is whatever amuses, suits or benefits me. . . . I lie but my lies become truths." When adventure coincided with impulse they were capable of heroism; when it did not they escaped into myth. By transforming their lives into legends, they lived out their private fantasies. Like Vincent Berger, the autobiographical hero of Malraux's *The Walnut Trees of Altenburg* (1945), "he could perhaps have found some means of destroying the mythical person he was growing into, had he been compelled. But he had no wish to do so. His reputation was flattering. What was more important, he enjoyed it."

Their works, like their lives, had important qualities in common. Both authors were strongly influenced by Joseph Conrad, whose *Heart of Darkness* profoundly shaped Malraux's story of the quest for a madman gone native in the jungle in *The Royal Way*. In a weird 1924 obituary notice of Conrad, Hemingway said he would gladly grind T. S. Eliot into a fine powder if that would bring Conrad back to life. He portrayed the great Conradian theme in *Lord Jim*, of moral failure and recovery of self-esteem, in "The Short Happy Life of Francis Macomber," and of victory in defeat in *The Old Man and the Sea*.

The two were, at first, generous in praising each other's major novels. Malraux considered *A Farewell to Arms* (1929) to be "the best love story written since Stendhal." Hemingway owned eight books by Malraux, four of them in French. In August 1935 he told the Russian journalist Ivan Kashkin that Malraux's *Man's Fate* (1933), a novel about the betrayal of the Communist revolution in Shanghai, "was the best book I have read in ten years" and added, "if you ever see him I wish that you would tell him so for me." But in the introduction to his anthology *Men at War* (1942), written after their personal relations had soured, he excluded that book and gratuitously attacked Malraux. He rightly called the famous scene where the prisoner-hero Katov, after giving away his cyanide pill, is waiting to be burned alive, "a marvelous piece of writing . . . magnificently written." He then lamely explained that he would have included it "for its literary value if I had not, knowing Malraux in Spain, come to doubt his accuracy. If there was any doubt as to the truth of the incident, I felt it should not be published in this book while we were at war, no matter how well written it was." This criticism was pointless, as Hemingway well knew, since factual accuracy is not essential in imaginative fiction. Hemingway would say almost anything to get the better of Malraux, especially if his rival was not able to respond.

Their first personal contacts, during the Spanish Civil War, provoked Hemingway's radical change from high praise to corrosive criticism. They met briefly at the Hotel Florida in Madrid in August 1937 and in Barcelona in November 1938. Malraux said that in New York in late 1937 Hemingway had talked about Shakespeare, in striking terms, just as he spoke "of life in his best writing." Both men were touring America to raise money to buy ambulances and medical supplies for the Spanish Loyalists. Malraux (his French translated for the Anglophone audiences) was a great orator; Hemingway, though less dramatic, was also an effective speaker. The only photo of them together was taken around the desk of Malraux's editor at Random House, Robert Haas, as they went over Malraux's fund-raising speech. Both writers wore suits and ties, and Malraux kept on his coat and scarf. Seated in the middle and looking down at his corrected typescript, Malraux seems to be speaking at the same time as Hemingway instead of listening to his advice. Hemingway, while staying overnight at the White House, also briefed President Roosevelt about the Spanish War.

Hemingway spoke fluent Spanish; Malraux knew little of the language. Emphasizing his rival's noncombatant role, Malraux said, "Hemingway had spent more time than I in Spain before the war, and he spent less time during it. In short, he knew a great number of civilian Spanish and I knew a great number of enlisted Spanish." Both authors wrote major novels about the Spanish War: Malraux's *Man's Hope* (1937) and Hemingway's *For Whom the Bell Tolls* (1940). Both portrayed in their novels their greatly admired friend, the Spanish general Gustavo Durán, and Hemingway was jealous of Malraux's friendship with him. Both made important films about the Spanish war. Hemingway wrote and narrated a documentary *The Spanish Earth* (1937); Malraux wrote and directed *L'Espoir* (also called *Sierra de Teruel*), a superb feature film that was shot during the war and finally released in 1945.

Though they fought for a common cause, the two literary titans, struggling for supremacy, inevitably clashed. Georges Soria, a French journalist who observed them in Madrid, noted Hemingway's obvious boredom with Malraux's torrential speeches, his criticism of Malraux's alliance with the Communists, and his dislike of Malraux's abstract theories and pompous predictions: "'Ernie,' staring at his glass and obviously 'turned off,' was waiting resignedly for Malraux to finish his breathless improvisations in order to get a word in edgewise. The two men respected, but hardly liked one another. 'Ernie' tended rather to seek the company of simple, quiet people and hated theorizing about politics or literature. Without malicious intentions, he called

Malraux 'Comrade Malreux'—a bad pun [on '*malheureux*,' unhappy] that expressed his aversion for this type of intellectualism."

Hemingway's satiric account, in a letter to General Buck Lanham in April 1948, about Malraux's supposed talk with the Polish General Walter expressed his own conviction that thought interferes with action in war: "Malraux, a phony, kept asking him questions like what do you think, mon general, about all sorts of things, le masturbation parmi le chinoise, le valeur devant le mort de les indigene du classe super-intellectuelle etc. [masturbation among the Chinese, the courage when faced with death of the native super-intellectual class]. Finally Walter said, 'Pour-quoi demande moi penser? *Penser*? Moi Generale sovietique. Moi pense jamais!'" [Why ask me to think? *Think*? I'm a Soviet general. I never think]. Malraux's abstract questions were absurdly inappropriate to a military conversation and there was no reason to believe that Walter would know the answers—if, indeed, there were any. Hemingway did not seem to realize that Walter may have been satirizing Communist control by saying that even Soviet generals merely obeyed orders and were not *allowed* to think. Hemingway's lively anecdotes were designed to amuse his correspondents and to enhance his reputation by denigrating his formidable adversary.

For personal reasons Hemingway was much more critical of *Man's Hope* than he was of *Man's Fate*. He was angry that Malraux, who'd achieved a fine record in Spain, had left the war to write a novel and published *Man's Hope* as early as 1937, before the real war began—even though the novel concluded *after* the Loyalists' great victory in the battle of Guadalajara in March. In May 1938 he boasted to his editor Max Perkins, in telegraphic style, that when the war is "finished am going to settle down and write and the pricks and fakers like Malraux who pulled out in Feb 37 to write gigantic masterpisses before it really started will have a good lesson when write ordinary sized book with the old stuff unfaked in it." But the real cause of his anger was that Malraux had pipped him at the post by publishing a Spanish War novel before he could bring out his own work. Provoked by Malraux's impressive achievement, he was determined to write a better book than *Man's Hope*.

Hemingway's argument with Malraux was specious and he was in no position to criticize the French war hero. Malraux went to Spain as soon as the war broke out in July 1936; Hemingway, coming from America, arrived as a war correspondent eight months later in March 1937. Malraux helped create the Loyalist air force with the Escuadra España, flew sixty-five combat missions as bombardier and gunner, and was wounded during one of the raids. Hemingway enviously allowed that Malraux must have acquired his nervous facial tic at well over ten thousand feet.

Hemingway didn't seem to see that in Malraux's *Man's Hope* the American character Slade (whom Olivier Todd and Isaiah Berlin strangely call "Shade") was partly based on himself. Malraux, noting Hemingway's emphasis on primitive feeling, wrote that "Slade was fifty. He had traveled a good deal and life had given him some nasty knocks—among others . . . the lingering, mortal illness of having loved a woman. And the only things to which he attached any importance he called idiotic or bestial; elemental things like pain and love, humiliation, innocence." Malraux attacked Hemingway's stubborn anti-intellectualism when Slade exclaims, "the only people I like are idiots—innocents. . . . Most people have the big head, and they can't do a thing with it." Deliberately or not, Hemingway's last sentence in *For Whom the Bell Tolls* echoes Malraux's last sentence in *Man's Hope*. Malraux concluded: "this new consciousness within him was . . . [as] profound and permanent as the beating of his heart." Hemingway ended: "He could feel his heart beating against the pine needle floor of the forest."

After trumping him in combat, fiction and film, Malraux could afford to be generous when *For Whom the Bell Tolls* came out three years after his own book. In a 1948 interview he compared Hemingway to two of the greatest novelists of all time—and to Stendhal for the second time: "I consider it a powerful work, with a bravura piece, a central moment—the sabotaged attack, the launching of the offensive—which is a model of descriptive literature and which, keeping everything in proportion, can be compared to Tolstoy . . . and to Stendhal." But in a second interview in the 1960s Malraux ignored the fact that both he and Hemingway had had love affairs in Spain, and expressed some illogical reservations about the novel: "When, like Hemingway, you introduce a love story into a revolutionary combat, you are pulling the reader's leg, because if you are having a love affair you are not in revolutionary combat." In fact, like Tolstoy in *War and Peace*, Hemingway intensified the emotions and deepened the drama of both *A Farewell to Arms* and *For Whom the Bell Tolls* by including love stories in the accounts of war. Malraux also committed an unforgivable solecism by declaring that William Faulkner, who had a considerable vogue in France, was a better writer than Hemingway. But

Hemingway cheeked Malraux by invading his literary territory and going to China in 1941 to cover the war with Japan.

After their ill-fated encounters Malraux criticized Hemingway's character as well as his novel. Bruce Chatwin concluded, "Hemingway thought 'Camarade Malraux' a poseur and Malraux thought Hemingway a fake tough . . . *c'est un fou qui a la folie de simplicité*" (a madman with delusions of simplicity). Some of Malraux's comments on his rival's public persona, myth-making and braggadocio also applied, quite precisely, to himself: "As to the man Hemingway, I have reservations. I am afraid the personage may spoil the writer, that the legend in which he revels is prejudicial to the courageous, infantile and boastful man he has always been." In conversation with Isaiah Berlin, he repeated the very word Hemingway had used to degrade him, "Hemingway was a phony *solitaire*, unconvincing, no good; he knocked him out."

Their most contentious and absurd confrontation took place at the Ritz Hotel just after the liberation of Paris in August 1944. Hemingway, in his most self-aggrandizing mood, often retold this story while exaggerating both the numbers and the dialogue. In a letter of June 1946 to the Russian writer Konstantin Simonov he wrote, "André Malraux came to see me and asked how many men I had commanded. I told him never more than 200 at the most and usually between 14 and 60. He was very happy and relieved because he had commanded 2,000 men, he said. So there was no question of literary prestige involved."

Hemingway sent this playlet version in a letter of February 1953 to Bernard Berenson.

> Malraux asked: "How many have you commanded?"
>
> Hemingway: "Dix aux douze. Au plus deux cent" (Ten to twelve, two hundred at the most).
>
> Malraux: "Moi: deux mille" (I commanded two thousand).
>
> Hemingway: "What a shame my colonel that we did not have the assistance of your force when we took this small town [of Paris]."

One of Hemingway's partisan bodyguards eagerly offered to end the conversation with Malraux by asking, "Papa, should we shoot this asshole?" But Hemingway mercifully "let him preen and jerk and twitch until he left." By the time this story got recycled by Malraux's biographer Pierre Galante, Malraux was astonished to find the voluptuary Hemingway "stark-naked, in the arms of two young women. The warrior's repose!"

It was ludicrous for Hemingway—rarely more than a journalistic observer—to compare himself with Malraux, who could have given a credible account of his war experience. He had been captured by the Germans in 1940 and escaped from a POW camp near Sens, southeast of Paris. He'd led 1,500 *maquis* in the Dordogne region of southwest France. He then commanded the Alsace-Lorraine Brigade under General Jacques Leclerc from September 1944, took part in the capture of Dannemarie in Alsace in November, the defense of Strasbourg—the last French city in German hands—against Gerd von Runstedt's offensive in December, the march on Colmar and Sainte-Odilie, and the triumphant entry into Stuttgart in April 1945. A wanted man, traveling with false papers, he'd been captured by the Gestapo in July 1945, and had escaped torture and death only weeks before he met Hemingway. Malraux, who'd been promoted from private soldier to lieutenant colonel, had achieved what Hemingway, fantasizing in the Ritz bar, had only dreamed of doing.

Hemingway's story "A Room on the Garden Side," set in the Ritz Hotel, contains yet another version of his now legendary conversation with Malraux. According to Susan Beegel's useful summary in *Studies in Short Fiction* (1994), Colonel André is dressed in a fancy uniform: cavalry pants, high polished boots and a tunic with stripes as long as a stepladder. Robert, the Hemingway-hero and real soldier, wears a uniform scavenged from dead Americans. They have the now familiar exchange about how many men each had commanded. "When asked how he was able to feed 2,000 irregulars, Malraux responds, 'We were among patriots.'" Claude, one of Hemingway's French companions, cuts him down with a speech about how hungry troops had rapidly eroded French patriotism. "Both Robert and André are talented writers not writing because they have chosen to follow the war. The story questions whether their contributions to the war merit such 'sacrifice' and whether they deserve their celebrity."

Their personal rivalry continued until Hemingway eliminated himself from the fight. He won the Nobel Prize in 1954. Malraux did not win it, though he deserved it and was a much better writer than the contemporary French winners: Roger Martin du Gard, François Mauriac and Jean-Paul Sartre. But he regretfully noted, "they will never give it to a Gaullist." Hemingway told the Paris-based journalist Janet Flanner he regretted that Malraux, often a rumored candidate, had not received the prize. He knew that Malraux had a suicidal father and feared that he might become depressed enough to kill himself.

Hemingway resented Malraux's shift to right-wing politics and acceptance of (his tremendously successful) high office, which took him away from writing novels, though he continued to publish innovative books on art. In another letter to Berenson of January 1953, Hemingway said that he's "the sort that gets to be Minister of Culture in a new chicken-shit Republic where there are no standards except charm." Ignoring his own lies, he once again condemned those of Malraux, "how you can tell a man who has killed men (armed) is that usually his eyes do not blink at all. A liar's eyes blink all the time. Meet Malraux sometime."

Malraux's final judgment in *Anti-Memoirs* (1967), six years after Hemingway's death, perceptively traced the pattern of his life and its reflection in his postwar novel *Across the River and Into the Trees* (1950), which called Malraux's commanding general "that jerk Leclerc." Malraux observed, "Hemingway, throughout the curve which begins with the young man in love with an older woman, then with a younger one, and ends—after God knows how many instances of impotence and suicide—with a sixty-year-old colonel in love with a young girl, never ceased to foreshadow his own fate."

Though often engaged in violent sports, Hemingway was more focused on his fiction and wrote greater novels and stories than Malraux. But Malraux, more intellectual and ambitious, had greater achievements as an explorer, editor at Gallimard, aviator, warrior, filmmaker, politician and art historian. Despite their acrimonious but fascinating disputes—which brought out the worst in the more insecure and offensive Hemingway and a lofty superiority in the more cerebral Malraux—the two authors, like extinct stars, continue to radiate light long after their deaths.

TWENTY-TWO

J. D. SALINGER

J. D. Salinger's path crossed Hemingway's in wartime Paris in August 1944 and on the road to Germany in September. Their momentous personal encounters were far more important to Salinger than Hemingway's literary influence. Salinger hero-worshipped Hemingway and regarded him as a confessional father-figure. He saw the parallel between Hemingway's injury in World War I and his own war trauma. But there is only a thin record of Hemingway's direct comments on Salinger, who was fascinated and inspired by Hemingway throughout his life. Salinger's credulous biographers have always accepted his own self-enhancing viewpoint, though his memory could be faulty. He claimed that Hemingway had praised Faulkner, whom he heartily disliked.

Casting a cold eye in 1962, Mary McCarthy identified the key elements of Hemingway's influence on *The Catcher in the Rye* (1953). Recalling Hemingway's patented "built-in shit-detector," she noted how Salinger adopted "the very image of the hero as pitiless phony-detector. . . . Like Hemingway, Salinger sees the world in terms of allies and enemies. He has a good deal of natural style, a cruel ear, a dislike of ideas . . . and a ventriloquist's knack of disguising his voice." The adolescent world of *The Catcher in the Rye* is "based on a scheme of exclusiveness. The characters are divided into those who belong to the club and those who don't." McCarthy didn't mention how Salinger's path crossed Hemingway's in wartime Paris in August 1944 and on the road to Germany in September.

Salinger, who briefly attended three universities without earning a degree from any of them, frequently sized up his older, famous and formidable competitor. On his first shot at Hemingway in his college newspaper, the *Ursinus*

Weekly of 1938, two years before the publication of *For Whom the Bell Tolls*, the nineteen-year-old Salinger revealed his mixture of adulation and envy. He referred to *The Fifth Column*, echoed Edmund Wilson's criticism of Hemingway's decline in the 1930s, and adopted a familiar and matey, cocky and condescending tone: "Hemingway has completed his first full-length play. We hope it is worthy of him. Ernest, we feel, has underworked and overdrooled ever since *The Sun Also Rises*, 'The Killers' and *A Farewell to Arms*."

Six years later the teenage critic had become a counter-intelligence soldier in wartime France and a published author who met Hemingway in his heroic role of war correspondent and returned Parisian. Hemingway was at his affable best after "liberating" the Ritz Hotel. He welcomed all American soldiers, as well as Malraux and Orwell, and provided abundant food and drink from the fabled wine cellar. Salinger, in military uniform, sought him out and the first of their two wartime meetings was for him an extraordinary event. Hemingway's early biographer Carlos Baker (paraphrasing a letter from Salinger to Hemingway that he was legally forbidden to quote) stated: "He found Hemingway both friendly and generous, not at all impressed by his own eminence, and 'soft'—as opposed to the hardness and toughness which some of his writing suggested. They got on very well, and Ernest volunteered to look at some of his work. Salinger returned to his unit in a state of mild exaltation."

Salinger's biographers Ian Hamilton and Kenneth Slawenski both paraphrase this same letter, in which Salinger was more egoistic and complacent: "The two authors seem to have spent most of their time praising each other. Hemingway certainly turned on the charm, telling Salinger he had seen his picture [and fiction 'The Heart of a Broken Story'] in *Esquire* and asking to see some of his new work." Salinger, who'd conveniently brought along a story, showed him "The Last Day of the Last Furlough" and reported that "Hemingway read the story and was impressed." In an even more exaggerated portrayal that appeared in *Time* magazine (September 15, 1961), two months after Hemingway's death, he is supposed to have ejaculated, "Jesus, he has a helluva talent." In these versions, which Salinger's biographers accept as valid, Hemingway not only received the young writer but also recognized him. It seems doubtful, however, that Hemingway had the time—in the crowded room and the midst of war—to read the story and to praise it. Finally, Salinger judged the world-famous author, man to man, was delighted by his fulsome compliment and found him up to the mark: "He was not at all pretentious or overly macho, as Salinger had feared. Instead, he found him to be gentle and well grounded: overall, a 'really good guy.'"

In September 1944, as the American army fought its way to Germany, Hemingway visited Salinger's unit as a war correspondent for *Collier's* magazine. Hamilton noted that Hemingway "got to arguing about the merits of a German Luger he was carrying as opposed to the U.S. .45, and blasted the head off a chicken to prove his point." Salinger, who'd slaughtered pigs in prewar Vienna and seen many dead men in combat, seemed to be "greatly shocked"—though the decapitated chicken was certainly doomed and destined for the pot. He transformed this event into a tragicomic incident in one of his best stories, "For Esmé—with Love and Squalor" (1953). The autobiographical Sergeant X explains, "that goddam cat I shot jumped up on the hood of the jeep. . . . I took a pot shot at it [because] I was temporarily insane. . . . That cat was a spy. You *had* to take a pot shot at it. It was a very clever German midget dressed up in a cheap fur coat. So there was absolutely nothing brutal, or cruel, or dirty." The sergeant's apparently rational excuse for shooting the cat shows that he really is crazy and not responsible for his strange behavior. Salinger seems to have forgiven Hemingway's violent act and justified the callousness that men are forced to adopt in war.

Sergeant Salinger had landed on Utah Beach on D-Day and served in a unit on the front lines. Both Hemingway and Salinger took part in the ferocious fighting in the Hürtgen Forest, between Aachen and Bonn in northwest Germany, from November 15 to December 4, 1944. In this battle Salinger went through the same war trauma that Hemingway had experienced on the Italian front in World War I. In one of the most costly attacks of the war, the Germans made a last stand on the frontier in "freezing rain, sleet, snow, flood, mud, pillboxes, and dense, dank woods straight out of German folk tales." An army historian wrote that in three days in mid-November the 22nd Infantry Regiment (to which Hemingway was attached), weakened by mines, enemy infiltration and shelling, had incurred more than 300 battle casualties. Despite this sacrifice, they advanced only a mile and a half after a five-day attack. By the time the battle had ended in December, 24,000 Americans had been killed, wounded, captured or missing. An officer who fought in this battle, which resembled the pointless slaughter of the Great War, "believed the entire Hürtgen operation was stupidly conceived, since it would have been relatively easy to bypass this muddy mass of mines, prepared positions, and fireplans for mortars and artillery." This fierce conflict inspired some of Richard Cantwell's most horrific memories in Hemingway's postwar novel *Across the River and into the Trees* (1950).

In "War in the Siegfried Line" (published in *Collier's* at the beginning of the battle on November 18, 1944), Hemingway cheered up the home front by stressing the heroic victory rather than the high cost of war: "The infantry cracked the Siegfried Line. . . . Beyond the black cloud of smoke and debris that rose, you saw two enemy half-tracks tearing up the white road that led into the German hills." Hemingway's friend Colonel Buck Lanham encouraged his troops by screaming: "Goddam, let's go get these Krauts! Come on! Nobody's going to stop here now!" But in a letter to his son Patrick, sent from the Hürtgen Forest the next day, Hemingway expressed hopes that were not realized and gave a more realistic description of the European war that would last until May 8, 1945: "We are in the middle of a terrific damned battle—that I hope will finish off the Kraut Army and end the war—and I cannot leave until our phase of it is over." Hemingway took great risks and even illegally led troops in combat. But after surviving his wounds in World War I, he thought he was invulnerable and was not afraid of death.

Hemingway's early stories describe ghastly wounds, shell shock and the traumatic effects of World War I. Interchapters VI and VII of *In Our Time* (1925), "Big Two-Hearted River" and "A Way You'll Never Be" are vivid evocations of his actual experience in a way his propagandistic war reporting could never be. The violent Interchapter VI describes Nick and Rinaldi, who are still exposed to fire, lying near a church which offers them no refuge. Hemingway once considered "a separate peace," which Russia had signed with Germany in order to withdraw from the war, as a possible title of *A Farewell to Arms* and uses the phrase for Nick's ironic observation: "Nick sat against the wall of the church where they had dragged him to be clear of the machine-gun fire in the street. Both legs stuck out awkwardly. He had been hit in the spine. . . . 'Senta [Listen] Rinaldi. Senta. You and me we've made a separate peace.' Rinaldi lay still in the sun breathing with difficulty." Nick may be paralyzed, Rinaldi may die, and they both share the ghastly comradeship of the mutilated and moribund.

Hemingway and Salinger had similar, bloody experiences, but wrote about them quite differently. Hemingway's violence was more forceful and direct, Salinger's rather precious and pretentious, oblique and subdued. Hamilton observed: "all the war service stories that he wrote around this time are focused on a single subject: the war-damaged survivor pitiably suspended between two worlds—the world of combat and the world of civilian readjustment." In "The Stranger" (a title lifted from Albert Camus), he describes the effect of an explosion rather than the actual event and writes that Vincent Caulfield had died in the Hürtgen Forest when a mortar blew up in his face. "'The Magic Foxhole' ends with Gardner, still hallucinating, confined in a military hospital, a victim of what the authorities call battle fatigue." "For Esmé" ironically describes Sergeant X as "a young man who had not come through the war with all his faculties intact." Salinger portrays the aftermath rather than the reality of battle. The sergeant's buddy exclaims: "you oughta see your goddam hands. Boy, have you got the shakes. . . . The goddam side of your face is jumping all over the place. . . . You had a nervous breakdown."

In July 1945 Salinger sent Hemingway a letter, addressed to Cuba, from a military hospital in Nürnberg. He was being treated for a nervous breakdown sustained in combat, a condition Hemingway was familiar with and which threatened to stigmatize Salinger with a potentially damaging psychiatric discharge. Hamilton observed that this letter "is almost manically cheerful. Indeed, its voice is precisely that of the eager, wise-cracking, full-of-himself young Salinger of 1939. The letter burbles on, boastful, flattering, facetious, as if to an old chum—although the probability is that he had met Hemingway but twice." Carlos Baker misdates and paraphrases this letter: "Salinger facetiously explained his temporary hospitalization in Nürnberg as an attempt to find a nurse who resembled Catherine Barkley [in *A Farewell to Arms*]. He had managed to accomplish some writing, including part of a play about a boy named Holden Caulfield and his sister Phoebe. The stage, said Salinger, had fascinated him ever since he had played the role of Raleigh in R. C. Sherriff's romantic war drama, *Journey's End*. . . . He recalled that his talks with Ernest in Europe had given him his only hopeful minutes of the entire war, and named himself national chairman of the Hemingway Fan Clubs." He ended the letter by discussing the personally relevant *Crack-Up* and expressing disapproval "of critics attacking Fitzgerald for his inability to develop as a writer. When an author produces a masterpiece like *The Great Gatsby* . . . he can't 'develop' beyond that."

Two other complimentary statements by Hemingway were reported indirectly four decades after his death. He bought his secretary, Valerie Danby-

Smith, a copy of *The Catcher in the Rye*, which he thought *she* would like. She reported that the English writer Gerald Brenan had told her that Hemingway had told him "the contemporary American writers he most admired were J. D. Salinger, Carson McCullers and Truman Capote." The subjects and style of these extremely mannered writers were quite different from the masculine authors he greatly admired: Tolstoy, Kipling, Stephen Crane and T. E. Lawrence. Nicolaus Mills noted that Lillian Ross—always unreliable—wrote in the *Observer* of 2010 that Salinger had showed her a wartime letter from Hemingway stating, "First you have a marvelous ear and you write tenderly and lovingly without getting wet."

Hemingway ignored the greatest postwar American writers, Vladimir Nabokov and Saul Bellow, and even the novels of his close friend Peter Viertel. He wasn't threatened by Salinger, who'd shared his combat experience in the Hürtgen Forest, as he was by his fierce rivals, the war novelists Norman Mailer, James Jones, and Irwin Shaw, who'd been Mary Welsh's lover before she married Hemingway. He may not have been entirely sincere in his generous judgments any more than he was when he ignored the greatest contemporary authors and said that three obvious noncontenders—Carl Sandburg, Bernard Berenson and Isak Dinesen—deserved the Nobel Prize.

In a rare moment of self-criticism Salinger later told a friend that he hated Hemingway's "overestimation of sheer physical courage, commonly called 'guts,' as a virtue. Probably because I'm short on it myself." This comment illuminates Holden Caulfield's attack—often misinterpreted as Salinger's own views—on Hemingway in *The Catcher in the Rye*. There is a clear echo of *A Farewell to Arms* in Salinger's novel when both writers describe learning important lessons. Hemingway wrote, "I did not know that then, although" and Salinger repeated, "I didn't know it then, though."

Holden's older brother D.B., a Hollywood writer, "got me to read this book *A Farewell to Arms* last summer. He said it was so terrific. That's what I can't understand. It had this guy in it named Lieutenant Henry that was supposed to be a nice guy and all. I don't see how D.B. could hate the Army and war and all so much and still like a phony like that." Holden objects to Hemingway's fundamental romanticism, his portrayal of the intensity of love amid overwhelming death. D.B.'s view of the novel is mature and sophisticated, Holden's is superficial and fatuous, as he rejects grown-up values yet desires adult certainty. D.B. could surely hate war *and* admire the tragic novel, which condemns rather than glorifies war. The contrasting views of D.B. and Holden suggest Salinger's continuing ambivalence about Hemingway's great themes and powerful style.

TWENTY-THREE

GEORGE ORWELL

In 1936 George Orwell published his best essay, "Shooting an Elephant," and Hemingway brought out one of his greatest stories, "The Short Happy Life of Francis Macomber." Both works, written in a famously austere style, were based on the young authors' personal experiences in exotic settings: Burma in 1926 and Kenya in 1933. The essay is political. The dying elephant symbolizes the dying British Empire, but Orwell presciently realizes that "it is a great deal better than the younger empires that are going to supplant it." The story is sexual. Macomber's loss of courage and flight from the wounded lion (a futile response) reveals his personal weakness and the fault line in his marriage. Orwell's first-person narrative condemns himself. He shoots the elephant "solely to avoid looking a fool." Hemingway's third-person narrative condemns Macomber's publicly exposed cowardice. Both characters are humiliated. Orwell, who hides his fear, is pressured by the crowd to uphold his official position and act against his true feelings. Macomber is forced to tolerate his wife's adultery with the white hunter Wilson.

The characters in these works assume uneasy roles as colonial policeman and as big-game hunter. They are expected to act in a certain way and follow the code of the sahib and bwana. Orwell insists, "A sahib has got to act like a sahib; he has got to appear resolute, to know his own mind and do definite things." In Africa, Wilson tells Macomber, you cannot shoot animals from a car and "no white man ever bolts." But Orwell has never killed an elephant and Macomber has never killed a lion. Both men are out of their depth and forced against their will to meet the expectations of others. Orwell is the only white man in the narrative. His slaughter of the elephant is witnessed by a hostile crowd of two thousand Burmese. Macomber's shameful behavior is witnessed by two hostile and critical whites, his wife Margot and the hunter Wilson, as well as by a few impassive African servants. Orwell's behavior becomes a public spectacle. Macomber's fear, Wilson's chasing animals in a car and Margot's crime are all kept secret.

Both works are suffused with hatred—and self-hatred. In his striking opening sentence Orwell writes, "In Moulmein, in Lower Burma, I was hated by large numbers of people." He fully reciprocates their taunts and hatred and "thought that the greatest joy in the world would be to drive a bayonet into a Buddhist priest's guts." Hemingway writes that the yellow eyes of the lion "narrowed with hate"; and after Macomber weakly accepts Margot's adultery with Wilson, he finds that "of all the many men that he had hated, he hated Robert Wilson the most." He also hates Margot for breaking her promise, "There wasn't going to be any of that," and for compounding his recent humiliation by sleeping with Wilson.

The characters face extreme and unusual dangers. During the rainy season in Burma the ground is too soft to approach the elephant. If Orwell misses him from a distance and the elephant charges, he would "have about as much chance as a toad under a stream-roller." Macomber, breaking the code, doesn't want to follow the wounded lion, who has flattened himself in the tall grass and is waiting to charge the hunter who pursues him. Both writers name the specific rifles they carry. Orwell exchanges a .44 Winchester, "much too small to kill an elephant," for a more powerful "German thing with cross-hair sights." Wilson carries a "short, ugly, shockingly big-bored .505 Gibbs."

The usually tame elephant, now in heat, has broken his chain, escaped from his handler, wrecked the bazaar and killed a coolie. But when Orwell catches up to him, he's peacefully eating grass and has (as Orwell subtly changes his sex) a "preoccupied grandmotherly air." Orwell does not want to kill it, but must do so to satisfy the demand of the crowd. The imperialist perceived that "when the white man turns tyrant it is his own freedom that he destroys."

Orwell describes the elephant from the outside, Hemingway gets inside the lion, and both sympathize with the wounded animals who announce their presence with a characteristic sound. The elephant trumpets, the lion roars. The potentially fatal bullets have no decisive effect, and both animals suffer and remain alive after being shot. Orwell needs five bullets to kill the elephant, who takes half an hour to die with a desperate slowness: "He looked suddenly stricken, shrunken, immensely old, as though the frightful impact of the bullet had paralysed him without knocking him down." Similarly, in Hemingway's story, "the bullets, all of them, hitting, had no effect on the buffalo." But Hemingway, in one of his greatest passages, describes the wounded lion and the strategy he devises against the unknown weapon from the animal's point of view: the bullet "crashed again and he felt the blow as it hit his lower ribs and ripped on through, blood sudden hot and frothy in his mouth, and he galloped toward the high grass where he could crouch and not be seen and make them bring the crashing thing close enough so he could make a rush and get the man that held it."

Both men feel guilty after their traumatic experience. Orwell sympathizes with the elephant, "dying very slowly and in great agony," and regrets having to kill the valuable work animal. Macomber fears the lion and is ashamed of running away from him. Orwell, a policeman, can kill the useful elephant and get away with it. Macomber has paid a lot of money to be able to kill the lion. He intends to kill it, but becomes frightened when it charges. Margot torments and betrays him. But when he recovers his courage, redeems himself by killing the buffalo, is sexually restored and seizes power from her, Margot fears he will leave her and shoots him in the skull from the car. Orwell's elephant is both real and symbolic. Hemingway's lion is real, plays an active role in the story and causes a crisis in Macomber's marriage. Orwell survives. Macomber, along with the lion and buffalo, is killed.

In 1936, the year these works were published, the Spanish Civil War broke out. Orwell went to Spain to fight, Hemingway went as an armed war correspondent. They met for the first and only time after the liberation of Paris in August 1944 when Orwell asked to borrow a pistol and Hemingway gave him a Colt .32. Their experience with weapons in Asia and Africa proved to be a valuable asset when they killed men instead of animals in wartime.

TWENTY-FOUR

TED HUGHES

Most great animal poems—by Rilke, Lawrence, Jeffers, Roethke, and Bishop—approach their subject from the author's point of view. They try to identify with and think like, penetrate and describe the mysterious inner life of these vital creatures. Hemingway and Ted Hughes do something more ambitious and difficult. They enter the animal's brain and describe the act of killing from the feral point of view.

By identifying consciousness in animals, and how humans can attempt to understand and represent it, Hemingway and Hughes anticipated a challenging and compelling scientific topic. Evidence about the social skills, attention and evolution of animals presents a strong case for their mental states or "creative consciousness." Thomas Nagel's famous article, "What Is It Like to Be a Bat?," describes bats as mammals with highly evolved sensory apparatus, and argues that an essential and often neglected component of consciousness is what it feels like to be a particular conscious thing.

Interchapter XII of Hemingway's *In Our Time* describes the matador facing the bull before the kill. He then personifies the bull and uses compression for intensity and present participles to suggest continuous action: "The bull looking at him straight in front, hating." In his bullfighting story "The Undefeated," he again goes inside the bull's head and employs simple sentences to animate the action and reveal the killer instincts of both animal and man: "The bull was suspicious. He wanted the man. No more barbs in the shoulder" from the *banderillos*.

The need to hate before the kill recurs in "The Short Happy Life of Francis Macomber." The eponymous hero hates his white hunter, Wilson, who's slept with Margot, Macomber's all-too-willing wife. He hates Margot for breaking her promise and having sex with Wilson. Macomber also hates himself for his cowardice with Margot and with the lion. The lion hates Macomber for wounding him. Hemingway achieves his brilliant effects and insights by subtly shifting the point of view back and forth from what the hunter sees to what the wounded lion feels, in a sequence of complex sentences connected by "and." Using his five senses, feeling the agonizing pain from his wound and devising his fatal strategy, the lion seeks protective cover before charging and trying to kill the killer:

> hesitating before going down the bank to drink, with such a thing opposite him, he saw a man figure detach itself from it and he turned his heavy head and swung away toward the cover of the trees as he heard a cracking crash and felt the slam of a .30-06 220-grain solid bullet that bit his flank and ripped in sudden hot scalding nausea through his stomach. He trotted, heavy, big-footed, swinging wounded full-bellied, through the trees toward the tall grass and cover, and the crash came again to go past him ripping the air apart. Then it crashed again and he felt the blow as it hit his lower ribs and ripped on through, blood sudden hot and frothy in his mouth, and he galloped toward the high grass where he could crouch and not be seen and make them bring the crashing thing close enough so he could make a rush and get the man that held it.

This searing description is surely based on the teenaged Hemingway's war wounds on the Italian front in 1918 when enemy mortar fire tore into his flesh. As Macomber, in the lion's eyes, changes from "thing" to "figure" to "man," the animal senses but does not fully understand what is happening to him. When Wilson forces Macomber to pursue the gut-shot lion, Hemingway shifts the focus from the hunter to his prey. After describing the terrible wound, Hemingway again emphasizes the lion's point of view and twice uses the crucial words "hate" and "hatred": "his big yellow eyes narrowed with hate, looked straight ahead, only blinking as the pain came as he breathed, and his claws dug in the soft baked earth. All of him, pain, sickness, hatred and all of his remaining strength, was tightening into an absolute concentration for a rush." Hemingway believed that the hunter, experiencing mutual hatred, must know how the animal thinks, feels and reacts before he kills him.

The three crashes in the first quotation—two hits and a miss—foreshadow what Macomber hears and feels, after he's recovered his courage and ability to dominate Margot, when she shoots him: "he felt a sudden white-hot, blinding flash, explode inside his head and that was all he ever felt." Macomber understands the lion's protracted pain and desire for vengeance, but does not feel them himself. Margot's perfect head-shot kills him instantly.

Like Hemingway, Ted Hughes is a tough, virile author, closely connected to the natural world, who expresses violence and visceral ferocity in his work. Both writers offer new insights about how wild creatures think. Hughes' "Hawk Roosting" is a murderous version of Gerard Manley Hopkins' religious poem "The Windhover," about a small, colorful kestrel. Hopkins praises "the mastery of the thing! / Brute beauty and valour and act, oh, air, pride, plume." The title of "Hawk Roosting" suggests quietude, quite the opposite of the savage feeling in this first-person, self-assured monologue. The poem, narrated from inside the hawk's head and with his sinister diction, portrays the evolutionary perfection of the predator and the egocentric horror of his worldview. He doesn't act, but merely surveys the world between "hooked head and hooked feet" while recalling and relishing his past kills:

I sit in the top of the wood, my eyes closed.
Inaction, no falsifying dream
Between my hooked head and hooked feet:
Or in sleep rehearse perfect kills and eat.

The hawk terrifies his prey with unbearable tension and tremendous horror, and represents the deadliness of the natural world. He imagines himself as an all-powerful hunter with nothing to stop him from tearing the entrails and killing his victims. Like the God of the Old Testament, he has total power over life and death: "Who hath prevented me? . . . Whatsoever is under the whole heaven is mine" (Job 41:11). High trees give him a formidable advantage. Undisturbed by reveries, he relies on instinct and pure sensation. The hawk does not actually use his physical perfection and fierce consciousness but, employing "sophistry," a philosophical term, constantly threatens everything his hawk-eye can see:

I kill where I please because it is all mine.
There is no sophistry in my body:
My manners are tearing off heads . . .

Nothing has changed since I began.
My eye has permitted no change.
I am going to keep things like this.

The narrative, told from within the hawk's feral brain, gives authority to the gradually realized theme of human conceit and propensity to violence.

Hughes gave several different explanations of the hawk, which is both symbolic and realistic. He first said he imagined "the hawk speaking to himself. He is like a dictator, who thinks he is God and invincible." He later denied that the hawk was a fascist or "symbol of some horrible genocidal dictator." He also told Ekbert Faas that through this egomaniacal raptor and oracle of destruction raw "Nature is thinking" and sounds "like Hitler's familiar spirit." The critic Yvonne Reddick thought the hawk was influenced by D. H. Lawrence's "Eagle in New Mexico" and represents the survival instinct. Both Hemingway's lion and Hughes' hawk feel hatred. But the lion is hunted, the hawk is the hunter. The lion knows what has hurt him, the hawk knows his own power.

TWENTY-FIVE

MARSHAL NEY

The paths of glory lead but to the grave.

—Thomas Gray, "Elegy Written in a Country Churchyard"

Michel Ney, one of Napoleon's original marshals, was renowned for his extraordinary courage in battle. One historian declared that Ney, who did not fear death, "had no use for money or ambition or politics or anything except military glory," yet his career ended in defeat at Waterloo, his life in disgrace and execution. The rise and fall of a tragic hero, noble in battle but flawed in political judgment, inspired various nineteenth-century novelists and his story continued to fascinate writers in the twentieth century.

The son of a humble barrel-maker, Ney (1769–1815) was born in a French enclave in the German Saarland and was bilingual. After leading the French army to victory in many great battles, he commanded the rear guard in the retreat from Moscow in 1812 and was known as the last Frenchman to leave Russian soil. In 1814 he pressured Napoleon to abdicate and accept exile on Elba, and was rewarded when the Bourbons regained the throne. When Napoleon escaped and returned to France in 1815, Ney promised to capture him and bring him back alive in an iron cage. Instead, believing that Napoleon could regain power, he joined him and fought under him at Waterloo, twelve miles south of Brussels.

Ney's cavalry overran the British cannons but, without infantry or artillery support, repeatedly failed to break the well-armed square-formations. His men were slaughtered as they tried to advance through the valley of death in the worst carnage Ney had ever seen. He led the charge over and over again and had five horses killed under him, but his reckless assaults were partly responsible for the French defeat in June 1815. Waterloo, the final battle of the Napoleonic wars, decided the fate of Europe.

One of the greatest soldiers in French history, Ney had survived every major campaign. When Napoleon was exiled for the second time, on St. Helena, Ney—who had changed sides too often—was tried for treason by the Royalists. In a judicial murder of December 1815 he was sentenced to execution by firing squad. Courageous to the end, Ney refused to wear a blindfold and was allowed to give his final order. He continued to justify himself and shouted: "Soldiers, when I give the command to fire, fire straight at my heart. Wait for the order. It will be my last to you. I protest against my condemnation. I have fought a hundred battles for France, and not one against her. . . . Soldiers, fire!" Napoleon had called Ney "the bravest of the brave" and given him command at Waterloo. But on St. Helena he was embittered by Ney's first betrayal and their disastrous last battle. He declared, despite Ney's formidable achievements, that he was "brave and nothing more . . . good at leading 10,000 men into battle, but other than that a real blockhead."

Ney's exploits and cruel fate fascinated and inspired Stendhal, Victor Hugo and Leo Tolstoy. Ney became a character in their novels and added a realistic element. Hemingway included both Stendhal's long description of the battle of Waterloo in *The Charterhouse of Parma* (1839) and Victor Hugo's account in *Les Misérables* (1862) in his propagandistic military anthology *Men at War* (1942). Stendhal portrays Ney through the eyes of the young Fabrizio, who is thrilled to catch sight of his glorious hero, the ruddy-complexioned Ney. He briefly joins Ney's escort, manages to identify and scrutinize him, sees him severely rebuke a subordinate, is overwhelmed by his reputation and dreams of achieving military glory:

> [His horse dashed off] to join the escort that was following the generals. Fabrizio counted four gold-laced hats. A quarter of an hour later, from a few words said by one hussar to the next, Fabrizio gathered that one of these generals was the famous Marshal Ney. His happiness knew no bounds; only he had no way of telling which of the four generals was Marshal Ney; he would have given everything in the world to know. . . .

> He noticed the biggest of these generals who was speaking to his neighbour, a general also, in a tone of authority and almost of reprimand; he was swearing. . . .
>
> "Who is that general who is *chewing up* the one next to him?"
>
> "Gad, it's the Marshal."
>
> "What Marshal?"
>
> "Marshal Ney, you fool! I say, where have you been serving?"
>
> Fabrizio, although highly susceptible, had no thought of resenting this insult; he was studying, lost in childish admiration, the famous Prince de la Moskowa, the "Bravest of the Brave."

Stendhal contrasts the bewildered but idealistic young Fabrizio with the authoritative commands of Marshal Ney; Hugo includes an omniscient historian's account of Waterloo in the midst of his novel. To maintain Ney's heroic stature, neither Stendhal nor Hugo describes his fatal cavalry charges. Hugo's viewpoint is more critical and incisive than that of Stendhal's young soldier Fabrizio. Stendhal gives brief glimpses of Ney advising the high-spirited and self-confident Napoleon, and appearing in battle, before finally summing up his reckless character: "[The rains] did not prevent Napoleon from exclaiming cheerfully to Ney, 'We have ninety chances out of a hundred.' . . . The Emperor jested with Ney, who had said, 'Wellington will not be so simple as to wait for Your Majesty.' . . . Wellington held the village and the plain; Ney had only the crest and the slope. . . . [Desperate for help,] Ney demanded infantry from Napoleon, and Napoleon exclaimed, 'Infantry! Where does he expect me to get it? Does he think I can make it?'"

Hugo portrays Ney after Waterloo as a disarmed, slashed, wounded, half-mad and suicidal warrior who wants to die in combat. In an overheated operatic passage, Hugo writes:

> Ney, bewildered, great with all the grandeur of accepted death, offered himself to all blows in that tempest. He had his fifth horse killed under him there. Perspiring, his eyes aflame, foam on his lips, with uniform unbuttoned, one of his epaulets half cut off by a sword-stroke from the horse-guard, his plaque with the great eagle dented by a bullet; bleeding, bemired, magnificent, a broken sword in his hand, he said,

> "Come and see how a Marshal of France dies on the field of battle!" But in vain; he did not die. He was haggard and angry. At [Marshal] Drouet d'Erlon he hurled this question, "Are you not going to get yourself killed?" In the midst of all that artillery engaged in crushing a handful of men, he shouted: "So there is nothing for me! Oh! I should like to have all these English bullets enter my chest!"

Hugo then alludes to the irony of Ney's tragic execution: "Unhappy man, thou wert reserved for French bullets!"

In a final heroic gesture Ney, stripped of his Marshal's insignia, tries and fails to rouse his retreating army, who can offer only vocal support: "The disintegration is unprecedented. Ney borrows a horse, leaps upon it, and without hat, cravat, or sword, dashes across the Brussels road, stopping both English and French. He strives to detain the army, he recalls it to its duty, he insults it, he clings to the route. He is overwhelmed. The soldiers fly from him, shouting, 'Long live Marshal Ney!'" Though Ney did not value the lives of his men, nor even his own, they continued to worship him. Robert Browning's "Incident of the French Camp" (1845) reveals the sacrifice Napoleon's soldiers were willing to make for their charismatic leaders. When a rider arrives to announce the capture of Ratisbon, Napoleon exclaims:

> "You're wounded!"—"Nay," the soldier's pride
> Touched to the quick, he said:
> "I'm killed, Sire!" And his chief beside,
> Smiling the boy fell dead.

In *War and Peace* (1867) Tolstoy describes the Russian victory in the 1812 battle of Borodino and shows how the decisions of the commanders affect the lives of his fictional characters. When one general proposed "to lead his division through the forest, Napoleon signified assent," but Ney, in a cautious but shrewd assessment, "ventured to observe that to move troops through woodland is risky." Tolstoy writes that all immediate decisions about cannons, infantry and cavalry were made on the spot "by the nearest officers in the ranks, without reference to Ney, Davoust, and Murat, far less to Napoleon himself." But he also notes that these commanders risked their lives by leading great numbers of troops into combat: "Napoleon's generals, Davoust, Ney, and Murat, who were close to that region of fire, and sometimes even rode into it, several times led immense masses of orderly troops into that region."

These great novels kept the figure of Ney alive in the literary imagination. Sixty years later Ford Madox Ford also thought Ney was a promising subject and describes a proposed collaboration with Conrad in his memoir *Joseph Conrad: A Personal Remembrance* (1924). Their hero "Assheton Smith was to have been the central figure of our novel about the [attempt to prevent the execution] of Ney—the Milord with the spleen intervening nearly successfully to save the beau sabreur"—the dashing adventurer. They also planned to describe the imaginary role played by the Tsar (hated by Conrad), who demanded the execution of the enemy who had devastated his country.

Like Ford, Robert Lowell focuses on Ney's death. Lowell's memoir "91 Revere Street" in *Life Studies* recalls playing, as a boy, with tall, hand-painted lead soldiers, "recognizable replicas of mounted Napoleonic captains: Kleber, Marshal Ney." His poem "Leaving Home, Marshal Ney" (*History*, 1973) echoes King Lear's lamentation for the dead Cordelia: "Why should a dog, a horse, a rat, have life, / And thou no breath at all?" and mourns Ney's unjust execution: "a Marshal of France, and shot for too much courage— / why should shark be eaten when bait swim free?"

Hemingway, an expert on military history, had a dozen books on Napoleon in his library. He idolized his military heroes and friends, Dorman-Smith and Buck Lanham, and identified with the courageous but tragic Marshal. Hemingway paid tribute to him in letters of April 1945 and July 1948, and wrote, "Been re-reading about Mike Ney. . . . He was not only a terrible [i.e., frightening] fighting man—he was a very good man." He also described, with some exaggeration, "Michel Ney the cooper's son who fought the 200 some rear-guard actions covering the retreat of the army from Moscow."

Ney's statue stood near the Paris flat where Hemingway lived in the early 1920s and in front of his favorite café, La Closerie des Lilas (the small lilac garden). In a richly compressed paragraph in *A Moveable Feast* (1964) he refers to him affectionately, as if his old companion were still alive, as Marshal Ney, Ney and, more familiarly, Mike Ney. He mentions but doesn't describe Ney's disastrous charges at Waterloo, alludes to the "Lost Generation" epigraph of *The Sun Also Rises* and makes Ney represent all the doomed heroes in history. Hemingway admires the beauty of the fierce statue and nostalgically recalls "the light on my old friend, the statue of Marshal Ney with his sword out and the shadows of the trees on the bronze, and he alone there and nobody behind him [in Moscow] and what a fiasco he'd made of Waterloo. I thought that all generations were lost by something and always had been and always would be and I stopped at the Lilas to keep the statue company . . . watching the statue and remembering how many days Ney had fought, personally, with the rear-guard on the retreat from Moscow that Napoleon had ridden away from in the coach with Caulaincourt." General Armand de Caulaincourt's memoir *With Napoleon in Russia* recalls that "We set out at exactly ten o'clock in the evening of December 5, 1812. The Emperor and I were in his sleeping coach." As Napoleon rode comfortably away, Ney remained behind to cover the retreat.

Four decades after Ney's death the Bourbons had left the scene and the French began to revalue his military career. During the dynastic reign of Napoleon III the heroic bronze statue of Marshal Ney by François Rude (1853) was placed on a high plinth on the avenue de l'Observatoire and near the place where he was executed. He triumphantly raises his sword in his right hand as if leading a cavalry charge and places his left hand on his scabbard. He looks to the left with an open mouth and seems to be defiantly shouting an order. He wears a bicorn hat, epaulets, decorations on his tunic, Marshal's sash across his chest and high riding boots with spurs, and has a cannon at his feet. Ney's rehabilitation continued fifteen years later in 1868 when Jean-Léon Gerôme painted *The Execution of Marshal Ney*. On a misty morning the officer and firing squad, their work finished, stand at ease on the left. Ney's bullet-ridden body lies face down on the ground before a yellow, pock-marked wall, with the dome of the Paris astronomy Observatory in the background.

Ney had turned against Napoleon and joined the Royalists, then left the Royalists and rejoined Napoleon, then behaved recklessly and was defeated at Waterloo. Both sides were furious with him and saw him as a turncoat. But the heartfelt tributes of leading artists and writers from Stendhal to Hemingway contrasted Ney's military triumphs with his involvement in politics and saw him as the embodiment of heroism betrayed by those in power. They all kept Ney's memory alive and redeemed their hero's honor and reputation.

TWENTY-SIX

PENINSULAR WAR

When I interviewed Martha Gellhorn for my biography of Hemingway, she told me that he'd been reading General Sir William Napier's *History of the War in the Peninsula* (1828–40) while writing *For Whom the Bell Tolls* (1940). During the Spanish Civil War, Hemingway made three trips to Spain as a journalist and reported the major battles with a novelist's eye. Fascinated by the patriotic fervor he observed in the peasants and workers, he noticed the striking parallels between the Peninsular War and the Civil War. He looked up Napier's eyewitness account, which led him to later histories.

The Peninsular War, in the early nineteenth century, was part of the costly and protracted struggle that opposed Napoleon's attempt to conquer Europe. The British, under Wellington, joined forces with the Spanish and Portuguese armies, raised the blockade of their ports and drove the French from Spain. This war saw the emergence of guerrillas (Spanish for "little wars"), in which mobile bands of freelance fighters harassed the enemy and helped the allies defeat the French. Ronald Fraser's *Napoleon's Cursed War: Spanish Popular Resistance in the Peninsular War, 1808–1814* (2008) describes the valuable contribution of these independent fighters.

Like the Peninsular War, the Spanish Civil War was international in scope. Fascist Germany and Italy intervened on the side of General Franco; Communist Russia supported the Loyalists. The volunteers on the Loyalist side came from every country in Europe and joined the militias that were affiliated with various left-wing parties. But there was an important and tragic difference between the earlier and the later wars. In the Peninsular War the guerrillas had a unifying common goal and fought to support the regular armies; in the

Civil War the Loyalists were not only overwhelmed by fascist military power, but rival militias also fought amongst themselves and the guerrillas disintegrated into brutal factions.

Hemingway learned of the guerrilla tradition, crucial to the idea of Spanish patriotism, from direct experience as well as from books. Broadcasting on Radio Madrid during the war, La Pasionaria, the famous Loyalist leader and orator, frequently evoked memories of the Spanish rising against Napoleon during the fight for independence in 1808. In *For Whom the Bell Tolls*, his particular blend of action, love story and documentary, Hemingway based the military leaders on real people and the progress of the war on actual events, but focused on how a particular guerrilla group actually fought. He recreated the background, politics and tactics of a heterogeneous guerrilla band, acting independently yet following the orders of the regular army, and invented typically Spanish characters, inspired by men he had known before and during the Spanish Civil War.

Into this context Hemingway placed his American volunteer hero, Robert Jordan, an anti-fascist but not a Marxist or Communist. He is a demolitions expert who has no contact with other American combatants in the International Brigades and fights an irregular war behind enemy lines. In a previous battle, he has been forced to kill his wounded Russian comrade, Kashkin, who was unable to move and unwilling to fall into the retributive hands of the enemy. Jordan's military mission is obstructed by his quarrel with Pablo, the treacherous leader of the guerrilla band. Their quarrel mirrors the conflict between the rival political factions on the left, whose internecine struggles were a major factor in the Loyalist defeat.

Fraser's description of the guerrilla bands in the Peninsular War illuminates the extensive parallels with the irregular bands that fought in the Spanish Civil War. The nineteenth-century guerrillas were small, mobile groups—with internal cohesion, collective identity and *esprit de corps*—that opposed a static regular army. They included some women; a significant number of outlaws, villains and troublemakers; and a number of foreign conscripts who had deserted from the French army. Most of the guerrillas and their leaders were peasants who had experienced collective violence at the hands of the enemy, "often with personal consequences: the death of close relatives, the abuse of female kin, forced labour in carrying or carting for the occupying army, the forcible seizure of food supplies and an infinity of individual indignities." There were two main kinds of guerrilla bands: "Those who took up arms without any authorization from either civilian or military authorities could be called *partisans*; those who asked for and received official authorization to create new groups . . . could be termed privateers."

Operating behind enemy lines, the fighters were essentially territorial. The deep gorges, hidden valleys and numerous mountain ranges in Spain were perfect guerrilla country. The French soldiers, trained for the traditional order of battle, were neutralized by the hostile terrain and the surprise attacks. The bands also provided valuable intelligence for their allies: "Small military groups reconnoitred and probed the enemy's lines, seizing prisoners to gain information on their opponents' strength, movements, food supplies and battle plans. . . . It was the first time that the guerrilla became a nationwide form of resistance and a sanctified right of self-defence." In this war, as in the Spanish Civil War, "reprisals on occasion rose to barbarous heights among the opponents in the guerrilla struggle."

At exactly the same time that he was fighting the Peninsular War in Spain, Napoleon rashly invaded Russia. Like the Spanish, the Russians opposed a superior army that had overextended itself into hostile territory. They avoided the confrontation of massive forces in traditional warfare, sanctified by Carl von Clausewitz, and concentrated that unknown quantity, the spirit of the army, in a series of sporadic guerrilla encounters. Leo Tolstoy had fought in the Caucasus (1852–53) and during the siege of Sebastopol in the Crimean War (1854–56). In a passage that Hemingway had certainly read, Tolstoy expounded the principles of the guerrilla war against Napoleon, used in Spain as well as in Russia, in a vital chapter of *War and Peace* (1869):

> One of the most conspicuous and advantageous departures from the so-called rules of warfare is the independent action of men acting separately against men huddled together in a mass. Such independent activity is always seen in a war that assumes a national character. In this kind of warfare, instead of forming in a crowd to attack a crowd, men disperse in small groups, attack singly and at once fly, when attacked by superior forces, and then attack again, when an opportunity presents itself. Such were the methods of the guerrillas in Spain; and of the mountain tribes in the Caucasus, and of the Russians in 1812.

As in the Peninsular War, the guerrillas in *For Whom the Bell Tolls* belong to a lawless mobile band that fight against a regular army; include women and foreigners; and recruit peasants who'd been persecuted by the enemy. They gather intelligence, are patriotic and territorial, and operate in a mountainous terrain that is hostile to the fascists. They carry out the same sudden and surprising, probing and withdrawing, hit-and-run attacks, ambush enemy columns and terrorize them in hand-to-hand encounters. They are quite capable of barbaric reprisals.

Hemingway based aspects of Robert Jordan on T. E. Lawrence, who adopted the tactics of his Spanish and Russian predecessors and used them while brilliantly leading the Arab revolt against the Turks in World War I. Both Lawrence and Jordan are foreign technical experts who assume command of a guerrilla group operating behind enemy lines. Both have a scholarly background, have spent many years in the country before the war, and have a sound knowledge of the language and culture of the people they lead. Both adopt the local customs, do not feel like outsiders and are not treated as such. Both take up an alien cause for their own idealistic reasons, destroy trains and bridges by detonating explosives, and are forced to kill their own wounded companions.

In *For Whom the Bell Tolls* hundreds of guerrillas are fighting in the mountains around Madrid. The most important group, led by El Sordo ("the deaf one"), join the attack on the bridge and are wiped out by enemy aircraft. In the novel all the guerrillas are peasants, and many—like Pablo and Anselmo—are illiterate. They all dress in black peasant smocks, stiff gray trousers and rope-soled shoes, and Jordan wears the same clothing. They use the familiar form of address, *tu* instead of *usted*; call each other *camarada* (comrade); and say *Don* and *Señor* only when they're joking.

Hemingway artfully combines many elements to suggest the difficulty of the undertaking and intensify the suspense. The mission must be timed precisely and Jordan must impose discipline upon the guerrillas, yet the group dynamics conspire against him. Pilar fatalistically prophesies that Jordan will meet his death, and Pablo treacherously undermines the attack. Jordan's love for and sex with Maria arouses Pilar's jealousy and the men's hostility. There is a heavy snowstorm, Pablo steals the detonators and the enemy discovers their plans. The cavalry patrols the area, the bridge is unexpectedly defended and fascist planes drop bombs. El Sordo's band is massacred, and Andrés is unable to deliver Jordan's message warning Golz to cancel his attack. Afterwards, the group finds it difficult to escape to the Gredos mountains.

At the end of the novel, when all Jordan's doubts and fears have been realized, he's forced to launch his "surprise attack" on an enemy who is expecting it. In this battle, the good men—Anselmo, Agustín, Fernando, Andrés, Eladio and Primitivo—are killed. Pablo and Rafael, who look out for themselves, manage to escape with Pilar and Maria. Jordan blows up the bridge, but breaks his leg when his horse is shot by the enemy and falls on him. Like Kashkin, he prefers to die rather than be captured, tortured and executed. He remains behind to kill the fascist Lieutenant Berrendo, who cut off the heads of El Sordo's men, and to be killed by his soldiers. The last sentence of *For Whom the Bell Tolls* leaves Jordan close to the earth but not yet in it: "He could feel his heart beating against the pine needle floor of the forest." It also repeats both the first sentence of the novel, completing the circular unity of the book, and echoes the last sentence of "The Snows of Kilimanjaro": "But she did not hear him for the beating of her heart."

Hemingway was pro-Loyalist but did not write propaganda. Critics on the left attacked his realistic portrait of guerrillas in action. His great novel, which drew on his reading about the Peninsular War as well as on his contemporary reporting in Spain, portrays both the triumphs and failures of the guerrilla war: the idealism and treachery, patriotism and cowardice, courage and brutality, sacrifice and selfishness, comradeship and anarchy, executions and remorse. Hemingway's vision of the world, embodied in Jordan, is essentially idealistic and romantic. He contrasts this view with the peasant cunning of Pablo. Jordan speaks for the author when he reflects on the fighting spirit and conflicting motives of the Spanish peasants. Alluding to Madame de Staël's maxim, "*Tout comprendre c'est tout pardonner*," Jordan concludes: "There is no finer and no worse people in the world. No kinder people and no crueler. And who understands them? Not me, because if I did I would forgive it all." In the twenty-first century guerrillas continue to pin down and damage well-trained regular armies, and have remained as ruthless, effective and flawed as Hemingway's Spanish fighters.

TWENTY-SEVEN

FIVE WARS

Both of Hemingway's grandfathers fought in the Civil War and he was proud of his family's military traditions. He was also fascinated by the wars at the turn of the century—the Spanish-American War, the Boer War, the Russo-Japanese War—and as a boy loved to read the Old Testament, which was full of battles. Though never a combatant, he went to all the major wars of his time. He volunteered as an ambulance driver with the Red Cross in Italy in 1918; and as a war correspondent covered the battles in Turkey and Greece during 1922, in Spain during 1937–38, in China during 1941, and in France and Germany during 1944.

The young Hemingway felt there hadn't been a real war to go to since his grandfather was shot in the Battle of Bull Run. He was eager to fight in the Great War, but was rejected by the army for defective vision. When he reached Paris with the Red Cross officers in June 1918, the city was bombarded by the Germans in the last main offensive of the war and final attempt to break through the front at Amiens. When he arrived in Milan, an ammunition factory exploded in the nearby Lombard countryside, and he had to carry mutilated corpses and human fragments detached from the barbed-wire fence that surrounded the plant.

Just after the explosion Hemingway was posted to an ambulance unit in Schio, east of Lake Garda, and evacuated the wounded in the top-heavy, blunt-nosed Fiats. He wanted to get closer to the fighting against the Austrians and volunteered to run a canteen on the Piave front. He was only forty yards from the Austrian lines, but had a rather trivial job dispensing chocolates and cigarettes to the soldiers.

Hemingway enjoyed the masculine comradeship of war, the brave commitment to battle, the constant test of courage and the real threat of death. In his bullfighting book, *Death in the Afternoon*, he said that bravery was "the ability to ignore possible consequences." In his anthology *Men at War*, he stated that imagination, the essential quality for a writer, was fatal for a soldier. He defined cowardice as "almost always simply a lack of ability to suspend the functioning of the imagination. Learning to live completely in the very second of the present minute with no before and no after is the greatest gift a soldier can acquire."

Hemingway was seriously wounded at midnight on July 8, 1918 at Fossalta di Piave. According to a contemporary report, written by his commanding officer, he was wounded "by the explosion of a shell which landed about three feet from him, killing a soldier who stood between him and the point of the explosion, and wounding the others." The shell was a muzzle-loaded Austrian trench mortar—a five-gallon can filled with explosives and scrap metal—fired from across the river. In a letter written to Hemingway's father six days after the event, a comrade stated that Hemingway, though badly wounded and nearly killed, had acted heroically: "The concussion of the explosion knocked him unconscious and buried him with earth. There was an Italian between Ernest and the shell. He was instantly killed while another, standing a few feet away, had both legs blown off. A third Italian was badly wounded and this one Ernest, after he had regained consciousness, picked up on his back and carried to the first aid dug-out. Although some 200 pieces of shell lodged in him none of them are above the hip joint."

Another friend, who saw Hemingway soon after he was wounded, explained that he "was picked up by the Austrian searchlights and took several big machine gun slugs in his legs while carrying a wounded Italian soldier back from the advanced listening post to the front line." The friend confirmed Hemingway's courage and added that he fully deserved the Silver Medal for Valour: "Ernie acquitted himself with real distinction and won real glory. The Italians were pretty generous with Croce di Guerras, but they were damn tough and tight about awarding the Medaglia d'Argento per Valore. Believe me, you had to be damn near killed, in a most honorable way, to get that."

The official Italian citation read: "Gravely wounded by numerous pieces of shrapnel from an enemy shell, with an admirable spirit of brotherhood, before taking care of himself, he rendered generous assistance to the Italian soldiers more seriously wounded by the same explosion and did not allow himself to be carried elsewhere until after they had been evacuated." Hemingway was carried on a stretcher for three kilometers to a dressing station. While he waited two hours in the roofless stable for an ambulance to arrive, he was given shots of morphine and anti-tetanus, and had about twenty-eight fragments removed from his legs. He was then taken to the field hospital in Fornaci, before being sent to the base hospital in Milan.

At the time of his wound Hemingway was tremendously idealistic—he had been in Italy for a very short time and had not seen the horrors of warfare on the western front—and seems to have genuinely believed all the war propaganda. Conscious of the fame he might achieve for his exploits in Italy, which were described in his hometown newspaper, he called his war experience "the next best thing to getting killed and reading your own obituary."

The idealism of 1918 provided a powerful contrast to the bitter disillusionment expressed in *A Farewell to Arms*. In his war novel, the wounded hero Frederic Henry reaches down to touch his knee and is horrified to find it "wasn't there." He also experiences the sensation of returning from death:

> Through the other noise I heard a cough, then came the chuh-chuh-chuh-chuh—then there was a flash as when a blast furnace door is swung open, and a roar that started white and went red and on and on in a rushing wind. I tried to breathe but my breath would not come and I felt myself rush bodily out of myself and out and out and out all the time bodily in the wind. I went out swiftly, all of myself, and I knew I was dead and that it had all been a mistake to think you just died. Then I floated, and instead of going on I felt myself slide back. I breathed and I was back.

Despite the wound, the tone of Hemingway's letters of 1918 is extremely positive and the photographs in the Milan hospital show a proud and happy young man, well on the way to recovery. Hemingway had proved his heroism in action and experienced a close encounter with death without suffering any permanent injuries. His behavior under fire gave him confidence in his courage and in his ability to act ably under stress. The wound not only made him aware that he could die, but also proved that he could survive. It made him feel invulnerable, made him live intensely, made him want to challenge fate rather than submit to it. He had endured trench mortar and machine-gun fire, and thought nothing could kill him.

Hemingway's experience at Fossalta led him to divide men into those who had been wounded and those who had not. Like Colonel Cantwell in *Across the River and Into the Trees*, "he only loved people who had fought or been mutilated." Though he was never a soldier, he had the combatant's hatred of the safe staff officer and believed you could not judge a man until you had seen him in action.

Hemingway's wound had a positive effect on his life. It was of course an accident, a mistake, a misfortune. He had been hurt—and had survived—by chance. Yet he was able to transform what had begun as a commonplace distribution of chocolate and cigarettes into something glorious and noble. Hemingway saw most clearly when he lived most intensely. He believed you "have to be hurt like hell before you can write seriously."

In the fall of 1922 Hemingway went to Turkey as a war correspondent for the *Toronto Star*. He took the Orient Express to Sofia, reached Constantinople on September 30 and soon contracted malaria. He arrived after the defeat, the retreat and the evacuation of the Greek army from Smyrna, after the fire and massacre that followed the Turkish occupation of the city. But he described the physical squalor and political situation in "Constan" and reported the signing of the armistice treaty that halted the Turkish pursuit of the Greeks into Europe. From a lice-ridden hotel on the frontier, he narrated the desperate flight of the Greek refugees. He sent dispatches on the character and ambitions of the Turkish general Mustapha Kemal. He was cynical about politicians, compassionate about civilian victims and sympathetic to the Greeks rather than to the cruelly victorious Turks. (Both sides had committed atrocities.)

In 1914 Smyrna (now Izmir) had been offered by the Allies to entice Greece into the war against the Central Powers. The occupation of the city by the Greeks in May 1919, followed by a massacre of the Turks, was the immediate cause of the Greco-Turkish War. The 600-year-old Ottoman Empire had been liquidated in Europe and Asia, but the Turks still fought fiercely to retain the cities and plains of their Anatolian homeland.

The final campaign of the war, which began (shortly before Hemingway arrived) on August 18, 1922, was a series of Turkish victories that quickly drove the Greeks 350 miles westward from Ankara to Smyrna. The Turks defeated the Greeks, north of Ankara, on August 20, and General Ismet Pasha broke through the front on August 26. The Turks advanced forty kilometers by the 29th and captured the Greek commander on September 2. They reoccupied Smyrna and completed the conquest of Anatolia on September 9.

In "The Snows of Kilimanjaro" the dying hero remembers when the Greek *evzones*, wearing their traditional dress, were mistakenly massacred by their own artillery and then deliberately slaughtered during their futile retreat (the officers shooting their own men) from the superior Turkish forces. The Greeks "made the attack with the newly arrived Constantine officers that did not know a god-damned thing, and the artillery had fired into the troops and the British observer had cried like a child. That was the day he'd first seen dead men wearing white ballet skirts and upturned shoes with pompoms on them. . . . Later he'd seen things that he could never think of and later still he had seen much worse."

The Turks immediately arrested vast numbers of Greeks and Armenians, suspected of being involved in the Smyrna massacre of May 1919, and Turkish troops started a fire in order to conceal the slaughter of 125,000 Christians. The remaining population swarmed to the water's edge at the western edge of the city while the fire raged behind them. In his story "On the Quai at Smyrna," Hemingway described the searchlight scanning the crowds who were screaming for survival, the women who gave birth to babies and the ones who would not give up their dead infants, and the drastic measures taken by the Greeks to prevent their valuable mules from falling into the hands of the enemy. When the Greeks "evacuated they had all their baggage animals they couldn't take off with them so they just broke their forelegs and dumped them into the shallow water."

Mustapha Kemal marched north from Smyrna to pursue the remnant of the Greek army and crossed the Dardanelles. But the armistice signed on October 11 ended the war and, Hemingway explained, "marked the beginning of the end of European domination in Asia." After the Greek defeat a million broken-spirited refugees sought safety across the Greek frontier. In *In Our Time* Hemingway described the silent, ghastly procession into Thrace: "Greek cavalry herded along the procession. . . . There was a woman having a kid with a young girl holding a blanket over her and crying. Scared sick of looking at it. It rained all through the evacuation."

Hemingway, nourished on the history of the American War Between the States, believed, "Civil War is the best war for a writer, the most complete." He was deeply attached to the country, culture and people of Spain. After Franco's fascists rose against the Republican government in July 1936, he was eager to devote himself to the Loyalist cause.

He made four separate trips to Spain as a war correspondent for the North American Newspaper Alliance and spent eight months there during 1937–38. He had shed blood for Italy, and was now being paid to expose himself to danger and write about the war. On his first and most significant tour in the spring of 1937, he reported the siege of Madrid and worked on the documentary film *The Spanish Earth*. The film included scenes of infantry and tanks in action, and was later shown to President Roosevelt in the White House. In the fall of 1937 he sent dispatches from Madrid and wrote his play, *The Fifth Column*, while under bombardment in the Hotel Florida. In the spring of 1938 he reported the battle of the Ebro Delta as the fascists lunged toward the Mediterranean, captured Tortosa on the coast road, and cut communications between Catalonia and Madrid. In November 1938 he witnessed the events that led to the fall of Barcelona.

During April 1937 Madrid was besieged by Franco's forces, which shelled the capital from University City but could not capture the town. The front was only a short ride from the Hotel Florida, which was hit by shells intended for the nearby telephone exchange. Hemingway's first reports celebrated the Loyalist victories over Italian troops at Guadalajara and Brihuega. He described the landscape, military action, strategic significance, political importance and effect on the civilian population. He also stressed the physical hardships and wrote, "The first thing you remember is how cold it was; how early you got up in the morning; how you were always so tired you could go to sleep at any time; how hard it was to get gasoline; how you were always hungry."

Herbert Matthews, the *New York Times* correspondent in Spain, described how Hemingway saved his life during a dangerous river crossing in November 1938:

> It was during the Ebro battle; we had to take a rowboat to get over from the west to the east bank because the bridges had been bombed down. The current was swift and there were some nasty rapids a few hundred

> yards down the river so the boat was being partly pulled across by a rope, which snapped. We started drifting swiftly toward the rapids. Hemingway quickly took the oars; another journalist acted as coxswain to pace his strokes with shouts, and by an extraordinary exhibition of strength, Ernest got us safely across. He was a good man in a pinch.

Everyone who knew Hemingway in Spain agreed that he showed the best side of his character, was generous and courageous, and did everything he could for the Loyalists. His fame gave him privileged status as a correspondent, the authorities allowed him a car and driver, and he had complete freedom of movement. He always shared his superior food and drink with his colleagues. He enjoyed the test of nerve in warfare, seemed to thrive during the bombardments at the front and contrasted his youthful reaction on the Piave to his mature response in Madrid: "in the war in Italy I was a boy and I had much fear. In Spain I had no fear after a couple of weeks and was very happy." His German friend Gustav Regler, who was seriously wounded while fighting with the Twelfth International Brigade, said, "For him we had the scent of death, like the bullfighters, and because of this he was invigorated in our company."

In January 1941, just after marrying, Hemingway and his third wife, Martha Gellhorn, went to China to report for *PM* and *Collier's*. His mission was to study the strategic situation, see how Chiang Kai-shek's war against Japan was progressing and (eleven months before the Japanese attacked Pearl Harbor) decide how the war affected American commercial and military interests in the Orient. The war in China was four years old and three-quarters of the country was occupied by the Japanese. The combination of civil war and foreign intervention in China seemed to repeat the struggle in Spain.

Their month in the interior began on March 25 when they flew north from Hong Kong, over the mountains and the Japanese lines to Namyung. They then spent seven horrible days traveling south by car, boat and horse, to the Canton front, just next to Hong Kong, which was the nearest sector held by Chiang's Kuomintang. After driving all day from Namyung to Shaokwan on roads that were rivers of mud strewn with boulders, they spent three days with the commanding general of the war zone. At the headquarters of the 12th army sector, the Chinese and Japanese machine guns were only three kilometers apart, but an undeclared truce was in effect. After visiting cadet training camp, Hemingway outdrank fourteen Chinese officers, who gradually collapsed and slithered under the table.

Hemingway spent forty-three hours on the boat back to Shaokwan and twenty-five hours on the 400-mile trip to a filthy hotel in Kweilin. He then flew northwest to Chungking (in Szechwan province, about 770 miles from Hong Kong), which was the wartime capital of China. The Japanese occasionally bombed the town, though not when Hemingway was there. In Chungking he had lunch with Chiang and his American-educated wife. The Generalissimo—who was "thin, straight-backed, impeccable in a plain grey uniform and looked embalmed"—discussed the Chinese Communists whom he feared more than the Japanese. The high point of the trip to the interior was a secret meeting with Chou En-lai, who was living underground and in constant danger in Chungking. During his debriefing in Washington, Hemingway accurately predicted that the Communists would take over China after the war.

While Martha remained in the capital, Hemingway flew north to Cheng-tu. He visited a Chinese military academy, established by the Germans, and watched 100,000 workers build an airfield. After his return to Chungking, they flew southwest over the Burma Road to Lashio and traveled by land to the sweltering cities: Mandalay and Rangoon. Hemingway called the saffron-robed Buddhist priests "religious bums." After leaving Burma, he returned to Hong Kong and (he claimed) spent an exhausting night with three beautiful Chinese girls.

Hemingway was always at his best in adversity. Martha praised his flexibility, patience, courtesy. During the "unspeakable horror journey" she constantly complained while he remained stoic; she had to endure the nightmare of China, he had to put up with both China and Martha. She admitted that "he saw the Chinese as people while I saw them as a mass of down trodden valiant doomed humanity." Hemingway's best story about the trip concerned the farmers' dissatisfaction with the quality of watery night soil during a cholera epidemic. When the buyers complained, the vendors allowed them to test the thickness of the product by sucking it up through straws.

Hemingway spent the early years of World War II in Cuban waters and eventually became a war correspondent for *Collier's*. In London on May 25, 1944, he suffered a severe concussion and needed fifty-seven stitches after his car struck a water tank during a blackout. But he left the hospital four days later to fly with the RAF and observe the D-Day landings in Normandy. He reported the war in France from mid-July. On July 26, after the breakout from St-Lô, he accompanied Colonel Buck Lanham as he led the 22nd Infantry Regiment of the Fourth Infantry Division, which spearheaded the Normandy advance, entered Paris, attacked the Siegfried Line and held a key salient in the Battle of the Bulge. Hemingway had what he called "a good war": short, irregular, exciting, comradely and lucky. His seven months' participation in the conflict (June–December 1944) were the happiest of his life.

In Saint-Pois on August 5, between the landings in Normandy and the liberation of Paris, Hemingway had a second serious accident. While riding on a motorcycle with the photographer Robert Capa, he was forced to leap into a ditch to avoid a German anti-tank gun, was fired on by a machine gun, banged his head on a boulder and suffered another concussion.

Hemingway's most controversial campaign in the war was the week of fighting around Rambouillet (twenty-three miles southwest of Paris) that led to the liberation of the capital on August 25. After accompanying a private group of Free French partisans into the city, he acted like a military governor, establishing headquarters and raising the American flag. More important, he secured valuable information about enemy defenses on the road to Paris that facilitated General Leclerc's triumphant entry. He also participated in the ferocious fighting in the Hürtgenwald, between Aachen and Bonn, from November 15 to December 16, 1944. One of the most costly attacks of the war took place as the Germans made a last stand on the frontier in freezing rain, sleet and snow. An army historian wrote that in three days in mid-November the 22nd Infantry Regiment, weakened by mud, mines, enemy infiltration and shelling, had incurred more than 300 battle casualties.

Hemingway liked combat, enjoyed killing and thought war was the greatest outdoor sport. A lifelong student of the natural history of the dead, he had slaughtered fish and animals since boyhood. He made comparisons between bullfighting and war, and derived vicarious pleasure from watching the matador assume godlike powers over life and death. He killed half-ton marlin in the Gulf Stream and dangerous lions in Africa; he watched soldiers kill the enemy in Spain; and killed men himself in World War II. Like Albert Camus, he believed that "absolute freedom is the freedom to kill." He learned the "fear-purged ecstasy of battle" and (like the hero of *For Whom the Bell Tolls*) admitted that he "liked to kill as all who are soldiers by choice have enjoyed."

Hemingway claimed to have killed a great many Germans and certainly killed a few of them. On August 3, 1944, at Villedieu-les-Poêles in Normandy, he threw grenades down a cellar where Nazi troops were supposed to be hiding, but did not check to see if they were actually there. He may have wanted to take credit for the action without confronting the fragmented remains of his victims. On November 22, armed with a machine gun, he definitely killed some Germans who attacked Lanham's headquarters in the Hürtgen Forest.

Wars, in which entire nations fought for their very existence, was for Hemingway the ultimate competitive struggle. He particularly enjoyed the exhilarating pleasure of absolute victory: "re-taking France and especially Paris made me feel the best I have ever felt. Ever since I had been a boy [in 1918] I had been in retreats, holding attacks, retreats, victories with no reserves to follow them up, etc., and I have never known how winning can make you feel." He achieved tremendous satisfaction after overcoming obstacles by heroic will, a transfiguring exaltation after passing through a dangerous storm of steel: "I think there is a steady renewal of immortality through storms, attacks, landings on beaches where landing is opposed, flying, when there are problems and many other things which are all awful and horrible and hateful to those who are not suited to them. These things make a katharsis which is not a pathological thing, nor a seeking after thrills, but it is an ennobling thing to those who are suited for them and have the luck so that they survive them."

TWENTY-EIGHT

MEN AT WAR

Hemingway's 1,100-page military anthology *Men at War* (1942)—published in his lean decade between *For Whom the Bell Tolls* (1940) and Colonel Cantwell's bitter memories of war in *Across the River and Into the Trees* (1950)—has received very little attention. But its contents and his Introduction reveal not only his wide knowledge of military history but also how his personal experience and literary taste influenced his attitude to war.

Hemingway had always been fascinated by war, which inspired the greatest material for his fiction. But this job was unusual; it gave him little satisfaction and insufficient control over the finished product. On August 25, 1942, just after completing it, Hemingway complained to his old friend Evan Shipman, then serving as a private in an armored unit: "I have edited an anthology of best writing on War from Caesar and Xenophon down. It goes over a thousand pages and was a godawful job." Even the Introduction he was asked to write had problems. Crown publishers "insisted on an Introduction of ten thousand words and over. I can say anything I want to say in from 200 to 2000 so Introduction probably not so good."

It's surprising, after capturing Hemingway and exploiting his prestige, that Crown did not defer to his literary reputation and superior judgment. He had to fight for the inclusions and exclusions he wanted, and write a much longer Introduction than he thought necessary. It was a tedious exercise that left him scant time for more important work. Weary of fighting over the contents with the publishers and eager to get back to his own fiction, Hemingway wanted to finish the job. Uncharacteristically, he submitted to the publisher's demands.

He referred to Nat Wartels, the Crown chairman, when he told Max Perkins about the difficulties of the project and his relief that it was done: "It is a fine feeling to have that Wartels book finally off our hands, but I wish you would have thought of it so that we could have done it together. It would have been a much more pleasant experience and we could have made a pot of money. I don't know whether it could have been a better book because we fought it out with them on all questions of taste." Hemingway probably didn't get paid for this patriotic work and, with no copyright acknowledgments, the publisher didn't seem to pay for extracts from living authors.

Perkins told Hemingway that Crown publishers "haven't a very high standing, but are perfectly reputable, and publish large collections and sell them at a low price relatively and *merchandise* them." Crown brought out *Men at War* on October 22, priced at three dollars and with a large first printing of 22,500 copies. The book sold well and on December 13, 1942 reached first place on the *New York Times Book Review* bestseller list.

Hemingway got useful advice about the contents from Perkins, Colonel Charles Sweeny and Marine Lt.-Col. John Thomason. Thomason was Chief of Naval Intelligence for Central America in World War II, when Hemingway was living in Cuba. Sweeny's Hemingway-titled *Moment of Truth* (1942) appeared too late to be included. Hemingway did not know Thomason well and misspelled his name in a letter to Perkins. He called Thomason's *Fix Bayonets* (1926) "very juvenile," but included four excerpts from it and from *Lone Star Preacher* (1941), no doubt strongly recommended by Thomason himself. His nearest rivals, each with three entries, were Tolstoy, Hemingway and the American journalist Marquis James.

The anthology contains sixty-three authors and eighty-two entries of fiction, history and memoirs, but no poetry. It has works from the Hebrew Bible, Greek, Latin, French, Spanish and German; from Xenophon and Caesar through Stendhal, Victor Hugo, Guy de Maupassant and William Faulkner, to accounts of the recent attack on Pearl Harbor and the American triumph in the Battle of Midway in June 1942. Hemingway also included the work of several friends: the war correspondent Alan Moorehead, the playwright Laurence Stallings and the satirist Dorothy Parker. The other women in the book were Charlotte Yonge, Mary Johnstone and Agnes Smedley. The many nonentities damaged the book that was not, as the subtitle boasted, "The Best War Stories of All Time."

The publisher thanked the editor and anthologist William Kozlenko for devising a plan that was actually very poor and should have been rejected. The selections are carelessly arranged by eight vague, overlapping themes. Admitting that the structure was weak, Hemingway writes in the Introduction: "the material has not been grouped chronologically but is rather placed under certain arbitrary heads and divisions. . . . Since all the selections deal with war, many of them would fit as well under one head as under another." The second section, for example, confuses the reader by leaping wildly from the American Civil War; naval action in World War I; the history of Rome; back to the Civil War; the biblical David and Goliath; the Spanish Civil War; the medieval King Arthur; the infantry in World War I; Thermopylae in 480 BC; Confederate soldiers, World War I and Oliver Cromwell; and the Alamo—all randomly collected under the heading "Danger and Courage."

There's no real difference, for example, between "War is the Province of Uncertainty" and "War is the Province of Chance"; and the last section heading, "War is Fought by Human Beings," is obvious and otiose. Each section begins with a long quote from Carl von Clausewitz's *On War* (1832), which is not directly related to the contents and is too general to be effective. A great many minor works, two of them anonymous, should have been deleted—how fast reputations, like those of many Nobel Prize winners, have disappeared—and replaced by superior pieces such as Isaac Babel's *Red Cavalry* (1926), Robert Graves' *Good-Bye to All That* (1929) and George Orwell's *Homage to Catalonia* (1938).

The anthology would also have been greatly improved if the entries had been arranged chronologically according to the dates of the battles. All works by the same author should have been placed together instead of being separated by unrelated entries. As Perkins told him, "those two Tolstoi pieces have almost perfect unity." If the text were much shorter and more readable, there could have been brief introductions to each author and entry, with publication dates and (where applicable) translators.

Hemingway's twenty-page Introduction, one of his most important essays, discusses the purpose of the anthology, the best entries, and his personal concept of truth and courage in war. He dedicates the book to his sons, aged eleven to nineteen, and directly addressing the reader, sheds light on the biographical context: "This introduction is written by a man who has three sons to whom he is responsible. Therefore, be pleased to regard this introduction as absolutely personal rather than impersonal writing. The book will contain truth about war as near as we can come by it, which was lacking to me when I needed it most."

Personal factors influenced the making of *Men at War*. The suicide of his father in 1928 damaged Hemingway's view of his father's manliness and his own self-image. His need to prove his courage in combat propelled him toward violence and self-destruction. Five serious accidents and concussions ruined his health, and affected his thinking and writing. He was unhappily estranged from his third wife, Martha Gellhorn, who'd left him to report the war in Europe, and felt compelled to follow and compete with her.

Winston Churchill, whose entry described his 1898 cavalry charge at Omdurman in the Sudan, declared "nothing in life is so exhilarating as to be shot at without result." But Hemingway, dangerously involved in five wars, had been hit by shell fragments while serving on the Italian front. He had reported wars in Turkey, Spain and China. He claimed to have hunted German submarines in the Caribbean—more of a lark than a threat—and soon became a grenade-throwing combatant before reporting the war against Germany.

He recalls his naive teenage belief in the Great War: "When you go to war as a boy you have a great illusion of immortality." But he was wounded, and quotes his favorite speech from Shakespeare's *Henry IV, Part 2*, which is also quoted by Frederic Manning. Alluding to "Chink" Dorman-Smith, whom he met in Milan in 1918, he writes: "[I had] the feeling of having a permanent protecting talisman when a young British officer I met when in the hospital first wrote out for me, so that I could remember them, these lines: 'a man can die but once; we owe God a death . . . and let it go which way it will, he that dies this year is quit for the next.'"

Insisting on the truth about war, Hemingway praises (without naming) the great German general Erwin Rommel: "one of the great advantages, in the tank warfare in North Africa, which the Germans have held, is that their Commander in Chief has always been up with the tanks to see that his orders have been carried out." He also describes the dark side of war: "The Axis would be happy and contented if we made no criticism and simply gloried in the valor of our soldiers, no matter what results were produced by that undeniable valor." He therefore included two entries from Richard Hillary's *Falling Through Air* (1942), with his shocking descriptions of being horribly burned in his airplane cockpit in September 1940 and the series of ghastly operations on his charred face. After his book was published and praised, and while he was still an invalid, the reckless Hillary was allowed to fly. In January 1943 he lost control of his plane and died in a crash.

The publisher does not identify the author called "Private 19022" as the Australian writer Frederic Manning. He does not state that in *Her Privates We* (1930), an expurgated version of Manning's *The Middle Parts of Fortune* (1929), the soldiers' realistic use of obscene words had been deleted. Hemingway admires Manning as a truthful touchstone and moral guide, and calls his work "the finest and noblest book of men in war that I have ever read. I read it over once each year to remember how things really were so that I will never lie to myself nor to anyone else about them."

The anthology appeared just before the crucial Allied victories—the British at El Alamein in North Africa, the Russians at Stalingrad—that turned the tide of war at the end of 1942. At the time it was compiled the prospect of victory seemed bleak. While Hemingway insisted on the value of truthful reporting, he wanted the book to explain the current war, increase morale, inspire the will to fight and be a "good weapon." He exclaims, "We must win this war at all costs and as soon as possible" and suggests what must be done: "The greatest danger that the allied cause faces is the possible disillusion of the people of China and Russia in regard to their allies. China must have aid in greatly increasing amounts." He wanted to use André Malraux's great novel *Man's Fate* (1933) and explains that he could not negatively portray a wartime ally. Malraux's hero is "waiting to be burned alive with some two hundred of his comrades after the suppression by Chiang Kai-shek of a Communist revolt. This is a marvelous piece of writing and would have been included in this book if we had not been at war and if Generalissimo Chiang Kai-shek had not been one of our allies."

Hemingway's most shocking statement, to excite hatred of the enemy and exact revenge, was made before medical experiments in the Nazi extermination camps became known. He suggests that after the Allied victory the best way to avoid future wars with endlessly belligerent Germany "can probably only be done by sterilization. This act can be accomplished by an operation little more painful than vaccination and as easily made compulsory. All members of Nazi party organizations should be submitted to it if we are ever to have a peace that is anything more than a breathing space between wars." With no volunteers, it would be difficult to choose the right victims. This half-serious statement, along with his criticism of the Germans and praise of the Russians, was deleted in Cold War reprints.

Despite the value he places on truth, Hemingway dismisses the element of high-minded persuasion: "The part this book can play in the winning of this war is to furnish certain information from former times. . . . This collection of stories, accounts and narratives is an attempt to give a true picture of men at war. It is not a propaganda book. It seeks to instruct and inform rather than to influence anyone's opinion. Its only and absolute standard for inclusion has been the soundness and truth of the material. . . . This book will tell you how all men from the earliest times we know have fought and died. . . . So learn about the human heart and the human mind in war from this book."

Hemingway's lifelong credo was that "a writer's job is to tell the truth. His standard of fidelity to the truth should be so high that his invention, out of his experience, should produce a truer account than anything factual can be." He had quarreled bitterly with his old friend John Dos Passos about the Loyalists' execution of Dos' comrade and translator during the Spanish Civil War. He now repays Dos Passos by excluding his novel *Three Soldiers* (1922) and criticizing it as untruthful: "on rereading it did not stand up. Try to read it yourself and you will see what I mean. The dialogue rings false and the actual combat is completely unconvincing."

Hemingway discusses three of the finest selections from a literary as well as an historical point of view. Stendhal, part of the French army that invaded Russia in 1812, described Napoleon's 1815 defeat in *The Charterhouse of Parma* (1837). Hemingway thinks "the best account of actual human beings behaving during a world shaking event is Stendhal's picture of young Fabrizio at the battle of Waterloo. You will have seen a small piece of war as closely and as clearly with Stendhal as any man has ever written of it. It is the classic account of a routed army."

Tolstoy fought as an artillery officer in the Crimean War in 1854. Disputing Tolstoy's belief that historical forces are greater than powerful leadership, Hemingway notes that in *War and Peace* (1867), Tolstoy "took one of the few really great generals of the world and, inspired by a mystic nationalism, tried to show that this general, Napoleon, did not truly intervene in the direction of his battles but was simply a puppet at the mercy of forces completely beyond his control. Yet when he was writing of the Russians, Tolstoy showed in the greatest and truest detail how the operations were directed. His hatred and contempt for Napoleon make the only weakness in that great book of men at war."

Hemingway includes the entire text of Crane's *The Red Badge of Courage* (1895), which at 90 pages is by far the longest entry in the book. Stendhal and Tolstoy had first-hand experience in war; Crane did not. Hemingway says, "Crane wrote it before he had ever seen any war. But he had read the contemporary accounts, had heard the old soldiers, they were not so old then, talk, and above all he had seen Mathew Brady's wonderful photographs. Creating his story out of this material he wrote that great boy's dream of war that was to be truer to how war is than any war the boy who wrote it would ever live to see. It is one of the finest books of our literature."

His most important statement concerns what Samuel Johnson in *Rasselas* called "the dangerous prevalence of imagination." Hemingway believes that thinking, anticipating fears, and morbid imagining about being captured, wounded or killed, can be fatal in battle. A soldier is more likely to survive in battle by combining careful training with instinct and impulse. He adopted this idea from two classic novels that were published shortly before and after he was born. As Henry Fleming goes into combat in *Red Badge*, Crane writes: "A little panic-fear grew in his mind. As his imagination went forward to a fight, he saw hideous possibilities. He contemplated the lurking menaces of the future, and failed in an effort to see himself standing stoutly in the midst of them."

In Joseph Conrad's *Lord Jim* (1900), Captain Brierly describes Jim having too much imagination just before he commits a cowardly act and jumps from his ship: "the matter was no doubt of the gravest import, one of those trifles that awaken ideas—start into life some thought with which a man unused to such a companionship finds it impossible to live." Echoing these beliefs in the Introduction, Hemingway expresses one of his most significant ideas: "Cowardice, as distinguished from panic, is almost always simply a lack of ability to suspend the functioning of the imagination. Learning to suspend your imagination and live completely in the very second of the present minute with no before and no after is the greatest gift a soldier can acquire." In his chapter on Hemingway in *The Wound and the Bow* (1941), Edmund Wilson shrewdly observed, "his heroes are almost always defeated physically, nervously, practically: their victories are moral ones."

TWENTY-NINE

GENERALS

Hemingway was never a soldier but had a lifelong fascination with war, battles, killing, wounds and death. As a teenager in World War I he was seriously wounded by shrapnel. Later on he reported on wars in Turkey, Spain and China. In World War II he went on government-authorized sub-hunting expeditions in Cuban waters, and accompanied American forces in France and Germany. He was one of the first American war correspondents to enter Paris and proudly claimed to have liberated the Ritz Hotel.

In Europe, Hemingway had what he called a good war, and portrayed it as the greatest outdoor sport, an extension of the hunting he had pursued all his life. In *Death in the Afternoon* (1932) he described the matador's godlike power over life and death. Just as he felt he had the right to glorify or criticize the bullfighters in this book, so later on he came to believe that his dangerous combat experience gave him the right to judge, even condemn, many military leaders. He began to see himself as a general *manqué*, a commander of men in battle. Most of all he worshipped courage and the display of courage; any performance that fell short of his heroic ideal disappointed and angered him. The advance on Paris, the battle of Hürtgen Forest, and the Allied victory were the high points of his enjoyment of war. Soon after these excitements and triumphs he wrote enthusiastic and admiring war dispatches and private letters about the most prominent American generals, many of them his close contemporaries. Yet a few years later, he has changed his mind completely, most notably in *Across the River* (1950). His canting hero Richard Cantwell, a retired soldier, expresses Hemingway's bitter disillusionment about what he had seen in World War II. It is worth exploring Hemingway's extreme change of heart.

Hemingway was ambivalent, even contradictory, about most military leaders. In a dispatch of January 27, 1923, he admired "that old, bald-headed, perhaps a little insane but thoroughly sincere, divinely brave swashbuckler, Gabriele D'Annunzio." In World War I this major Italian writer (1863–1938) fought with the elite *Arditi* shock troops and dropped propaganda pamphlets on a dangerous flight over Vienna. Defying the decision of the Versailles conference in 1919, he captured the Adriatic city of Fiume and held it for more than a year. Though a rival of Mussolini, his ideas influenced the theatrical aspects of Italian fascism. In *Across the River* Cantwell praises D'Annunzio's military exploits in the air and on land and sea as well as his poem about his temporary blindness after an air crash. But he also puts the knife in at the end: "writer, poet, national hero, phraser of the dialectic of Fascism, macabre egotist, aviator, commander, or rider, in the first of the fast torpedo attack boats, Lieutenant Colonel of Infantry without knowing how to command a company, nor a platoon properly, the great, lovely writer of *Notturno* whom we respect, and jerk"—by which he means presumptuous and annoying.

In letter of July 23, 1945 (two months after V-E Day) to Max Perkins, who would never dare challenge his *Diktats*, Hemingway patriotically praised the American victors: "Eisenhower has a hell of a good head and is a fine man. . . . Bradley a much better General. I think probably as good as [the Civil War general William Tecumseh] Sherman. Patton, if not such an impossible histrionic character and an unmitigated liar is an excellent General officer." But only five years later, when the glory began to fade—though Eisenhower would be elected president in 1952—Hemingway felt obliged to diminish their extraordinary achievements and cut them all down to size. Omar Bradley (1893–1981) was demoted to "the schoolmaster." Eisenhower (1890–1969) belonged with the provincial American Methodist Youth Organization and was "strictly Epworth League. . . . An excellent politician. Political General. Very able at it."

The tactical speed and aggressive action, the colorful character and reckless bravado of George Patton (1885–1945), enhanced by his pearl-handled pistol, should have appealed to Hemingway. Despite his death in a car crash in December 1945, he too had to be pulled off his self-created pedestal. Hemingway's letters help explain his irrational hostility to Patton. Writing to General Raymond Barton on June 9, 1948, he diminished Patton by using a childish form of his first name and employing a football metaphor to describe the delayed breakout after the invasion of Normandy. Few battles were "more balled up than one of Georgie Patton's columns held up by two burp guns [machine pistols] before the Great End Run" to Paris. Patton's egoism and self-glorification were too close to Hemingway's own character. In *Across the River* Hemingway described, with a mild qualifier, "Georgie Patton who possibly never told the truth in his life." In a letter to Charles Scribner of September 9, 1950, Hemingway, awarding Patton an ironic title, invented his own untruthful statement. His allegation, based on scandalous gossip and far-fetched hearsay that extended over three generations, claimed that "the daughter of some one I know [had a] daughter allegedly raped by the Hon. Georgie Patton when she was a child."

Hemingway's hostility to three other generals—the American Walter Bedell Smith, the French Philippe Leclerc and the English Bernard Law Montgomery—was provoked by personal grudges. Smith (1895–1961) was Eisenhower's chief of staff in North Africa, Italy and Western Europe from 1942 to 1945, and later became ambassador to Russia and head of the CIA. Hemingway witnessed Smith's misguided briefing about a battle in northwest Germany. Though Smith was confident and reassuring, the high-casualty combat turned out to be much fiercer than expected. In *Across the River* Hemingway contrasted with heavy irony the difference between planning staff and combat troops: "General Walter Bedell Smith explained to all of us how easy the operation that later took the name of Hürtgen Forest would be. . . . So after I had the privilege of hearing General Walter Bedell Smith explain the facility of the attack, we made it." Hemingway completely identified with the troops sent into battle and included himself in the "we."

Leclerc (1902–1947) came from an aristocratic family that had taken part in the Crusades and was educated at Saint-Cyr military academy. He fought in the North African campaign, landed in Normandy under Patton, and liberated Paris and Strasbourg. He died in a plane crash in Algeria and was posthumously elevated to Marshal of France. Hemingway tangled with Leclerc in Rambouillet in August 1944. Ahead of the regular army, Hemingway led a private group of Free French partisans into the town and held it for a day after the Germans had retreated. He gathered useful intelligence, made judicial decisions about captured Germans, conducted counterespionage operations, and competed with both reporters and the French army. The Americans held back to let the French, for political reasons, be the first to liberate Paris. Hemingway's interference with this high-level plan could have caused serious friction between the Allies. The American authorities investigated his wild behavior but, to avoid bad publicity, did not punish him. Any other correspondent would have lost his credentials and been sent home in disgrace.

Leclerc was furious that Hemingway, violating his status as a war correspondent by using weapons, had interfered with his military objectives and tried to race to Paris before the French army. In a dispatch of October 7, 1944 for *Collier's* magazine, Hemingway described, with heavy irony and inevitable euphemisms, how Leclerc had insulted instead of thanking him: "Never can I describe to you the emotions I felt on the arrival of the armoured column of General Leclerc south-east [*sic*] of Paris. . . . We advanced in some state toward the general. His greeting—unprintable—will live in my ears forever. 'Buzz off, you unspeakables,' the gallant general said. . . . In war, my experience has been that a rude general is a nervous general."

In a letter of June 9, 1948 to General Barton—who would not swallow his stories as readily as Perkins and Scribner—Hemingway falsely claimed that he had cleared Leclerc's path to Paris and saved the lives of many French soldiers: "the work I did about Rambouillet laying out everything so Leclerc (am glad that prick is dead) went in on a dime where it would have cost him at least $8.95." In *Across the River*, rhyming "Leclerc" and "jerk," "dead" and "said" for comic effect, Hemingway-Cantwell concedes Leclerc's bravery before condemning him as he did D'Annunzio: "Leclerc was a high-born jerk as I think I've explained. Very brave, very arrogant, and extremely ambitious. He is dead, as I said." In a mean-minded and vindictive passage that exposed the negative side of his character he also claimed, using a jewelry metaphor and snobbishly specifying his champagne, that Leclerc tried to diminish the American victory by using and wasting American ammunition to make his limited triumph seem more significant: "The people of Leclerc, another jerk of the third or fourth water, whose death I celebrated with a magnum of Perrier-Jouet Brut 1942, shot a great number of rounds to make it seem important because we had given them what they had to shoot with. But it was not important."

Hemingway poured much of this vitriol into *Across the River*. In this flawed but revealing novel Cantwell's adoring young companion Renata knows nothing and cares nothing about his caustic opinions of the generals. She feigns interest because she cannot stop his obsessive monologues nor challenge his savage outbursts. Like Desdemona with Othello, another foreign soldier in

Venice, she loves him for the dangers he had passed, and he loves her that she did pity them. Cantwell says, "You wouldn't understand the campaigns." Renata submissively replies, "I only want what you will tell me."

Hemingway's denigration of Montgomery (1887–1976) in letters and in the novel, was closely connected to his adoration of another military hero, Captain Eric Edward "Chink" Dorman-Smith of the Fifth Northumberland Fusiliers, whom he had met on November 3, 1918 in Milan as he recovered from his wounds. Chink (1895–1969) had gone from Sandhurst to the front at Mons, Belgium, and commanded a battalion at Passchendaele. He'd been wounded three times and won the Military Cross at Ypres for conspicuous gallantry under fire. Six feet tall and very thin, he had blue eyes, black hair and a clipped moustache. Gentle, quiet, introspective and intellectual, he could be both charming and caustic. Hemingway called him "my best friend."

In a letter of May 2, 1950, four months before *Across the River* was published, he wildly exaggerated the number of his own victims, punned (in the last word) on Monty's middle name and told the famously reticent Chink that he wanted to kill the British commander: "In this next book I speak rather irreverently of the good Monte. . . . I have it completely accurate and straight now that [I] have killed 122 (armed not counting possible or necessary shootings) and this Monte still escapes one. There should be a law." A distinguished military historian observed that "Montgomery was deliberate, a cautious calculator of hazard and advantage, prone to overinsurance. . . . Montgomery thus refused battle, where possible, unless the odds were highly favourable. . . . He never fought an unsuccessful battle" and turned the tide of war by defeating Rommel in North Africa.

Hemingway admired the dashing but defeated Rommel much more than the cautious but triumphant Monty, who seemed to take unfair advantage of the enemy with overwhelming manpower and superior weapons, and achieved only lopsided victories. On April 15, 1950 Hemingway told his military friend Buck Lanham that the British "had Rommel beaten when he could not take Alexandria [in Egypt] and they were just recuperating and getting ready to run him out on a cheap basis when in comes Monty with his 14/1 or I won't move concept of war. Chink says that when Monty taught tactics at the war college his only conception was to break a hazel nut with a sledge hammer."

Hemingway repeated this charge in *Across the River* when Cantwell, alluding to the North African desert and equating the ratio of gin to vermouth with

Monty's advantage over Rommel, orders "two very dry Martinis. . . . Montgomerys. Fifteen to one." Though every general has to create a heroic public persona—the physically thin Monty wore a distinctive beret—Cantwell then explains to the glassy-eyed Renata:

> "Monty was a character who needed fifteen to one to move, and then moved tardily. . . . He was not [a great general]. The worst part was he knew it. I have seen him come into a hotel and change from his proper uniform into a crowd-catching kit to go out in the evening to animate the populace." . . .
>
> "But he beat General Rommel."
>
> "Yes. And you don't think any one else had softened him up? And who can't win with fifteen to one?"

Hemingway ignores the obvious point that one object of war is to defeat the enemy while sustaining the minimum number of casualties.

In a moment of rare insight Cantwell admits that he criticizes the universally admired heroes of the war—Patton, Leclerc and Montgomery—because "I have failed and I speak badly of all who had succeeded." His caustic references to Monty are actually central to the meaning of the novel. Monty had adopted Chink's battle plan of July 1942, which provided the "blueprint" for his first success in North Africa at the battle of Alam Halfa in September. The fascinating story of how Chink "softened up" Rommel explains why Hemingway denigrated Monty's achievement, attacked him in the novel for sartorial showmanship and criticized him for delaying the capture of Paris during the famous battle south of Caen in Normandy in the summer of 1944: "[Monty] was unable to close, even, the gap at Falaise and found the going rather sticky and could not quite get there on time."

Hemingway's heroes, by contrast, included two German and two American generals. In *Across the River* he cryptically wrote, "Ernst Udet I liked the best." His namesake (three years older than Hemingway), an ace pilot in World War I, was unjustly blamed for the defeat of the Luftwaffe in the Battle of Britain and killed himself in 1941. His suicide was concealed from the German people and he was praised as a war hero who died in a plane crash.

Identifying with Rommel (1891–1944), Cantwell tells Renata, "when I was a boy, I fought against Erwin Rommel half way from Cortina to the Grappa, where we held." But Cantwell's experience fighting the Austrians in the Italian Alps does not match Hemingway's. As a young officer Rommel had fought the Italians on the Isonzo Front and the Piave River from October to December 1917. Hemingway was wounded on that Front, six months later, in July 1918. In July 1944, after the failure of the plot to kill Hitler, Rommel, who had opposed Hitler's disastrous military policies, was forced to commit suicide. As with Udet, his suicide was hidden and the public was told that he died of a heart attack. W. H. Auden had famously said, "History to the defeated / May say Alas but cannot help nor pardon." Cantwell chivalrously questions the status of the defeated when the puzzled Renata elicits his illuminating response:

> "Did you really like Rommel?"
> "Very much."
> "But he was your enemy."
> "I love my enemies, sometimes more than my friends."

It is ironic that after surviving many battles, five of Hemingway's twelve generals died violent deaths. D'Annunzio was murdered by the fascists. Patton and Leclerc died in car and in plane crashes. Udet committed suicide and Rommel was forced to kill himself to avoid a show trial and the severe punishment of his family. Always troubled by his own suicidal urges, Hemingway felt a deep kinship with Udet and Rommel.

Hemingway admired "Lightning Joe" Lawton Collins (1896–1987) who took part in the Normandy invasion and fought in France and Germany until the enemy surrendered in May 1945. In *Across the River* Hemingway listed the qualities he valued and wrote, "Lightning Joe was a good one. Very good. . . . Commanded the Seventh Corps when I was there. Very sound. Rapid. Accurate. Now chief of staff."

After his adventures in Rambouillet and the liberation of Paris, Hemingway was embedded with Buck Lanham's 22nd Infantry Regiment for four weeks, entered Germany with the first American tanks on September 12, and covered the heavy fighting around the fortified Siegfried Line and the Hürtgen Forest. In his dispatch of November 18, 1944 Hemingway coyly called Lanham (1902–1978) "the Colonel" instead of naming him. He quoted Lanham encouraging his regiment, the first to crack the Siegfried Line, with the Hemingwayesque exhortation, "Goddam, let's go get these Krauts!"

In his greatest tribute, Hemingway extolled his friend as "one of the finest, most skillful, and most intelligent infantry officers" he had ever known. Though a gallant soldier, Lanham was old-fashioned, strait-laced, thoroughly conventional, personally unimpressive and surprisingly dull. Hemingway's alter ego was one of his greatest fictional creations. He was idealized to heroic proportions to match Hemingway's urgent need for a wartime comrade who would reflect, confirm, exalt and perpetuate his own martial expertise and daring exploits.

Between 1945 and 1950 Hemingway became embittered and changed his view of several military leaders. He attacked the leading Allied commanders, admired the German enemies, blindly but loyally defended his friends and glorified his own achievements. He feared that his first novel in ten years would be a comparative failure after the tremendous success of *For Whom the Bell Tolls*, and he was right. As the weakening of his creative powers coincided with the growth of his megalomania, he felt the need to topple the wartime idols. His self-serving judgments of the generals, in which personal feelings prevailed over objective facts, fatally weaken his central character. Cantwell is a tragic figure who dies aware of his failure to achieve his goals, but Hemingway cannot persuade us to sympathize with him. His great war novels, *A Farewell to Arms* and *For Whom the Bell Tolls*, described romantic and idealized human struggles. *Across the River* describes the death of his old idealism.

THIRTY

FIDEL CASTRO

Hemingway's long involvement with Cuba illuminates the diplomatic relations between the United States and that country. Hemingway lived in Cuba for twenty years and instinctively sympathized with Fidel Castro and the Cuban Revolution. In the spring of 1939, just after the Loyalists had been defeated in the Spanish Civil War, Hemingway's third wife, Martha Gellhorn, found the Finca Vigía (Lookout Farm) in the village of San Francisco de Paula, twelve miles southeast of Havana. The one-story, run-down Spanish colonial house had high ceilings, tile floors, a sixty-foot living room, swimming pool and tennis court. It was surrounded by fifteen sprawling acres and stood on a 468-foot hill that caught the breezes and had a fine view of the lights of the capital.

In a letter of 1952 Hemingway described his Cuban house, routine and habitual diversions: "It is a good place to work because it is out of town and on a hill so that it is cool at night. I wake up when the sun rises and go to work and when I finish I get a swim and have a drink and read the New York and Miami papers. After work you can fish or go bird shooting and in the evening my wife and I read and listen to music." At his favorite bar, La Floridita, he piously covered the bronze bust of himself during Lent. During his years in Cuba he finished *For Whom the Bell Tolls* and wrote *Across the River and Into the Trees*, *The Old Man and the Sea* and the posthumously published *A Moveable Feast* and *Islands in the Stream*.

When Hemingway lived in Cuba the country was ruled by Fulgencio Batista. He had overthrown the government in 1934 and governed by patronage rather than by terror until 1944. He lived in Florida for the next eight years and returned in a coup in 1952. He promised to restore normal conditions after several chaotic years, but became a brutal dictator, repressed the universities and crushed Castro's first attempt to revolt in 1953.

During World War II, Hemingway organized a private spy network, which he jokingly called the Crook Factory, and gathered information about Nazi sympathizers on the island. But in a secret, 124-page report on Hemingway, the FBI—which feared his personal prestige and political power—expressed resentment at his amateur but alarming intrusion into their territory, and unsuccessfully attempted to control and vilify him.

In October 1942 the local FBI agent told J. Edgar Hoover that the American ambassador had granted Hemingway's request "to patrol certain areas where German submarine activity has been reported" and had given him scarce gasoline for this purpose. Hemingway thought that his boat, the *Pilar*, fully manned and heavily armed but disguised for fishing, would attract the attention of a German submarine. The sub would signal the *Pilar* to come alongside in order to requisition supplies of fresh water and food. As the sub approached, Hemingway's men would machine-gun the crew on deck while a Spanish jai alai player would throw a small bomb into the conning tower. Fortunately, for both Hemingway and the Germans, he never actually encountered an enemy submarine.

After reporting the war in Europe in 1944–45, he returned to Cuba with his fourth wife, Mary Welsh. During his years of fame, he won the Pulitzer Prize in 1953 and the Nobel Prize the following year. He gave his gold Nobel medal to the shrine of the national saint, the Virgen de Cobre. On January 1, 1959 Castro seized power and Batista fled to the Dominican Republic. Acknowledging Hemingway's influence, Castro told the English author Kenneth Tynan, "we took *For Whom the Bell Tolls* to the hills with us, and it taught us about guerrilla warfare."

Out of the country at the time, Hemingway had not seen the bloody fighting and the consolidation of power when Batista fled in December 1958. His own house and property had not been harmed. After Castro had ruled for ten months, Hemingway's nostalgic support for the Spanish Left and distaste for Batista's cruel regime inspired a public statement when he flew into the Havana airport on November 3, 1959. The American Embassy reported to the State Department that Hemingway told journalists:

1. He supported the Castro government and all its acts completely, and thought it was the best thing that had ever happened to Cuba.

2. He had not believed any of the information published abroad against Cuba. He sympathized with the Cuban government, and all *our* difficulties.

3. Hemingway emphasized the *our*, and was asked about it. He said that he hoped Cubans would regard him not as a *Yanqui* (his word), but as another Cuban. With that, he kissed the Cuban flag.

In those early days of hope, when Fidel greatly improved schools, hospitals and transport on the island, Hemingway naturally expressed support for the new regime. He told Tynan that he thoroughly approved of Castro and said, "This is a good revolution, an *honest* revolution." In May 1960 Castro won a fishing competition and Hemingway presented him with the prize. When interviewed about Castro, Hemingway contrasted a commonplace uprising in a banana republic to this "real revolution" and stated his admiration for Fidel. In April he compared the Castro government to the Spanish Republic and expressed cautious hope in a letter to a Polish friend: "This is a very pure and beautiful revolution so far—Naturally I do not know how it will come out. But I hope for the best—So far it is what we hoped for, in intent, when they made the Republic in Spain (and which never arrived). I hope things will go well—The people who are being shot deserve it." But he scrupulously paid his American taxes, and remained a United States citizen and patriot. He would not have stayed in Cuba if his presence there hurt American interests.

In July 1960 Hemingway left Cuba for his new home in Ketchum, Idaho. In January 1961, after Castro had nationalized most of the American property on the island, the United States broke off diplomatic relations with Cuba. The disastrous American Bay of Pigs invasion followed in April. A few days after Hemingway's funeral in July 1961, his boat and possessions were expropriated by the Castro regime. Mary explained, "I had a phone call in Ketchum from the Cuban government asking me whether I would consent to donate our home in Cuba as a museum. In exchange I would be allowed to remove all the papers from the Bank and my personal belongings. I accepted. At the time I was so grief-stricken that I didn't care about giving up the house."

The State Department arranged Mary's visit to Cuba that July. She was forced to give up the house. But Castro, who came to the Finca to see Mary, allowed her to keep her clothes and jewelry, twenty-five precious books, paintings by Joan Miró, Juan Gris, Paul Klee and André Masson (a Braque had been stolen in their absence), all of Hemingway's papers and forty pounds of manuscript from the bank vault. The *Pilar* was hauled onto the grounds and the Finca became the Hemingway Museum. In 1972 Mary gave all the surviving papers to the Hemingway Collection in the John F. Kennedy presidential library in Boston.

Hemingway was a shrewd political observer. As early as 1922 he'd interviewed and satirized Mussolini, and had reported five wars. He thought Castro was a welcome change from the repressive Batista regime, and supported the Revolution before Castro had established his own dictatorship, declared himself a Communist and opposed America. If the United States had adopted Hemingway's sympathetic attitude and maintained relations with Cuba instead of trying to overthrow that government and adhering to a policy that has failed for more than fifty years, the people of both countries would have benefited.

THIRTY-ONE

HOLLYWOOD

Hemingway never wrote screenplays, but many of his novels were made into films. His second wife's wealth and his growing success as a writer allowed him to live a flamboyant and adventurous life, fishing for marlin in the Gulf Stream and hunting lions in Africa. Like a film star, he was handsome, glamorous, wealthy, well traveled and much married. His slow destruction and dramatic death traced the pattern of a movie idol's career.

While doing research for my biography of Hemingway I spent a week with his three sons and conducted interviews with his third wife and his sisters, with well-known authors, bullfighters, film directors and screenwriters. But whenever I tried to penetrate the mysteries of Hemingway's relations with film stars, with actresses surrounded by rumors of love affairs with the macho writer, I encountered nothing but frustration and failure.

I had read letters, interviews and memoirs in order to find out everything I could about Hemingway's wide circle of friends. But books on film stars had only brief references to him. I wanted to investigate and describe his relations with actors in the same way I did with his other friends and was not concerned with discovering the "real" Marlene Dietrich. But it was not until I started looking into the lives of these actors that I realized there was no "real" person. They had retired from the world, refused to see anyone and hid their private lives. The lack of substance in printed sources and the total silence from the actors themselves made me wonder if Hemingway's relations with film stars were necessarily superficial, if both actor and author had become frozen in their images and could never get beyond play-acting, narcissism, flattery and mutual exploitation. My approaches to and rejection by Hollywood actors revealed the difficulty of discovering the truth, as opposed to the scandal, about Hemingway and the Hollywood connection. My desire to find the facts and to read Hemingway's letters clashed with their wish to maintain privacy, and inevitably led to a crisp, automatic dismissal.

Hemingway met Marlene Dietrich in March 1934 while sailing back to New York on the *Île de France* after his first African safari. They were genuinely fond of each other, met in Paris and New York, and corresponded during the last decade of his life. He affectionately called her The Kraut and they exchanged public compliments. His flattering "Tribute to Mamma from Papa Hemingway" (*Life*, August 18, 1952) was answered by her banal ghostwritten article, "The Most Fascinating Man I Know" (*This Week*, February 13, 1955). In his posthumous novel *Islands in the Stream*, Hemingway fantasized about sexual relations with Dietrich, the model for the hero's actress-wife. But Lillian Ross' *New Yorker* profile of Hemingway (May 13, 1950) aroused Dietrich's fury by revealing that she used towels from the Plaza Hotel to clean her daughter's house.

My young daughter pronounced her name Díet-rich, with three syllables, and pictured her as a fat lady who stuffed herself with food. I imagined her as a ravaged skeleton, hiding in the shadows of her suite to preserve the faded image of her beauty. It was even difficult to find out her exact date of birth. But Irwin Shaw, who had recently been in touch with her, gave me her address on the Avenue Montaigne in Paris and said I could use his name as an introduction.

When I arrived in Paris I wrote a letter stating my credentials and explaining my serious purpose, walked across the Seine to the Right Bank and in hesitant French asked, pleaded and finally begged the concierge of her well-guarded fortress to present my letter to her. But the uniformed young man (not the crone I had expected) insisted that Dietrich no longer lived in the building and was terribly vague about whether she was in Paris, New York or Los Angeles. He would not accept my letter "in case she suddenly appeared" and was irritated by my awkward persistence. I tried to break the impasse with a series of frantic French gestures, awkwardly chopping up the air with the sides of my hands and blowing out my cheeks in exasperation. I knew he was lying and his hauteur suggested a bribe (but how much?) would be futile, so I reluctantly abandoned my quest. I imagined Dietrich, behind a twitching curtain, watching me slink sadly away.

Hemingway met Ingrid Bergman in San Francisco when he was en route to China in January 1941. He skied with her in Sun Valley, Idaho, in the early

1940s and, though her appearance was extremely Nordic, wanted her to play the Spanish heroine in the film of *For Whom the Bell Tolls* (1943). He was disappointed in the chaste cinematic version of the intensely erotic sleeping-bag scene, in which both lovers were fully clothed, and had some harsh things to say about Roberto Rossellini when the "sweet and good and honest" Bergman ran off with that "22-pound rat."

I'd seen Bergman act on stage in Paris, and in 1974, before I thought of writing Hemingway's life, I dined at the table next to her at the Connaught Hotel in London. She was tall and distinguished-looking, and spoke Swedish with elderly friends who looked like a couple of spooky neurotics from an Ingmar Bergman film. Two days later, when I saw her by chance in Brook Street, wearing a silk scarf and trench coat, the "real" Bergman looked like a well-bred housewife. When Bergman was alive I missed my chance to talk to her. Now that she was dead, I couldn't even see her daughter.

When I wrote to Bergman's last husband, Lars Schmidt, he promptly replied that her actress-daughter, Pia Lindstrom-Daly, had all her letters and he was "sure she will answer you." Technically, she did respond, and sent a postcard with her phone number at NBC. When I came to New York from Colorado, Pia was in Europe. When I wrote again, asking if she would either send me photocopies of Hemingway's letters or allow me to read them in New York, she didn't answer. When I came to New York for the last time before completing my book, she failed to return my call. I never found Pia's home phone number, never met her, never read the Hemingway-Bergman letters.

Hemingway visited Ava Gardner and Luis Miguel Dominguín at his bull ranch near Madrid in the spring of 1954, and later comforted Ava when she was in the hospital for a week trying to pass a painful kidney stone. She had starred in *The Killers* (1946), *The Snows of Kilimanjaro* (1952) and *The Sun Also Rises* (1957). Ava lived in Ennismore Gardens in London, where I was writing the biography. I obtained her address and an introduction from the director Fred Zinnemann. I knew she had been hurt by a particularly nasty article by Rex Reed, who portrayed her as a vulgar alcoholic. So I tried to arouse her interest by mentioning that I had just interviewed Dominguín and hoped she would accept my assurance that I was only seeking information about Hemingway. Her secretary answered, on embossed stationery, rather archly refusing my request for an interview: "I am afraid she will be unable to do so as she does not participate in this form of endeavour." Undaunted, I went round to her house, looking for the famous profile and voluptuous form behind the flickering curtain. While I was hanging about, hoping for a bit of luck, Ava's maid came out to walk her poodle. I asked them a few questions, but the servant responded in an outlandish tongue and I could not get more than a few barks out of the dog. A photograph of Ava and Dominguín appears in my book, and I sometimes look at it longingly.

Patricia Neal had visited Hemingway's Finca Vigía in Havana in 1950 to gain some privacy during her affair with Gary Cooper. I tried to convince her (as I'd tried to convince Ava) that I was not interested in her sexual liaison, but her impressions of Hemingway's friendship with Cooper. In order to encourage her response I mentioned that her novelist-husband Roald Dahl, who had known Hemingway in London in 1944, had sent me a friendly reply. Why didn't she follow his splendid example? I learned only later that they were divorced in 1983. It was terribly hard to keep up with the private lives of actors.

The minor actress Beverly Bentley had been part of Hemingway's entourage at Pamplona in the late 1950s and was a friend of Hemingway's son Gregory. She had once been married to Norman Mailer, who had written an introduction to Gregory's book about his father. Though I received an extremely interesting response from Mailer, as I had from Roald Dahl, Bentley did not bother to reply.

The most tantalizing of all the Hollywood women was Nancy "Slim" Hawks Hayward, who had known Hemingway in Key West in the 1930s, visited him in Cuba and fished on the *Pilar*, and nearly blown his head off in a hunting accident in 1946. Slim had discovered Lauren Bacall, who starred in *To Have and Have Not* (screenplay by William Faulkner). Like Nancy and Howard Hawks in real life, Bacall and Bogart called each other Slim and Steve in the film. Hemingway's fourth wife, Mary, said that Slim was one of Hemingway's "admired and admiring girl friends," and felt that Slim threatened her marriage. Many friends believed that Hemingway was in love with Slim and may have had an affair with her.

Slim, who lived around the corner from Mary in Manhattan, fired my interest and frustration by writing: "I do have a great many letters from Ernest Hemingway. However they are of a very personal nature and I would not at all be disposed to making them available to stranger. . . . So I am afraid I can be of no help to you." I fantasized about applying for a job as her butler and reading the letters when she was out of the house. In desperation I wrote to her last husband, Lord Keith, who said, "I regret that I cannot be of much help to you as I have not seen my former wife for some twelve years—and Hemingway was, I think, dead before I met her."

Orson Welles recorded the script of *The Spanish Earth* (1937), the documentary film Hemingway and Joris Ivens made about the Spanish Civil War. But Welles' delivery was considered too theatrical, so he was replaced by Hemingway himself and became the voice on the recording-room floor. In *Cahiers du Cinema* (5: 1966), Welles provided an absurdly fanciful account of how he bear-baited and scuffled with Hemingway during the recording session. But Welles proved as mysterious, elusive and difficult to find as the Third Man. My letters came winging back from the canyons of New York and Los Angeles, and I never found out where he was until after his death.

Hemingway's most significant friendship was with Gary Cooper, the son of a judge from Montana, whom he met while hunting and skiing in Sun Valley in the autumn of 1940. Cooper starred in the first version of *A Farewell to Arms* (1932) and in *For Whom the Bell Tolls*. Hemingway thought Cooper was "a fine man: as honest and straight and friendly and unspoiled as he looks." But he later criticized Cooper's love of money and conversion to Catholicism. In May 1961, when he was dying of cancer, Cooper told Hemingway, "I bet I make it to the barn before you do." He kept his word and died on May 13, less than two months before Hemingway killed himself.

After my biography was in the press, I traced Cooper's widow and daughter through the Academy of Motion Picture Arts and Sciences and received a charming letter from Maria Cooper (who was married to the pianist Byron Janis) suggesting I phone her mother. I was not sure, without my notes, if Cooper's widow was the same woman who had known Hemingway in Sun Valley and tactfully decided not to mention Patricia Neal. She was indeed the one and only Rocky. Though she did not tell me anything new about Hemingway's friendship with Cooper, she made some sharp comments about Martha Gellhorn. Rocky thought she had letters from Hemingway, but had no idea where they were.

My best informant was Henry Fonda's fourth wife, Afdera Franchetti, a lifelong friend of Hemingway's Italian love Adriana Ivancich. Though Afdera forgot our appointment and was asleep when I arrived, she soon woke up, talked like a rocket and confirmed (as I had suspected) that Adriana's suicide in 1983 was connected to her involvement with Hemingway in 1950.

The biographer, like the journalist, is inevitably a suppliant—waiting for letters or hanging on the end of a phone—subject to the whims and rudeness of his informants. My long round of refusals and rejections revealed the implacable opposition between the scholar's and the star's point of view. These actors did not have much interest in or place much value on documents, facts or the biographer's quest. They had no clear conception of what I was trying to do, and my reputation as a scholar and writer meant nothing to them. They could not understand why I wanted to talk to them about *someone else*—even someone as famous as Hemingway. They were famous and wealthy, wanted to protect their privacy and wished to hide, rather than reveal, the truth. They could not be bothered to distinguish between a serious literary study and a superficial Hollywood biography that wavered between idealized fantasy and sensational scandal.

Actors, whose tender egos are frequently hurt by the press, were naturally wary of interviews. Their publicity value was so great and so marketable that they could not conceive of a scholarly inquiry. They did not trust introductions, even from their friends, so it was extremely difficult to break into their remote, hermetic existence. They were creatures of fantasy and often inhabited a fantastic world. The once-beautiful women did not want to expose their aged faces to a writer. They had no disinterested motives themselves and could not credit me with having them. Since I was not writing publicity for them, they had nothing to gain from talking to me and refused to answer my letters or grant an interview. I was merely another member of the clamorous public, forever beating on their doors. If everyone had responded as selfishly as the actors did, it would have been impossible to complete my book.

It is highly ironic that Hemingway and the Hollywood images have now merged. When people heard I was writing Hemingway's biography, they frequently asked, "did you meet his daughters?" In fact, Margaux and Mariel—named for a French wine and Cuban port—are Hemingway's *grand*-daughters. But they looked remarkably like him and continued, as models and movie stars, the glamorous Hemingway tradition.

THIRTY-TWO

JOHN HUSTON

Andrew Sarris called Huston "a Hemingway character lost in a Dostoyevsky novel." Norman Mailer—who portrayed Huston as Charles Eitel in *The Deer Park* (1955)—observed that he is "the only celebrated film artist to bear comparison with Hemingway. His life celebrates a style more important to him than film." In an interview Huston said of Hemingway, "I was very influenced by his writing and by his thinking. . . . His values, his reassessment of the things that make life go." These suggestive statements merely hint at the striking parallels between the two men. Both sought to live a life filled with the action, adventure and romance they created in their work. Keen sportsmen who courted danger and took risks, they enjoyed early success, cultivated a Byronic persona and knew the satisfactions of celebrity and the perils of fame. Hemingway's character, virile ethos and code of honor strongly influenced Huston, whose best films can be thematically defined by Hemingway's titles: *Men Without Women* and *Winner Take Nothing*.

Both Hemingway and Huston had grandfathers who fought with the Union army in the Civil War, and both men were born in the Midwest at the turn of the century: Hemingway in 1899, Huston in 1906. Their mothers had dominant personalities and professional careers. Both men refused to attend college, set out to learn from direct experience in the world, lived in Paris in their twenties and began their writing careers as journalists. Both were enthusiastic about Latin culture: Hemingway about Spain and tropical Cuba, Huston about tropical Mexico, where he made four movies and spent the last years of his life.

Both were powerful boxers in their youth and in later life. Hemingway's opponents included Ezra Pound, William Carlos Williams and the Canadian novelist Morley Callaghan, with Scott Fitzgerald as incompetent timekeeper. The young Huston won twenty-three out of twenty-five amateur bouts, breaking his nose in one of them, and became a ranking California lightweight before abandoning the sport. Both were heavy drinkers, but did not let alcohol interfere with their work.

Huston shared with Hemingway a fascination with cruelty, wounds and death. Hemingway witnessed this on the Italian front. Huston had ridden with Mexican cavalry in his early twenties. Both participated in fierce fighting in World War II in Europe, Hemingway as a war correspondent, Huston as a documentary filmmaker. They enjoyed testing their own courage in difficult situations, and liked to subject their friends to danger to see how they'd react. Their overpowering personalities dominated everyone around them. Hemingway constantly challenged competitors. Huston took great risks with the lives and health of his actors and crew. On separate occasions both men intimidated Tennessee Williams with their aggressive *machismo*.

Hemingway and Huston felt compelled to demonstrate their toughness and strength. Huston followed Hemingway, made his own way through the Master's tumultuous wake and practiced the same dangerous masculine pursuits: bicycle racing, horseback riding (and betting on horses), marlin fishing, bullfighting, hunting elephants and big cats. In December 1954 a friend wrote that the forty-eight-year-old Huston had actually "fought a bull in Madrid, made quite a few good passes and has the photos to prove it."

The Maharajah of Cooch Behar, a bullfight aficionado and friend of Hemingway, organized a tiger hunt in Assam, in the foothills of the Himalayas, for Huston. On August 25, 1955 Huston sent an enthusiastic cable to Clark Gable, a keen hunter, urging him to join their expedition: "Am seizing opportunity and joining Maharajah of Cooch Behar hunt on 18th. This last of great hunts sixty elephants all the trimmings. Only be four guns. One gun still open. Would you like me to make res for you." Gable, confined by a movie contract, was forced to refuse.

After Huston had climbed the ladder to the shooting platform on his elephant, the huge beast (he wrote) "suddenly began to trumpet . . . and out came [the tiger], fast as a flaring bird. . . . As I pulled the trigger, my elephant swayed wildly, throwing me to one side. I fired again, knowing I'd miss, as the yellow-and-black devil darted away into the brush. . . . He'd covered 200 yards in under 10 seconds." Though Huston missed his first shot, he got his second and bagged a tiger that was eight-and-a-half-feet long. In Peter Viertel's novel *White Hunter, Black Heart* (1954), the character based on Huston says that Hemingway's "Francis Macomber experiences the greatest sensation of his life after he has killed his first buffalo. He has overcome fear. We're after those same sensations."

Both men, for all their obsession with courage, danger and the elemental struggles of mankind, had romantic natures and domestic inclinations. Hemingway had four wives, Huston had five (and all five divorced him). Hemingway shot a lion; his fourth wife ate lion; Huston's fifth wife boldly *rode* a lion—and has the photos to prove it. Each married increasingly younger women and, while married, fell in love with a series of women even younger than their wives. Huston, however, was unashamedly promiscuous, while Hemingway was a guilt-ridden serial monogamist. Both had three children and were difficult, demanding and frequently absent fathers. Both owned large houses and retreats from the world, which displayed their trophy wives and hunting trophies, and both were connoisseurs of art and had fine collections of modern paintings. Hemingway had a grand house in Key West, and then the Finca Vigía near Havana, and owned works of art and several valuable bullfight posters. Huston owned St. Clarens, his Georgian mansion in Ireland, where he displayed works by Klee, Gris, Monet, Modigliani, Chaim Soutine and several night-life posters by Lautrec.

The novelist and screenwriter Peter Viertel, their mutual friend, introduced the eccentric and ebullient Huston to Hemingway in May 1948, when Huston was in Havana to make *We Were Strangers* (1949), a movie about Cuban revolutionaries. At the time Viertel was more worried about Huston's reaction than Hemingway's. "I was never quite sure how [Huston] would react in any given situation," Viertel recalled. "I knew he could be violent if provoked." But Huston loved trials, hardships and disasters, and was soon given the chance to test his strength and courage. At first Hemingway challenged him to a boxing match and threatened to "cool" the gangling lightweight. Anticipating Huston's tactics, he said, "With those long arms you might just stand off and keep jabbing me in the nose, mightn't you? Maybe cut me up?" Huston chivalrously replied, "I wouldn't dream of doing that, Papa." But the match did not come off. Mary Hemingway told Huston that Papa was ill and begged him not to fight.

Inevitably the two, so similar in character, engaged in a competitive test.

Hemingway invited Huston and Viertel on his boat, the *Pilar*, where they discussed Havana and war, writing and potential movie deals. Huston shot an iguana, and Hemingway insisted he retrieve it. Huston and Viertel searched for it in the crevices of the rocks and saw some spots of blood, but gave up after forty minutes and swam back to the boat. Though dissatisfied with their inept performance, Hemingway did not send them back. Instead, he himself searched for two more hours, among the rocks and under the blazing sun, put a bullet through its head and brought back the hideous trophy.

It may have seemed pointless, even foolish, to search through burning rocks for a dying iguana instead of enjoying the tropical breeze, cool shade and icy drinks on his boat. But the arduous quest was an important example of Hemingway's personal courage, showy endurance, sense of duty and moral lesson to his younger disciples. In this Day of the Iguana episode, Hemingway also meant to humiliate Huston by showing that he was (though seven years older) a tougher man who lived by his own virile code. In *Green Hills of Africa* (1935), Hemingway justified his passion for hunting when he identified with his wounded prey. He remarked, "I did nothing that had not been done to me. I had been shot and I had been crippled and gotten away."

Huston liked the challenge of shooting his films in distant and difficult locales, and Hemingway's books had drawn him to Africa. The burning of the missionary outpost in *The African Queen* (1951) was filmed in Butiaba, near Lake Albert and Murchison Falls in Uganda, where Hemingway had two plane crashes and was reported dead in January 1954. Hemingway's pilot, Roy Marsh, was the same former RAF officer who'd flown Huston around central Africa. And the *Murchison*, the boat that rescued Hemingway after a plane crash, was the same one that Huston had rented while making *The African Queen*.

Huston always tried to keep in touch. In 1954, amidst his hectic film schedule, he reminded himself: "11:00. Call Papa—Palace Hotel, Madrid." Later that year, on November 21, he congratulated Hemingway on winning the Nobel Prize and mentioned the overwhelming problems on his current picture: "*Moby Dick* is a tough one to make. I have been at the actual shooting four months now and don't see daylight even yet. Misfortunes multiply as we go along; the only thing that hasn't happened yet is for somebody to get killed"—though there were a few close calls. In 1956, when *Moby Dick* was released, an English journalist, sensing the parallels between Hemingway's work and Huston's films, parodied the style of *The Old Man and the Sea* when describing Melville's novel: "He was an old Huston who filmed alone, and he had gone many days now without making a film. . . . 'I fear the Dick of Moby,' the boy said, 'It is difficult to make and will cost many dollars.' 'I do not fear,' said the old Huston, 'I know many tricks and I have faith.'"

On the last day of 1956, Huston suggested meeting for a drink before he started to read *The Old Man and the Sea* (actually, one of Hemingway's worst books): "It seemed to me, before starting one of your finest books, I should talk or anyway have a drink with you. I even imagined that you would consider my not coming to see you a rudeness. . . . In any case, there was no thought in my mind of asking for your help on the screenplay. I mean, I only wanted to come in and get warm." He didn't want to seem as rude as David O. Selznick, who had infuriated Hemingway by failing to stand up when his wife Mary came into the room. But Hemingway did not know that Selznick, in his underwear, had good reason to stay where he was.

Huston was one of the best screenwriters in the business, and Hemingway had never written a screenplay (and was proud of it). But Huston—who deferred to no one but his actor-father, Walter Huston—felt obliged to assume an extremely deferential tone with the hypersensitive novelist and assure him that he was *not* seeking help with a script. Aware of Hemingway's touchiness and competitiveness, and admiring his writing, Huston had a unique relationship with him.

Though they met only a few times and corresponded rarely, Huston (with some exaggeration) claimed that Hemingway "was a very close personal friend of mine." He then nailed down Hemingway's impact: his values, ideals and courage. "I've enormous admiration for Hemingway," he said, "and to my generation he was a great influence. . . . Hemingway laid down a certain set of standards for my time, standards of behavior. He made some effort to describe tastes and the good things of life and put them down on record, evaluating their importance. . . . It was important for a man to be brave and have valor. . . . They influenced my generation to the point of being . . . almost a new religion."

When Hemingway committed suicide, Huston "approved completely." He felt that if Hemingway could not live a heroic life, it was better not to live at all. Best, Huston felt, to die while sane than exist while crazy: "He knew he was on the way out; his mind was gone. Papa had been having persecution complexes, phobias, and life was dreadful for him. He had a moment or two of sanity and killed himself in one of those moments."

Both Hemingway and Huston admired Kipling, a major influence on their work, who taught them a colloquial and laconic, skeptical and stoical, belligerently masculine style. Huston, director of *The Man Who Would Be King*, was repeatedly drawn to a group of intensely masculine writers—Melville, Crane, Kipling and Hemingway—whose adventurous heroes stood at a slight angle to the universe. His early fiction portrayed this type of character, who often reappeared in his films.

Huston's two early boxing stories—"Fool" (March 1929) and "Figures of Fighting Men" (May 1931)—published in H. L. Mencken's prestigious *American Mercury*, were strongly influenced by Hemingway's prose style, bitter stoicism and theme of victory in defeat. In the second story, Huston wrote that "a second-rater dipped his gloves in rosin and rubbed them in the old-timer's eyes during a clinch. His sight was ruined, but his fighting days were not over. Now he showed them he could take it. He became a punching bag in the small clubs. His pretty-boy face was knocked lop-sided. In a few months he was one of the old men of the ring."

The blasphemy at the end of the first story—the idea that Christ and Judas were in cahoots and the Crucifixion was fixed—recalls the blasphemy in Hemingway's playlet, "Today is Friday" (1926), in which three Roman soldiers callously discuss the Crucifixion in a modern idiom. He later made an excellent picture about washed-up boxers, *Fat City* (1972). James Agee, Huston's most perceptive critic, alluded to Hemingway's famous phrase "grace under pressure" and seemed to be talking about the novelist when describing Huston's films: "his movies have centered on men under pressure, have usually involved violence and have occasionally verged on a kind of romanticism about danger."

Most of Huston's films were adaptations of serious novels. As a reader, writer and director with a powerful connection to literature, Huston liked to quote Hemingway's views on writing. "There was no greater feeling in the world," Hemingway said, "than anchoring your words firmly on paper . . . when the words took wing." Comparing Hemingway to his leading contemporary, Huston told the screenwriter of *Under the Volcano* that Hemingway's work was essential to his own filmmaking: "Scott Fitzgerald is not as visceral as Hemingway, who gets you into the scenes, not just into the words." He later added that Hemingway had an uncanny ability to bring scenes and characters to life: "Certain American writers have . . . a peculiar ability to re-create, to make you feel that you are actually present in something. If Hemingway had anything, he had that." This was the great goal of twentieth-century moviemaking: to give the audience an even more intimate and immediate connection with the characters and action on the screen than readers could have with a novel.

Huston specialized in movies about male comradeship during violent conflict: *The Treasure of the Sierra Madre* (1948), *The Red Badge of Courage* (1951), *Moby Dick* (1956), *The Man Who Would Be King* (1975), and *Victory* (1981). Hemingway was also a great admirer of Crane's work and of the coarse-grained texture and white sky of the Mathew Brady photographs that inspired both the novel and Huston's film. *The Killers* (1946), directed by Robert Siodmak, could have been an ordinary film noir but, elevated by the screenplay written by Huston with his friend and longtime collaborator Anthony Veiller, became an important picture. It was the only film based on his work that Hemingway actually liked. In Hemingway's story (which reads like a screenplay) the killers, awaiting the arrival of their victim, taunt and intimidate the workers in a diner with a series of insults that require immediate assent.

In the film version Huston recreated Hemingway's hardened hero, torn between ironic fatalism and despairing courage, who seeks authentic values and adheres to a strict code of honor. *The Killers* opens as the gangsters enter a diner that recalls a classic Edward Hopper painting. They are not smartly dressed, as in the story, but make a lot of menacing wisecracks. The workers, who are frightened and don't understand what's going on, are ironically called "bright boy." The haunted victim, played by Burt Lancaster, is about to be murdered for stealing the gang's money after a successful robbery (rather than for failing to throw a fight and betraying the gamblers, as in the story). Just before his death Lancaster, with stoic resignation, says, "There's nothing I can do about it. . . . Once I did something wrong. . . . I'm through with all that runnin' around." After he's killed, the insurance investigator, played by Edmund O'Brien, discovers through a series of flashbacks the reason for his death.

Huston planned to make another movie based on three Hemingway stories, which would be directed by himself and two Europeans: his mentor William Wyler and his friend Billy Wilder—a strange choice for a work by Hemingway. On July 5, 1954 Huston wrote to his longtime agent, Paul Kohner, "I would be delighted to do either 'Fifty Grand' or 'The Undefeated.' Now it's up to them to make their choices." These stories of courageous losers had a strong appeal. In "Fifty Grand" (1927) an aging boxer bets $50,000 against himself in a hopeless match. He almost wins when he's fouled by a painful low blow, but survives to lose the fight and win his bet. In "The Undefeated" (1925, also in *Men Without Women*) an old wounded bullfighter attempts a comeback in a Madrid night fight. Though tossed twice and gored, he kills the bull on the sixth try and is rushed to the hospital. "'I was going good,' Manuel said weakly. 'I was going great. . . . I didn't have any luck. That was all.'" Though the subject, style and theme of these stories were a perfect match for Huston, the movie—because of complications with the other directors—was never made.

In 1954 Huston also tried to coax Hemingway, who staunchly resisted all temptations from Hollywood (and condemned Faulkner for swallowing the bait and selling out), to take part in another film based on the greatest bullfighter of the time: "I think the idea of you and Peter [Viertel] and me doing the one with [Luis Miguel] Dominguín is great and an absolute must." Huston, a keen aficionado, had also been considering Barnaby Conrad's bestselling *Matador* (1952), based on his career as an American bullfighter. But Huston told Kohner that he preferred the Hemingway project: "I don't think [*Matador*] would have the immediate and widespread appeal as *Death in the Afternoon* by Ernest Hemingway. And I believe Papa could be coaxed into doing the script himself or perhaps himself with Peter. If the three [Hemingway] stories idea falls by the wayside, I would like to aim for that. I couldn't guarantee it would come off, but, if it did, it would certainly be big medicine." The producer Harold Mirisch was keen on this idea and cabled Huston: "Everyone here terrifically enthusiastic over Hemingway idea. You have our blessings. Investigate possibilities of subject." But Hemingway could not be coaxed and the project was dropped.

Huston was asked to direct *The Old Man and the Sea*, with a screenplay by Peter Viertel, "but couldn't see the old Cuban fisherman played by a [professional] actor, and the studio couldn't risk doing it without one." In 1958 the movie, leadenly directed by John Sturges, starred the rotund, red-faced and absurdly miscast Irish-American, Spencer Tracy, who owned the rights and was coproducer.

Despite these ill-fated setbacks, Huston was still determined to make a Hemingway film. The producer David Selznick, a long-standing friend, wanted to remake *A Farewell to Arms* (the 1932 movie had starred Gary Cooper and Helen Hayes) starring Rock Hudson and his own adored wife Jennifer Jones. The budget was $4.2 million and Huston's unusually high fee was $250,000. On

October 25, 1956 Selznick cabled Huston: "Could you concentrate wholly on *Farewell [to Arms]* until completion photography, after which believe you would feel safe leaving post-production, including editing, entirely in my hands?"

Far from feeling safe with Selznick, who wanted complete control and appropriated the power that traditionally belonged to the director, Huston sensed the danger and felt extremely uneasy. Selznick, hand over heart, falsely claimed "there have been few books ever transcribed to the screen with the studied and loving care that [Ben] Hecht and I gave this one through many weary months." But Huston realized at the outset that their debased version had turned one of Hemingway's greatest novels into a banal and cliché-ridden romance. In his autobiography, *An Open Book*, Huston recalled, "From the moment I saw the script, David and I were in conflict. Through David's influence on Hecht, the Hemingway story had simply become a vehicle for the female lead—Jennifer Jones." Well aware of the challenge, the strong-willed Huston pretended to agree with Selznick while plunging ahead and making the movie his own way.

Selznick's biographer remarked that Huston criticized all the material which was not in the novel and which Selznick and Hecht had put into their ninth draft. Following his habitual method, he insisted that "they should stay as close as possible to Hemingway's original scenes." In typical Hollywood fashion, which Huston strenuously opposed, Selznick had paid a fortune for a brilliant novel and then ruined it with his own inept additions.

Selznick's biographer also explained the irreconcilable differences between the two powerful egos: "Huston liked to keep himself open to any new ideas he might have until just before shooting a scene, which meant that camera set-ups could be—and usually were—changed, lines of dialogue altered, blocking and other staging details revamped, thus giving his scenes an edgy, almost improvised spontaneity. Selznick, on the other hand, wanted as much control as possible." After spending an entire day with three secretaries, Selznick sent Huston a tedious and offensive sixteen-page memo that criticized Huston's careful planning and accused him of procrastination. The secretaries warned Selznick that the memo would have a disastrous effect, but he preferred a showdown and sent the ultimatum.

> I should be less than candid with you [Selznick wrote] if I didn't tell you that I am most desperately unhappy about the way things are going.

> It is an experience completely unique in my very long career. It is an experience that I feel is going to lead us, not to a better picture . . . but to a worse one.
>
> Fervently as I want you to direct the picture, I would rather face the awful consequence of your not directing it than to go through what I am presently going through.

Though Selznick emphatically maintained, "I have learned that *nothing matters but the final picture*," the only thing that really mattered to him was Jennifer Jones.

Before he'd finished the memo, Huston—generous, extravagant and always short of cash, but unwilling to bend the knee—immediately packed his bags, left the film and surrendered his lucrative fee. Unable to protect the integrity of the novel, he was immensely relieved to abandon the project that he knew Hemingway would hate and that would destroy their precious friendship. Huston was replaced by the plodding Charles Vidor. Released in 1957, the picture did not make a profit and Hemingway never got the additional $100,000 that Selznick had promised to give him. When describing his response to this debacle, Huston quoted Hemingway's story about a *picador*'s comments after his matador's disastrous performance: "There was a division of opinion. Some wanted to shit on his father, some wanted to shit on his mother."

Though Huston had failed to direct a film by Hemingway, he did play him on the screen. In the early 1970s Huston took on the role of James Hanneford, a movie director modeled on Hemingway in Orson Welles' *The Other Side of the Wind*. Welles had observed Hemingway and his followers at bullfights in Spain. But Welles, who had more unfinished projects than Leonardo da Vinci, never completed this picture.

Hemingway was writing his Venetian novel, *Across the River and Into the Trees*, his first book since the tremendously successful *For Whom the Bell Tolls*, when he first met Huston and they had discussed the possibility of making a film of the book. In 1975–76 Huston and his longtime mistress, secretary and collaborator, Gladys Hill, worked on a script of the movie that he planned to direct. He knew the difficulties—no real action and a lot of repetitive scenes and boring dialogue—and explained that Hemingway "was trying something that didn't come off—it's an experiment, a kind of indulgence." He also told the *New York Times* that "the book, which was largely a disaster, is a dialogue between a colonel who is dying and a very young Italian girl. Papa was very dejected by the reception of the book and I've got correspondence from him [now lost] which was written when he was so down about it. I know the background, a lot of personal things. He really exposes himself in the book and it is hard to draw the line between Hemingway and the old colonel." Armed with inside knowledge, Huston cut to the essence of the novel. The film would show "the compassionate and sensitive side" of Hemingway and define "what it means to be a soldier."

It's interesting to see how, with all their considerable skill, Huston and Hill failed to master a hopeless project and dramatize dead words and lifeless scenes. (I've tried to write the script myself; it can't be done.) In this case, Huston (awed by Hemingway) followed the novel too faithfully instead of inventing new scenes (as he did in *The Killers*) to flesh out and vitalize the story. The 117-page typescript in the Herrick Library begins with Colonel Richard Cantwell driving in a jeep with Sergeant Jackson and remembering his past. There are flashbacks to battles in World War II; an allusion to duck shooting in the Venetian marshes; and a reference to the always obliging porter and bartender in the luxurious Hotel Gritti on the Grand Canal. There's a good deal of arch conversation, and scenes in the streets of Venice and in Harry's bar. Cantwell talks to his friend Alvarito; meets the beautiful young aristocrat Renata (his rebirth) and asks her, "Would you ever like to run for Queen of Heaven?"

After another flashback to the war, Cantwell says, "I don't care about our losses—because the moon is our mother and our father." (Imitation bad Hemingway is even worse than real bad Hemingway.) Renata keeps asking him to recount his tedious war exploits. Thus encouraged, Cantwell disparages the generals who'd destroyed his career. He then tells her, "We are devotees of the pictorial arts." They take a gondola ride (like a couple of tourists) and she urges him to "hold me tight and try to love me true." When they dock at St. Mark's Square, Cantwell, despite his weak heart, gallantly punches two American sailors whom he thinks have made insulting remarks about his true love. He and Renata admire her portrait, which he has commissioned; and he ungallantly tells her younger sister Vittoria (Huston's invention), "You are so god-damned beautiful it's heart-breaking. Also, you are jail bait."

Well aware of his physical decline, Cantwell tells himself, "You are half a hundred years old, you beat up old bastard you." Hemingway reveals in this autobiographical novel that he regarded himself as old and finished at fifty, his age when he wrote the book. Cantwell makes plans for the future in America. He talks to the headwaiter at the Gritti Palace, whom he elevates to *Gran Maestro*, and discusses their fanciful *Ordine Militar*. He bitterly and obsessively recalls the hopeless attack whose failure demoted him from general to colonel. The duck hunt, the best scene in the book, is shifted to the end of the film, and the boatman, who suggests Charon, the oarsman of the Underworld, foreshadows the colonel's death. The script returns to the opening scene, and Cantwell dies in the jeep, leaving written orders to give the portrait to Renata and his guns to Alvarito. As the jeep drives off, the movie ends. The second version, dated April 2, 1976, is revised but essentially the same. Huston could not solve the intractable, impossible problem: that nothing much, and nothing interesting, ever happens in the novel or the film.

Huston confessed in an interview that, with all his strenuous efforts, "I never got a proper script. I worked on it myself, but I never got it. . . . I did use flashbacks, but the script never came off." It was terribly sad for the careers of both Hemingway and Huston, despite the perfect match of novelist and director, that none of Huston's ambitious and promising projects to put Hemingway on film was ever realized. For all his admiration and passionate commitment to Hemingway, Huston never directed a film based on his friend's work.

Hemingway and Huston lived egoistic, adventurous and dangerous lives. They nurtured in themselves and their friends a cult of masculinity and often reckless courage, which inspired some of their finest artistic achievements. They were lionized in the 1940s, but Lillian Ross, of the *New Yorker*, wrote satiric portraits of Hemingway in 1950 and of Huston in 1952. Both men, toward the end of their lives, had some failures, and both had an entourage of courtiers and camp followers, flatterers and parasites. But after being written off, they made a strong finish: Hemingway with the posthumous *A Moveable Feast* (1964) and Huston with a final cinematic masterpiece, *The Dead* (1987).

THIRTY-THREE

EDUCATED WIVES

St. Louis woman, stole the heart of my big boy.

Stung by Hemingway's attack on her character and writing, Gertrude Stein retaliated with a notorious wisecrack, "anyone who's married three girls from St. Louis hasn't learned much." Stein sneered at Hemingway for choosing provincial women, but St. Louis also produced T. S. Eliot, Marianne Moore, Walker Evans and William Burroughs. Hemingway, who did not go to a university, was attracted by the wealthy background, ladylike demeanor and superior education of his series of wives—classy consorts for a young journalist who became a prominent writer. His first three wives took years of French at school, which gave them a head start in Paris. Hadley Richardson was the nicest wife, Pauline Pfeiffer the richest, Martha Gellhorn the most beautiful and independent. Hadley became a housewife and good sport; Pauline, who graduated from the Journalism School of the University of Missouri, became a fashion journalist; Martha Gellhorn became a war correspondent and novelist. Hemingway, who divorced three all increasingly young wives, left Hadley for Pauline and abandoned Pauline for Martha. After Martha left him, he followed the pattern and married Mary Welsh, another Protestant midwestern journalist.

Bernice Kert's *The Hemingway Women* and the books on Hadley and Pauline paid very little attention to their education; the biographies of Martha were more thorough. Unpublished material generously sent by the schools they attended illuminate a crucial aspect of their lives, and show how their education shaped their character and foreshadowed their future. Hadley attended the Mary Institute. The pamphlet published in 2009 on its 150th anniversary states that William Greenleaf Eliot—minister, Harvard graduate and grandfather of the poet—founded the school in 1859 based on the radical idea that women's intellectual abilities were equal to those of men. He named the Institute after his oldest daughter, Mary, who died at the age of sixteen. The original six-member faculty taught English, French, natural history, music, drawing and calisthenics. Girls could also take courses in mathematics and science at nearby Washington University. In 1891 the school moved away from the "almost exclusive focus on rigorous, strenuous scholarship and embraced the virtues of a full, well rounded life for young women that included entertainments, exhibitions, festivities, recreations and pastimes." The girls were mainly trained to be wives and mothers.

Hadley, born in 1891, entered the Institute in 1902, studied there from the fifth through twelfth grades and graduated with honors in 1910. In a photo that appeared in the senior yearbook she has a gentle smile and wears a white jacket, blouse and large satin bow around her neck. A gigantic furred, feathered and billowing turban-like hat covers her brow and drops down to the left. She went to her mother's college, Bryn Mawr near Philadelphia, but poor health forced her to drop out after a year. Later on, the glamorous actress and wartime pin-up Betty Grable graduated from the Mary Institute in 1934; and after a hiatus the study of Greek was reintroduced in 1956.

In an obscure lecture published in the *Centennial Issue* of the Mary Institute (December 1959), T. S. Eliot reminisced about his early memories of the school, which was adjacent to his home, and said, "but for the difference of sex my brother and I would also have graduated from Mary Institute." He fondly recalled the school janitor, who possessed a parrot, "was reputed to have been a runaway slave and certainly had one mutilated ear." He also appropriately stressed the importance of education, and read "The Dry Salvages"—"I think that the river / Is a strong brown god"—from the *Four Quartets* "because it's about the river and the sea, the Mississippi and the Atlantic Ocean on the coast of New England, the two great natural forces which impressed my childhood imagination."

Pauline Pfeiffer, whose devout mother had her own private chapel at home, entered the Academy of the Visitation in 1901 when her younger sister Virginia was also a student. The name of the convent school refers to the visit of Mary to her cousin Elizabeth (Luke 1:39–56), which brings divine grace to Elizabeth and her unborn child, John the Baptist. The Order of the Visitation was founded in France in 1610 by St. Francis de Sales and introduced to America in 1799. The St. Louis Academy was founded in 1833 and located in the countryside half an hour from the city center.

The *Annual Announcement* of 1912–13, Pauline's senior year, explained that "The object of the Academy is to provide for the students a thorough, systematic, Christian education, training not only the minds of its pupils, but also their hearts, that they may go forth, 'Great, strong, valiant women, to stand for virtue, to stand for God.'" Pauline's biographer wrote, "The rigorous academic program included a philosophy based on 'Gospel virtues of optimism, gentleness, joy, humility and inner freedom.'" The school had its own ornate chapel, and some of the girls later became nuns and joined the convent. Pauline took her First Communion in May 1907. The more worldly girls were escorted to the spectacular St. Louis World's Fair, which opened in April 1904.

Tuition was $350 per year, with extra charges for music, art, chemistry and a private room. The rules about dress and visitors were strict. The students wore at all times a deliberately unfashionable black serge uniform. The *Annual Announcement* stated, "The young ladies receive visits on Sundays and Thursdays, but these visits must be authorized by parents, as well as sanctioned by the Directress. . . . Letters written or received by pupils are subject to inspection."

Most of the classes were taught by Sisters, and the students recited Dante and studied Shakespeare, Dickens and Longfellow. In addition to academic subjects, as well as music and art, the girls mastered sewing, mending and embroidery. As Yeats observed in "Among School Children," "The children learn to cipher and to sing, / To study reading-books and history, / To cut and sew, be neat in everything." Handwritten entries on a ledger for Pauline's last years record additional charges for soap, needles, thread, stamps, books, reading glasses, violin strings and candy.

The Academy bountifully bestowed awards, prizes and medals so that most girls would get something to please them and gratify their parents. Pauline received awards for neatness and order, improvement and application, polite deportment, pen[wo]manship, French recitation and good grades (91 out of 100 percent). She graduated in June 1913 when she was eighteen, and seven of her classmates came from Missouri. Her graduation photo shows her, with eight other girls, standing at the end of a row and tilting her head toward the center. Dressed in white, she wears a full-length gown and frilly blouse, tight sash, long gloves, with the tip of her shoe pointing out beneath her hem.

In 1921 Pauline wrote the Alumnae Association that she was "continuing her journalistic work in New York and is now a member of the *Vogue* writing staff." She made a six months' tour of Europe in 1922–23 and spent the winter of 1925 in Paris. In 1930 she was listed as Mrs. William [*sic*] Ernest Hemingway of Key West, Florida.

A letter to her former teacher Sister Alexis Phelan, sent while Pauline was working for *Vogue*, describes her life in Paris. Published in the school magazine, it was prefaced by a gushing editorial comment that exaggerated her influence: "had we foreseen her then as the future arbitrator of American fashions how we would have aped her variations of that old black uniform!" Pauline tells the Sister that she feels a little desolate as Virginia has just left to spend the winter with the family. She's so busy with work on *Vogue* that she thinks she might be in Paris for the rest of her life. But, she adds, "unless you are in a convent, you can't always be sure you are anywhere for life, can you? I thought I should always live in New York four years ago." She's had some difficulty adjusting from schoolgirl to Parisian French and confesses: "not speaking it fluently gives me a feeling of being robbed all the time. And I can understand none of the jokes in French farces—which you would say perhaps is just as well."

She then criticizes lax French Catholics and implicitly contrasts them to the properly bred convent girls at Visitation: "They are a genre to themselves. I fear their consciences were not prudently formed when they were children, for they follow their own inclinations in all things. They eat meat on Friday, arrive at Mass at any time, if at all." However, she hastens to assure Sr. Phelan that she's staying with a strictly observant Catholic family and has received "nineteen rosaries blessed by the Pope, all given me by fervent pilgrims to Rome." Pauline tells the Sister what she wants to hear and is tactfully silent about her social, drinking and sexual life (if any) in that depraved city of sin. Hadley, sealing her doom, befriended Pauline when they met in Paris in 1925. Two years later, after her secret affair with Hemingway, Pauline married him.

The current Prospectus of the John Burroughs School, which Martha (born in 1908) attended, idealistically states that it "was founded in 1923 by a group of parents who sought to establish a new type of school in St. Louis. It was to be coeducational, nonsectarian and college preparatory. Our founders believed in simplicity, service, concern for nature, democracy, individuality and the highest academic standards." On September 21, 2017, the current headmaster, Andy Abbott, wrote me about the origin of the school:

> Martha Gellhorn not only attended Burroughs, but she is often cited as one of the reasons for the school's existence. . . . The school was founded by a group of parents in 1923 and her father was one of the founders. They were all parents of girls, and at the time the only schools for girls were very traditional—the two most popular and well regarded were Mary Institute where Hemingway's first wife attended and Visitation, a parochial school, where his second wife went to school.
>
> Dr. Gellhorn, according to legend, wanted a school for girls that "taught biology below the neck" and that embraced John Dewey's ideas of progressive education. He and the other parents approached the existing schools about making their curricula more progressive, but they all refused and so the parents decided to start their own school. They reached out to the presidents of some of the top women's colleges in the East to ask about progressive education for women, and those presidents said that if the school wanted to be truly progressive, they should be co-educational, and so Burroughs was co-ed at the outset.
>
> Martha Gellhorn [who transferred from the Mary Institute] was a student when the school opened in October of 1923 and she was in the first graduating class of seniors in the spring of 1926.

Named after the American naturalist John Burroughs, the school began with seventy-five pupils and ten teachers. It was located in the countryside near St. Louis and emphasized outdoor life and individual development. A long-winded peroration in the *Announcement* of May 1924 declared it was "founded upon the conviction that each normal child has latent possibilities of power, and that it is the chief purpose of the school to cooperate with parents in discovering, fostering and developing that power in order that, in adulthood, he shall perform his satisfying work, and that he shall make his contribution to the improvement of human society." The prosperous parents also had to make a considerable contribution of $1,000 a year tuition, almost three times the cost of Visitation.

Martha, involved in all the activities of the school, was an energetic leader. She was Speaker of the Assembly, President of the Athletic Association and member of the Hockey Team. As President of the Dramatic Association she played a leading role in John Masefield's *The Locked Chest* which, her biographer Carl Rollyson writes, portrays "a woman who leaves her cowardly husband for refusing to shelter a relative falsely accused of murder."

She was also on the board of the *John Burroughs Review*, where she published several works. With strained humor she praised an old hat that was remodeled as an Easter bonnet. In an ironic defense of her young life, "Apologia Pro Vita Sua," she rebelled against social conventions and argued that good intentions could lead to bad results. She concluded by vowing: "I will prepare my lessons, and someone else may receive the master's scorn. I will seethe loudly and furiously when next my desk mate mutilates my eraser. I will get the car every morning and cause some innocent person to be uncomfortable. I will eat only half my brother's candy, leaving enough for him to get sick on." The following year, aged seventeen, she apologized to her mother for the faults she had described in her story: "My extreme selfishness . . . made me indifferent to you and to everyone except myself." The *Senior Annals* that year politely but inaccurately praised her as "the magnificent Martie . . . sane and sweet-tempered." Her untitled "Poem" of 1926 was more mature and accomplished. Her chromatic and overwrought paean to the power and beauty of the sun repeats "I have watched" at dawn, noon and evening, and concludes with the hope "That Life will be / As strong, and proud, and beautiful, / As the magnificent Sun." Martha, like Hadley, also followed her mother to Bryn Mawr, but became bored after her third year and left college to pursue her career in the real world.

Hemingway's wives had a superior education in three elite but very different institutions in St. Louis. Hadley—a pleasant, conventional, slightly dowdy wife—had a son with Hemingway. But when he felt she was not a suitable wife for a successful author, she reluctantly agreed to a divorce. She then had a happy second marriage to the journalist Paul Mowrer, and died at the age of eighty-seven in 1979.

Despite her strict Catholic upbringing and studies, Pauline conducted a predatory adulterous affair with Hemingway and stole her best friend's husband. Yet the guilt-ridden convent girl continued to be a strict Catholic and tried unsuccessfully to convert Hemingway to the faith. She had two sons with him, but her refusal to use contraceptives (he later said) hurt their sexual life and ruined their marriage. Pauline's sister Virginia was a lesbian, and after her divorce Pauline also had lesbian liaisons with the poet Elizabeth Bishop and other women. She died, aged fifty-six in 1951, during a minor operation.

Martha fulfilled her early promise, fought for many just causes and had a distinguished career. In 1998, at the end of her long life, the ninety-two-year-old Martha, stricken by liver cancer and nearly blind, committed suicide by swallowing a cyanide pill. Hadley's school was traditional, Pauline's parochial, Martha's progressive. Hadley and the more ambitious Martha were positively influenced by their education, Pauline rebelled against and then returned to her Catholic background.

THIRTY-FOUR

WOMEN'S VOICES

Hemingway has always been considered the quintessential *macho* writer, but his best fiction shows how sensitively attuned he was to women's speech. He listened carefully to exactly how women expressed their feelings, and created their characters through suggestive dramatic dialogue without the narrator's comments. Though his women are always seen through the eyes of his male hero, their voices define the emotional scenes: they complain, provoke, flirt, adore and condemn. His women were based on significant people in his life: on his mother, his first wife Hadley, the English Duff Twysden, his American nurse Agnes von Kurowsky, his third wife Martha Gellhorn, the aristocratic Italian Adriana Ivancich, his lover Jane Mason and his former mentor Gertrude Stein. Hemingway's mother is sentimental and misguided, Hadley is obsessively materialistic in one story and bitterly disillusioned in another. The fictional Brett Ashley, Catherine Barkley and Maria have been wounded and traumatized by war. Maria and Renata are teenaged Latin mistresses. Margot Macomber, like Brett, is ironic and bitchy. Gertrude Stein is dogmatic and self-condemned.

Harold Krebs in "Soldier's Home" (1925) has survived the war and come back to face his unpleasant mother, whose stifling love is even more difficult to bear than her nagging criticism of his postwar life. After her whining platitudes and religiose pieties, his mother wants her son to affirm his love for her and, despite his lack of faith, to pray with her. Her phony tears force him to suppress his undefined anger, betray his real beliefs and feel revulsion for himself as well as for her:

> "Don't you love your mother, dear boy?"
> "No," Krebs said.
> His mother looked at him across the table. Her eyes were shiny. She started crying.
> "I don't love anybody," Krebs said.
> It wasn't any good. He couldn't tell her, he couldn't make her see it. . . .
> "I didn't mean it," he said. "I was just angry at something. I didn't mean I didn't love you."
> His mother went on crying. Krebs put his arm on her shoulder.
> "Can't you believe me, mother?"
> His mother shook her head.
> "Please, please, mother. Please believe me."
> "All right," his mother said chokily. She looked up at him. "I believe you, Harold."
> Krebs kissed her hair. She put her face up to him.
> "I'm your mother," she said. "I held you next to my heart when you were a tiny baby."
> Krebs felt sick and vaguely nauseated.

Krebs' extreme reaction clashes effectively with his mother's cloying sentimentality. Her attempt at emotional blackmail and reminder of his childhood dependence make him realize that he must escape from her clutches and find a newspaper job in Kansas City just as he had previously escaped to war. The effective contrast of their two voices, of her speech and his thoughts, show her complete lack of awareness about what her son has suffered in war.

Hemingway was aware that many people deliberately repeat themselves to express their emotions, force their listeners to pay attention, emphasize a point and drive home their argument. In "Cat in the Rain" (1925) the bored and restless wife is dissatisfied with her self-absorbed and unresponsive husband George, who tries to ignore her and continues to read. Hemingway satirizes the recently married Hadley as an acquisitive American woman who expresses her spoiled and compulsive character in a series of disparate desires and repeats "I want" eleven times:

> "I want to pull my hair back tight and smooth and make a big knot at the back that I can feel," she said. "I want to have a kitty to sit on my

> lap and purr when I stroke her." . . .
>
> "And I want to eat at a table with my own silver and I want candles. And I want it to be spring and I want to brush my hair out in front of a mirror and I want a kitty and I want some new clothes."
>
> "Oh, shut up and get something to read." . . .
>
> "Anyway, I want a cat," she said, "I want a cat. I want a cat now. If I can't have long hair or any fun, I can have a cat."

Most of her personal wants, from long hair to silver and candles, are superficial yet tangible. But it's impossible for her to summon up spring and difficult to have fun with George. "Anyway" continues her lament despite his interruption. Stroking the cat and making a big knot she can feel have sexual connotations. The cat in the rain, which she fails to rescue, symbolizes her isolation, need for protection and desire to have a baby. The childish Hadley, eight years older than Hemingway, got her wish. The story is set in a Rapallo hotel in January 1923; their son Jack was born ten months later in November.

The woman in "Cat in the Rain" wants to have a baby. In "Hills Like White Elephants" (1927), a more subtle and profound story about Hadley's pregnancy, the man wants to get rid of it. Hemingway criticizes the superficial woman in "Cat." But in "Hills" he sympathizes with the woman's furious hostility to her unmarried lover rather than with the selfish man. The bored and unhappy couple are waiting for a train in the desolate landscape of the Ebro (which suggests "embryo") Valley in Spain. She thinks the dry white hills look like the skin of elephants. But the literal-minded man rejects her imaginative perception and their different visions separate them. He cannot understand what she would have to endure in an abortion—a word that's never mentioned. She perceives the physical and emotional suffering all too well:

> "Then I'll do it. Because I don't care about me."
>
> "What do you mean?"
>
> "I don't care about me."
>
> "Well, I care about you."
>
> "Oh, yes. But I don't care about me. And I'll do it and then everything will be fine." . . .
>
> "And we could have everything and every day we make it more impossible."

"What did you say?"

"I said we could have everything."

"We can have everything."

"No, we can't."

"We can have the whole world."

"No, we can't."

"We can go everywhere."

"No, we can't. It isn't ours any more."

"It's ours."

"No, it isn't. And once they take it away, you never get it back."

Hemingway expresses the women's deepest emotions in the simplest sentences and monosyllabic words. The repetitive, contradictory dialogue suggests their alienation as he tries to convince her to have the operation that she doesn't want. The woman's self-sacrificial dissociation from her own feelings and well-being is shocking. At one point he doesn't hear or understand what she's saying, she repeats herself but leaves out "make it more impossible" and he tries to convert her "could have" into an unconvincing "can have." In the last line the undefined "it"—baby and love—is tragic.

She finally begs him: "Would you please please please please please please please stop talking?" Everything he says is a self-serving lie and proves that he doesn't really love her. It's not true that abortions are simple, safe and perfectly natural, and that many people have them. Paradoxically, if she agrees to have an abortion to regain his love, she will never be able to love him again. The two Hadley stories suggest serious problems in their marriage, which ended in 1926 when Hemingway fell in love with Pauline.

In *The Sun Also Rises* the volatile Brett Ashley is mannish and sexy, sophisticated and witty, bitter and pathetic. She drops in and out of the novel as she moves from France and through Spain, becomes serially involved with Jake Barnes, his friend Robert Cohn, her bankrupt fiancé Mike Campbell and the bullfighter Pedro Romero, and bounces back at the end to her hopeless relations with Jake. Brett, Hemingway's most complex woman character, appears in his first and best novel. She's introduced in Paris, appears with a group of homosexuals and asks to "give a chap a brandy and soda." Provocative and witty, she teases Jake for spoiling things by bringing a prostitute into their social circle:

> "It's a fine crowd you're with, Brett," [Jake] said.
> "Aren't they lovely? And you, my dear. Where did you get it?"
> "At the Napolitain [café]."
> "And have you had a lovely evening?"
> "Oh, priceless," I said.
> Brett laughed. "It's wrong of you, Jake. It's an insult to all of us" . . .
> "It's in restraint of trade," Brett said. She laughed again.
> "You're wonderfully sober," I said.
> "Yes. Aren't I? And when one's with the crowd I'm with, one can drink in such safety, too."

In this brief but telling exchange, Brett and Jake, old frustrated friends, taunt each other about having inappropriate sexual partners instead of being with each other. She laughs twice at her own witty remark about the prostitute's "restraint of trade" and he comments on the unusual sobriety of his alcoholic friend. At the end of that scene she tells Jake, her sympathetic confessor, that despite her superficial jollity, "I've been so miserable."

In the next scene the passionate, regretful and guilty Brett is frustrated by Jake's sexual impotence. She still desires him, though she can't have him either emotionally or physically:

> "Don't touch me," she said. "Please don't touch me." . . .
> "I can't stand it." . . .
> "You mustn't. You must know. I can't stand it, that's all. Oh, darling, please understand!"
> "Don't you love me?"
> "Love you? I simply turn all to jelly when you touch me."
> "Isn't there anything we can do about it?" . . .
> "There's not a damn thing we could do." . . .
> "But, darling, I have to see you." . . .
> "When I think of the hell I put chaps through. I'm paying for it all now."

In the most subtle scene she manages to give him some sort of sexual satisfaction. Jake is now unusually hopeful about the possibility of having chaste relations. Brett is more realistic. The nymphomaniac confesses that she could never control herself and would always deceive and wound him.

In Pamplona during the *feria* Jake vicariously excites and humiliates himself by helping to arrange Brett's affair with Romero. She *thinks* she loves him and admits that she's habitually out of control. Though she's not restrained by Jake's rational warning, she still wants his blessing:

> "Do you still love me, Jake?"
> "Yes," I said.
> "Because I'm a goner," Brett said.
> "How?"
> "I'm a goner. I'm mad about the Romero boy. I'm in love with him, I think."
> "I wouldn't be if I were you."
> "I can't help it. I'm a goner. It's tearing me all up inside."
> "Don't do it."
> "I can't help it. I've never been able to help anything."

After her brief affair with the teenaged Romero, Brett does the right thing and makes a *gran rifiuto*. Still childishly dependent, she confesses her first decent and moral act to Father Jake:

> "Darling! I've had such a hell of a time."
> "Tell me about it."
> "Nothing to tell. He only left yesterday. I made him go."
> "Why didn't you keep him?"
> "I don't know. It isn't the sort of thing one does. I don't think I hurt him any." . . .
> "He wanted me to grow my hair out. Me, with long hair. I'd look so like hell." . . .
> "He wanted to marry me, finally." . . .
> "Maybe he thought that would make him Lord Ashley." . . .
> "You know it makes one feel rather good deciding not to be a bitch."
> . . . "It's sort of what we have instead of God."

Brett, with her fashionably boyish hair, notes that long Spanish hair is out of the question. But she is justly proud (in an iambic pentameter last line) of her selfless renunciation. Jake, unimpressed and knowing she'll return to her usual reckless behavior, dismisses her decent decision with a far-fetched joke about her husband's title. But the pagan enchantress, who's been compared to Circe and refused entry to a church, has followed her idiosyncratic religious beliefs. Hemingway's dialogue captures the ironic voice of the fascinating Duff Twysden. He lusted after Duff and transformed his sexual frustration with her into a bitterly romantic novel with an impotent hero.

Both Brett and Catherine Barkley in *A Farewell to Arms* (1929) are British and worked as assistant nurses in a Voluntary Aid Detachment. Both women have been mentally deranged by the traumatic loss of their lovers killed in the war, but respond in different ways. The sexy Brett, experienced and sophisticated, predatory and bitchy, seeks a replacement in a series of unsatisfactory affairs. Her terse, sharp dialogue swirls from brash to sad to morally triumphant, yet she ends as hopeless and miserable as she began. The sex scenes in Hemingway's novels emphasize physical attraction and the last chance for love before impending death. But the suggestion of degrading sex in the empty glasses on the dirty café table, which Jake sees after Brett has left with Romero, is more effective than realistic descriptions of sex.

The virginal Catherine, though sometimes a "bit crazy," is a good nurse. Innocent and devoted, passive and benign, she withdraws into herself, falls deeply in love with Frederic and surrenders her individual identity. Her voice, though occasionally witty, is submissive and sentimental. After *The Sun Also Rises* Hemingway's increasingly egocentric fictional heroes want adoration rather than rivalry and the women become mere adjuncts to the men who accept their love as their due. In their first significant meeting the still traumatized Catherine confuses Frederic Henry with her dead lover and tries to reestablish her identity through him. He accepts his new therapeutic role, dutifully repeats her instructions and has to lie about love in order to cure her:

> "You did say you loved me, didn't you?"
> "Yes," I lied. "I love you." I had not said it before.
> "And you call me Catherine?"
> "Catherine." We walked on a way and stopped under a tree.
> "Say, 'I've come back to Catherine in the night.'"
> "I've come back to Catherine in the night."

> "Oh, darling, you have come back, haven't you?"
> "Yes."
> "I love you and it's been so awful. You won't go away?"
> "No. I'll always come back."

In the end, however, she's the one who "goes away."

After offering more reassurance the man—as in "Soldier's Home" and "Hills Like White Elephants"—must reaffirm his love. Though Catherine seems to overcome her delusions and regain her sanity, her fragile condition foreshadows her tragic fate.

> "You don't have to pretend you love me. That's over for the evening. Is there anything you'd like to talk about?"
> "But I do love you."
> "Please let's not lie when we don't have to. I had a fine little show and I'm all right now. You see I'm not mad and I'm not gone off. It's only a little sometimes."

During their first sexual encounter she questions him about his past lovers, which he falsely claims were unimportant. She then alludes to Hemingway's favorite passage about the faithful wife from Ruth 1:16: "Whither thou goest I will go; and where thou lodgest, I will lodge; thy people shall be my people, and thy God my God."

> "I'll say just what you wish and I'll do what you wish and then you will never want any other girls, will you?" She looked at me very happily. "I'll do what you want and say what you want and then I'll be a great success, won't I?" . . .
> "I do anything you want."
> "You're so lovely."
> "I'm afraid I'm not very good at it yet."
> "You're lovely."
> "I want what you want. There isn't any me any more. Just what you want."

Her rhetorical questions suggest her uneasiness about his love and their future. Like the tormented woman in "Hills" who doesn't "care about me,"

Catherine willingly surrenders her selfhood and submerges herself in Frederic. Though a sexual novice, she also changes from the future "I'll do" to the present "I do" and offers to gratify all his sexual desires.

Frederic seeks pleasure and excitement with her hair, which could make them look like twins and merge their identity in a kind of tonsorial orgasm. (The hair theme reaches full growth in his posthumous novel *The Garden of Eden.*) But when Catherine becomes accidentally pregnant, she's afraid that Frederic feels trapped and angry, and promises not to cause trouble—though her death is big trouble. Catherine's unwanted pregnancy foreshadows her disastrous fate, and she and Frederic must pay for illicit sex with death. Hemingway's fictional women long for a child, resist an abortion and die like Catherine with her stillborn baby. Their unborn children represent the truly lost generation.

The romances in *A Farewell to Arms* and *For Whom the Bell Tolls* (1940) are intensified by the psychological wounds and the pressure of war. Catherine has been traumatized by the death of her fiancé; Maria by her brutal rape by the fascists. Regenerative love helps to heal and obliterate both tragedies. Frederic replaces Catherine's lost fiancé; Robert Jordan's love cancels the rape, imaginatively restores Maria's virginity and triumphs over his rivals in the band of guerrillas. Jordan's sexual encounters with Maria, brief peaceful interludes during the war, mark the passage of the three nights in which the book takes place. Like Jake with Brett in *The Sun Also Rises*, Pilar vicariously participates in the love life of Jordan and Maria.

When they first meet, Jordan immediately notices Maria's hair, which had been shaved in prison by the fascists, has recently grown out and now merges into the Spanish landscape: "Her hair was the golden brown of a grain field that had been burned dark in the sun but it was cut short all over her head so that it was but little longer than the fur on a beaver pelt. . . . He looked at her hair that was as thick and short and rippling when she passed her hand over it, now in embarrassment, as a grain field in the wind on a hillside." After defying Pilar, and with his swelling throat and thick voice suggesting an erection, he boldly "ran his hand over the top of her head. He had been wanting to do that all day and now he did it, he could feel his throat swelling. . . . 'Do it again,' she said. 'I wanted you to do that all day.' 'Later,' Robert Jordan said and his voice was thick. 'And me,' the woman of Pablo said in her booming voice. 'I am expected to watch all this? I am expected not to be moved?'"

On their first sexual encounter in Jordan's sleeping bag Maria is first shy, then eager. He commands her and tenderly calls her "rabbit"—*conejo* in Spanish and slang for "pussy":

> "I am ashamed," she said, her face away from him.
> "No. You must not be. Here. Now."
> "No. I must not. I am ashamed and frightened."
> "No. My rabbit. Please."
> "I must not. If thou dost not love me."
> "I love thee."

In a delightful question when they're kissing, she innocently wonders, "Where do the noses go?" He erases her past to suit the present: "if we do everything together, the others maybe never will have been."

On their second encounter Maria asks, in a famous phrase, "Did the earth never move for thee before?" The literary source may have been T. S. Eliot's *Murder in the Cathedral* (1935): "The heaving of earth at nightfall." The real-life inspiration was the bombardment of the Hotel Florida in Madrid while Hemingway was in bed with his future wife, the blonde Martha Gellhorn. Martha found sexual intercourse painful; Maria feels "great soreness and much pain" from her rape, but is "thankful too to have been another time in *la gloria*." Like Catherine, the ultra-submissive Maria says, "I will do anything for thee that thou should wish" and offers to pleasure Jordan in another way: "Is there not some other thing that I can do for thee?"

In one of her longer speeches Maria, always eager for sexual and practical tuition, plans their future and declares in her awkwardly translated speech:

> "I will learn from Pilar what I should do to take care of a man well and those things I will do," Maria said. "Then, as I learn, I will discover things for myself and other things you can tell me."

But, shifting from the future tense to the subjunctive, she'll also be prepared for the worst:

> "If you will teach me to shoot either one of us could shoot the other and himself, or herself, if one were wounded and it were necessary to avoid capture."

Maria's foreignness, rape and threat of death intensify their brief love affair. Her slightly archaic ("dost not") speech has youthful innocence and charm. In the end, the mortally wounded Jordan persuades Maria to escape without him.

Hemingway's women reveal recurrent themes in his fiction. In *The Sun Also Rises* Brett is thirty-four, Romero nineteen; in *Across the River* Richard Cantwell is fifty, Renata also nineteen. The fascists have killed both Maria's father and Renata's father. Maria speaks Spanish using the familiar *tu*, Renata is learning English, and both are comparatively inarticulate. Like Brett, Catherine and Maria, Renata, like an actress on stage, makes a dramatic appearance. As always, Hemingway emphasizes the woman's full-grown, wind-blown "dark hair, of an alive texture, that hung down over her shoulders."

Hemingway's hero Lord Byron, his nineteen-year-old Italian lover Teresa Guiccioli and her young brother Pietro Gamba were the prototypes of Hemingway, his adored Venetian Adriana Ivancich and her younger brother Gianfranco. Unfortunately, Renata and Cantwell have nothing significant to say to each other and talk endlessly about food. Her persistent questions provide an excuse for his egoistic lectures, she nods her head in tacit agreement and even falls asleep as he continues to talk. She concentrates on meals, sex and Cantwell, lives in the present moment and insists: "Please let's not think of anything, or anything, or anything." Yet she can sometimes be quite sharp, as when she says:

> "What is your great sorrow?"
> "Other people's orders," he said. "What's yours?"
> "You."

She's even surprisingly witty when, learning to speak American, she exclaims (in Hemingway's self-parody): "Put it there, Pal. This grub is tops" and "Listen, Mac. You hired out to be tough, didn't you?"

As in the two previous novels, the young woman wishes to serve the experienced older man who initiates the virgin into the pleasures of sex. Renata and Cantwell have difficulty in finding a private place before performing precariously in a gliding gondola. Renata contradicts herself by swearing, "I have never cared what anyone thought, ever," but she also wants to protect her reputation and refuses to go to his hotel room because "Everything is known in Venice anyway. But it is also known who my family are and that I am a good girl. Also they know it is you and it is I." Hemingway's novels compensated for his sexual frustration. Both Agnes von Kurowsky and Adriana Ivancich were angry that though they did not sleep with Hemingway in real life, the characters they inspired had sex with the hero in the novels. Duff Twysden didn't give a damn.

Like Maria with Jordan, Renata bids farewell to Cantwell just before his death, and like Catherine with Frederic she becomes extremely emotional:

> "Can't I ride with you to the garage?"
> "It would be just as bad at the garage."
> "Please let me ride to the garage." . . .
> The girl was crying, finally, although she had made the decision never to cry. . . .
> "I've stopped," she said. "I'm not an hysterical."

There's a striking contrast between the poignant, hopeless conclusion of *The Sun Also Rises*,

> "Oh, Jake," Brett said, "we could have had such a damned good time together." . . .
> "Yes," I said. "Isn't it pretty to think so?"

and Cantwell's rather stilted and affectless goodbye:

> There are some things that a person cannot do. You know about that. You cannot marry me and I understand that, although I do not approve it.

He's too old and sick; she's too young and innocent, and her aristocratic family would never allow her to marry him.

Hemingway must have been deeply wounded by the end of his affair with the model for Margot Macomber, the exceptionally wild and beautiful Jane Mason who went on her own African safari. His brilliantly repetitious dialogue is better in his stories and memoir than in his later novels. "The Short Happy Life of Francis Macomber" (1936) returns to the terse and ironic speech of the 1920s, and Margot's voice is more like Brett's than like Catherine's and Maria's. This bitter tale of a predatory, treacherous and murderous female emphasizes the connection between shooting and sex, and shatters the possibility of romantic love in the glamorous setting of big-game hunting in Africa. Wilson, the white hunter, tries to exclude Margot from their hunt, but she insists on joining them and mocking them:

> "We'll put on another show for you tomorrow," Francis Macomber said.
> "You're not coming," Wilson said.
> "You're very mistaken," she told him. "And I want *so* to see you perform again. You were lovely this morning. That is if blowing things' heads off is lovely." . . .
> "Why not let up on the bitchery just a little, Margot." . . .
> "I suppose I could," she said, "since you put it so prettily."

After Macomber reveals his cowardice by running away from the lion, Margot, moving in for the kill, taunts and humiliates him by shamelessly sleeping with Wilson. Her satiric barbs, while she holds power over Macomber, are devastating. When Margot returns to their tent after sex with Wilson she's mendacious, defiant and unregenerate, and assumes that only the brave deserve the fair:

> "Where have you been?"
> "I just went out to get a breath of air."
> "You did, like hell."
> "What do you want me to say, darling?"
> "Where have you been?"
> "Out to get a breath of air."
> "That's a new name for it. You *are* a bitch."
> "Well, you're a coward." . . .
> "There wasn't going to be any of that. You promised there wouldn't be."
> "Well, there is now," she said sweetly.

Macomber gains a slight advantage by challenging Margot, who's dependent on his wealth but won't give up Wilson:

> "If you make a scene I'll leave you, darling," Margot said quietly.
> "No, you won't."

> "You can try it and see."
> "You won't leave me."
> "No," she said. "I won't leave you and you'll behave yourself."
> "Behave myself? That's a way to talk. Behave myself."
> "Yes. Behave yourself."
> "Why don't *you* try behaving?"
> "I've tried it so long. So very long."
> "I hate that red-faced swine," Macomber said. "I loathe the sight of him."
> "He's really *very* nice."

As "I'll leave" subtly merges with "you'll behave," Margot, having bed-tested Wilson, puts the knife in by praising his character. Hemingway, who does not want to be distracted from his rapid-fire dialogues, almost always uses "said" instead of variants to identify the speakers.

When Wilson sees Margot murder her husband, who'd redeemed himself by confronting a lion, he now has her in *his* power:

> "That was a pretty thing to do," [Wilson] said in a toneless voice. "He *would* have left you too."
> "Stop it," she said.
> "Of course it's an accident," he said. "I know that."
> "Stop it," she said.
> "Don't worry," he said. There will be a certain amount of unpleasantness but . . . you're perfectly all right."
> "Stop it," she said. . . .
> "Why didn't you poison him? That's what they do in England."
> "Stop it. Stop it. Stop it," the woman cried. . . .
> "Oh, please stop it," she said. "Please, please stop it."
> "That's better," Wilson said. "Please is much better. Now I'll stop."

Having lost her advantage, Margot is reduced to eight frantic repetitions of the monosyllabic "stop" and, like the woman in "Hills," to three utterances of "please"—both words repeated by Wilson in the last sentence of Hemingway's greatest story.

Hemingway may have taken the title of *A Moveable Feast* (1964) from Albert Camus' *The Stranger* (1942). His posthumously published memoir retaliates for Gertrude Stein's attacks on him after they'd left Paris and uses her own voice as he remembered or imagined it. Dogmatic, censorious and speaking *ex-synagoga*, she orders him not to "argue with me." She insists that the sex scenes in his early story "Up in Michigan," like a painting that is too obscene to hang, cannot appear in print—though he published it in 1923. Not content with criticizing his fiction, she lays down the law about how he must live as a writer. Ignoring the needs of Hadley, whose trust fund supported the family, Stein declares that he has to follow her example, "You can either buy clothes or buy pictures. No one who is not very rich can do both."

Like Hemingway's attacks in *Across the River*, from Dante's *Inferno* (his "Notes from Underground") to works by D'Annunzio and Sinclair Lewis, Stein tries to defend her turf by attacking authors greater than herself. She claims that "Huxley is a dead man" and that the tubercular D. H. Lawrence is "impossible. He's pathetic and preposterous. He writes like a sick man." In a swingeing mood, she also condemns Hemingway and all his companions: "You are all a *génération perdue*. . . . You have no respect for anything. You drink yourselves to death." He liked this well enough to use it as an epigraph in *The Sun Also Rises*.

In a feeble but nasty attack Stein castigates homosexuals as "criminals and perverts. . . . Those people are sick and cannot help themselves and you should pity them." She also calls the unnamed Jean Cocteau a truly vicious man who "corrupts for the pleasure of corruption and he leads people into other vicious practices as well. Drugs, for example." In a blatant, self-serving defense of her own lesbian relations, Stein exclaims, "the act male homosexuals commit is ugly and repugnant and afterwards they are disgusted with themselves. . . . In women it is the opposite. They do nothing that they are disgusted by and nothing that is repulsive and afterwards they are happy and they can lead happy lives together."

Hemingway completely demolishes her absurd argument in a savage passage when he accidentally overhears Stein and Alice Toklas having a degrading, disgusting and extremely unhappy sexual quarrel. His devastating sentences parody Stein's crude mode of repetition, which he had refined into an infinitely superior style: "I heard someone speaking to Miss Stein as I had never heard one person speak to another; never, anywhere, ever. Then Miss Stein's voice came pleading and begging, saying, 'Don't, pussy, Don't. Don't, please don't. I'll do anything, pussy, but please don't do it. Please, don't. Please don't, pussy.'" Stein's words recall Maria's "I will do anything" as well as the woman in "Hills" pleading and begging the man to stop talking. By not revealing the reason for the quarrel, Hemingway intensifies our curiosity about what Toklas, addressed as "pussy," threatened to do to the supposedly dominant but actually subservient Stein. As Hemingway writes in "Macomber," he "suddenly felt as though he had opened the wrong door in a hotel and seen something shameful."

Hemingway satirized his mother (born 1872) and Stein (born 1874), who both had an imposing statuesque appearance and a formidable overbearing personality. The portrait of Stein in Paris in the mid-1920s returns to the start of his career when he wrote the two Hadley stories and *The Sun Also Rises* (all set in Europe). As his novels progress, the women with alluring hair change from bold and assertive to adoring and submissive, and frequently plead with the men to confirm their love.

THIRTY-FIVE

PAULINE PFEIFFER

In recent years four writers have attempted to rehabilitate Hemingway's second wife, Pauline Pfeiffer. The first of these came in 2009, when her son and grandson published a radical revision of his autobiographical work *A Moveable Feast* that tried to change her negative image. Since then there have been two further attempts to exonerate her.

Who was Pauline Pfeiffer (1895–1951)? She was born in Iowa and grew up in Piggott, Arkansas. Her father Paul owned the local bank, the land office, the cotton gin company, and ruled the region like a feudal lord. Her Uncle Gustavus Adolphus Pfeiffer (named after a Swedish warrior-king) was a multimillionaire who owned several worldwide pharmaceutical corporations that were finally bought by Pfizer.

Pauline graduated from a Catholic high school in St. Louis and from the School of Journalism at the University of Missouri. She worked on two newspapers and the magazine *Vanity Fair*, and had been engaged in New York to her cousin Matthew Herold. After graduating from Harvard Law School, he became the attorney for the Pfeiffer companies. Pauline and her younger sister Jinny went to Paris in 1921. She worked for Main Bocher, editor of the French *Vogue*, attended fashion shows and sent in reports.

Small and dark, with a boyish figure, bobbed hair and cloche hat, Pauline was spoiled, self-assured and ambitious. Like all the Pfeiffers she was used to getting whatever she wanted. Like the acquisitive and demanding young woman in Hemingway's story "Cat in the Rain" who insists—"I want to eat at a table with my own silver and I want candles. And I want it to be spring and I want to brush my hair out in front of a mirror and I want a kitty and I want some new clothes"—Pauline wrote to Hadley, "I'm going to get a bicycle and ride in the *Bois*. I am going to get a saddle too. I am going to get everything I want."

There's no information about Pauline's sex life before she met Hemingway in Paris in March 1925. But she was far from home and parents, moved in a sophisticated and sexually free society. So she was probably not a virgin at the age of thirty—rather late in those days to remain unmarried. Bored with the matronly Hadley and eager for stimulating new experience, Hemingway was attracted to Pauline's chic style and impressive wealth. She was exciting, flattered him, took the initiative and seduced him.

In January 1926 Pauline joined the Hemingways, who were skiing in Shruns, Austria. In February, while Hemingway was en route to New York for publishing business, Pauline met him in Paris. She disingenuously wrote to Hadley, who remained in Austria, "your husband, Ernest, was a delight to me. I tried to see him as much as he would see me and was possible." She told her family, more frankly, "I feel he should be warned that I'm going to cling to him like a millstone and old moss and winter ivy." She showered praise on *The Torrents of Spring* (1926), his satire on Sherwood Anderson, at a time when Hadley, his friends and editors disliked the book.

They had few common interests. Hemingway cared nothing about Piggott (her home town), the Catholic Church, women's fashion, expensive men's clothing, pricey restaurants, luxurious furnishings and Spanish antiques. Pauline was not athletic but, like a good sport, went along with Hemingway's passion for Austrian skiing, German bike races, Spanish bullfighting and African big-game hunting. She disliked Caribbean deep-sea fishing and the rough life on the *Pilar*. In the late 1930s Hemingway was deeply committed to the Republican side in the Spanish Civil War and risked his life while reporting from the front. In a rare but damaging disagreement, Pauline (as a loyal Catholic) supported Franco's fascists.

In Paris in 1925, just before he met Pauline, Hemingway had felt frustrated by his longing for the attractive and promiscuous Duff Twysden, and he turned to Pauline for satisfaction. She knew that if she wanted to capture Hemingway she would have to sleep with him, and they became lovers when they met in Paris. Her biographer Ruth Hawkins reports that in their hotel on the French Riviera in the summer of 1926, "Pauline, an early riser, came to the Hemingways' bedroom each morning, wearing a robe over tomboy pajamas, and crawled into bed with them. The three shared breakfast in bed along with a lot of playfulness that took on sexual overtones." These daily frolics were even more exciting when Hadley watched him fooling around with Pauline. He liked the snake in the garden, the thrill, devotion and loyalty of his lover, and even claimed that his affair made him more kind and responsive to Hadley.

When Hadley finally confronted Hemingway and asked if he loved Pauline, he was not apologetic or contrite, acted as if nothing had happened and continued to see her. Hadley recalled that he even blamed her for forcing the issue: "If she hadn't brought the affair out in the open, it would not be a problem. He saw nothing wrong with the status quo." Hadley then insisted that Hemingway and Pauline should separate for 100 days, and if they still loved each other after that time she would agree to divorce him. She later thought she should have allowed him to burn out his passion for Pauline: keeping them apart merely increased their desire.

Pauline returned to Piggott. During their separation and despite their lack of common interests, she excused their adultery by claiming their love was unique and that *amor omnia vincit* (love conquers everything): "We are the same guy. . . . You and I have something that only about two persons in one or several centuries get. And having it . . . we can't face life without each other."

She felt that if someone must sacrifice and suffer it had to be Hadley, and even took responsibility for their affair: "We tried to be so swell (and who were swell) didn't give Hadley a chance. We were so scared we might lose each other—at least I was—that Hadley got locked out. I don't think you did this the way I did. I think the times Hadley doesn't hate me she must know that I was just blind dumb." In an unpublished story Hemingway's hero rejects Pauline's justification and believes that they were guilty: "She had thought it was a great sin, however, and it was only justified to her by how much they loved each other. Even then it was not justified. It was too great a sin."

By September 1926 the unregenerate Pauline, unconcerned about her reputation, told Hemingway she'd proudly proclaim that she now possessed a lover: "I don't care if you say to Hadley that we were living together in Paris. I don't care at all. I mean this. You tell anybody anything you want." It was difficult to reconcile her behavior with her Catholic beliefs, but Pauline wanted to please him sexually. Since she feared pregnancy they must have used contraceptives before they married. Once she had snared him, she became guilt-ridden and pious, and refused to use them.

But their precautions didn't always work, and there are hints of an abortion in Hemingway's letters and fiction. In November–December 1926 he compared their separation to an abortion and revealed that Pauline had had that operation: "I think that when two people love each other terribly much and need each other in every way and then go away from each other it works almost as bad as an abortion. . . . Maybe we'll have a little guts and not try self-sacrifices [and separations] in the middle of surgical operations."

In "Hills Like White Elephants" (1927), a man tries to persuade his reluctant lover to have an abortion. In *To Have and Have Not* (1937), the furious wife mentions the disastrous effects of abortion pills and screams at her husband who'd forced her to take them: "Love is ergoapiol pills to make me come around because you were afraid to have a baby. . . . Love is that dirty aborting horror that you took me to. Love is my insides all messed up."

Hadley divorced Hemingway in January 1927 and, still in Paris, he married Pauline in May. They moved into an elegant apartment in a high-windowed, four-story house with a courtyard at 6 rue Férou, a quiet narrow street off the Jardin du Luxembourg. It had a large bedroom, living and dining rooms, small study, child's room, two bathrooms and a well-appointed kitchen. The outdoor toilet and old sawmill of his dreary flat with Hadley were left far behind. (This change resembled Picasso's transformation from humble to luxurious quarters after he married a Russian ballerina.)

Uncle Gus advanced the money to pay for the flat, just as he later paid for their Ford car in 1929, the grand house in Key West in 1931 and $25,000 for their African safari during the Depression in 1934. He created trust funds for Hemingway's widowed mother and oldest son Jack, advised him about investments and in 1935 even offered to put up $800,000 to build a bullring in Havana.

The bountiful and generous Gus, who had no children, gave Hemingway the kind of creative and adventurous life he would have liked to have if he hadn't devoted himself to making money. (Hemingway slyly revealed that Gus made perfume for a few cents a bottle and sold it for a dollar.) At Gus' death in 1953, his estate was valued at $15 million. In exchange, it must be noted, Hemingway dedicated *A Farewell to Arms* to Gus, and gave him the manuscripts of that novel and *For Whom the Bell Tolls*, "Fifty Grand," "The Killers," "The Undefeated" and two *Esquire* articles—all of which became tremendously valuable as their author's fame increased.

The advantages of Gus' wealth were simultaneously undermined by the drawbacks of Pauline's Catholicism, a crucial factor in her character, her affair with Hemingway, their marriage and their divorce. She felt guilty before her marriage and penitential after it. She adjusted her religion to suit herself, embraced or abandoned it according to her needs, and risked her soul to get Hemingway. She was an observant Catholic, yet committed adultery and broke up the marriage of a close friend who had a small child. At the same time she encouraged Hemingway to attend Mass. Since the Church did not recognize his Methodist marriage (which made Jack a bastard), she was able to marry a divorced man in church. She insisted that Hemingway had indeed become a Catholic when, wounded and unconscious in a wartime Milan hospital, he was baptized by an Italian priest. Hemingway cynically remarked, "Hell, any man could become a Catholic for a million bucks." He hated the prohibition of contraceptives, which (he believed) made many women, including Pauline, risk death by going through a dangerous pregnancy soon after a difficult childbirth. Pauline later regretted her intransigence and told Hemingway's fourth wife, Mary, "If I hadn't been such a bloody fool practicing Catholic, I wouldn't have lost my husband."

Pauline later confessed to Gregory, "Gig, I just don't have much of what's called a maternal instinct, I guess. I can't *stand* horrid little children until they are five or six—though they're still pretty awful then." She always put her husband before her children. In 1928 she left the infant Patrick with her parents and followed Hemingway for hunting in Wyoming; in 1934 she left the baby Gregory at home with his fierce nanny Ada Stern and went on the African safari.

Jack and Patrick both hated Ada, who had a violent temper and called Greg "a little shitsky." A silent, tyrannical, blue-eyed Prussian spinster from Syracuse, New York, Ada had a disastrous effect on Greg's personality and later life. Her rages terrified him and intensified his emotional dependence. He wrote that in his childhood "any infraction of her innumerable rules would cause her to fly into a screaming fit. . . . She would pack her bags and go hobbling down the stairs with me clinging to her skirts, screaming, 'Ada, don't leave me, please don't leave me.'" Patrick confirmed that Ada had serious emotional problems and was a secret drinker, a lesbian and a "pretty monstrous woman." Indifferent to Ada's cruelty, Pauline failed to rescue Greg from her clutches and give him the maternal love he desperately needed.

In July 1932, eight months after Greg's birth, another marital crisis erupted when Pauline became pregnant again. The panic-stricken but still joking

Hemingway wrote to Dr. Carlos Guffey, who'd delivered their second baby in Kansas City: "I could not believe she was pregnant as have either practiced withdrawal or used Havana's best Safeties *and withdrawal*. . . . Frankly I do not see how she could be starting to be pregnant as have never relaxed vigilance. . . . However a certain amount of semen gets splattered around and this of mine seems very virulent. Pauline's religion prevented her from taking precautions. To hell with religion in this respect." It seems that *she* would not take precautions, but would allow him to use several kinds of birth control. This time Pauline took abortion pills again, resumed her periods and had no more children. The next month Hemingway told Pauline's devout Irish-Catholic mother that he had driven a 372-mile round trip to get the guilt-ridden Pauline to the nearest Catholic church in Montana for Easter service.

Hemingway once warned Pauline's Key West friend Lorine Thompson, "You must not get too attached to things and people in life, you know, because of the disappointment in having to give them up eventually." He had an affair in Havana with the wild and stunning Jane Mason in the early 1930s; and with the dazzling journalist and novelist Martha Gellhorn, whom he'd met in Key West, when they were reporting the Spanish Civil War in 1937. He married Martha in 1940.

Hemingway's affair with Martha had an uncanny resemblance to his affair with Pauline. Like Pauline, Martha was a youthful, attractive, glamorous and fashionably dressed woman. She too insinuated herself into the household, courted the passive Hemingway, who became her athletic instructor while his wife was preoccupied with domestic duties, and wrote endearing letters thanking the wife for her kind hospitality. In both cases the affair was conducted secretly and at a safe distance. When Pauline discovered it, she (like Hadley) remained tolerant, struggled to hold onto her husband and maintain her marriage. But the lover eventually displaced the wife.

Hemingway often unloaded his own guilt onto convenient scapegoats. He blamed his mother for his father's suicide, Pauline for the breakup of his first marriage, Greg for Pauline's death. When Martha threatened their marriage, Pauline's betrayal of Hadley justified Martha's betrayal of Pauline. Hemingway fatalistically declared, "If you deceive and lie with one person against another you will eventually do it again." Though Pauline chose to be a wife more than a mother, she lost both her husband and the affection of her younger son. Lorine Thompson thought that if they had remained married, Pauline's spoiled and self-indulgent character would have prevented her from taking proper care of the sick and depressed Hemingway: "it would have been very difficult for Pauline, because of the type of person she was, to live with Ernest in his last years."

Pauline's younger sister Jinny was the longtime lover of Laura Archera, the wife of Aldous Huxley, both before and after her marriage. Patrick recalled that "Jinny was lesbian and she was quite keen on getting my mother to be homosexual as well." After her divorce in November 1940 Pauline lost interest in sexual relations with men. In 1946 she turned to her own sex for consolation and had affairs with the poet Elizabeth Bishop and several other women.

In Los Angeles in late September 1951 Greg, wearing ladies' clothing, was arrested in a women's bathroom. When Pauline phoned Hemingway with the evil tidings, he blamed her for Greg's condition, they quarreled bitterly and she sobbed uncontrollably. On October 1 she had an agonizing hemorrhage and died unexpectedly on the operating table. Hemingway wounded Greg by blaming him for her death, and they never met during the last decade of his life. When Greg became a doctor he read Pauline's autopsy report and was relieved to find that he had not been responsible. She died, in fact, from a rare tumor of the adrenal gland. Since Pauline's marriage had ended in divorce she could not, as she wished, be buried in a Catholic cemetery.

Greg had a disastrous life. He suffered from alcoholism and manic depression. He went through four broken marriages, transvestism, mental breakdowns, confinement in asylums, scores of self-prescribed shock treatments and unsuccessful sex change operations. In September 2001 Greg (now renamed Gloria), while walking naked in public and carrying women's clothing, was arrested in Florida for indecent exposure and had a fatal heart attack in a women's prison in Miami.

In 2012 Pauline's biographer and defender Ruth Hawkins (who says nothing about her *Vogue* articles or lesbian affairs) claimed that the worldly fashion reporter was quite innocent and argued that she was unable to distinguish between good and evil: "Rather than Pauline being the shrewd man-hunting female who calculatedly took Hemingway away from his first wife . . . she was a naïve woman, inexperienced with men, who became enamored with Ernest beyond all ability to judge or care about right or wrong."

In *Vogue* of June 8, 2016 Lesley Blume, who wrote a poor book on Hemingway, insisted, "What gets overlooked, however, are Pauline's own hard-earned accomplishments . . . as a successful fashion journalist for *Vogue*." Pauline's accomplishments, such as they are, have nothing to do with her treacherous behavior towards Hadley.

Blume maintains that Pauline was "smart, witty, stylish," but offers no examples of her wit. She quotes Pauline emphasizing the liberating break with her background by stating, "I certainly never expected that I should become a new woman. No one in my family was ever anything new." Her frenetic existence, Blume writes, was "filled with reporter's notebooks, fashion shows, boutique visits and copy: she covered accessories, apparel and general trends and happenings in the world of la mode." Blume claims that Pauline and Hemingway "spoke a common language and lived in overlapping spheres of high-stakes journalistic pressure." But his work as a foreign correspondent and war reporter was completely different from her gossipy and cliché-ridden reports for a women's magazine. Blume compares Pauline's description of a fashionable Italian shoemaker, which silently quotes Thomas Carlyle's definition of genius in his *Frederick the Great*, to Hemingway's superb achievement. The shoemaker "gives the impression of great energy and tremendous earnestness—both excellent qualities for a creator. Untold labor is involved in his designs. Genius still remains an infinite capacity for taking pains." "This" (writes Blume) "was the *same sort* of summary pronouncement that Hemingway specialised in when describing his own journalistic subjects" (emphasis mine). But Blume's tin-eared comparison is absurd. She concludes with a weak argument: "Pauline as husband bait, Pauline as predator: This is how she has been portrayed. . . . But it takes two to participate in a successful seduction." But Hemingway's obvious involvement in their affair does not excuse Pauline's behavior.

In the last chapter of the posthumously published *A Moveable Feast* (1964), Hemingway blamed the breakup of his first marriage on Pauline, who (he says) was encouraged by his treacherous friends John Dos Passos and Gerald and Sara Murphy. The title of his memoir, which refers to the shifting dates of feast days such as Easter in the Church calendar, alludes to the "Tables and Rules for the Moveable and Immovable Feasts" in the Anglican *Book of Common Prayer* (1549). In *The Stranger* (1942) Albert Camus called the different times of lunch "a moveable feast." Hemingway subtly changed the title from a positive to a transient and evanescent meaning. In *Across the River* he wrote, "Happiness, as you know, is a moveable feast" that's likely to disappear. In *True at First Light* (published posthumously in 1999), he repeated that "Love . . . is a moveable feast" that could vanish at any time.

Patrick Hemingway, who controls Ernest's Estate, has authorized extreme changes in the original text of *A Moveable Feast*, which had been edited by Mary Hemingway. The misnamed *Restored Edition* of 2009 cut a whole chapter instead of adding new material. Patrick, Pauline's son (in an irrelevant Foreword that compared different versions of the Bible) and Sean Hemingway, her grandson (in an Introduction) attempted to whitewash and rehabilitate Pauline. Ignoring her behavior, responsibility and guilt, and placing the blame on Hemingway, Sean wrote of "his betrayal of Hadley with Pauline . . . the remorse that Hemingway expresses and the responsibility that he accepts for the breakup. . . . He comes across in the posthumous first edition as something of an unknowing victim, which clearly he was not"—though his role as victim is not at all clear.

Sean deleted the last chapter of the 1964 edition, so the incomplete and misleading text of the *Restored Edition* ends with a satire on Scott Fitzgerald—instead of the original final chapter that concluded by criticizing Pauline and praising Hadley. Sean then shifted the original last chapter to a new section called "Additional Paris Sketches," but his reasoning fails to justify the radical change: "[Hemingway] decided that it was not the ending he wanted since he considered his marriage to Pauline a beginning, and this ending clearly left the heroine of the book, Hadley, abandoned and alone." But Ernest Hemingway himself gave a very different meaning of Hadley "alone" at the end of that chapter: "I loved her and I loved no one else and we had a lovely magic time while we were alone."

Hemingway's unpublished passage on *A Moveable Feast* in the Kennedy Library in Boston, not quoted by Sean, contradicts his grandson's distorted view and reveals Hemingway's intention to tell the truth about Pauline: "[The memoir] could be a good book because it tells many things that no one knows or can ever know and it has love, remorse, contrition, and unbelievable happiness and final sorrow."

The deleted and shifted last chapter contains, paradoxically, some new passages that emphasize *Pauline's* betrayal of Hadley. The unnamed Pauline first demanded that he choose between them and give her all his love: "The new one says you cannot really love her if you love your wife too. . . . The one who is relentless wins." Referring to their skiing holiday in Austria, he describes

Pauline's diabolical deceit, her apparently innocent betrayal of Hadley and the separation that intensified his passion: "sometime in the middle of winter she began to move steadily and relentlessly toward marriage; never breaking her friendship with your wife, never losing any advantage of position, always preserving an appearance of complete innocence, going away elaborately but only being away at any time long enough so that you would miss her too badly." He disapproved of Pauline's cunning maneuvers but admired the love that inspired them. Hemingway concludes by stressing Pauline's deep-rooted guilt that could not be extinguished and helped destroy their marriage: "[She] made only one grave mistake. She undervalued the power of remorse . . . so the black remorse came and hatred of the sin and no contrition, only a terrible remorse. . . . For the girl to deceive her friend was a terrible thing."

To answer Pauline's unconvincing defenders and conclude the case against her: In a prolonged and deliberate deception she befriended Hadley and her little boy, stole her husband and had an adulterous affair with him. She became a zealous Catholic while attempting to assuage her sin and guilt, forbade the use of contraceptives, spoiled their sex life and damaged their marriage. She made him accept his involuntary baptism, invalidated his first marriage and persuaded the skeptic (who carried a lucky rabbit's foot) to attend church. She left Greg for many months with a cruel nanny, never rescued him and ruined his life. She protected Hemingway instead of helping Greg when he was arrested. No amount of tinkering with a well-established text, in print for nearly sixty years, can change these facts.

THIRTY-SIX

FEASTS

The Hemingway hero, like the author himself, is always hungry and a good dinner puts him in a good mood. The descriptions of food and drink in Hemingway's work—from youthful journalism to posthumously published fiction, from obscurity to fame—are both autobiographical and literary. His taste in food, as well as his prose style, changes as his travels broaden and his career develops. He describes meals to reveal character and express ideas, convey a mood, set the scene and evoke the spirit of a foreign place. His characters move around a lot—Hemingway himself ranged from China to Peru—and you can tell where they are by what they eat.

There's a radical change from Hemingway's early to late descriptions of food. They range from *vin ordinaire* to the finest vintages, from crude fare when camping in the woods, during wars and on his boat to *haute cuisine* of grand hotels in Venice and elegant restaurants in Paris; from rough to refined, simple to sophisticated, provincial to cosmopolitan, naive to pretentious. In the transformation from Brown's Beanery in *The Torrents of Spring* (1926) and the humble diner in "The Killers" to the increasingly elaborate feasts, beginning with *Across the River and Into the Trees* (1950), eating replaces action and becomes an end in itself. The shift from the portrayal of food as an essential part of the country and culture to the glorification of the wealthy gourmet's status and taste, signaled by excessive description and a mannered style, reveals the decline of Hemingway's character and his loss of inspiration.

In his youth the foreign food Hemingway knew ranged from spaghetti joints, associated with Italian gangsters, to dreary chop suey parlors. But the rich food and wine he discovered, while still in his teens in wartime Italy, added a new dimension to his life. His celebration of drinking in Europe in the 1920s, when the dollar was strong and alcohol cheap, titillated his readers back home, who were constrained by Prohibition and confined to bootleg whisky and sacramental wine.

In *A Moveable Feast*, Hemingway claimed to have been poorer than he really was and said he caught pigeons when food was scarce. He wrote that hunger was worse in Paris because he was constantly tempted by the sight and smell of delectable dishes: "You got very hungry when you did not eat enough in Paris because all the bakery shops had such good things in the windows and people ate outside at tables on the sidewalk so that you saw and smelled the food." But he also maintained, when identifying with his heavy-drinking and sometimes alcoholic friends, that lack of food intensified artistic awareness. Hunger, he felt, "sharpens all of your perceptions, and I found that many of the people I wrote about had very strong appetites and a great taste and desire for food, and most of them were looking forward to having a drink."

In "Camping Out" (June 26, 1920), an early evocative article sent from Europe to the *Toronto Star*, Hemingway, interested in cooking as well as eating, gave exact instructions about how to fry just-caught trout over a coal fire. He based this display of expertise in the rough on his earliest cooking experience and encouraged his readers to follow his example. The pleasure was increased by the androgynous trout: obviously phallic but suggesting, more subtly, the female genitals: "Put the bacon in and when it is about half cooked lay the trout in the hot grease, dipping them in cornmeal first. Then put the bacon on top of the trout and it will baste them as it slowly cooks. . . . The trout are crisp outside and firm and pink inside and the bacon is well done—but not too done."

This newspaper article foreshadowed the more resonant description of campfire cooking in "Big Two-Hearted River," the longest and most important story in his first trade book, *In Our Time* (1925). In this story Hemingway uses characteristically short words and simple sentences as well as effective repetition. He shows how the shell-shocked Nick Adams, his appetite intensified by the smell of the food, tries to hold himself together, and prevent another crack-up, through the rituals of cooking and fishing in the healing wilderness. The crucial words in this passage, "with difficulty," suggest that the bubbles rising to the hot surface are like the thoughts of war he's desperately trying to suppress: "Nick put the frying pan on the grill over the flames. He was hungrier. The beans and spaghetti warmed. Nick stirred them and mixed them together. They began to bubble, making little bubbles that rose with difficulty to the surface. There was a good smell. Nick got out a bottle of tomato catchup and cut four slices of bread. The little bubbles were coming faster now."

A newspaper article, sent from Germany in September 1922 and peppered with satiric comments, hints at the severe hardships caused by postwar inflation. Hemingway recreates the atmosphere of a rough inn in the Black Forest by describing bare-armed laborers in undershirts cutting the dark loaves with their own knives. He joins the two basic elements of the simple meal (which could be had for only a few cents) by warning that the communal bread and wine are both sour: "The beer is good, the wine is bad, dinner is at noon, you have to select your piece of black bread carefully to make sure you are missing a sour one. . . . Workmen with their suspenders over their undershirts eat hunks of black bread they carve off a loaf with a pocket knife and wash down with sour wine."

A year later, in the more self-assured and amusing "Wild Gastronomic Adventures of a Gourmet" (November 24, 1923), Hemingway uses the effective variation of "I have eaten" and the highfalutin diction of "toothsome," inside information from Indians and familiarity with French horsemeat restaurants (which still exist), tall tales and backwoods lore, heroic boasting and manly swagger, incongruous catalogs of revolting food and deliberately anticlimactic letdowns (spaghetti, doughnuts and fritto misto) to shock and even nauseate his timorous readers:

> I have eaten Chinese sea slugs, muskrat, porcupine, beaver tail, birds' nests, octopus and horse meat.
>
> I have also eaten snails, eels, sparrows, caviar and spaghetti. All shapes.
>
> I must confess to having eaten mule meat, bear meat, moose meat, frogs legs and fritto misto. . . .
>
> There is very little one can say for mule meat. It makes little appeal to either the esthetic sense or the palate. In ranking foods, it should be placed somewhere between boiled moccassin and the more toothsome of the tallow candles. . . .
>
> [He dubiously claims that] on a bet I ate a fair-sized quantity of poison ivy. . . .

> Just after the sea-slugs . . . came ancient eggs. One-hundred-year-old eggs. Dark green in color. . . . Lay off ancient eggs. . . . .
>
> [*Escargots*] remind you most of an inner tube. Cross an inner tube with a live frog, and make the product slippery, and you have the texture. . . .
>
> There are two common animals that taste like very good young pork. One is the opossum. . . . The other is the common porcupine. . . .
>
> Muskrats are good eating, too, as any Indian can tell you. The meat is as tender as chicken. . . .
>
> Sometimes [octopus] is good and sometimes it is very tough and leathery. . . .
>
> For weeks I ate horsemeat before I discovered it. . . . The meat is like beef, but stringy. . . .
>
> After years of adventurous eating there are only a few things that I dislike. One of them is parsnips. Another is the doughnut. Another is Yorkshire pudding. Another is boiled potatoes.

The young Hemingway, who'd been eating in Europe since he was eighteen, reels off a catalog of exotic and disgusting dishes for his squeamish midwestern readers, and ends by comically rejecting some commonplace foods.

The following month, in "Christmas on the Roof of the World" (December 22, 1923), Hemingway recalled the wintry feeling in wartime Milan—"drinking hot rum punches inside the cafés"—and suggested (as in the first paragraph of "In Another Country," 1927) that the dead game resembled the stiff corpses of soldiers at the front: "Foxes, deer, pheasants, rabbits, hanging before the butcher shops." He concluded the three-part article with a sentimental, nostalgic, anti-romantic account of a young man and woman, homesick and lonely after only three days in Paris, eating their dreadful Christmas dinner ("They attack. . . . They attack") far from their families and familiar American food: "They attack the special Christmas dinner. The turkey . . . seems to include a small taste of meat, a great deal of gristle and a large piece of bone. . . . They attack the potatoes, which are fried with too much grease. . . . They ate the dessert, and neither one mentioned the fact that it was slightly burned. . . . 'I didn't know Paris was like this,' she said. 'I thought it was gay and full of light and beautiful.'" The disastrous attempt to create an American dinner accentuates their desolate mood.

The Torrents of Spring (1926), Hemingway's satire on the phony primitivism of Sherwood Anderson, takes place in Petoskey, in northern Michigan. The specialty of Brown's Beanery, with its catchy slogan "The Best by Test," recalls the crudely cooked beans in "Big Two-Hearted River." The hypnotic description of the Beanery ("There was. . . . There was") foreshadows the much darker opening paragraphs of *A Farewell to Arms* (1929). While evoking the all-too-familiar lunchroom setting in *Torrents*, Hemingway mentions the condiments that are needed to spice up the bland food and the down-home humor of the waitress: "There was the long counter, the salt cellars, the sugar containers, the ketchup bottle, the Worcestershire Sauce bottle. . . . There [was] a pile of doughnuts under a glass cover. . . . 'I would like to have some [pork] and beans for myself.' . . . 'A pig and the noisy ones,' the waitress called" out to the cook.

Toward the end of *Torrents* Hemingway shifts the scene, with a sudden jolt, from Petoskey to Paris, where he's writing this very book. And he describes a lavish luncheon with his writer-friend John Dos Passos to show how far he had come. To emphasize the contrast between *basse* and *haute cuisine* and convey the flavor of the moment, he gives the dishes fancy French names while translating them into English for the benefit of his wide-eyed American audience. Hemingway lords it over the provincial reader by ordering almost everything on the menu, which he could do when the dollar was strong in France. He also stretches credulity by claiming that he drank, in midday, four bottles of wine and two fiery brandies. The somewhat unrefined expression "washed down" (conveyed with a familiar aside to the reader), reveals the American background of this worldly expatriate: "We lunched on *rollmops*, *sole meunière*, *civet de lièvre à la cocotte*, *marmelade de pommes*, and washed it all down, as we used to say (eh, reader?) with a bottle of Montrachet 1919 with the sole, and a bottle of Hospice de Beaune 1919 apiece with the jugged hare. Mr. Dos Passos, I believe, shared a bottle of Chambertin with me over the *marmelade de pommes* (Eng., apple sauce). We drank two *vieux marcs*."

In *The Sun Also Rises* (1926), Hemingway's most artistically perfect book, food helps define the mood of the characters in four different locales in France and Spain. In Paris the lonely and frustrated Jake Barnes does some sophisticated but rather desperate slumming with a Belgian prostitute and has a perfectly rotten time. Prostitutes (whose slang name also means "hen") are not known for their sparkling conversation; and the stolid Belgians, addicted to *moules et frites*, are the perennial targets of the French. At both the beginning and the end of the novel Jake, impotent from a war wound, substitutes unspecified food for sex:

> I had picked her up because of a vague sentimental idea that it would be nice to eat with some one. It was a long time since I had dined with a *poule*, and I had forgotten how dull it could be. . . . Georgette cheered up a little under the food.
> "It isn't bad here," she said. "It isn't chic, but the food is all right." . . .
> We had another bottle of wine and Georgette made a joke. She smiled and showed all her bad teeth.

Later on, Jake and Bill Gorton dine in a restaurant on the fashionable Île St. Louis in the Seine. But it had been mentioned in an American guide book and had suddenly become very popular:

> We ate dinner at Madame Lecomte's restaurant on the far side of the island. It was crowded with Americans and we had to stand up and wait for a place. . . .
> We had a good meal, a roast chicken, new green beans, mashed potatoes, a salad, and some apple-pie and cheese. . . . After the coffee and a *fine* [brandy] we got the bill, chalked up the same as ever on a slate, that was doubtless one of the "quaint" features, paid it, shook hands, and went out.
> "You never come here any more, Monsieur Barnes," Madame Lecomte said.
> "Too many compatriots."

It's ironic that Jake, a regular customer who knows the owner but is degraded to the status of a tourist, orders a quintessentially American meal. The American clients prefer their own kind of food and the restaurant provides what they want.

On their fishing trip to Burguete, in the Pyrenees of northeast Spain, the waitress serves the hungry sportsmen large portions of hearty mountain food, with local fish and fruit, and plentiful cheap wine: "The girl brought in a big bowl of hot vegetable soup and the wine. We had fried trout afterward and some sort of a stew and a big bowl full of wild strawberries. We did not lose money on the wine."

At the end of the novel Jake is reunited with Brett Ashley, who's left the young bullfighter Pedro Romero. He meets her at Botin's in Madrid—founded in the eighteenth century, located off the Plaza Mayor and famous for its suckling pig. In a bittersweet reprise of his earlier meal with Georgette, the impotent Jake—for whom too much is just enough—consumes a huge meal and wants to have dessert. By contrast, the sexually satisfied Brett, smoking to cut her appetite, eats very little and refuses the sweet. Hemingway falters slightly in this near-perfect scene with the redundant "young suckling pig," and ends with Jake's caustic hint about the things he cannot do:

> We lunched upstairs at Botin's. It is one of the best restaurants in the world. We had roast young suckling pig and drank *rioja alta*. Brett did not eat much. She never ate much. I ate a very big meal and drank three bottles of *rioja alta*.
>
> "How do you feel, Jake?" Brett asked. "My God! what a meal you've eaten."
>
> "I feel fine. Do you want a dessert?"
>
> "Lord, no."
>
> Brett was smoking.
>
> "You like to eat, don't you," she said.
>
> "Yes," I said. "I like to do a lot of things."

Three stories in *Men Without Women* (1927) use food in America, Switzerland and Italy to define the essence of these countries. In "The Killers" two criminals, awaiting the arrival of their victim in a dismal diner, taunt, intimidate and insult the workers:

> "I'll have a roast pork tenderloin with apple sauce and mashed potatoes," the first man said.
>
> "It isn't ready yet."
>
> "What the hell do you put it on the card for?" . . .

> "I can give you any kind of sandwiches," George said. "You can have ham and eggs, bacon and eggs, liver and bacon, or a steak."
> "Give me chicken croquettes with green peas and cream sauce and mashed potatoes."
> "That's the dinner."
> "Everything we want's the dinner, eh? That's the way you work it." . . .
> "I'll take ham and eggs," the man called Al said. . . .
> "Give me bacon and eggs," said the other man. . . .
> George put the two platters, one of ham and eggs, the other of bacon and eggs, on the counter. . . .
> Both men ate with their gloves on.

The killers, full of misunderstanding and menace, deliberately order dishes that are not available. They are in town to kill, not to eat, and wear their gloves to assert their status.

The macabre theme of the ironically titled "An Alpine Idyll" is sandwiched between the start and finish of a Swiss-German meal. The narrator asks,

> "What is there to eat?"
> "Anything you want. The girl will bring you the eating card [a literal translation of *Spiesekarte*]. . . .
> The menu was written in ink on a card and the card slipped into a wooden paddle.

Before the food is served, a peasant at the inn tells his story. His wife had died in the winter and couldn't be buried until the snow thawed, so he stored her in the woodshed like a frozen slab of meat: "'When I started to use the big wood she was stiff and I put her up against the wall. Her mouth was open and when I came in to the shed at night to cut up the big wood, I hung my lantern from it.' . . . 'Say,' said John. 'How about eating?' 'All right,' I said." The meal—its wooden paddle hinting at the woodshed—allows them to continue their normal, ongoing life and to ignore the horrors of the story.

In "Che Ti Dice La Patria?" (What Does the Country Tell You?), a patriotic slogan invented by Gabriele D'Annunzio and adopted by the fascists, Hemingway and his American-journalist friend Guy Hickok stop for a meal at La Spezia, on the Ligurian coast south of Genoa:

> "Let's eat somewhere simple," Guy said. . . .
> The girl who took our order put her arm around Guy's neck while we were looking at the menu. . . .
> The girl who had taken our order came in from the kitchen with spaghetti. She put it on the table and brought a bottle of red wine and sat down at the table.
> "Well," I said to Guy, "you wanted to eat some place simple."
> "This isn't simple. This is complicated." . . .
> "What's the mechanics of this place?" Guy asked. "Do I have to let her put her arm around my neck?"
> "Certainly," I said. "Mussolini has abolished the brothels. This is a restaurant."

In this witty scene, a contrast to Jake Barnes' sad meal with a prostitute, two Americans (Hickok possibly set up by the more worldly Hemingway) wind up in a transparently disguised whorehouse. Hemingway uses this incident—and the overeager waitress—to criticize the moral hypocrisy of the fascist regime.

A Farewell to Arms, like *The Sun Also Rises*, uses food scenes in a subtle and thematic way. In the alternating scenes of war and peace, there's rough fare at the front and more refined food in the peaceful cities. Just before he's wounded by an Austrian mortar shell, Frederic Henry shares food and danger with his Italian comrades, and finds comic relief in his perennial struggle with the elusive spaghetti: "Gavuzzi handed me the basin of macaroni. . . . I lifted it to arm's length and the strands cleared. I lowered it into the mouth, sucked and snapped in the ends, and chewed, then took a bite of the cheese, chewed, and then a drink of the wine. It tasted of rusty metal. . . . 'It's rotten,' he said. 'It's been in there too long.'" The wine, like the war, is rotten and the soldiers have been in it too long.

Frederic and Catherine Barkley escape from the war in Italy by rowing up Lake Maggiore from Stresa to Brissago in neutral Switzerland. Exhausted and ravenously hungry, they head straight for breakfast in a café, whose proverbial Swiss cleanness provides a striking contrast to the filth of war:

> We went inside the café and sat down at a clean wooden table. We were cockeyed excited. A splendid clean-looking woman with an apron came and asked us what we wanted.

"Rolls and jam and coffee," Catherine said. . . .
"I want some eggs fried too."
"How many eggs for the gentleman?"
"Three."
"Take four, darling."
"Four eggs." . . .
"I suppose pretty soon they will arrest us."
"Never mind, darling. We'll have breakfast first. You won't mind being arrested after breakfast."

They are arrested, but are given Swiss visas and rent a chalet in a village above Montreux on Lake Geneva. After a brief idyll Frederic, unaware that Catherine is dying in childbirth and eating his last supper, tries in a time of extreme stress to establish contact with another human being. As the waiter repeats the names of the dishes, he reassures Frederic with a soothing, "'That's true,' he said. 'That's true.'" But his resonant phrase "It is finished"—Christ's last words on the Cross in John 19:30—suggest that Catherine has become a Christlike sacrifice for her unwanted pregnancy and his military desertion:

I sat down and asked the waiter what the *plat du jour* was.
"Veal stew—but it is finished."
"What can I have to eat?"
"Ham and eggs, eggs with cheese, or *choucroute*."
"I had *choucroute* this noon," I said.
"That's true," he said. "That's true. You ate *choucroute* this noon." He was a middle-aged man with a bald top to his head and his hair slicked over it. He had a kind face.
"What do you want? Ham and eggs or eggs with cheese?"
"Ham and eggs," I said, "and beer."
"A demi-blonde?"
"Yes," I said.
"I remembered," he said. "You took a demi-blonde this noon."

In the 1930s, after he'd left Europe and returned to more meager rations during the Depression in America, food became less significant in Hemingway's work. He did, however, manage to escape to Africa. In *Green Hills of Africa* (1935), an account of his first hunting safari in Kenya, Hemingway describes breakfast, lunch and dinner, which was often extracted from tins, but also included a roast of Grant's gazelle and a long-awaited Christmas pudding. In a sly, ironic letter written during his second African safari in 1953 to the refined aesthete Bernard Berenson, who was unlikely to taste the dish, Hemingway explained that "lion is very good to eat. The tenderloin tastes like wiener schnitzel when it is breaded." In her memoir *How It Was*, his fourth wife, Mary, also compared lion steak to veal and wrote that the raw "clean pink flesh [was] delicious, steak tartare without the capers. . . . Thereafter Ernest and I had the lion marinated in sherry with some herbs grilled over [the] cookfire. It was firmer than Italian veal."

Hemingway was omnivorous. His library contained books on French, Italian, Spanish, American, Chinese and African cuisine, as well as Brillat-Savarin's *The Physiology of Taste* and *La guide gastronomique de la France*. After World War II—when he became rich and famous, consorted with celebrities and began to imitate his public persona—a radical change took place in his taste in food, choice of restaurants and description of meals. Flattered by deferential and well-paid headwaiters at posh establishments, Hemingway now described meals as if they were intrinsically significant rather than events that conveyed the mood and theme of his books. Food became an absurd substitute for conversation and a narcissistic display of the diner's palate. In the food scenes of *Across the River* he lapsed into embarrassing self-parody as his bitter hero, Colonel Richard Cantwell, displayed to the adoring novice, Renata, his inside knowledge of everything from opening wine to cutting clams.

Cantwell, dining at the luxurious Gritti Palace Hotel on the Grand Canal in Venice, tries with moderate success to explain how it feels to be a lobster, whose hostility has disappeared with his death: "The lobster was imposing. He was double the size a lobster should be, and his unfriendliness had gone with the boiling, so that he now looked a monument to his dead self; complete with protruding eyes and his delicate, far-extended antennae that were for knowing what rather stupid eyes could not tell him. He looks a little bit like Georgie Patton, the Colonel thought." Hemingway's hero also seems like a ghost of his dead self. And the demeaning comparison of General Patton, Hemingway's *bête noir*, to a crustacean badly misfires.

In another pointless and interminable scene in the Gritti Palace, which goes on for eighteen pages, Cantwell orders the steak in three languages, though the all-too-familiar waiter is undoubtedly multilingual:

> "There is one very good steak," the *Gran Maestro* said, reappearing.
> "You take it, Daughter. I get them all the time in the mess. Do you want it rare?"
> "Quite rare, please."
> "*Al sangue*," the Colonel said. . . . "*Crudo, bleu*, or just make it very rare."
> "It's rare," the *Gran Maestro* said. "And you, my Colonel?"
> "The scaloppini with Marsala, and the cauliflower braised with butter. Plus an artichoke vinaigrette if you can find one. What do you want, Daughter?"
> "Mashed potatoes and a plain salad."

Renata's simple, almost American choice, perhaps in deference to her host, makes Cantwell's order seem pretentious.

As the scene continues, Hemingway seems to be writing, automatically, a novel called *Tender Is the Loin*. His account of Renata's mastication is absurd, the last repetition ("saucer of *sauce*") awkward. The meaningless dialogue reveals that the lovers, outside of bed, have absolutely nothing to say to each other:

> Then she chewed well and solidly on her steak. . . .
> "Is the steak good?" the Colonel asked.
> "It's wonderful. How are your scaloppini?"
> "Very tender and the sauce is not at all sweet. Do you like the vegetables?"
> "The cauliflower is almost crisp; like celery."
> "We should have some celery." . . .
> He started to eat the artichoke, taking a leaf at a time, and dipping them, heavy side down, in the deep saucer of *sauce vinaigrette*.

Finally, when it's time to order the *formaggio*, Hemingway suddenly becomes tone deaf ("Cheese . . . Please. What cheese?") and his dialogue increasingly inept:

"What do you want for the end of the meal?" . . .

"Cheese," she said. "Please."

"What cheese?"

"We will devote ourselves to the cheese." . . .

"We will dedicate ourselves to the cheese with happiness."

Later on in the novel, when Cantwell buys some sausage in a Venetian street market, the first, adverbial part of the sentence is overelaborate; the second part, by contrast, combining taste with knowledge to give meaning to the quality of the meat, is very effective: "She cut a thin, paper thin, slice for him, ferociously, and lovingly, / and when the Colonel tasted it, there was the half smokey, black pepper-corned, true flavor of the meat from the hogs that ate acorns in the mountains."

The delightful meals in the well-named *A Moveable Feast* range from a simple lunch prepared by his first wife, Hadley—"little radishes, and good *foie de veau* with mashed potatoes and an endive salad. Apple tart"—and dinner on Lake Geneva, to Lipp's Brasserie, an unnamed but extremely expensive restaurant and a pick-up dinner on the road with Scott Fitzgerald. This memoir, written in a simpler style between 1957 and 1960, shows—as food triggers rich memories—an impressive recovery of his formidable powers.

Addressing Hadley by her nickname and referring to the local wine, Hemingway remembers the simple food in a dazzling Alpine setting: "the Sion wine was even better. Do you remember how Mrs. Gangeswisch cooked the trout *au bleu* when we got back to the chalet? They were such wonderful trout, Tatie, and we drank the Sion wine and ate out on the porch with the mountainside dropping off below and we could look across the lake and see the Dent du Midi with the snow half down it and the trees at the mouth of the Rhône where it flowed into the lake." The wine flows through their dinner as naturally as the water flows into the lake. This idyllic meal summons up a simpler time and contented marriage, when he was poor and ambitious.

Hemingway often rewarded himself with a rich meal after a good stint at his desk. Equating writing with hunger, food with sex, he alluded to the well-known postcoital *tristesse*: "After writing a story I was always empty and both sad and happy, as though I had made love." He was particularly fond of oysters (describing them three times in *A Moveable Feast*), which were supposed to be an aphrodisiac and to resemble the female genitals in appearance, texture and taste. He writes that the expatriate poet Ernest Walsh, after winning a large prize from *Dial* magazine, "asked me to lunch one day at a restaurant that was the best and the most expensive in the Boulevard St.-Michel quarter, [with] oysters, expensive flat faintly coppery *marennes*, not the familiar, deep inexpensive *portugaises*, and a bottle of Pouilly Fuissé." Since Walsh was the host on this notable occasion, Hemingway recalls, "I began my second dozen of the flat oysters . . . watching their unbelievably delicate brown edges react and cringe as I squeezed lemon juice on them and separated the holding muscle from the shell and lifted them to chew them carefully." Observing precisely, as always, he intensified the hedonistic experience by watching the oysters squirm in the zesty juice before he devoured them.

In the spring of 1925 Hemingway joined Scott Fitzgerald to retrieve his car in Lyon and drive it back to Paris. They stopped for the night at a hotel in Châlon-sur-Saône, between Dijon and Lyon. Hemingway ordered *escargots*, which he'd recently described as rubbery and slippery, but now liked so well that he also ate Fitzgerald's portion: "When he came back I said I would get him some more snails but he said he did not want any. He wanted something simple. He did not want a steak, nor liver and bacon, nor an omelette. He would take chicken. We had eaten very good cold chicken at noon but this was still famous chicken country, so we had *poularde de Bresse* and a bottle of Montagny, a light, pleasant wine of the neighborhood." Hemingway knows what he wants and eats everything in sight. Fitzgerald, indecisive and with a more delicate stomach, wants (like Guy Hickok in "Che Ti Dice") something simple. He chooses the regional specialty—local poultry from nearby Bresse, which were famously fat and well fed—and (like Brett and Renata) eats moderately.

In Cuba near the end of his life, suffering from depression and worried about his health, he had a very simple diet. Valerie Hemingway, who worked as Ernest's secretary during the last years of his life and later married his youngest son, Gregory, described the food in the Finca and in the homely restaurants of Havana:

> Hemingway makes it clear in his writings that he was very fond of food, even simple food like a cheese and onion sandwich—which he often ate when we were on the road. He had calf's liver with bacon and onions every day we were in Madrid in 1960. He loved fish and he loved Chinese food. In 1960 the food at the Finca was both minimal

> and simple. Fish, mostly poached, and which he had caught, perhaps five times a week, with a vegetable and salad. Both he and Mary were trying to lose weight. Plain fruit for dessert. Mangoes were taken directly from the trees. When we ate out, it was at the Floridita, where he often had lamb; El Pacífico, which was Chinese; or La Terraza, where lobster was the specialty. I don't recall him eating much meat or even chicken. Those things were barely available in Cuba at the time. There was always plenty of wine with meals. Usually a whiskey or gin and tonic before dinner, but not before lunch. We never had spirits before 5 p.m. Nor did we have hors d'oeuvres or nibbles with drinks before dinner. Mary ran a very tight ship.

Hemingway's heroes have the same appetite for food as they do for hunting and fishing, boxing and war, women and sex, and meals remain a touchstone of their existence. Though tragedy destroys many of his heroes, rich feasts, devoured with gusto, are a constant source of sensual pleasure. As he wrote in "Wild Gastronomic Adventures": "I have discovered that there is romance in food when romance has disappeared from everywhere else. And as long as my digestion holds out I will follow romance."

THIRTY-SEVEN

HUMOR

Hemingway's fame rests on his tragic romances of love and death; his evocative stories crafted in spare prose; his vivid war reporting and travel books. He was not a comic writer, and when he tried to be funny he could be heavy-handed, as in his parody *The Torrents of Spring*, or embarrassingly arch, as in the tedious conversations with the Old Lady in the otherwise fascinating *Death in the Afternoon*. Yet his most underrated quality was his lively sense of humor. In his personal life he was hard on himself and on others; in letters he could be savagely funny and satiric, contemptuous and malicious, even nasty. He liked elaborate, excessive insults and coined some colorful phrases. In his writing his wit could be charming and tender, mordant and cynical, his humor sly and clever. In the most serious contexts, flashes of amusement relieve the tension of the drama or cast realistic light on a romantic situation.

John Dos Passos once remarked that "Hem was the only man I ever knew who really hated his mother." She was the focus of his youthful resentment as well as his bitter humor about women. In 1918, in New York and about to work for the Red Cross in Italy, the teenaged Hemingway rebelled against her puritanism and propriety. As a practical joke, he announced his "engagement" to the film star Mae Marsh, whom he'd never met. His parents failed to get the joke, and his father wrote to complain that it "had taken five nights sleep from your mother . . . who was broken hearted." Finally, Hemingway had to explain that it was all pure fantasy. While living in decadent Paris after the war, matured by his experience, married and embarked on his career, he adopted a more sophisticated tone. Using one of Grace Hemingway's favorite clichés, he told his father that she had an overdeveloped sense of sin: "I remember Mother saying once that she would rather see me in my grave than something—I forget what—smoking cigarettes perhaps."

Later on he blamed his mother for his father's suicide, and portrayed Ed as a castrated weakling, dominated by the monstrous Grace. In what was surely a ludicrous exaggeration, he told his fourth wife, Mary, that Grace "never forgave me for not getting killed in World War I, so she could be a Gold Star Mother." On another occasion, opposing a conventional with a contemptuous response, he dramatically exclaimed: "Jesus, is it Mother's Day? Then I'll have to send the old bitch a wire."

Despite his crude talk in speech and letters, Hemingway was sensitive and vulnerable. He had a corresponding impulse to retaliate for slights, to hit out against family, wives, friends and literary rivals. This defensive urge provoked his comic and grotesque putdowns. Enraged at his older sister, Marcelline, for criticizing his divorce from his first wife, Hadley, he compared his sister to a coffin and called her "a bitch complete with handles." His younger brother Leicester, who feebly imitated Hemingway and tried to cash in on his reputation, portrayed him as the swaggering Rando Granham in his autobiographical novel *The Sound of the Trumpet*. Hemingway called it "a chickenshit abortion filled with the worst crap he had ever read. The few good parts were like ripe plums in vomit."

Hemingway was deeply romantic about women. His serial loves and marriages were essential to his emotional life and inspired his work. But when these relationships disintegrated he adopted an aggressive posture and shot off witty remarks or retaliatory barbs. When living with his second wife, Pauline, in Key West in the 1930s, he had a mistress, Jane Mason, in Havana. Beautiful but emotionally unstable, Jane jumped out of a window in her house and broke her back. Hemingway, detaching himself from the disaster, portrayed himself as the indifferent male and called her "the girl who fell for him literally." When he finally asked Pauline for a divorce, she vindictively said: "Ernest, if you divorce me I'll take everything you've got," and he replied: "Pauline, if you let me have a divorce, you can have everything I've got." He felt it would be worth everything he had to get rid of her—though much of what he had, his house, boat (and African safari), had been paid for by her generous rich uncle Gus. But the facts were less important than getting back at his wife and making himself the victim.

His third wife, Martha, his most engaging victim and the only woman who left him, admitted that Hemingway could always make her laugh, even when she wanted to murder him. Martha had a mania for cleanliness and called Hemingway (none too fondly) "The Pig." He complained to Aaron Hotchner that "her father was a doctor, so she made our house look as much like a hospital as possible." As their marriage began to disintegrate, right after it began, he became increasingly critical. Using a racing metaphor for that thoroughbred, he remarked that she "had but three gaits"—two fast, one slow—"running away, over-work, and sleep." He claimed that Martha, who'd attended Bryn Mawr and rivaled him as a foreign correspondent, "had made more money writing about atrocities than any woman since Harriet Beecher Stowe." When she took off to report the Russo-Finnish War in 1940, Hemingway, in a joke tinged with self-pity, portrayed himself in tropical Cuba as a tribesman who needed female warmth in his teepee: "What old Indian likes to lose his squaw with a hard winter coming on?" Fearing Martha's independence would lead to infidelity, he also insisted: "I need my wife in bed and not in the most widely circulated magazines."

After their divorce Hemingway, suggesting that most upper-class women had sexual difficulties, told Bernard Berenson that Martha "was not built for bed but few nice people are." After Martha had an operation, their sex life improved. It was like entering a cathedral, he exclaimed, "like coming into Penn Station." After their marriage collapsed, Hemingway called one of his cats Mooky, a nickname she hated, and told his publisher Charles Scribner: "Have a new house-maid named Martha and certainly is a pleasure to give her orders."

Ever the romantic, Hemingway overflowed with sentimental endearments while courting his fourth wife, Mary, whom he met in wartime London. But after they were married he soon began to resent her, and when she had an accident he was more annoyed than sympathetic. As with Martha, he compared Mary to a horse and reported that she had broken "her near hind leg." When she became jealous of the young Italian Adriana Ivancich (the model for Renata in *Across the River*), he blamed Mary for his own dangerous flirtation, compared her to the sadistic Spanish Inquisitor-General and told her: "You have the face of a Torquemada."

Proud and touchy, Hemingway had a hair-trigger temper and got even angrier as he got older. As early as 1922, as a young foreign correspondent, he was enraged when the International News Service questioned his travel expenses and sent them a terse telegram in cablese: "SUGGEST YOU UPSTICK BOOKS ASSWARDS." Hemingway used letters to let off steam, retaliate against enemies and express what couldn't be printed. He used his cruel wit to pay off old grudges, elaborating his abuse and enjoying his own nastiness. In a letter of 1948, unhappy about the Belgians' role in the war and the crude postwar Belgian tourists, he described their distinctive repulsiveness in terms of offensive odors: "Been trying to think of what a Belgian smells like. . . . It is a blend of traitorous King, toe-jam, un-washed navels, old bicycle saddles, (sweated), paving stones . . . with a touch of leek soup and cooking parsnips." Hemingway had always felt that writing was a rather unmanly profession and cultivated a compensatory tough persona. If writers were suspect, critics were much worse. He hated the critics, who turned against him in the early 1930s, as much as the Belgians, and referred to them in letters as "the eunuchs of art" and "the lice who crawl on literature."

Aware of and even perhaps embarrassed by his role as a rich and successful author who needed dependents to sustain his prestigious way of life, Hemingway made many mordant wisecracks about parasites and followers. Punning on the title of Richard Llewellyn's Welsh coal-mining novel, he remarked of a new manservant: "how green was my valet." He defined the roles of the hard-drinking, down-home Toby Bruce as "secretary, treasurer, chauffeur, valet and procurer." His unfortunately named German translator "may have made errors but was always Horschitz." Though unaware that his lawyer Alfred Rice was swindling him by taking a 30 percent (instead of the usual 10 percent) commission, Hemingway stressed his incompetence by grotesquely calling him "the reserve outfielder on my paraplegic baseball team." In Cuba, when the Basque priest Father Andrés—who drank, cursed and refused to behave like a priest—arrived at the Finca smelling like a billy goat, Hemingway would order the maid to launder his habit and remove his sweaty "odor of sanctity."

Even friends did not escape censure. Though Hemingway admired Gary Cooper's portrayal of Robert Jordan in *For Whom the Bell Tolls* and valued him as a sporting companion, he felt the rich but tight-fisted Cooper loved money more than most people loved God. He was critical about Cooper's late conversion to Catholicism to please his wife (perhaps because he'd done the same thing when he married Pauline), and told a friend that Cooper now had both money and God.

Literary rivals came in for the same colorful rejection as wives. In a bilious letter of 1951 to Charles Scribner, Hemingway blasted the firm's leading editor and authors. Max Perkins had "an idiot wife," Thomas Wolfe was "a glandular giant with the brains and guts of three mice," Scott Fitzgerald was "a dishonest and easily frightened angel." The following year, when he saw the stage version of *The Great Gatsby* in New York, he said "he paid to get in and would gladly have paid to get out."

His intense rivalry with Fitzgerald began with their first meeting in Paris in April 1925, when Fitzgerald had just published *The Great Gatsby* and Hemingway was still unknown. Fitzgerald introduced him to Perkins and to Scribners, which became his lifelong publishers. But helping Hemingway was always dangerous. As early as July 1925 he wrote to Fitzgerald, mildly mocking his intellectual limitations (though he'd been to Princeton and Hemingway had not gone to college), his snobbery, his alcoholism and his unwarranted devotion to the destructive Zelda. He gave a brilliant satiric sketch of Fitzgerald's self-indulgent life, so different from his own: "I wonder what your idea of heaven would be—A beautiful vacuum filled with wealthy monogamists, all powerful and members of the best families, all drinking themselves to death."

Hemingway sometimes attacked other writers as a way of staking out his own territory. He felt his early experience in battle enabled him to distinguish between authentic and phony writing about war and death. Combining a business metaphor with military slang in a letter to the critic Malcolm Cowley, Hemingway attacked Archibald MacLeish for the unjust appropriation of public grief, for whoring at *Fortune* magazine and for exploiting his brother's death in leaden poetry: "Does Archie still write anything except Patriotic? I read some awfully lifeless lines to a Dead Soldier by him. . . . I thought good old Allen Tate could write the lifeless-est lines to Dead Soldiers ever read but Archie is going good. His brother Kenny was killed in the last war flying and I always felt Archie felt that sort of gave him a controlling interest in all deads."

Hemingway, boasting in childhood that he was "'fraid of nothing," always took great risks. But fearful that he might die violently, he superstitiously joked about death. After the Great War he wrote that my "living grandfather, not the dead one, he's dead, toted me to luncheon." In Paris he said of the editor Ernest Walsh, stricken by tuberculosis and marked for an early death, "now that he is dying is getting to be a pretty nice guy." Charles Fenton, author of an intrusive book on Hemingway's literary apprenticeship, "set a bad example to other biographers by jumping to his death from a hotel window."

Making a witty remark out of the obvious, Hemingway was fond of observing: "Men are dying this year who have never died before." When Tennessee Williams, who'd known Pauline in Key West, asked about her death, Hemingway rudely crushed him with: "She died like everyone else . . . and after that she was dead." Recovering from the war in 1918, he claimed that being wounded and surviving was "the next best thing to getting killed and reading your own obituaries." Thirty-six years later, after his second African plane crash, he did read his obituaries and maintained: "I could never have written them nearly as well myself."

In the 1920s Hemingway displayed his wit in a range of literary work. He wrote verse parodies and his burlesque novel *The Torrents of Spring*. He blended reportage and mocking satire in the interchapters of *In Our Time*, wrote sophisticated, romantic and cynical comic dialogue in *The Sun Also Rises* and black comedy in "The Killers." Even his serious stories of love and death are streaked with wit. Humor lightened the tragic element in his minor works: *Death in the Afternoon*, *Green Hills of Africa*, *To Have and Have Not* and *Across the River*. He particularly mocked his favorite targets: Martha Gellhorn in a play and a story, and Scott Fitzgerald in *A Moveable Feast*.

Hemingway's parody of Pound's "Hugh Selwyn Mauberley" ("The age demanded an image / Of its accelerated grimace") in "The Age Demanded," written a few years after the Great War, expressed the prevailing antiwar sentiment of the time in a rudely obscene rejection of his parents' prewar values, beginning: "The age demanded that we dance / and jammed us into iron pants." In a swipe against his religious upbringing he parodied the famous Psalm 23, "The Lord is my shepherd, I shall not / want him for long," in his mocking, pretentiously titled "Neothomist Poem." Similarly, in the deliberately provocative story "Today is Friday," he described two Roman soldiers casually commenting on the crucifixion as if Christ were a prizefighter in a boxing match:

> "He was pretty good in there today."
> "Why didn't he come down off the cross?"
> "He didn't want to come down off the cross. That's not his play."

In another early poem, "The Earnest Liberal's Lament," he punned on his own much-disliked first name and cynically mocked attempts to change the world:

I know monks masturbate at night,
That pet cats screw,
That some girls bite,
And yet
What can I do
To set things right?

In *The Torrents of Spring* Hemingway jeered at Sherwood Anderson's fashionable but often absurd racial and sexual primitivism and set his story in northern Michigan. The Indian Red Dog, trying to identify Yogi Johnson's origins, comically abbreviates the Indian names: "'Your tribe. What are you—Sac and Fox? Jibway? Cree, I imagine.' 'Oh,' said Yogi. 'My parents came from Sweden.'" Parodying his own fondness for the word "commence" as well as Anderson's style, Hemingway solemnly noted that "spring had not yet come, and the men who had commenced their orgies were halted by the chill in the air."

In the Red Cross and as a journalist the young Hemingway had witnessed five wars. He knew the suffering of common soldiers and refugees, and always took a dim view of politicians and generals. Reporting the Genoa Economic Conference for the *Toronto Star* in 1922, he wrote that the Soviet Foreign Minister Georgi Chicherin was obsessed by his gaudy uniform, his deputy Maxim Litvinov had a ham-like face and the German Chancellor Karl Wirth looked like the tuba player in a Bavarian band. Interviewing Mussolini just after he seized power that year, Hemingway immediately saw through the Duce's theatrical mask and wrote: "there is something wrong, even histrionically, with a man who wears white spats with a black shirt." He called him "the biggest bluff in Europe," and concluded "you will see the weakness in his mouth which forces him to scowl the famous Mussolini scowl."

In *In Our Time* Hemingway found a way to combine objective and imaginative writing, to express the range of powerful feelings he'd experienced in war. "L'Envoi," the last vignette, balances brutal descriptions of the Greco-Turkish War with a satirical portrait of King George II of Greece. He used indirect speech, a playfully ironic tone and the language of nursery rhyme: "The king was working in the garden. . . . This is the queen, he said. She was clipping a rose bush. . . . Plastiras is a very good man I believe, he said, but frightfully difficult. I think he did right though shooting those chaps. . . . Of course the great thing in this sort of affair is not to be shot oneself! . . . Like all Greeks he wanted to go to America." The queen, clipping a rose bush like any suburban housewife, is utterly conventional; the king, under house arrest, rather petulantly complains of his restriction to the grounds of the palace. He cynically believes in the importance of survival, but has only four months left to rule. He would soon be deposed by General Nicholas Plastiras, who'd executed six ministers after the revolution of 1922 but whom King George calls "a very good man." Despite his taste for whiskey and soda and for British diction ("frightfully," "chaps"), the insecure and unhappy king is democratically reduced to the level of the immigrant peasant who dreams of opening a diner in America.

Hemingway's return to Oak Park after his war wound became an important theme in his stories, and he used humorous irony to reveal the contrast between the cynical young man and his conventional family. In "The Last Good Country" he indirectly alluded to his mother's dislike of his writing when the young Nick Adams responds with mock-solemnity to his sister's objection:

> "But *St. Nicholas* is our favorite magazine."
> "I know," said Nick. "But I'm too morbid for it already. And I'm not even grown-up."

In "Soldier's Home" the mother exerts pressure on her traumatized son to start work, which he doesn't want to do, and uses the language of religion, which he's rejected. Numbed and embittered, Krebs unintentionally wounds his mother. She resorts to emotional blackmail and creates a scene that makes her stifling maternal love more difficult to bear than her hostility. The contrast between her demands and his response is painfully ludicrous.

Witty dialogue established both the cynical views of the expatriate characters and the disillusioned tone of *The Sun Also Rises*. Speaking of an exhausted hack-writer based on the once-renowned Joseph Hergesheimer, a character maintains: "He's through now. . . . He's written about all the things he knows, and now he's on all the things he doesn't know." When Bill Gorton asks the once affluent Campbell, "how did you go bankrupt?," Mike replies: "Two ways. . . . Gradually and then suddenly."

Jake Barnes, alluding to a prostitute's mind rather than her body (which his war wound prevents him from using), remarks: "It was a long time since I had dined with a *poule*, and I had forgotten how dull it could be." By contrast, the woman he loves, Brett Ashley, a reckless English aristocrat down on her luck, is exciting but unreliable. When she fails to show up for a rendezvous at an elegant hotel, Jake stoically if sentimentally consoles himself. He observes that Brett is never there when he needs her, though he's always there for her, "so I sat down and wrote some letters. They were not very good letters but I hoped their being on Crillon stationery would help them." Hemingway often translated Spanish into English literally, to reproduce the formality of Spanish in comical English. At the end of the novel Jake answers Brett's desperate summons to the Hotel Montana in Madrid. The manager insists that "the personages of this establishment were rigidly selectioned." But Jake skeptically responds: "I was happy to hear it. Nevertheless I would welcome the upbringal of my bags."

Brett, a breathtakingly outrageous woman, provides much of the novel's wit. Though she loves Jake, she has affairs with the alcoholic Mike Campbell, the Princetonian Robert Cohn and the bullfighter Pedro Romero. Referring to a louche hotel that rented rooms by the hour for sex, Brett crassly tells Jake that they asked her and Mike "if we wanted a room for the afternoon only. Seemed frightfully pleased we were going to stay all night." In this voyeuristic novel (with a hero who cannot have sex) the characters look lustfully at each other. When Jake sees the Jewish Cohn staring longingly at the seductive Brett, he mock-heroically compares him to Moses after forty years in the wilderness: "He looked a great deal as his compatriot must have looked when he saw the promised land." Admiring Romero in his sparkling, tight-fitting *traje de luces*, Brett suggests her interest in seeing him naked as well as dressed: "how I would love to see him get into those clothes. He must use a shoe horn."

Death, an ever-present theme in Hemingway, could be the occasion of black comedy. The murderers in "The Killers"—who wear natty clothes, use mock-polite diction and incongruously appear in a small-town diner—are compared to a cocky vaudeville team. One of them "wore a derby hat and a black overcoat buttoned across the chest. His face was small and white and he had tight lips. He wore a silk muffler and gloves." His coat is as tight as his lips because he's trying to hide a shotgun underneath it. Awaiting the arrival of their fatally resigned victim, the hitmen entertain themselves by intimidating the men in the diner with laconic insults that require immediate assent. Hemingway based "The Killers" on the comical-sinister gangsters of Al Capone's

Chicago. The sharp cinematic scenes and the wisecracking dialogue, contrasting the banality of the characters with the violent conclusion, influenced the portrayal of underworld characters in American gangster films.

Though the focus of *Death in the Afternoon* is the balletic ritual of death in the bullfight, Hemingway leavened the subject with amusing passages that place the *corrida* in the context of Spanish culture. Speaking of Madrid (where both inhabitants and visitors often dine at midnight and always stay up late) but remembering his days as a war reporter in the early 1920s, he noted: "in no other town that I have ever lived in, except Constantinople during the period of the Allied occupation, is there less going to bed for sleeping purposes." He liked to joke, half-seriously, about the debilitating exactions of women, and said that retired matadors sometimes came back to fight "because the intensity of their domestic relations has relaxed."

Hemingway made strenuous efforts to break from his Victorian past, but always retained an element of midwestern puritanism. His glossary provided definitions that revealed his amused fascination with sexual commerce. He broadly explained *puta* as "whore, harlot, jade, broad, chippy, tart or prostitute," adding of *hijo de puta* (son of a whore): "In Spanish they insult most fully when speaking or wishing ill of the parents rather than of the person directly." Homosexuality, which repelled as it fascinated him, was always an absurd sort of joke to him. Referring to the flourishes of a style inappropriate to the strict rules of the *corrida*, he defined *maricón* (a derisive word for homosexual) as "a sort of exterior decorator of bullfighting." Speaking of Jean Cocteau's lover Raymond Radiguet in the text, the narrator punningly explains: "He was a young French writer who knew how to make his career not only with his pen but with his pencil if you follow me." He then quotes Cocteau's ironic comment on Radiguet: "Bébé est vicieuse—il aime les femmes." Hemingway used the feminine form of the word for "vicious" (instead of *vicieux*) to suggest that Cocteau was speaking as if his lover were a woman.

Hemingway also used the glossary to describe, with comic exaggeration, one of the dangers of foreign travel, which he called "heel rape": "ambulatory vendors will come up to you while you are seated in the café, [and] cut the heel off your shoe with a sort of instant-acting leather-cutting pincers they carry, in order to force you to put on a rubber heel." Hinting at a milder form of crucifixion, he suggested an absurd solution to the problem. The best thing to do when you see one of them approaching "is to take off your shoes and put them inside your shirt. If he then attempts to attach rubber heels to your bare feet, send for the American or British Consul." Speaking of pickpockets in his gloss on *maleante* (corrupter), Hemingway remarked that "in their own walk of life these gentry combine the same qualities that Montés listed as indispensable to a bullfighter—lightness, valor, and a perfect knowledge of their profession."

In a letter to Gertrude Stein, who first told him about the bullfights in Spain, Hemingway delighted in the grisly aftermath of the *corrida*, and liked to imagine how the experience would shock the folks back home. The triumphant matador, awarded an ear, had honored Hemingway's wife with his bloody trophy: "Hadley got the ear given to her and wrapped it up in a handkerchief which, thank God, was Don Stewart's. I tell her she ought to throw it away or cut it up into pieces and send them in letters to her friends in St. Louis but she won't let it go and it is doing very nicely." Describing the horrid ear as if it were a newborn infant, he added, with "thank God," just the right touch to this delightful vignette.

Hemingway saw both humor and anguish in sex, a subject which provoked a great many wisecracks and witticisms. Nick Adams has a series of sexual intimations and experiences. In "Fathers and Sons," his father challenges the young Nick for using an improper word:

> "The little bugger," Nick said.
> "Do you know what a bugger is?" his father asked him.
> "We call anything a bugger," Nick said.
> "A bugger is a man who has intercourse with animals."
> "Why?" Nick said.
> "I don't know," his father said. "But it is a heinous crime."

Though he objects to Nick's use of the word, the father provides a deliberately incomplete definition of "bugger." He avoids discussing sodomy between humans and talks instead of the far less common bestiality, which he doesn't understand. To disguise his meaning he uses the word "heinous," which Nick doesn't understand. His intervention exposes his own prudery and leaves Nick confused. This funny and sad conversation shows how fathers want to hide and to explain the truth about sex, and how sons have to pick up as much of the puzzle as they can.

Nick's sexual initiation continues when his Indian friend Billy asks him if he wants to go another round with his sister Trudy. (Like her real life model Prudy Boulton, she "did first what no one has ever done better"):

"You want Trudy again?"
"You want to?"
"Un Huh."
"Come on."
"No, here."
"But Billy—"
"I no mind Billy. He my brother."

When Nick asks Trudy the same question that Billy asked him, she apparently assents with an inarticulate "Un Huh." Though Billy drops out of the conversation during their next exchange, he remains a formidable presence. Nick doesn't understand Indian sexual customs or Billy's attempt at male bonding. But he realizes from her casual non sequitur ("He my brother") that she doesn't mind doing it again while Billy's watching. (In "Summer People" an older Nick Adams jokes about the sexual promiscuity of the lower classes when he asks: "Why weren't there any virgins in state universities?")

"Fathers and Sons" connects Nick's sexual experience with memories of his father's death. In his description of how the cosmetic mortician reconstructed his father's gun-shattered face, Hemingway wittily contrasted the undertaker's complacency with his dubious repairs: "The undertaker had been both proud and smugly pleased. But it was not the undertaker that had given him that last face. The undertaker had only made certain dashingly executed repairs of doubtful artistic merit. The face had been making itself and being made [by his father's sad life] for a long time." Hemingway found a wry irony indispensable when writing about the most agonizing experiences of his life.

In the Foreword to *Green Hills of Africa*, about hunting big game on his first safari, Hemingway joked about the essential requirement of popular books: "Anyone not finding sufficient love interest is at liberty, while reading it, to insert whatever love interest he or she may have at the time." His work in fact is full of "love interest" and he wrote about all the women he loved. He idealized the women in *A Farewell to Arms* and *Across the River*, but his wives were usually satiric targets. The perfect tone and petulant repetition of "Cat in the Rain" captured the character of the childish American wife, based on Hadley—spoiled, demanding and irrational: "'Anyway, I want a cat,' she said. 'I want a cat. I want a cat now. If I can't have long hair or any fun, I can have a cat.'" (Hemingway's ear for dialogue was especially accurate in this story. In a letter of May 1915, Katherine Mansfield said something very similar: "Why haven't I got a Chinese nurse with green trousers and two babies who rush at me and clasp my knees—I'm not a girl—I'm a woman. I *want* things. Shall I ever have them?") In his African book Hemingway gently punctured the vanity and fantasies of his petite, small-boned wife Pauline. She "disliked intensely being compared to a little terrier. If she must be like any dog, and she did not wish to be, she would prefer a wolfhound, something lean, racy, long-legged and ornamental."

To Have and Have Not (1937), set in Key West and Havana and partly based on his affair with Jane Mason, describes a voyeuristic intrusion and a farcical coitus interruptus. Tommy Bradley opens the door of the bedroom and observes his wife, Helène, and the writer Richard Gordon making love in his house. As the distracted Gordon sees Bradley and squirms with discomfort, Helène exclaims: "Don't stop. . . . Please don't stop. . . . Don't mind him. Don't mind anything. Don't you see you can't stop now? . . . That's only Tommy. . . . He knows all about these things. Don't mind him. Come on, darling. Please do." Gordon is unable to continue but Helène assumes they can carry on as if nothing has happened. She angrily asks: "My God, don't you know anything? Haven't you any regard for a woman?" Attacking the predatory, sexually demanding woman after both Tommy and Richard have tactfully withdrawn, Hemingway emphasizes the habitual offender's crass dismissal of her husband: "That's only Tommy. . . . He knows all about these things."

Martha Gellhorn was a frequent target of Hemingway's cruel wit. While they were still married he satirized her as Dorothy Bridges in his play, *The Fifth Column* (1938). The hero Philip Rawlings wants to marry Dorothy but disapproves of her luxurious tastes, and his friend warns her: "Don't be a bored Vassar bitch." Infatuated with her but aware of her flaws, Rawlings calls her "lazy and spoiled, and rather stupid, and enormously on the make." Apparently clairvoyant about their troubled future, Hemingway has Rawlings explain: "I'm afraid that's the whole trouble. I want to make an absolutely colossal mistake." In his postwar story "It Was Very Cold in England," the Hemingway character has an acerbic exchange with an unnamed woman based on Martha.

As they stir up their old rivalry as war correspondents, he hints at her infidelity. Then, using a sexual pun and describing their tempestuous marriage in terms of war, he compares her to a dud mine that fails to detonate when properly rammed: "You remind me of the old, badly laid mines . . . that wash up years afterwards along the coast after the big fall and winter storms."

For Whom the Bell Tolls marked a return to the idealistic love of *A Farewell to Arms*. The young Maria, who's been raped by the fascists, retains her innocence and Robert Jordan treats her like a virgin. The first time they kiss and make love, in a lyrical interlude between her violation and his death, she asks, in a famous and charming line: "Where do the noses go? I always wondered where the noses would go" (the use of "would" is masterful). In contrast to Maria, Hemingway created the earthy, sharp-tongued Pilar, the quintessential Spaniard, the gypsy and past mistress of bullfighters, the sexual expert and dominant female. Giving a new spin to regional fruit, she maintains: "The melon of Castile is for self abuse. The melon of Valencia for eating." And she quickly demolishes her boastful, alcoholic and finally submissive husband Pablo:

> "In those days I was very barbarous."
> "And now you are drunk," Pilar said.
> "Yes," Pablo said. "With your permission."
> "I liked you better when you were barbarous."

Hemingway described Colonel Cantwell's romance with the young Italian girl in *Across the River* in an arch and often irritating tone, but balanced the love affair with the hero's bitter gibes and reflections on war. A Milanese war profiteer "accused his young wife . . . of having deprived him of his judgment through her extraordinary sexual demands." In a grisly pun on "impression," Cantwell's driver (who pronounces "vehicles" with a long "i") warns him: "Sir, there is a dead GI in the middle of the road up ahead, and every time any vehicle goes through they have to run over him, and I'm afraid it is making a bad impression on the troops." In another grotesque incident Cantwell, combining the rational with the absurd in a solemn ritual, uses geometry to blot out the effects of his youthful battle trauma on the Italian front. Squatting on the bank of a river, he "relieved himself in the exact place where he had determined, by triangulation, that he had been badly wounded thirty years before."

Quoting a popular line from *The Merchant of Venice*, Cantwell asks: "what's the news from the Rialto now?" The waiter at his favorite bar, alluding to the back-biting gossip in Venice, replies: "You will get it all at Harry's except the part you figure in." Hemingway, quite good at backbiting, particularly disliked the overly cautious Field Marshal Bernard Montgomery. In the novel Cantwell asks for "Two very dry Martinis. . . . Montgomerys. Fifteen to one." This punning order alludes not only to the extreme proportion of gin to vermouth in the martini (also the name of a rifle) and to Monty's campaigns in the dry North African desert, but also to the commander's need for overwhelming superiority before he would risk confrontation with the enemy.

In his later works Hemingway does not always achieve the fine balance of light humor and tragic defeat that stamps his greatest work. Instead, he aggressively used his fiction to retaliate against rivals and enemies. In *Across the River* he unleashed his most devastating vitriol on Sinclair Lewis who, like Faulkner and Hemingway, was an alcoholic and, after winning the Nobel Prize in 1930, had gone into a sharp decline. His attack on Lewis—so unsympathetic, extreme and unnerving—has an element of repulsive wit. Readers who recognized Lewis as the unnamed American spotted by Cantwell at a nearby table in Harry's Bar, would probably have known that Lewis suffered from skin cancer that had to be burned off every few months by cobalt treatments and that his raw red skin had horrible pock marks coated with pus. Emphasizing his physical revulsion, as he did with Ford Madox Ford and Wyndham Lewis in *A Moveable Feast*, Hemingway described Sinclair Lewis' ferret features, ghastly craters "and black hair that seemed to have no connection with the human race. The man looked as though he had been scalped and then the hair replaced. . . . He looks like a caricature of an American who has been run one half way through a meat chopper and then been boiled, slightly, in oil."

Hemingway's attacks on Fitzgerald, though not quite as nasty, had a devastating effect on Scott's character and reputation. In *Torrents of Spring* he good-naturedly alluded to Fitzgerald's irritating habit of dropping in unannounced in Paris and getting self-destructively drunk: "Fitzgerald came to our home one afternoon, and after remaining for quite a while suddenly sat down in the fireplace and would not (or was it could not, reader?) get up and let the fire burn something else."

By 1936 Fitzgerald, like Sinclair Lewis, had become for Hemingway a frightening example of a writer who'd betrayed his talent and been destroyed by popular success. The hostile reference to Fitzgerald in the *Esquire* version of "The Snows of Kilimanjaro" originated with the Irish writer Mary Colum, who'd put down Hemingway with a witty remark. He avenged himself by appropriating her comment and by victimizing Fitzgerald, who'd just revealed his disastrous personal life in "The Crack-Up" and was particularly vulnerable: "he remembered poor Scott Fitzgerald and his romantic awe of [the rich] and how he started a story once that began, 'The very rich are different from you and me.' And how some one had said to Scott, Yes, they have more money." That same year, stressing Fitzgerald's permanent immaturity, Hemingway told Max Perkins that "it was a terrible thing for him to love youth so much that he jumped straight from youth to senility without going through manhood." A decade after Fitzgerald's premature death, he told Scott's future biographer that, derailed by Zelda, he'd suffered a sharp decline: "He had a very steep trajectory and was almost like a guided missile with no one guiding him."

Despite Hemingway's almost affectionate account of their ludicrous, rain-soaked trip from Lyon back to Paris in a small Renault whose top Zelda had willfully removed, his man-of-the-world indictment in *A Moveable Feast* was even more crushing. Long before they set out for Lyon, Hemingway rather cryptically noted that Fitzgerald's "delicate long-lipped Irish mouth . . . worried you until you knew him and then it worried you more"—when you realized the weakness it revealed. Fitzgerald drank Mâcon wine from the bottle while they were traveling in the car and "it was exciting to him as though he were slumming or as a girl might be excited by going swimming for the first time without a bathing suit."

The comical high point of the trip occurs in their hotel room in Lyon. Fitzgerald, with a low fever, lies on his bed looking "like a little dead crusader." Hemingway, his attendant and nursemaid, says with deadpan humor: "I was getting tired of the literary life." Charging Hemingway with callous indifference, Fitzgerald exclaims: "You can sit there and read that dirty French rag of a paper and it doesn't mean a thing to you that I am dying." He insists that his temperature be taken and Hemingway, having acquired a large thermometer designed to test bathwater, shakes it down professionally and warns him: "You're lucky it's not a rectal thermometer." Hemingway portrayed Fitzgerald as naive and gauche, sexually and psychologically inexperienced, troublesome and irritating, hypochondriac and insecure, dependent upon and dominated by Zelda, a complacent and self-confessed cuckold. His emphasis on the weak, feminine side of Scott's character subtly yet cruelly confirms Zelda's accusations of his sexual inadequacy.

In this book Hemingway portrays all the characters, comically but venomously, as he saw them after they had quarreled. Ford Madox Ford was not "the heavy, wheezing ignoble . . . up-ended hogshead" until their battle over the *Transatlantic Review* in 1924. Gertrude Stein was not a "disgusting lesbian" until after she'd demeaned him in her *Autobiography of Alice B. Toklas* in 1933. Wyndham Lewis did not have the eyes of an "unsuccessful rapist" until he attacked Hemingway in "The Dumb Ox" in 1934. Fitzgerald was not an "alcoholic failure" until "The Crack-Up" articles appeared in 1936. Dos Passos was not a "sycophantic and destructive toady" until their fight about Spanish politics in 1937. Pauline was not a "predatory bitch" until he left her in 1939, and Martha was not a "crass careerist" until their marriage fell apart. Throughout his career Hemingway's satiric humor was his weapon against the demons of sex and death. Anger inspired his wit and drove him to elaborately comic metaphors. *A Moveable Feast*, his posthumous time bomb, gave him the last word.

THIRTY-EIGHT

QUARRELS

Hemingway had deep sympathy with the underdog: with American Indians, wounded soldiers, Greek refugees, damaged veterans, Spanish guerrillas, Chinese casualties and Castro revolutionaries. But he had a satiric streak and frequently used his formidable strength against his adversaries. He struggled for dominance and thought his enemies had to be publicly punished. He engaged in physical and intellectual combat, with many threats and some real punches, and saw it as a literary version of bullfighting and big-game hunting. Some of the combatants had helped him, others had attacked him. Asserting his originality and independence, he was aggressive with Sherwood Anderson, Ford Madox Ford, Scott Fitzgerald and Sinclair Lewis, who'd praised his books. Touchy and easily offended, he also had corrosive quarrels with Gertrude Stein, Wyndham Lewis, Robert McAlmon, Harold Loeb, Max Eastman, Wallace Stevens and John Dos Passos, mainly provoked by their negative criticism of his character and work.

Though Hemingway had many lifelong friends—youthful comrades, admired authors and older mentors—he was notorious for his well-publicized disputes, many of them vividly portrayed in his posthumous time bomb, *A Moveable Feast*. Sex is the powerful engine that drives this memoir. It has a strong emotional impact, and provides psychological insight into his personality and dramatic intensity to his book. Bitter jealousy, women's power over men and insecurity about his own sexuality are the subtle yet forceful undercurrents in his relations with almost all the characters. He is jealous of Ford's liaison with Jean Rhys and of Loeb's with Duff Twysden, angry about Zelda's emotional castration of Fitzgerald, disgusted by Stein's lesbianism, repelled by

Lewis' appearance, furious about McAlmon's accusations of homosexuality, enraged by Eastman's and Stevens' attacks on his manhood.

Hemingway also quarreled bitterly with all his wives and divorced three of them. He thought Hadley was dowdy and never forgave her for losing his precious manuscripts. Pauline was fanatically Catholic and refused to use contraceptives. Martha was sexually frigid as well as selfish and independent. Mary had no self-respect and cravenly accepted his abuse. He both idealized his love for Hadley and blamed Pauline (long dead and now expendable) for his betrayal of Hadley.

Hemingway could be loyal, but had a quick temper, was aggressive and hypersensitive to personal affronts. He didn't start most fights, but when provoked or attacked he reacted angrily, even violently. Since he was taller and more powerful than his enemies, he felt that disputes, like duels, could be settled by force or, at least, by caustic satire. He was able to take physical punishment, whether accidentally self-inflicted or during fistfights. He had physical struggles with Robert McAlmon, Max Eastman and Wallace Stevens, and defeated them. He also attacked adversaries, like Ford Madox Ford and Sinclair Lewis, who were ugly and older. He also defended James Joyce in quarrels.

His violent reactions were part of the tough-guy persona he created in the 1930s in order to demonstrate that an author could also be a man of action. After he became famous, he hated literary competitors. He was generous with young unknown writers and with mediocrities, but was extremely reluctant to praise serious rivals. He believed that exposing himself to violence tested his values and confirmed the close connection between physical courage and moral strength in both his life and art.

Hemingway's *The Torrents of Spring* (1926) was the first of many gratuitous personal attacks, intended to wound and destroy the reputation of writers who had once helped him and had been his close friends. Sherwood Anderson, the first successful writer he had ever met, had urged Liveright to publish Hemingway's first trade book, *In Our Time* (1924). Hemingway rightly insisted that his early stories were not like Anderson's and that he had not been inspired by them. He wrote *Torrents* to dissociate himself from Anderson's influence and to satirize his latest book, *Dark Laughter* (1925). Hemingway's ability to parody Anderson shows how well he had learned and then rejected his lesson. He mocked Anderson's fashionable assumption that the emotional and sensual life of the Black race was superior to that of the white, and condemned his sentimental primitivism: "His dark face shone. Sharply, without explanation, he broke into high-pitched uncontrollable laughter. The dark laughter of the negro."

Ford Madox Ford published Hemingway's early stories in the *Transatlantic Review* and allowed him to edit the American issue in August 1924. On the dust wrapper of *In Our Time* Ford generously proclaimed, "The best writer in America at this time . . . the most conscientious, the most master of his craft, the most consummate, is Ernest Hemingway." In his introduction to *A Farewell to Arms* Ford handsomely ranked Hemingway with Joseph Conrad and W. H. Hudson as one of "the three impeccable writers of English prose that I have come across in fifty years or so of reading." But Hemingway loathed Ford's physically revolting appearance and his gratitude soon turned to wrath. He was thoroughly "sick of Ford and his megalomaniac blundering." He compared the older writer to an "up-ended hogshead" and described him as pedantic, rude, affected, snobbish and mendacious.

Hemingway admired Scott Fitzgerald in the mid-1920s, became more critical as he knew him better in the late 1920s and cruelly attacked him in the 1930s. But no friend did more for Hemingway than Fitzgerald. In *A Moveable Feast* he cruelly retaliated for Fitzgerald's extraordinary generosity and kindness. He portrayed his old friend as rude to all foreigners, childish and gauche, wasteful and irresponsible, quarrelsome and irritating, an artistic whore and destroyer of his own talent. A ludicrous and self-indulgent hypochondriac, he interfered with Hemingway's writing.

Sinclair Lewis called *A Farewell to Arms* "superb" and wrote a favorable introduction to a handsome edition of *For Whom the Bell Tolls*. Yet Hemingway felt Lewis was guilty on several counts. Lewis had won the Nobel Prize in 1930 and had helped him. But he had a repulsive complexion from skin cancer that recalled his own unsightly skin disease, and his life foreshadowed Hemingway's own alcoholism and literary decline. In *Across the River* Hemingway wrote that his thin ferret features and ghastly skin craters looked "like Goebbels' face, if Herr Goebbels had ever been in a plane that burned, and not been able to bail out before the fire reached him."

Gertrude Stein had studied Hemingway's weaknesses and knew how to hurt him. In her *Autobiography of Alice B. Toklas* (1933) she said Hemingway, who prided himself on his courage, was "yellow." He thought he was sophisticated and cosmopolitan; she reduced him to an Oak Park provincial and claimed he was "ninety percent Rotarian." In *A Moveable Feast* he explained that his relations with Stein abruptly ended when he unintentionally overheard a sadomasochistic lesbian quarrel, including Stein pleading with the dominant Toklas, which shocked and repelled him. He foreshadowed his own destructive tendency when he wrote of Stein: "She had, or Alice had, a sort of necessity to break off friendships and she only gave real loyalty to people who were inferior to her. She had to attack me because she learned to write dialogue from me."

In his incisive chapter in *Men Without Art* (1934) Wyndham Lewis criticized the very things Hemingway was proud of: his originality, sophistication and fictional heroes. He also shot barbs into Hemingway's most vulnerable spots: his embarrassing indebtedness to the stylistic repetitions of Stein, his lack of political awareness and his passive characters with the soul of a "dumb ox": "Hemingway invariably invokes a dull-witted, bovine, monosyllabic simpleton, a lethargic and stuttering dummy . . . a super-innocent, queerly sensitive, village-idiot of few words and fewer ideas." Though Lewis was a handsome ladies' man, Hemingway retaliated by stating, "He had a face that reminded me of a frog, not a bullfrog but just any frog. . . . I do not think I had ever seen a nastier-looking man. . . . Lewis did not show evil; he just looked nasty. . . . The eyes had been those of an unsuccessful rapist."

Robert McAlmon's Contact Editions published Hemingway's first pamphlet, *Three Stories and Ten Poems* (1923), when he was unable to place his work anywhere else. McAlmon's alcoholism, homosexuality and malice inevitably led to a rupture of their precarious relationship. McAlmon spread rumors that Hemingway had beaten Hadley when she was pregnant, that he was a homosexual and that his second wife, Pauline, was a lesbian. Hemingway threatened to beat the man he called a skinny, disappointed, half-assed, ass-licking, "fairy," fake husband, literary type. In 1934 he confronted McAlmon in a Parisian bar, accused him of nasty gossip and smashed his passive opponent with a short left hook. Fifty years later, when I said Hemingway had been viciously provoked and defended his behavior, McAlmon's friend Kay Boyle was still furious and claimed that his assault was unforgivable.

Hemingway was madly attracted to Duff Twysden and was jealous of Harold Loeb's affair with her. At the end of the Pamplona fiesta Hemingway bitterly attacked Loeb, who lost his temper and challenged him to a fistfight. As they prepared for combat, both men admitted that they didn't really want to hit each other. But it was very rare for him to offer an abject apology, which he did in a letter to Loeb: "I wish I could wipe out all the mean-ness and I suppose I can't but this is to let you know that I'm thoroughly ashamed of the way I acted and the stinking, unjust uncalled for things I said." But Hemingway's contrition was short-lived and he satirized Loeb as the pushy and irritating Robert Cohn in his Spanish-fiesta novel.

Max Eastman's "Bull in the Afternoon," a damaging review of *Death in the Afternoon*, exposed Hemingway's posturings and seemed to question his sexual capacity: "Hemingway lacks the serene confidence that he *is* a full-sized man. . . . He has the obligation to put forth evidences of red-blooded masculinity" and has developed "a literary style of wearing false hair on the chest." Max Perkins recalled that when Hemingway ran into Eastman in Scribner's offices, he "ripped open his shirt and exposed a chest which was certainly hairy enough for anybody." He then became truculent and asked, "What do you mean accusing me of impotence?" He hit Eastman with a book and threw him to the ground. But, as with Harold Loeb, he realized he was out of control and regained his temper.

During the Spanish Civil War, Hemingway had a political dispute with John Dos Passos about the latter's close friend and translator, the Loyalist colonel José Robles. After Robles was arrested by the Communists, Hemingway learned that he'd been accused of espionage and executed. He assumed Robles was guilty; but Dos, deeply shocked, refused to believe his friend was treacherous. He became furious when Hemingway suggested he was politically naive. In *A Moveable Feast* he characterized his old friend as a pilot fish who led the rich sharks, Gerald and Sara Murphy, to their innocent prey and (like Pauline) helped destroy his marriage to Hadley. After Dos was half-blinded in a car accident that killed his wife, Katy (Hemingway's childhood friend), he emphasized Dos' Latin origins and illegitimate birth by calling him a "one-eyed Portuguese bastard." Hemingway did not portray most of the characters as they were in the 1920s, but as he saw them after the quarrels of the 1930s.

Hemingway did not seem to regret the loss of these friends who were easily replaced. He remained loyal to many lifelong companions who were exempt from censure: the war hero Chink Dorman-Smith, the white hunter Philip Percival, the Loyalist general Gustavo Durán, the editor Max Perkins and the American soldier Buck Lanham.

Hemingway's attacks on old friends and new enemies followed a recurrent pattern. His reaction to them changed from extreme enthusiasm to vengeful disillusionment. When he became bored with his friends, discovered their faults, found a real or imaginary grievance or had no further use for them, he would ruthlessly, relentlessly and suddenly break off the friendships. The screenwriter Donald Ogden Stewart, a friend and victim, gave a perceptive analysis of this destructive syndrome and attributed it to Hemingway's fear of creating personal obligations that he found impossible to fulfill: "The minute he began to love you, or the minute he began to have some sort of obligation to you of love or friendship or something, then is when he had to kill you. Then you were too close to something he was protecting. He, one-by-one, knocked off the best friendships he ever had. He did it with Scott; he did it with Dos Passos—with everybody. I think it was a psychological fear he had that you might ask something from him."

After 1937 Hemingway had no close writer-friends. Jealousy, bitterness, arrogance, ambition, pride, politics and especially threats to his sexuality drove them all out of his life. In the 1940s and 1950s he knew soldiers, sportsmen, cronies, millionaires, actors, playboys and self-abasing parasites like Aaron Hotchner, who made a fortune by exploiting Hemingway. But there were no intellectuals, authors or artists. Their absence coincided with the emergence of the still combative Papa Hemingway, his last public persona. His lifelong conflicts enhanced his reputation and increased his fame. His suicide—aggression turned against himself—seemed a fitting climax to his furious and violent life.

THIRTY-NINE

SELF-CONDEMNATION

The 1920s were Hemingway's golden age as a man and a writer. In the last half of the decade he published *In Our Time* (1925), *The Sun Also Rises* (1926), *Men Without Women* (1927) and *A Farewell to Arms* (1929). During this time of brilliant achievement and early fame he was, by all accounts, a charming man and loyal friend. But *Death in the Afternoon* (1932), his first full-length nonfiction work, signaled an abrupt decline in his character and work. In this book he began to glorify blood sports, cultivate a self-consciously macho image, develop a swaggering and pompous persona, and attack other writers. The radical shift in style and tone, from laconic to loquacious, is immediately apparent if we compare the pure and lucid prose of *A Farewell to Arms* to the labored and tedious conversations with the Old Lady in *Death in the Afternoon*.

D. H. Lawrence, who believed in the therapeutic effect of writing, observed that "one sheds one's sicknesses in books—repeats and presents again one's emotions, to be master of them." In his early work Hemingway purged his fears and sadness, converting his experience into art; in his later books he shed his sicknesses, but put them on display instead of mastering them. His death-haunted books were a means of expressing his anger with himself and the world, of challenging readers to accept him with all his flaws.

With *Death in the Afternoon* Hemingway took off his fictional disguise, became a public figure and began to impersonate his own characters. He generated valuable publicity for this brashly self-confident image and attracted a new audience. He not only meant to impress his readers with his talent, skill, courage and heroic achievement, but also to confess his own misdeeds: his guilt, his failure and his corruption. In a recurrent pattern that has not been previously noticed, *Death in the Afternoon*, *Green Hills of Africa*, "The Snows of Kilimanjaro," *Across the River* and *A Moveable Feast*—like spikes on a fever chart—trace the progress of his literary pathology. Not waving but drowning, he clearly sees his own decline, but can do nothing to arrest it. Eventually, the question of his moral and artistic decline becomes the underlying subject of each book. The tone of these works is disturbing, an uneasy blend of self-glorification and ruthless self-laceration. Equally disturbing is the overkill of his assault on literary rivals. More interested in retribution than reflection, he has no desire nor ability to learn from his contemporaries. Yet Hemingway would not be Hemingway without the extraordinary honesty and perception with which he condemns himself. Like the alligator in Elizabeth Bishop's poem "Florida," Hemingway has five distinct voices: "friendliness, love, mating, war, and a warning."

In the most revealing passage in *Green Hills of Africa*, the white hunter asks, "what are the things, the actual, concrete things that harm a writer?" and Hemingway fatalistically diagnoses his own disease: "Politics, women, drink, money, ambition. And the lack of politics, women, drink, money and ambition." He wanted the worldly excitement these five things represent, but feared that excess could ruin him. His politics, in fact, were far from extreme. Though he never swallowed the Communist line, nor moved to the right as he got older, he actively supported the Loyalists in the Spanish Civil War and paid the price for his political engagement. His left-wing activities aroused the suspicions of the FBI, and later on, in the 1950s, his suspicion that federal agents were following him contributed to his mental breakdown. Even paranoids have real enemies.

A serial monogamist, Hemingway needed love as much as Fitzgerald needed drink. He never forgave himself for his betrayal of his first wife, Hadley, whom he still loved but found boring. He married his second wife, Pauline, in 1927, enchanted by her elegant clothes and her wealth that bought the big house in Key West, the fishing boat and the African safari. Guilt-ridden, he soon felt corrupted by the easy life money could buy. Drink finally wrecked his liver and damaged his ability to write. Overweening ambition made him see writing as a gladiatorial sport in which he was compelled to denigrate and defeat his rivals, both living and dead. As Gore Vidal, playing the game Hemingway invented, observed, "It's not enough to succeed. Others must fail."

Death in the Afternoon is a hybrid of two books. The first is *the* classic study of bullfighting in English; the second—more personal and interesting, but also more opinionated and irritating—is grafted onto the first to make the bullfight material more palatable to Anglo-Saxon readers. In the opening pages, Hemingway tries to explain the appeal of the *corrida*: "At the first bullfight I ever went to I expected to be horrified and perhaps sickened by what I had been told would happen to the horses. . . . I thought [the bullfights] would be simple and barbarous and cruel." But he insists that, "the only place where you could see life and death, i.e., violent death, now that the wars were over, was in the bull ring." Connecting the bullfight to fishing and hunting—other masculine arts that require skill, endurance and courage, and relate to the eternal struggle to survive—he maintains that "killing cleanly and in a way which gives you aesthetic pleasure and pride has always been one of the greatest enjoyments." In a statement that anticipates Camus' *The Stranger* and *The Rebel*, he adds that "when a man is still in rebellion against death he has pleasure in taking to himself one of the Godlike attributes: that of giving it." Hemingway equates killing bulls in the ring with killing the enemy in war. Both give men, while risking their own lives, the freedom to inflict death.

In his longest nonfiction book, Hemingway speaks as an expert to novices. He's pedantic and enthusiastic, dogmatic and provocative; obsessed by homosexuals, prostitutes and venereal disease, by cowardice, suicide and death. He discusses various obscure matadors, both cowardly and brave, but readers can't tell the difference and have to accept Hemingway's *ex cathedra* pronouncements. To break up the encyclopedic narrative with some diverting dialogue, he introduces the Old Lady—one of his most unfortunate inventions. Since she's interested in and even likes the bullfight, he hopes his equally naive readers will agree with her. This aged and incongruous character allows him to display his new persona and engage in some self-mockery. When telling her about the admirable Maera, Hemingway identifies with the bullfighter and seems to describe his own character: "He was generous, humorous, proud, bitter, foul-mouthed and a great drinker." He also exposes his own braggadocio when discussing Ignacio Sanchez Mejías (the subject of a fine elegy by García Lorca): "he laid his bravery on as with a trowel. It was as though he were constantly showing you the quantity of hair on his chest." (Max Eastman pounced on Hemingway's *machismo* in "Bull in the Afternoon," a vitriolic review of this book that provoked a fistfight with Hemingway.) In a third revealing passage about himself, Hemingway admits that he's biased, opinionated and self-deceiving: "rarely will you meet a more prejudiced man nor one who tells himself he keeps his mind more open."

Hemingway allows the Old Lady to defy him and expose his own faults. When he admits with mock humility that his comparison to Whittier's sentimental "Snowbound" is quite mistaken, she punctures his heroic image by bluntly stating, "I like you less and less the more I know you." She condemns him for criticizing matadors "very meanly" and admits that she sometimes tires of his talk. On page 190, he suddenly tires of *her*. She's served her purpose and is comically dismissed: "What about the Old Lady? She's gone. We threw her out of the book, finally. A little late you say. Yes, perhaps a little late."

Writing nonfiction seemed to bring out Hemingway's tendency to pontificate. Ranging over the literary landscape, Hemingway refers to his friendships with Gertrude Stein and the turf writer Evan Shipman; quotes Shakespeare, Marvell, Longfellow and Matthew Arnold; and offers faint praise for the naturalists Gilbert White and W. H. Hudson. But, for the first time in a major work, he also assaults his contemporaries and rivals. He dislikes Virginia Woolf's feminism, Waldo Frank's bedside mysticism, Dashiell Hammett's bloodthirsty murders, William Faulkner's logorrheic outpourings and sensational content. In "Foreheads Villainous Low" (1931), Aldous Huxley had accused him of feigning stupidity. Hemingway ignores this charge, but counterattacks by calling Huxley dishonest. He accuses him of putting "his own intellectual musings, which might sell for a low price as essays, into the mouths of artificially constructed characters which are more remunerative when issued as people in a novel." Hemingway's attacks on other writers also demolish the literary genres he despises and clear the way for his own work. He felt Huxley's talky, intellectual novels were unreal and out of date.

Hemingway's attacks on "fairies" in a book that glorifies the slaughter of animals for sport has damaged his reputation today, but his opinions are as vivid as they are intolerant. He castigates not only Ronald Firbank, Jean Cocteau and his lover Raymond Radiguet, but also—in a savage passage—"the prissy exhibitionistic, aunt-like, withered old maid moral arrogance of a Gide; the lazy, conceited debauchery of a Wilde, who betrayed a generation; the nasty, sentimental pawing of humanity of a Whitman and all the mincing gentry." Hemingway dislikes Gide's defense of homosexuality in *Corydon* (1920).

He's angry on behalf of the 1890s generation who adored Wilde's reckless wit and believed in him as a writer. And he scores a hit against Whitman's fervent but often creepy embracing of humanity. But this passage reveals more about Hemingway than about men who then were outcasts and are now considered brave defenders of sexual freedom. Like all excessively macho men, he felt threatened by homosexuals, who seemed to deny their own manhood and undermine his own insecure masculinity. It's highly ironic that he often exalts his friend and traveling companion Sidney Franklin, the Jewish-American bullfighter, without ever realizing that he was also a secret homosexual.

Green Hills of Africa, like *Death in the Afternoon*, is about killing animals and risking death, about the competitive struggle for superiority and the put-down of rivals in sport and art. Since big-game hunting in Africa does not lend itself to romance, Hemingway playfully challenges his audience by refusing to cater to their tastes. He says that "any one not finding sufficient love interest is at liberty, while reading it, to insert whatever love interest he or she may have at the time." If they don't have any love interest, they will have to do without it.

As in the Spanish book, Hemingway both exalts and condemns himself. The African natives (his paid servants) adore his manly virtues. They're astonished that the sharp-eyed Bwana can aim accurately when others cannot even see and (though he says it himself) "could shoot a rifle on game as well as any son of a bitch that ever lived." The English white hunter Philip Percival (called "Pop") was Pauline's "ideal of how a man should be, brave, gentle, comic, never losing his temper, never bragging, never complaining." Hemingway, by contrast, not afraid to expose the worst side of his character, seems pleased to flaunt his belligerent tone and egoistic behavior. Pauline begs him, in vain, to "try to act like a human being." But he finds it impossible to suppress his bad temper, competitive instinct and poisonous envy, which spoil the hunt.

It is a short step from describing his bad behavior to discussing his fear of literary failure. Hemingway connects his personal shortcomings on safari and his artistic failings, the betrayal of ideal standards of behavior and the corruption of his talent. In another acute, self-reflective diagnosis, he moves from his own example to a generalization about writers in America. He explains that "something happens to our good writers at a certain age." We destroy them economically and critically: "Our writers when they have made some money increase their standard of living and they are caught. They have to write to keep up their establishments, their wives, and so on, and they write slop."

Death in the Afternoon had been hammered by the reviewers, "the lice who crawl on literature." He's tried to ignore their poisonous remarks and now mentions other victims: "at present we have two good writers [Sherwood Anderson and Scott Fitzgerald] who cannot write because they have lost confidence through reading critics." He concludes by connecting art, as he's connected bullfighting and hunting, to virility: "So now they cannot write at all. The critics have made them impotent."

Though authors are born unto trouble, as the sparks fly upwards, Hemingway (like the critics) intensifies their woes by offering a few compliments and then attacking his literary rivals. He fondly remembers Joyce, Pound and Dos Passos as drinking companions; praises the heroic Russians: Turgenev, Dostoyevsky and Tolstoy, the artistically refined Frenchmen: Stendhal and Flaubert, and the "good" American writers: James, Crane and Twain. His strangely stilted praise of the vernacular style—"All modern American literature comes from one book by Mark Twain called *Huckleberry Finn*. . . . There was nothing before. There has been nothing as good since"—is both inaccurate and absurd. It both dismisses Poe and the writers of the American Renaissance, and ignores the genteel tradition and novel of manners that runs from James and Wharton, through Fitzgerald, to Marquand and O'Hara. Among living writers, he praises Kipling and Mann's *Buddenbrooks*; and puts in a good word for two mediocre non-starters: the American novelist Winston Churchill and the "splendid" German Joachim Ringelnatz. Though it's easier to see what Hemingway dislikes than what he admires, *Green Hills of Africa* suggests (between his savage comments) that he values discipline and talent; the experience of war and ability to recreate battle scenes; a good story and colloquial style; vivid details and memorable descriptions of landscapes and seasons.

After these grudging tributes, Hemingway comes out swinging, defines what literature should be and claims superiority for his own style and practice. In *Death in the Afternoon* he'd rephrased Pound's aesthetic belief by elegantly stating, "Prose is architecture, not interior decoration, and the Baroque is over." In *Green Hills of Africa* he condemns Poe's fine writing, Melville's windy rhetoric and Thoreau's mannered style. Though nourished by several mentors in Paris, he insists that writers should work alone. The incestuous groupies—Emerson, Hawthorne and Whittier (he of the sentimental "Snowbound")—are "all angleworms in a bottle, trying to derive knowledge and nourishment from their own contact and from the bottle." Sinclair Lewis (who favored another sort of bottle) is nothing; Heinrich Mann no good; Valéry and Rilke both intolerable snobs.

Gertrude Stein, who'd introduced Hemingway to the *corrida*, escaped whipping in *Death in the Afternoon*. But in 1933 his former tutor published *The Autobiography of Alice B. Toklas* and hit a raw nerve by calling him a coward. Now he returned the favor by characterizing Stein as "jealous and malicious . . . with all that talent gone to malice and nonsense and self-praise." Reversing their roles, Hemingway claimed he'd not only helped to publish her work, but also taught her how to write dialogue: "She could never forgive learning that and she was afraid people would notice it, where she'd learned it, so she had to attack me."

In *Green Hills of Africa*, despite the luxurious paraphernalia of a modern safari, Hemingway exalted big-game hunting as the heroic struggle to survive. Justifying the killing, he illogically claimed that he'd suffered, in war and in violent accidents, the same wounds and pain he inflicted on dangerous animals: "I did nothing that had not been done to me. I had been shot and I had been crippled and gotten away. I expected, always, to be killed by one thing or another." But the man who would later kill himself also seemed to enjoy revealing the pain of self-inflicted wounds. In these two nonfiction books, Hemingway held forth in what he knew was a challenging, provocative way, giving us the benefit of his expertise as he pronounced on courage, sexuality and literature. At the same time he revealed, even gloried in, the worst aspects of his character.

By contrast, "The Snows of Kilimanjaro," the richest trophy of his safari and Hemingway's boldest and most searing self-exposure, transformed his African experience into art. By the time he wrote this story, he'd turned against Pauline, whose rich uncle had paid $25,000 for the safari and who'd featured in *Green Hills of Africa* as the (mostly) worshipful camp-follower, P.O.M. (Poor Old Mama). Collapsing the distinction between the narrator and the character, Hemingway, in the voice of Harry, the dying hero, denies he ever loved Pauline and idealizes Hadley as the true love he destroyed. Harry asks, "It was strange, wasn't it, that when he fell in love with another woman, that woman should always have more money than the last one?" He calls her a "rich bitch" and blames her for his own corruption.

Harry has sold out for money, betrayed his ideals and wasted his talent. Filled with self-hatred, he realizes too late that "he would never write the things he had saved to write until he knew enough to write them well. . . . He would never do it, because each day of not writing, of comfort, of being that which he despised, dulled his ability and softened his will to work so that, finally, he did no work at all." Struggling to see the truth about himself, Harry is torn between blaming his wife for his own deterioration and accepting responsibility for it. He first calls his wife "this kindly caretaker and destroyer of his talent." Then, in a realistic anatomy of his own malaise, he contradicts himself: "Nonsense. He had destroyed his talent himself. Why should he blame this woman because she kept him well? He had destroyed his talent by not using it, by betrayals of himself and what he believed in, by drinking so much that he blunted the edge of his perceptions, by laziness, by sloth, and by snobbery." Harry reflects that "he had never quarrelled much with this woman, while with the women that he loved he had quarrelled so much they had finally, always, with the corrosion of quarrelling, killed what they had together. He had loved too much, demanded too much, and he wore it all out."

Scott Fitzgerald, who'd just published the self-abasing and confessional "Crack-Up" articles (1936)—only two years after *Tender Is the Night*—was then in a state of radical collapse. Yet, like the critics he loathed, Hemingway continued to undermine Fitzgerald's self-confidence. Following the mean-spirited pattern of *Death in the Afternoon* and *Green Hills of Africa*, not content to condemn his own snobbery and seduction by the rich, he also projects his own faults onto his vulnerable friend and victim. Alluding to Fitzgerald's story "The Rich Boy," Harry "remembered poor Julian and his romantic awe of [the rich] and how he had started a story once that began, 'The rich are different from you and me.' And how some one had said to Julian, Yes, they have more money. But that was not humorous to Julian. He thought they were a special glamorous race and when he found they weren't it wrecked him just as much as any other thing that wrecked him." In fact, Hemingway did not put down Fitzgerald with the wisecrack about the rich. He was himself put down in a sharp exchange with the Irish writer Mary Colum.

At the end of the African story the ravenous hyenas smell Harry's rot and circle his camp. Though the water flows in his dream of being rescued, he dies near the wasteland of the dry water hole. But there's another ironic twist to this story. The brilliant flashbacks reveal that the threat of death has concentrated Harry's mind, that he did have a great and genuine talent, and that he could have fulfilled his promise and ensured his salvation if he had only been able to record—as Hemingway did—the vivid memories that show him at the very height of his creative powers.

In *Across the River*, as in "The Snows of Kilimanjaro," Hemingway closely identifies with another bitter, failed hero. Like Harry, Richard Cantwell suffers from a fatal disease; he dies of a heart attack at the end of the novel. But Cantwell (who talks pretentiously, as his name suggests) is a mouthpiece for Hemingway's obsessions, opinions and regrets. A professional soldier, who has been demoted from general to colonel, he suggests the sharp decline in Hemingway's literary reputation and demotion from the highest rank in literature. Through Cantwell, Hemingway attacks his literary rivals and previous wife (after he had divorced Martha Gellhorn and married Mary Welsh), combines bitterness with self-pity, blames others for his own faults and offers a scathing analysis of his profoundly flawed character.

We're supposed to admire Cantwell, who has some impressive qualities. He's served bravely in two world wars, and has been unjustly victimized by his military superiors. Though often concussed and seriously wounded, he's still quite tough and not afraid of death. He has an expert knowledge of many aspects of life, from wine to weapons, and is devoted to the young Italian woman, Renata, who adores him. Though she's a native of Venice and he's a sophisticated insider (well liked in the city and admired by the servants, as Hemingway was by the Africans), they haunt the most popular tourist spots: Harry's Bar on the Calle Valaresso, Florian's Café in Piazza San Marco and the posh restaurant in the Gritti Palace Hotel on the Canale Grande. (It's worth noting that Hemingway makes eight references to hanging, and that in March 1983 Adriana Ivancich, the model for Renata, hanged herself from a tree on her farm.)

Cantwell embodies Hemingway's midlife fantasies. He slips into the "Papa" mode, calls Renata "Daughter" and frequently repeats certain trivial phrases, like "complete with handles" (as on a coffin). But the major flaws of his character are glaringly obvious. Though he loves men who (like bullfighters) have fought and been wounded, he's more worried about his demotion than about his slain soldiers. By his own account, he is a know-it-all, a shit, a mean son of a bitch, a stupid and brusque, brutal and beat-up bastard. Wildly truculent, always eager for a fight, he can be ruthless, and loves his enemies more than his friends. Worst of all, Cantwell, obsessed with his misfortunes in war, can be tiresome, even phony. Like Hemingway with the Old Lady, he constantly lectures Renata, who falls asleep during one of his tirades. Cantwell could say, with Dylan Thomas, "somebody's boring me and I think it's me."

In one of his most insightful moments, Cantwell calls himself "an unjust bitter criticizer" and confesses, "I have failed and I speak badly of all who have succeeded." He exposes another unpleasant aspect of his character by persistently attacking not only the eminent military and political leaders of World War II, but also (when defending his turf) authors associated with Venice: Gabriele D'Annunzio and Sinclair Lewis. He condemns the overinflated narcissism and political ideology of that talented, brave and half-crazed Italian soldier, D'Annunzio: "writer, poet, national hero, phraser of the dialectic of Fascism, macabre egotist, aviator, commander, or rider, in the first of the fast torpedo attack boats, Lieutenant Colonel of Infantry without knowing how to command a company, nor a platoon properly, the great, lovely writer of *Notturno* whom we respect, and jerk."

Hemingway's nasty, exaggerated attack on Sinclair Lewis weakens the novel. He had been feuding with Lewis, on and off, since 1922, and the older writer had repaid his attacks with generosity and a few satiric barbs. He felt Lewis (still alive in 1950) was guilty not only of pustulating skin cancer and a radium-burned complexion, but also of winning the Nobel Prize in 1930, of helping Hemingway (always dangerous), and of foreshadowing his own alcoholism and literary decline. Fixated on Lewis' physical repulsiveness, which (like a neo-Platonist) he interprets as the outward sign of his moral defects, the handsome Hemingway provides a savage description of his deeply pitted compatriot and denigrates him five more times after that: "He had a strange face like an over-enlarged, disappointed weasel or ferret. It looked as pock-marked and as blemished as the mountains of the moon." Though Lewis' dermatological disease has nothing to do with his character or work, Hemingway's overkill reduces him to a mass of scars and craters, to a leper compelled to expose his sores.

Hemingway fearlessly and foolishly, unwittingly and obsessively reveals his own envy, bitterness and deterioration. Constantly picking at his sores, he never quite realizes, as he states in *Green Hills of Africa*, that "every damned thing is your own fault if you're any good." In great stories like "The Snows of Kilimanjaro" he created a character, a version of his inner self, who embodies tragic failure. But with Cantwell in the Venetian novel, he disturbingly mixes self-praise and self-disparagement.

This curious blend of self-aggrandizement and self-abasement continued in another sphere, when Hemingway submitted to a two-day interview with Lillian Ross. During their interview he played the fool and was taken for one. Ross repaid his generosity by taking his behavior at face value, and presenting the boring braggart as the real Hemingway. In the *New Yorker* of May 13, 1950, four months before the appearance of *Across the River*, Ross published the satiric portrait that dealt a devastating blow to his legend and prepared readers for the intolerable autobiographical hero in his novel. In her dishonest preface to the hardcover edition, published right after Hemingway's violent death in July 1961, Ross (whom Hemingway had liked and trusted) claimed that she'd written down only what she'd seen and heard, had not intended to ridicule or attack him, and was a sympathetic, affectionate and admiring observer.

Hemingway said he spoke a "joke language" with his "Kraut" friend Marlene Dietrich, who called him Papa and he called Daughter, though he was only two years older than her. But Ross took his actions and words seriously when he punched himself in the stomach, repeated the meaningless phrase, "How do you like it now, gentlemen?" and puffed up *Across the River* in self-exalting Indian talk: "Book start slow, then increase in pace till it becomes impossible to stand. I bring emotion up to where you can't stand it, then we level off, so we won't have to provide oxygen tents for readers." In fact, though he didn't realize it, the opposite is true. The best part of the novel, the first chapter, on shooting ducks in the Venetian lagoon, describes the natural world of men without women. But when Cantwell meets Renata, the novel becomes quite static and goes downhill all the way.

Fixated, as he always was, on rival authors, Hemingway (who particularly admired the account of the battle of Waterloo in *The Charterhouse of Parma*) allowed that he'd learned about writing from Stendhal as well as from Maupassant, Dumas and Daudet—though it's doubtful that the last two taught him anything. Instead of seriously discussing what major French authors meant to him, he clowned around by describing them in fragmented sentences and absurd baseball metaphors: "Mr. Flaubert, who always threw them perfectly straight, hard, high, and inside. Then Mr. Baudelaire, that I learned my knuckle ball from, and Mr. Rimbaud, who never threw a fast ball in his life. Mr. Gide and Mr. Valéry I couldn't learn from. I think Mr. Valéry was too smart for me."

He also permitted Ross to portray him as an arrogant fool by bringing the Slavic fighters into the arena and describing them in gladiatorial metaphors: "I started out very quiet and I beat Mr. Turgenev. Then I trained hard and I beat Mr. de Maupassant. I've fought two draws with Mr. Stendhal [the battle scenes in *A Farewell to Arms* and *For Whom the Bell Tolls*], and I think I had an edge in the last one. But nobody's going to get me in any ring with Mr. Tolstoy unless I'm crazy or I keep getting better"—though this ridiculous statement clearly proves that he was getting worse. As Norman Mailer observed of Hemingway's competitive instinct in his imitation-Hemingway *Advertisements for Myself*, his "irrepressible tantrum [is] that he is the champion writer of this time, and of all time, and that if anyone can pin Tolstoy, it is Ernest H."

In his last major work, *A Moveable Feast*, Hemingway circles back to his early years in Paris, before he succumbed to the corruption and decline he both predicted and portrayed in his previous works. In his return to the age of innocence, to his pristine youth before his expulsion from the Garden of Eden, he characterizes himself as poor, modest, eager, idealistic and just hitting his stride as a writer. He enjoys the simple pleasures of life, and simplistically equates poverty with purity, wealth with wickedness.

When describing his early reading, Hemingway pays tribute to the heavyweight sluggers: Stendhal, Turgenev, Dostoyevsky and Tolstoy. He exalts Ezra Pound, who gave him valuable help and advice, as "a great poet and a gentle and generous man," but is caustic about his other contemporaries. Hemingway admits that "in those days [as well as later on] I had a very bad, quick temper," which often flares up in his memoir. His anger fuels a series of brutal and venomous, but obviously exaggerated and highly entertaining *ad hominem* counterattacks. He licks old wounds and settles old scores with Stein, Huxley and Wyndham Lewis, who'd unwisely provoked retaliation from a formidable adversary. But all these quarrels took place in the 1930s, after the first symptoms of Hemingway's decline. He retroactively transposed them to the previous decade to maintain the unity of the book, and enjoy some long-delayed retaliation.

Hemingway tries a new ploy in *A Moveable Feast* by putting his own condemnations into the mouth of Gertrude Stein. In a series of papal pronouncements, she calls Huxley a "dead man," and dismisses D. H. Lawrence's novels as pathetic, preposterous and impossible to read. She despises Jean Cocteau as a drug addict and vicious corrupter of youth, but claims there is nothing disgusting about the activities of lesbians like Alice Toklas and herself. But Hemingway soon condemns Stein for the very viciousness she denies. In *Death in the Afternoon* he'd told the story of a journalist-friend who overheard a homosexual begging and crying about an intolerable perversion, "'I didn't know it was that. Oh, I didn't know it was that. I won't! I won't!' followed by . . . a despairing scream." Hemingway himself is similarly horrified in his memoir. Feigning sexual naivete and effectively imitating Stein's repetitive style, he overhears Toklas suggestively and repulsively "speaking to Miss Stein as I had never heard one person speak to another; never, anywhere, ever. Then Miss Stein's voice came pleading, and begging, saying, 'Don't, pussy. Don't. Don't, please don't. I'll do anything, pussy, but please don't do it. Please don't. Please don't, pussy.' . . . It was bad to hear and the answers were worse."

Hemingway himself first praises Katherine Mansfield, who died in 1923, as a "great short-story writer." But he immediately undermines this praise by stating that compared to her master, Anton Chekhov, her work seemed like the "artificial tales of a young old maid." In fact, Mansfield, far from being an old maid, had a recklessly adventurous sex life that had fascinated the repressed Virginia Woolf.

Hemingway reserves his heaviest artillery for three major authors: Ford Madox Ford, Wyndham Lewis and Scott Fitzgerald. But (as with Sinclair Lewis) he criticizes their appearance and character rather than their works. The more he recognized his own decline, the more he lashed out at other writers. He portrays the genial Ford as pedantic, rude, affected, snobbish and mendacious. And he describes the physically unattractive writer—who was overweight and had been gassed while fighting in the war—with intense but unexplained personal vitriol. He calls him an "up-ended hogshead . . . a heavy, wheezing, ignoble presence," whom he found repulsive and tried unsuccessfully to avoid.

Wyndham Lewis, who had skewered Hemingway in "The Dumb-Ox" (1934), was duly repaid in *A Moveable Feast*. As with Ford, he satirizes Lewis' physical appearance, and gives no indication that the man he portrays as a fraudulent bohemian was a brilliant painter and writer. In Lewis' novel *Tarr*, the anti-hero Kreisler rapes a woman. In his memoir, Hemingway describes Lewis as a nasty-looking frog with the eyes of an "unsuccessful rapist." This misleading phrase suggests that Lewis became impotent when he found a victim. But in 1922, when they first met, Lewis was a strikingly handsome man and a great seducer of many rich, beautiful and talented women.

In his memoir, Hemingway launched another cruel assault on the once vulnerable and long-dead Fitzgerald, which began in "The Snows of Kilimanjaro." Though Fitzgerald, like Hemingway, was extraordinarily good-looking, Hemingway emphasizes his feminine appearance by declaring that he "looked like a boy with a face between handsome and pretty. . . . The mouth worried you until you knew him and then it worried you more." When the alcoholic failure, who gets easily drunk, reveals his hypochondriac streak, Hemingway likens him to a "little dead crusader" and demeans him by taking his temperature with a huge bathtub thermometer. Hemingway attacked these authors because Ford had helped him, Lewis had criticized him and Fitzgerald had foreshadowed his own failure.

Like Cantwell in *Across the River*, Hemingway refuses to take responsibility for his own actions and condemns other people for his faults. He blames Dos Passos, the pilot fish, for leading Gerald and Sara Murphy, the sharks, to Hemingway, their innocent prey. He also blames Pauline (as he'd blamed Martha in *Across the River*) for ruining his marriage to Hadley. He claims, with three subtly progressive adverbs, that he was deceived by Pauline's treacherous infiltration: "an unmarried young woman becomes the temporary best friend of another young woman who is married, goes to live with the husband and wife and then unknowingly, innocently and unrelentingly sets out to marry the husband."

But Hemingway was not quite as passive and easily deceived as he pretended to be. In one of his most incisive passages (partly cut from the printed version of *A Moveable Feast*), he writes that when he returned to Paris after a business trip to New York, he should have caught the first train to Austria, where the faithful Hadley was waiting for him. But Pauline, "the girl I was in love with was in Paris then, and where we went and what we did, and the unbelievable wrenching, killing happiness, selfishness and treachery of everything we did gave me such a terrible remorse [that] I did not take the first train, or the second or the third. When I saw my wife again standing by the tracks as the train came in by the piled logs at the station, I wished I had died before I ever loved anyone but her." It was winter, they'd gone to Austria to ski and the logs were piled up to heat the station. This scene recalls his remorseful reflection in *Death in the Afternoon*: "I would sooner have the pox than to fall in love with another woman loving the one I have." Hemingway, an idealistic and romantic puritan, usually married the women he slept with. Though he returned to Hadley, he soon left her for Pauline, and Hadley was the only one he asked to forgive him. These guilt-ridden experiences (love affairs, divorces, new marriages) were the very stuff of art and enabled him to relive the cycle of romance and loss that had first inspired him as a writer.

In *The Autobiography of Alice B. Toklas*, Stein had urged Hemingway to explore and reveal his inner life: "What a book . . . would be the real story of Hemingway, not those he writes but the confessions of the real Ernest Hemingway." Though Stein didn't realize it, Hemingway would follow her advice for the last thirty years of his life. Though sensitive and concerned with his literary reputation, he repeatedly exposed the dark side of his character and then made himself seem even worse by attacking and blaming others. Strangely compelled to expose his faults and reveal his failures, he wrote his confessions with a brave, self-tormenting honesty. He acknowledged his faults, yet dared his audience to accept him. As Hamlet said of his father, "He was a man, take him for all in all, / I shall not look upon his like again."

FORTY

NOBEL PRIZE

The deliberations of the Nobel Prize committee are as famously secret as the papal conclave, and books like Kjell Espmark's *The Nobel Prize in Literature* (1991) do not explain how specific authors are chosen. Joseph Brodsky (who won in 1987) told his translator, "nobody knows how that happened. It's a kind of accident." Though extraliterary factors influence the judges—health and age, political ideas, time spent in prison or exile as well as pressure from powerful nations and need to award countries that haven't won—and they have made some weird choices, from Sully Prudhomme to Dario Fo, the procedure is quite deliberate. Twenty-two pages of unpublished material in the archives of the Swedish Academy, including three new letters by Hemingway, illuminate the Byzantine process that led to his prize in 1954. (Per Hallström's reports were translated by Charlotta Elmgren, Anders Österling's by James Spohrer.)

Hemingway was nominated by Per Hallström in 1947, 1953 and 1954, and his reports reveal how the writer was perceived in Europe. Hallström (1866–1960) had worked in London and Chicago as a chemist before becoming a writer of stories, plays and poems, and translator of Shakespeare. He joined the Swedish Academy in 1908 and was Permanent Secretary from 1931 to 1941. Once highly regarded, he's now fallen into oblivion.

In a seven-page, postwar report of 1947—written between the publication of *For Whom the Bell Tolls* and *Across the River*—Hallström provided some brief biographical background and made a few factual errors. Hemingway was born in 1899 (not 1898), served in World War I with the American Red Cross (not the Italian army) and was twenty-three (not twenty-one) when he first married. Hallström, whose country was neutral in both World Wars, believed that Hemingway and the men of the Lost Generation "had been driven to war by the . . . longing for eternal peace of their native country," though Hemingway mainly wanted to experience the thrill and danger of battle. Praising Hemingway's innovative technique, Hallström wrote, "the originality of his stories was in the surprisingly abrupt way they began, without introductory words, without presenting the characters or accounting for their situations, which gives the reader an immediate experience of reality." One of Hemingway's "most appealing qualities," he felt, "was the freedom from political prejudice, from every trace of hatred and agitation toward the enemy when he writes about war."

With plot summaries and superficial descriptions, Hallström outlined Hemingway's work for colleagues who didn't seem to know much about him. Missing the biblical source in Ecclesiastes 1:5 of the title, *The Sun Also Rises*, he offered a misleading, even ludicrous account of the novel: "It is about the erotic and bacchanalian confusion in a small group of American and English gentlemen and ladies in Paris, who have nothing else to do but nurse and increase this mayhem to monumental dimensions. . . . But one cannot say he was dull, for his vitality flowed through all this madness and his style maintained its rapid pace. . . . His courage made him a model for several Swedish writers."

"The ending of *A Farewell to Arms*," Hallström said, "is moving and completely beautiful, and lends the novel its strangeness." Focusing on the most violent and contentious scene in *For Whom the Bell Tolls*, when the Reds in Pilar's village beat the fascists to death and throw them off a cliff, he stated, "the most gruesome part of the novel is an extremely detailed description of the massacre . . . of cold-blooded cruelty during the revolution," which made the critic accuse Hemingway of a "taste for sadism and delight in human suffering."

Hallström rightly dismissed Hemingway's play, *The Fifth Column*, as a minor work; admired the incisive psychology, bitter satire on American women and diamond sharp prose of "The Short Happy Life of Francis Macomber"; and was surprisingly sympathetic to *Death in the Afternoon*, in which he found everything faultlessly balanced: "He thoroughly studies the psychology of the animals and brilliantly describes the bullfights for both the eye and the mind."

To Have and Have Not interested Hallström for its new social awareness and for "adding to Hemingway's views on the human condition. Until now, he has ignored economic conditions and social questions" and emphasized the hedonism of his characters. He hoped the novel "provides some indication of Hemingway's broadened and deepened interest in the world, which he's previously regarded as a hunting ground for pleasurable sensations."

Hallström seemed to conclude positively by maintaining that Hemingway "is an extraordinary artist, through his uncommonly keen and rapid eye for earthly objects, through his strength of perceptions and through his ability to make them immediate to the reader." But Hemingway's strongest advocate then added an unexpectedly harsh judgment that ruined the candidate's prospects in 1947: "From a stricter aesthetic point of view he is probably not a great writer and has not created any truly admirable novel."

Between 1947 and Hallström's second report in 1953 the competition intensified and seven distinguished writers (two of them American) won the prize: André Gide, T. S. Eliot, William Faulkner, Bertrand Russell, the Swede Pär Lagerkvist, François Mauriac and Winston Churchill. Hallström, who apparently had not read Philip Young's pioneering and perceptive *Ernest Hemingway: A Reconsideration* (1952), discussed the most recent novels. He was unaware of the autobiographical revelations in *Across the River*, and was puzzled by the strangely elusive novel that he vaguely said was "impossible to summarize because it doesn't tell us anything directly, but tries to provide an absolute explanation of life and the world." He dismissed the best scene in the novel by saying that Richard Cantwell "shoots some ducks, yet the reader doesn't get a great deal from this introduction to his character." But he concluded that the novel was "a previously unmatched example of Hemingway's masterful cinematic style."

Hallström was much more enthusiastic about *The Old Man and the Sea*: "This is a real tour de force achieved through his firm grasp of the subject, and through his close observation of the sea and the sky natural beauty has now become part of his inexhaustible expertise. . . . The novella is a work of uncommon strength and clarity." It's ironic that the committee's leading expert on Hemingway had such a poor grasp of his entire oeuvre.

Since any national academy or university professor can nominate candidates simply by writing a letter with supporting documents (I've done it myself), twenty-seven writers were proposed in 1954. To see what Hemingway, a great competitor, was up against, the list that year can conveniently be divided into four categories. I. Future winners (usually nominated several times before they are actually chosen): the Icelandic Halldór Laxness, who'd translated *A*

Farewell to Arms and won in 1955; the Spanish poet Juan Ramón Jiménez, who won in 1956; Albert Camus, who won in 1957 but died in a car crash in 1960; and the Czech poet Jaroslav Seifert, who had to wait for three decades but finally won in 1984. II. Serious competitors (who deserved the prize but never won): André Malraux, E. M. Forster, Gottfried Benn, Nikos Kazantzakis and Robert Frost, who was twenty-five years older than Hemingway and, with his help, had saved the wartime traitor Ezra Pound from execution. III. Non-creative writers (following the award to Theodor Mommsen and Henri Bergson): Carl Jung, Martin Buber, the French philosopher Julien Benda, the Austrian cultural philosopher Rudolf Kassner and the Spanish philologist-historian Ramón Menéndez Pidal. IV. Obscure minor writers proposed as long shots by their own countrymen: three from Belgium, two from Norway, two from Spain and one each from France, Italy, Austria, Greece and Russia.

Jacinto Benavente, winner in 1922, nominated Concha Espina who, like himself, had supported the fascists in the Spanish Civil War, instead of the more eminent Jiménez, who'd gone into exile. Forster was proposed by three influential figures from Oxford (rather than from his own Cambridge University): Lord David Cecil, J. R. R. Tolkien and F. P. Wilson. Jiménez and Camus, as well as Kazantzakis and Frost, were nominated by Swedish Academicians. Laxness got the most nominations, including those from Prince Wilhelm of Sweden, representing the PEN organization; professors from Reykjavik, Copenhagen, Kiel and Oxford; and the Scandinavian scholar Kemp Malone from Johns Hopkins.

Hemingway was not nominated by an American, but by Prof. Dr. Leo von Hibler, Head of the English-American Department of the University of Vienna and author (in German) of *The American Short Story* (1947). He justified the nomination "by the amount and value of Mr. Hemingway's work as well as by the great influence which this work has had on American and European literature." The previous American winners had been a wildly mixed bag: Eliot, Faulkner and O'Neill as well as Sinclair Lewis and Pearl Buck, whose novel Hemingway referred to as *The Bad Earth*. Hemingway was appalled when Lewis snagged the prize and later savaged him in *Across the River*. He was jealous when Faulkner got it and bitterly declared that "as long as I am alive he has to drink to feel good about having the Nobel prize."

The material in the Swedish Academy archive casts new light not only on the candidates, but also on the deliberations of the Nobel committee. In his third report, in 1954, Hallström discussed a book he'd just discovered, *Green Hills of Africa*, which led him "to review Hemingway's originality as a storyteller and stylist," and his theory, expressed in this work, that the "writer must not depict anything but what he directly perceives with his senses." In Africa, Hemingway appears in his "massive embodiment, with hardboiled eyes and hardboiled indifference to everything but his detailed observation of the soulless objects around him."

The committee members were very divided and some even suggested that the prize should not be awarded that year. The novelist Sigfrid Siwertz (1882–1970), clearly not enthusiastic about either Hemingway or his main rival Laxness, went so far as to exclaim that both men "are impossible as Nobel candidates." However, as his divided colleagues struggled to reach a decision, he reluctantly agreed that Hemingway was the stronger candidate.

The poet Anders Österling (1884–1981), Permanent Secretary of the Swedish Academy, evaluated the four leading contenders. He grudgingly wrote of Kazantzakis, "I am cautious, if not dismissive." He praised the "classic beauty" of Camus' latest book, *L'Été* (*The Summer*, 1954), a collection of lyrical essays about his native Algeria. Afraid of offending people by rewarding an author perceived to be offensive, he chauvinistically reproached Laxness for his "rancorous and polemical portrayal of [the medieval] King Olav Haraldsson" (995–1030), who was killed in the battle of Stiklestad, was later canonized as Saint Olav and is still greatly revered in Norway.

Österling, more sophisticated than Hallström and echoing his praise of Hemingway's novella, wrote:

> Ernest Hemingway's candidacy had been discussed earlier on a couple of occasions, but then set aside pending the arrival of a new work which would show his storytelling at its full strength. Such a work is *The Old Man and the Sea*, which to outward appearances is only a novel about the sport of fishing, but which within this framework opens up an impressive perspective, and which in its calm mastery can be counted as the finest in modern prose poetry. Hemingway's earlier writings have demonstrated a brutal and cynical, hardboiled side, which certainly seemed at first to be in conflict with the Nobel Prize value of idealism. On the other hand, there is the Hemingway of heroic pathos, of the very deep layers of his feelings for life, with a

male predilection for danger and adventure, and a natural admiration for the individuals who go to fight in the reality that is overshadowed by violence and death.

Starting with *A Farewell to Arms*, signifying his real breakthrough, he has portrayed war as controlling the tragic fate of his generation, without sentimentality but with a laconic realism of extraordinary effect. Hemingway's importance as one of the era's real trendsetters cannot yet be fully analyzed, but it will be clearly felt in both the U.S. and European narrative art from the last quarter century. In particular, the pattern of his dramatic and lively dialogue has been difficult to equal. It is a literary-historical fact, which cannot be effaced by argument, although it is always debatable, whether Hemingway's influence is in every way valuable.

If the nomination were to take into account the interest of the Academy, the attribution of the award should not be delayed or postponed. The now 56-year-old Hemingway is in any case the most significant name on this year's list, and in my opinion it would be both fair and appropriate to acknowledge his efforts at a time when a fresh masterpiece exists and can be recognized.

Alfred Nobel's will specified that the prize should be given to authors with an idealistic tendency, but many of the Nobel winners, especially Sartre and Beckett later on, cannot be called idealists. It's ironic that Hallström didn't really understand Hemingway's work and Österling didn't even mention Hemingway's two greatest novels, *The Sun Also Rises* and *For Whom the Bell Tolls*, which *is* idealistic, for Robert Jordan sacrifices his life while fighting the fascists. Both critics perversely praised his worst book, *The Old Man and the Sea*. In that novella, first published in *Life*, Hemingway cynically expressed his contempt for his magazine, his publisher, his readers, his critics and religion by writing an ironic and mock-serious fable that provided a pretense of culture with a shot of moral uplift. The work suffers from sentimentality and self-pity, crude Christian symbolism and self-parodic banalities disguised as peasant wisdom: "The setting of the sun is a difficult time for all fish. . . . Fish, I love you and respect you very much."

Confused by truly innovative authors, the Nobel committee has often compromised by awarding the prize to mediocrities and been notorious for ignoring (sometimes for political reasons) many great writers of the twentieth century. The distinguished rejections include Ibsen and Strindberg; Tolstoy, Akhmatova and Nabokov; Rilke, Musil and Kafka; Proust and Valéry; D'Annunzio and Lampedusa; Lorca and Borges; Hardy, Conrad, Ford, Joyce, Woolf, Lawrence, Orwell, Waugh and Auden; Henry James, Stevens, Pound, Fitzgerald and Robert Lowell.

So it's amazing, when the smoke puffed out of the Stockholm chimney, that the creaky fossils—stumbling blindly and for the wrong reasons—managed to choose the best writer and make Hemingway the current pope of literature. The official statement, signed by the committee secretary on September 1, 1954, declared that the $35,000 prize was awarded to Hemingway, with Laxness as second choice. The official citation criticized his early and best writing as "brutal, cynical and callous," but praised his "powerful, style-making mastery of the art of modern narration." Hemingway did not actually lobby for what he refused to name and superstitiously called "the Swedish thing." Though he rightly felt he deserved the prize, he was surprised when he actually got it. He was helped by two previous nominations, strong supporters on the committee and comparatively weak competition from Laxness. When he got his gold medal, he insouciantly gave it to the shrine of the Virgen del Cobre, the patron saint of Cuba.

When interviewed about the prize, Hemingway shrewdly and safely praised an art critic and two aging minor writers—rather than more potent contemporaries like John Steinbeck—and said that Bernard Berenson, Carl Sandburg and Isak Dinesen deserved the award. He wanted to puncture all pomposity and wrote his sister (with uncertain arithmetic) that he had completed 4,500 imperishable words that week, guaranteed by eighteen Swedes who had drunk too much aquavit and immortalized him by a vote of nine to seven, with one abstention.

Hemingway had been seriously injured in two nearly fatal African plane crashes in January 1954, which led to the premature publication of his obituaries and gave the committee a new sense of urgency. He exacerbated his internal damage by drinking heavily to dull the pain, and had traveled in Italy and Spain for three months after the accidents. But the man who sometimes wore bloodstained fishing shorts to his own dinner parties was not keen to attend the formal ceremonies in Sweden. Writing to Österling from the Finca Vigía in Cuba on October 29, 1954, the potential star of the ceremony rather stiffly explained—in a letter dictated to and perhaps written by the secretary who typed it—why he could not appear in person. He was pleased and honored to accept the Nobel Prize. But doctors' orders made it impossible for him to come to Stockholm in December to accept it from the king. He deeply regretted that he could not be there. He'd suffered serious injuries, aggravated by burns, and had to follow the effective treatment and regime that were helping him to recover. He was sure the Swedish Academy would understand his prudence and pardon him for giving up the great pleasure of a personal visit.

A month later, on November 30, Hemingway graciously complied with Österling's requests. He's given the American Embassy in Havana the text of his acceptance speech, which will be delivered by the American ambassador to Sweden at the banquet for the prizewinners. This speech will be sent to Stockholm together with the recording that will be broadcast on Swedish radio. He insists that he feels badly about being unable to attend the Nobel festival. He's also sent the Nobel Foundation on Sturegatan a photograph and biographical note to go with the text that will appear in the annual book of winners' biographies and speeches, "Le Prix Nobel." But he's not giving or sending a formal Nobel lecture.

That same day, again enlivening the formal "banquet" by calling it a "festival" (or Spanish *fiesta*), he wrote to Nils Stahle, the head of the Nobel Foundation, without giving his account number or the exact address of his bank. He repeated that it was a misfortune for him to be unable to attend the Nobel festival. He thanked Stahle for telling him about the details of the ceremony and for the concern about his health. He's been following the doctors' orders and should fully recover within a year. He asked that the prize money be deposited in his account at the Guaranty Trust Company on Fifth Avenue in New York.

Hemingway's perceptive speech, which diagnosed the dangers of literary life even as he reaped its rewards, was a sad acknowledgment of solitude, uncertainty and personal failure: "Writing, at its best, is a lonely life. Organizations for writers palliate the writer's loneliness but I doubt if they improve his writing. He grows in public stature as he sheds his loneliness and often his work deteriorates. For he does his work alone and if he is a good enough writer he must face eternity, or the lack of it, each day.

FORTY-ONE

UNWRITTEN WORKS

Many writers, to soothe their egos, inflate their reputations and warn off competitors, claim to be working on a book they are not really writing or have not even begun. But all authors reflect on what they have already done and consider ideas and subjects they might write about in the future. Hemingway wrote an autobiographical story about his unwritten books. He offers real insight into the beginnings and origins of things, the hidden sources and mysterious powers that inspire creativity.

Hemingway, who rarely praised his contemporaries, paid tribute to Mann in his letters. In December 1925 he wrote, "*Buddenbrooks* is a pretty damned good book." Five years later he said that Mann winning the Nobel Prize in 1929 "made me damned happy." His favorite Mann story was "Disorder and Early Sorrow" about a father who feels rejected when his favorite daughter becomes attracted to a young man.

In contrast to the dedicated Gustav von Aschenbach in "Death in Venice," Hemingway's writer Harry, dying of gangrene at the foot of the mountain in Kenya, has sold his vitality and destroyed his talent. The recurrent theme of "The Snows of Kilimanjaro" (1936) is *corruptio optimi pessima*: the corruption of the best is the worst. Hemingway writes of Harry, in a subtle mixture of flashbacks and narrative: "*He had seen the world change; not just the events. . . . He had been in it and he had watched it and it was his duty to write of it; but now he never would. . . .* Each day of not writing, of comfort, of being that which he despised, dulled his ability and softened his will to work so that, finally, he did no work at all."

Unlike Aschenbach, whose works foreshadow those that Mann would write, Harry reflects sadly on those he hasn't written. Hemingway describes material he's already used to supply the five flashbacks, the most brilliant part of the story, and to illustrate the work that Harry says he will never be able to write. They include vivid memories of the war in Turkey and Greece (in *in our time*), skiing in Austria (with the former enemies who had tried to kill him in the Italian Alps, described in *A Farewell to Arms*), fishing in Germany (in *Dateline: Toronto*), boyhood brutality in Michigan and violence in Wyoming, writing in Paris (in *A Moveable Feast*) and the horribly wounded British officer in World War I (also in *in our time*).

The best passages describe memories of Hemingway's great themes: war and love. He recalls leaving Turkey with the Greek refugees after their defeat in October 1922: "*Now in his mind he saw a railway station at Karagatch and he was standing with his pack and that was the headlight of the Simplon-Orient* [train] *cutting the dark now and he was leaving Thrace then after the retreat.*" He also longs for the unattainable American nurse (as Aschenbach longs for Tadzio), who had jilted him when he was recovering from his war wound in Milan: "*he had written her, the first one, the one who left him, a letter telling her how he had never been able to kill it. . . . How every one he had slept with had only made him miss her more. How what she had done could never matter since he knew he could not cure himself of loving her.*" After whoring in Constantinople and getting into a fistfight over a "hot Armenian slut," he meekly returns to his devoted wife in Paris, "that now he loved again."

Both Aschenbach and Harry, striving for perfection, die tragically in a foreign country and of repulsive afflictions: cholera and gangrene. There's a strong contrast between Harry's idealized past and diseased present. Yet as Friedrich Nietzsche writes in *The Will to Power*, "The sick and weak have had fascination on their side. . . . The great adventurers and criminals are sick at certain periods of their lives: the great emotions, the passions of power, love, revenge, are accompanied by profound disturbances."

The snows of Kilimanjaro and the snows of the Alps in the first flashback are *les neiges d'antan*, pure, high and unbelievably white in the sun—but forever unreachable. The ironic theme of "Snows" is that the dying Harry "would never write the things that he had saved to write until he knew enough to write them well." His mental flashbacks contrast his great potential with his tragic failure, yet also reveal that he had an impressive talent and lived more intensely just before his death. He could have fulfilled his promise and achieved artistic salvation if he had only been able to reject his decadent life and record the vivid recollections that show him (again like Aschenbach) at the very height of his powers. Harry *does* write these stories in his imagination, though it is too late to put them on paper, and his redemptive memories show that his life has not been completely wasted.

Hemingway's story is a self-portrait, a warning about what he could become if he failed. It shows how strange and absorbing it is to give in to the artistic life and what he suffers in the process: his inability to fulfill his great ambitions. In "Kilimanjaro" he brilliantly turns the theme of artistic impotence into an incisive analysis of the creative process.

FORTY-TWO

SUICIDE

Like Robert Graves in the Great War, Hemingway was mistakenly reported dead—after a car crash during the London blackout in May 1944 and after two African plane crashes in January 1954—and was able to read the reports of his own death. He once remarked that surviving a war was "the next best thing to getting killed and reading your own obituary."

In his essay "The Christmas Gift," published soon after the African accidents in April–May 1954, he rejected the idea that he was much possessed by death and saw the skull beneath the skin. His motto was "*Il faut d'abord durer*" (first, one must last), he suggested that he was a survivor, and it seemed that nothing could destroy the tough guy who'd lived up to the legend of the mythical Papa: "In all obituaries, or almost all, it was emphasized that I had sought death all my life. Can one imagine that if a man sought death all of his life he could not have found her before the age of 54? It is one thing to be in the proximity of death, to know more or less what she is, and it is quite another thing to seek her. . . . So much for the constant pursuit of death."

In *The Myth of Sisyphus* (1942), Albert Camus observed, "There is but one truly serious philosophical problem and that is suicide. Judging whether life is or is not worth living amounts to answering the fundamental question of philosophy." As a volunteer and reporter Hemingway had managed through luck and skill to fend off everything that had been trying to kill him: shrapnel wounds in World War I, battles in Turkey, Spain, China and France, German submarines, raging bulls and charging lions—until he finally decided to kill himself.

In "Montparnasse," an early poem published in Paris in 1923, Hemingway mocked the fashionable attempted suicides among the "people one knows," who are always rescued and continue to reappear:

There are never any suicides in the quarter among people one knows
No successful suicides.
A Chinese boy kills himself and is dead.
(They continue to place his mail in the letter rack at the Dôme)
A Norwegian boy kills himself and is dead
(No one knows where the other Norwegian boy has gone)
They find a model dead.
Alone in bed and very dead.
(It made almost unbearable trouble for the concierge)
Sweet oil, the white of eggs, mustard and water soapsuds and stomach pumps rescue the people one knows.
Every afternoon the people one knows can be found at the café.

In *A Moveable Feast* he mentioned the real suicide of Jules Pascin, his artist-friend in Paris, and suggested that it was preordained: "afterwards, when he had hanged himself, I liked to remember him as he was that night at the Dôme. They say the seeds of what we will do are in all of us."

In his story "A Clean, Well-Lighted Place" (1933), two waiters talk about a regular customer who was cut down before he could choke to death:

"Last week he tried to commit suicide," one waiter said.
"Why?"
"He was in despair."
"What about?"
"Nothing."

When the old man leaves, the compassionate waiter defines "nothing" by mocking the Lord's Prayer to suggest the overwhelming sensation of nothingness: "Our nada who art in nada, nada be thy name. . . ."

By 1961 Hemingway himself had been severely damaged by accidents, alcoholism, physical disease, paranoia and disastrous shock treatments. He suffered from profound depression and could not write nor even speak. On

July 2 he put the barrel of his shotgun against his forehead, pulled the trigger and blasted away the upper half of his head. Blood, brains, bones, teeth, hair and flesh were flung against the ceiling, walls and floor of the room. His fourth wife, Mary, who'd locked up the guns but left the keys out in the kitchen, had to step over the shattered parts of his head when she was awakened by the shot and came down the stairs to find him. I've been in that room and spoken to the woman who cleaned up the carnage.

In 1928 his father had also killed himself with a gunshot inside his house. Later on, Hemingway's brother and sister committed suicide. Mary confused matters by falsely claiming that he died while cleaning his gun or in a hunting accident. But his friends did not believe her and the truth soon came out. Twenty-three writers—old companions, young disciples and some who would themselves die by suicide pondering the possibility of their own tragic fates—were shocked by the sudden loss and the shot heard round the world. They were all eager to record their reactions, explain his character and pay homage to the work of the titanic figure.

In a strange foreshadowing of his own self-destruction, Hemingway predicted, even hoped, that James Jones would kill himself. He considered World War II his exclusive literary property and bore like the Turk no rival near the throne. After his war novel *Across the River* had been savaged by the critics, he manically attacked James Jones' highly successful *From Here to Eternity* (1951). In a letter of April 12 to their mutual publisher Charles Scribner, he asked how Jones "could announce in his publicity in this year 1951 that 'he went over the hill' [and deserted] in 1944. Things will catch up with him and he will probably commit suicide. . . . All I hope is that you can make all the money in the world out of him before he takes the overdose of sleeping pills or whatever other exit he elects or is forced into. In the meantime, I wish him no luck at all and hope he goes out and hangs himself as soon as plausible." Irwin Shaw, who knew both writers, noted that "Jones grappled with the ghost of Hemingway all his life, excoriating him, mocking him, worried about what Hemingway meant to him"—unable to equal or even approach his achievement.

By contrast, two old friends remembered him fondly, as he'd remembered Jules Pascin. John Dos Passos, who'd quarreled bitterly with Hemingway about politics during the Spanish Civil War, wrote to their mutual friend Sara Murphy: "Until I read of his poor death I didn't realize how fond I'd been of the old Monster. In Madrid I found myself in places I'd been with him." The Russian writer Ilya Ehrenburg, a rare survivor of Stalin's Purges, had also known Hemingway in Spain. He recalled that "Hemingway's death meant the loss not only of a writer whom I love, but also of a man whose friendship I was proud. In my memory he lives on as a tall sturdy man with a sad expression and a vague smile."

In his excellent memoir *Dangerous Friends* (1992), Hemingway's comrade Peter Viertel recalled his response to the news and doubts about the accident. He connected it to the death of Hemingway's father and the radical deterioration of his health. He then quoted two matadors who shared Hemingway's code:

> I've just heard that Hemingway had been killed in a hunting accident in Ketchum, Idaho. I was stunned. . . . Knowing how careful Hemingway had always been with weapons, I still refused to believe the news. . . . His death had been confirmed and it was believed he had committed suicide. It seemed incredible, and yet he had spoken so often of his father's suicide that the fact that he had chosen the same fate had a frightening logic. . . . He had been unable to write or read. The shock treatments he had been submitted to at the Mayo Clinic to cure him of his deep depressions had left him a shadow of his former self.

The matadors agreed about his suicide. The old Juan Belmonte said "*He hecho bien, Don Ernesto*—Ernest did the right thing." The young Antonio Ordóñez, whom Hemingway had praised in *The Dangerous Summer*, thought "It's better for him, even if it's bad for us." The matadors, whose profession was suicidal, saw the positive aspects of his suicide. They believed he had the courage to overcome the fear of death and choose when to die instead of passively accepting his mental and physical collapse.

The poet Anne Sexton, who killed herself by carbon monoxide in 1974, and Martha Gellhorn, Hemingway's third wife, who killed herself with cyanide in 1998, agreed with the matadors. Sexton observed: "Hemingway did the right thing. . . . To shoot himself with a gun in the mouth is the greatest act of courage I can think of. I worry about the minutes before you die, that fear of death. I don't have it with the sleeping pills, but with a gun there'd be a minute when you'd know a terrible fear. I'd do anything to escape that fear; death would be a friend, then." Gellhorn stated that Hemingway was "not murdering himself with hate, but simply leaving while there was time, from the empty ruins of life, because he knew—and I think rightly—that he had finished, and that what remained was going to be bleak and belittling."

John Steinbeck, Hemingway's old rival, also doubted that his death was accidental, and related it to the dominant idea in his work: "Although something of this sort might have been expected, I find it shocking. He had only one theme—only one. A man contends with the forces of the world, called fate, and meets them with courage. Surely a man has the right to remove his own life but you'll find no such possibility in any of H's heroes. The sad thing is that I think he would have hated accident much more than suicide." In Hemingway's story "Indian Camp," however, an Indian kills himself after witnessing the unbearable pain of his wife in childbirth.

Like James Jones and Irwin Shaw, Norman Mailer and Nelson Algren were strongly influenced by Hemingway. Mailer missed his final illuminating word and called his suicide "the most difficult death in America since Roosevelt": "Hemingway constituted the walls of the fort: Hemingway had given the power to believe you could still shout down the corridor of the hospital, live next to the breath of the beast, accept your portion of dread each day. Now the greatest living romantic was dead." Algren perceptively saw his hero as a sacrificial victim who portrayed America's tragedy in his art: "In truth, he was a broken man who had seen more loss of life than anyone should have to, and expressed in his writing, the whole buried burden of American guilt, the self-destructiveness of a people who felt their lives were being lived by somebody else."

Anthony Burgess agreed that Hemingway had inevitably become his own casualty: "He had reached a plateau of achievement and could not move. He was paralysed and might as well be dead. To impose a melodramatic end on a failed life, he had to be his own big game." In Italy, Hemingway's old friend Ezra Pound repeated the belief that the country ruined its authors, that there was something wrong with the culture as well as with the man. He'd heard about Hemingway's death but didn't know it was by suicide. When he learned the truth he became upset and lamented that America destroyed its best writers—including himself.

In a letter to me, using Hemingway's famous phrase, the Catholic novelist J. F. Powers noted the decline of his literary work and related his death to his lack of religious belief: "My feeling is that his built-in shit detector wasn't working too well at times, certainly not toward the end; actually, long before that, maybe even from the start. Still, he was great in his way. My dislike was and is mostly of his philosophy, and that is what makes his end so sad, as it failed him as it naturally would, as it's failed everybody who ever held it."

Like Powers, in his little-known "An Elegy for Ernest Hemingway" the Trappist monk Thomas Merton contrasts the spiritual element to Hemingway's "brave illusion." Merton uses Latin phrases translated as "you won't die in darkness" and "for the dead." He alludes to Hemingway's works: *For Whom the Bell Tolls* (which now tolls for him), *The Sun Also Rises* and—with "far country" and "forgotten war"—"In Another Country": "In the fall the war was always there but we did not go to it anymore." As Hemingway becomes his own prey, a single shot leads the adventurer to a quick death. Though suicide is a mortal sin, nuns in convents and monks in monasteries pray for his salvation and hope for mercy.

> Now for the first time on the night of your death
> your name is mentioned in convents, *ne cadas in*
> *obscurum.*
>
> Now with a true bell your story becomes final. Now
> men in monasteries, men of requiems, familiar with
> the dead, include you in their offices.
>
> You stand anonymous among thousands, waiting in
> the dark at great stations on the edge of countries
> known to prayer alone, where fires are not merciless,
> we hope, and not without end.
>
> You pass through our midst. Your books and
> writing have not been consulted. Our prayers are
> *pro defuncto.*
>
> Yet some look up, as though among a crowd of prisoners
> or displaced persons, they recognized a friend
> once known in a far country. For these the sun also
> rose after a forgotten war upon an idiom you made
> great. They have not forgotten you. In their silence
> you are still famous, no ritual shade.

How slowly this bell tolls in a monastery tower for a
whole age, and for the quick death of an unready
dynasty, and for that brave illusion: the adventurous self!

For with one shot the whole hunt is ended!

Robert Frost had helped Hemingway oppose Pound's execution for treasonous wartime broadcasts on fascist radio, and in 1958 had cooperated with Hemingway in securing Pound's release from his insane asylum. Thinking of his own son Carol who'd killed himself, Frost intuitively knew Hemingway's death was not an accident and understood the dark impulses that had driven him to suicide. He felt sympathy for Hemingway and insisted that he had shown great courage by killing himself when he'd lost the ability to write. In the *New York Times* he praised his strength of character and his pure style: "He was rough and unsparing with himself. Fortunately for us, he gave himself time to make his greatness. His style dominated our story-telling long and short. I remember the fascination that made me want to read aloud 'The Killers' to everybody that came along. He was a friend I shall miss. The country is in mourning. A brave man has gone where we all must go."

Both André Malraux and Cyril Connolly thought Hemingway was destined to die violently. Malraux alluded to Agnes von Kurowsky, Hemingway's nurse in the Milan hospital in 1918, and to Adriana Ivancich, the Venetian heroine of *Across the River*: "Hemingway, throughout the curve which begins with the young man in love with an older woman, then with a younger one and ends—after God knows how many [fictional] instances of impotence and suicide—with the sixty-year-old colonel in love with a young girl, never ceased to foreshadow his own fate." The English critic Cyril Connolly wrote admiringly in the London *Sunday Times*: "By the death of Ernest Hemingway we have lost a Titan: whatever judgment we make upon his books the man was of the stature of a great novelist. . . . He must have had from boyhood a preoccupation with death and violence, an imagination drawn irresistibly towards the macabre—a common attribute of genius" since the Romantic era.

Two of Hemingway's most distinguished contemporaries took a negative view of his suicide. Edmund Wilson had been the first important critic to praise his early work. In his diary *The Sixties* Wilson wrote: "The death of Hemingway upset me very much. Absurd and insufferable though he often was, he was one of the foundation stones of my generation, and to have him commit suicide is to have a prop knocked out. I have now been told that his mind had been going and that he had had shock treatments in Rochester; I hear reports that he was quite demoralized and could sometimes hardly talk intelligently. But at the time I was depressed by the notion that, after encouraging writers 'to last and get their work done,' he should have died in such a panicky and undignified way as by blowing his head off with a shotgun. The desperation in his stories had always been real: his most convincing characters are always just a few jumps ahead of death."

William Faulkner, critical and quite upset, considered it unmanly. His biographer wrote, "he knew that Hemingway was ill, but also felt that beneath the Hemingway persona there was another being who was neither tough nor virile. He suspected it was suicide, and felt Hemingway had constructed a fierce male exterior to shield him from whatever he was." His illness and suicide were all linked to fears in Faulkner himself. The death of a figure like Hemingway, two years younger, when they had been bracketed for years, was deeply disturbing.

Other authors took his death personally and even feared for their own lives. As his own writing became more and more difficult, Graham Greene noted, "There were moments when I realized perfectly why Hemingway shot himself." Christopher Isherwood, an English writer living in America, wrote in his diary: "Hemingway is dead; he probably did it deliberately, suddenly sick of it all, including his legend! No wonder. I understand senile dementia now." John O'Hara's biographer recorded his self-reflective response: "O'Hara was deeply affected by the death of Hemingway. After fetching a photograph showing the two of them together, he sat down and wept. He was depressed by Hemingway's suicide because he 'understood it so well.' He had noted a deterioration in Hemingway and was distressed by his 'petulant arrogance' and his allowing himself to be familiar with his inferiors. Hemingway had everything O'Hara yearned for, including the Nobel Prize, but watching his last years, he could see the terrible destructiveness which he knew so well in himself."

In Archibald MacLeish's elegy, published in the *Atlantic* (November 1961), the past is like a film reel winding in reverse. He alludes to Anton Chekhov's famous statement that if a gun is mentioned in the first act of a play it must go off in the last. MacLeish names three locales where Hemingway hunted, fished and lived. The Closerie (Lilac Garden) was a favorite café in Paris. The flash of life led to the flash of death, and his violent end was fatally predetermined.

HEMINGWAY

In some inexplicable way an accident.
—Mary Hemingway

Oh, not inexplicable. Death explains,
that kind of death: rewinds remembrance
backward like a film track till the laughing man
among the lilacs, peeling the green stem,
waits for the gunshot where the play began;

rewinds those Africas and Idahos and Spains
to find the table at the Closerie des Lilas,
sticky with syrup, where the flash of joy
flamed into blackness like that flash of steel.

The gun between the teeth explains.
The shattered mouth foretells the singing boy.

John Berryman had the most personal and agonizing reaction. Also dying by suicide, like Sexton and Gellhorn, he jumped off a bridge in Minneapolis in 1972 and landed on the rocks. He had wept like O'Hara when he heard the news and exclaimed: "Hemingway's defection bothered me; I cried; I didn't blame him—it's his own business—but I felt bad." His biographer wrote: "Although no one yet knew the manner of Hemingway's death, Berryman told a friend, 'The poor son-of-a-bitch blew his fucking head off.'"

In his elegy on Hemingway, "Dream Song 235," Berryman, another suicidal son of a suicidal father, identified with the dead man and took him as the model of the self-destructive artist. Berryman damned his father for leaving his son the fatal legacy of a disastrous youth and tragic death. He pleaded with his dead father not to pull the trigger of his gun, which would kill his love as well as himself and condemn his son to lifelong suffering:

Tears Henry shed for poor old Hemingway
Hemingway in despair, Hemingway at the end,
the end of Hemingway,
tears in a diningroom in Indiana
and that was years ago, before his marriage say,
God to him no worse luck send.

Save us from shotguns & fathers' suicides.
It all depends on who you're the father *of*
if you want to kill yourself—
a bad example, murder of oneself,
the final death, in a paroxysm, of love
for which good mercy hides? . . .

Mercy! my father; do not pull the trigger
or all my life I'll suffer from your anger
killing what you began.

As Auden observed in his elegy on Yeats: "By mourning tongues / The death of the poet was kept from his poems." Hemingway's suicide left a great emptiness that no one else could fill. The obituaries confirmed that his work lived on and, like an extinct star, continued to radiate light long after his death.

FORTY-THREE

ACHIEVEMENT

Hemingway died by his own hand on July 2, 1961. His fame rests on his evocative stories crafted in spare prose, his tragic romances of love and death, his vivid war reporting and his travel books. He was an uneven author, but wrote at least one great work in every decade of his career. His description of the Greek refugees retreating after a Turkish victory—"Minarets stuck up in the rain out of Adrianople across the mud flats"—appeared in his first and best book of stories, *In Our Time*. The novelist Ford Madox Ford praised the perfection of Hemingway's pure, skeptical and stoical style by observing, "his pages have the effect of a brook-bottom into which you look down through the flowing water."

The Sun Also Rises, published during the repressive Prohibition era in America, portrayed the self-destructive life of American expatriates in France and Spain, personified by Jake Barnes, rendered impotent by a war wound. Jake's hopeless love for Brett Ashley, a promiscuous and exciting English aristocrat, provides the core of the novel. But his tragedy is assuaged by the beauty of the natural landscape, which "abideth forever," and by the hope of a new and more promising generation.

A Farewell to Arms develops the brilliant opening sentence of "In Another Country" (1927): "In the fall the war was always there, but we did not go to it any more." Hemingway portrays his bitter disillusionment in the wound of Frederic Henry, the retreat from Caporetto, the arduous escape by rowboat into Switzerland and the death of Catherine Barkley in childbirth.

Hemingway's swaggering public image first appeared in two minor works: his Bible of bullfighting, *Death in the Afternoon*, and account of his first safari,

Green Hills of Africa. The former describes the deadly Spanish drama that combines pagan ritual, skillful technique and high courage. The latter conveys the excitement of closing in on dangerous animals in their natural setting, but patronizes the Africans and glorifies his own exploits. When Hemingway writes in the first person, he tends to become foolish and ponderous. *To Have and Have Not*, a weak but socially committed novel set in Key West and Cuba, was made into a good Howard Hawks film, with Bogart and Bacall. Hemingway redeemed the 1930s with two superb African stories: "The Short Happy Life of Francis Macomber," about corruption, self-betrayal and guilt, and "The Snows of Kilimanjaro" (both 1936), with poignant flashbacks that mix memory and desire.

The ambitious *For Whom the Bell Tolls*, which continues the love and war themes of *A Farewell to Arms*, is the best political novel by an American writer. In contrast to the gentle Maria, raped by the fascists, the earthy, sharp-tongued Pilar is a gypsy, sexual expert and powerful woman who dominates the guerrilla fighters. Hemingway's sympathy for Brett and Pilar, as well as for the young woman who refuses to have an abortion in "Hills Like White Elephants" (1927), refutes the fatuous criticism that he was unable to create credible female characters.

Hemingway's weaker novels are more autobiographically revealing than his best fiction. He was a battle correspondent in World War II, and published *Across the River* in 1950. A sad and rather interesting failure, it opens with a fine duck-hunting scene in the Venetian lagoons. But it descends into uneventful talks between an embittered American army colonel and his young Italian lover—a fictional compensation for Hemingway's inability to get her real-life counterpart into bed. *The Old Man and the Sea* was his most popular and most overrated novel. Serialized in *Life* magazine, this deliberately ironic and mock-serious fable—with simple-minded dialogue and painfully obvious Christian symbolism—expressed his contempt for the reading public, the critics and religion.

After two near-fatal African plane crashes in January 1954—which enabled him to read his own obituaries—Hemingway continued to drink heavily, though his damaged internal organs could no longer tolerate alcohol. Despite severe depression, exacerbated by shock treatments at the Mayo Clinic, he completed *A Moveable Feast*. This comic masterpiece satirized his old friends and enemies—Ford Madox Ford, Gertrude Stein, Wyndham Lewis, John Dos

Passos and even Scott Fitzgerald—and proved that he was still at the height of his powers.

His other posthumous books—not good enough, he thought, to be published in his lifetime—were often revealing, but added nothing to his literary reputation. *Islands in the Stream* described his relations with his three sons, especially with the troubled Gregory who, after four marriages and many children, had a sex change operation and died in jail. *The Dangerous Summer* describes the rivalry of the two greatest contemporary bullfighters—Luis-Miguel Dominguín and Antonio Ordóñez—focusing on their nerves, courage and grace when pitted against "a half ton of charging animal with a deadly weapon on each side of its head." *The Garden of Eden* (1986), about his marriage to Pauline Pfeiffer, limply dramatizes adultery, lesbianism and madness among idle Americans in the South of France. *True at First Light* (1999) familiarly reprises his second safari with his fourth wife in 1954.

Most modern American writers, from Frank Norris to Thomas Wolfe, are now mostly forgotten and little read. Hemingway, along with Fitzgerald and Faulkner, provides the gold standard for the twentieth century. His literary virtues are intense curiosity, passion for learning and mastery, and willingness to test himself under violent conditions.

BIBLIOGRAPHY

Asbury, Herbert. *The Gangs of Chicago*. NY: Thunder's Mouth Press, 2002.

Babel, Isaac. *Collected Stories*. Trans. Peter Constantine. NY: Norton, 2002.

Berryman, John. *The Dream Songs*. NY: Farrar, Straus and Giroux, 1969.

———. *Selected Letters*. Cambridge, MA: Harvard UP, 2020.

Butler, Samuel. *Life and Habit*. London: Fifield, 1878.

———. *The Way of All Flesh*. Oxford: Oxford UP, 1993.

Camus, Albert. *The Myth of Sisyphus*. Trans. Justin O'Brien. NY: Vintage, 1959.

———. *The Stranger*. Trans. Stuart Gilbert. NY: Vintage, 1954.

Caulaincourt, Armand de. *With Napoleon in Russia*. Trans. George Libaire. NY: Morrow, 1935.

Conrad, Joseph. *Lord Jim*. NY: Modern Library, 1921.

Danchev, Alex. *Cézanne: A Life*. NY: Pantheon, 2012.

Davies, Norman. *God's Playground: A History of Poland*. 2 vols. NY: Columbia UP, 1982.

Diliberto, Gioia. *Hadley*. NY: Ticknor & Fields, 1992.

Donaldson, Scott. *Archibald MacLeish*. Boston: Houghton Mifflin, 1992.

Dostoyevsky, Fyodor. *The Brothers Karamazov*. Trans. Constance Garnett. NY: Modern Library, 1943.

Espmark, Kjell. *The Nobel Prize in Literature*. Trans. Robin Macpherson. Boston: G. K. Hall, 1991.

Faas, Ekbert. *Ted Hughes: The Unaccommodated Universe*. Santa Barbara: Black Sparrow, 1980.

FBI file on Hemingway.

Fenton, Charles. *The Apprenticeship of Ernest Hemingway*. NY: Farrar, Straus and Cudahy, 1954.

Fitzgerald, F. Scott. *The Great Gatsby*. NY: Scribner's, 1925.

——. *This Side of Paradise*. NY: Scribner's, 1920.

Ford, Ford Madox. *Joseph Conrad: A Personal Remembrance*. London: Duckworth, 1924.

Fraser, Ronald. *Napoleon's Cursed War*. NY: Verso, 2008.

Fry, Roger. *Cézanne: A Study of His Development*. NY: Macmillan, 1952.

Gellhorn, Martha. *The Weather in Africa*. NY: Dodd, Mead, 1978.

Gilot, Françoise and Carlton Lake. *Life with Picasso*. NY: McGraw-Hill, 1964.

Góngora, Luis de. *Selected Poems*. Trans. John Dent-Young. Chicago: University of Chicago Press, 2007.

Haacke, Wilmont. *Alfred Flechtheim: Sammler, Kunsthändler, Verleger*. Düsseldorf: Kunstmuseum, 1987.

Hamilton, Ian. *In Search of Salinger*. NY: Vintage, 1989.

Hemingway, Ernest. *Across the River and into the Trees*. NY: Scribner's, 1950.

——. *By-Line: Ernest Hemingway*. NY: Scribner's, 1967.

——. *Collected Short Stories*. NY: Scribner's, 1938.

——. *The Dangerous Summer*. NY: Scribner's, 1985.

——. *Dateline: Toronto*. NY: Scribner's, 1985.

——. *Death in the Afternoon*. NY: Scribner's, 1932.

——. *88 Poems*. NY: Harcourt, Brace and Jovanovich, 1979.

——. *A Farewell to Arms*. NY: Scribner's, 1929.

——. *The Fifth Column*. NY: Scribner's, 1938.

——. *For Whom the Bell Tolls*. NY: Scribner's, 1940.

——. *The Garden of Eden*. NY: Scribner's, 1986.

——. *Green Hills of Africa*. NY: Scribner's, 1935.

——. *Islands in the Stream*. NY: Scribner's, 1970.

——. *Letters, 1904–1931*. Vols. 1–4. Cambridge, England: Cambridge UP, 2011–2018.

——. *Men at War*. NY: Crown, 1942.

——. *Men Without Women*. NY: Scribner's, 1927.

——. *A Moveable Feast*. NY: Scribner's, 1964.

——. *Selected Letters, 1917–1961*. NY: Scribner's, 1981.

——. *The Spanish Earth*. Cleveland: Savage, 1938.

——. *The Sun Also Rises*. NY: Scribner's, 1926.

——. *Three Stories and Ten Poems*. Paris: Contact, 1923.

——. *To Have and Have Not*. NY: Scribner's, 1937.

——. *The Torrents of Spring*. London: Penguin, 1966.

——. *True at First Light*. NY: Scribner's, 1999.

Hemingway, Mary. *How It Was*. NY: Knopf, 1976.

Houghton, Walter. *The Victorian Frame of Mind*. New Haven: Yale UP, 1957.

Huntford, Roland. *Nansen*. London: Duckworth, 1997.

Huxley, Aldous. "Foreheads Villainous Low." *Music at Night*. London: Chatto & Windus, 1931.

Kert, Bernice. *The Hemingway Women*. NY: Norton, 1983.

Lawrence, D. H. *Lady Chatterley's Lover*. NY: Signet, 1959.

——. *Phoenix*. London: Heinemann, 1936.

Lewis, Wyndham. *Men Without Art*. London: Cassell, 1934.

Lowell, Robert. *Collected Poems*. NY: Farrar, Straus and Giroux, 2003.

Mailer, Norman. *The Deer Park*. London: Corgi, 1962.

Malraux, André. *Antimemoirs*. Trans. Terence Kilmartin. Holt, Rinehart & Winston, 1968.

——. *Man's Hope*. Trans. Stuart Gilbert. NY: Random House, 1938.

——. *The Royal Way*. Trans. Stuart Gilbert. NY: Random House, 1935.

——. *The Walnut Trees of Altenburg*. Trans. A. W. Fielding. London: John Lehmann, 1952.

Matthews, Herbert. *The Yoke and the Arrows*. NY: Braziller, 1957.

McCormick, Donald. *One Man's Wars: The Story of Charles Sweeny*. London: Barker, 1972.

Merton, Thomas. "An Elegy for Ernest Hemingway." *Commonweal* (September 22, 1961).

Meyers, Jeffrey. *Hemingway: A Biography*. NY: Harper & Row, 1985.

——. *Hemingway: The Critical Heritage*. London: Routledge & Kegan Paul, 1982.

——. *John Huston: Courage and Art*. NY: Crown, 2011.

——. *Privileged Moments*. Madison: University of Wisconsin Press, 2000.

O'Connor, Frank. *The Lonely Voice*. Cleveland: World, 1965.

Orwell, George. "Shooting an Elephant." *A Collection of Essays*. NY: Anchor, 1954.

Richardson, John. *The Sorcerer's Apprentice*. NY: Knopf, 1996.

Rilke, Rainer Maria. *Letters on Cézanne*. Trans. Joel Agee. NY: Fromm, 1985.

Roberts, Charley, and Charles Hess. *Charles Sweeny, the Man Who Inspired Hemingway*. Jefferson, NC: McFarland, 2017.

Rollyson, Carl. *Nothing Ever Happens to the Brave: The Story of Martha Gellhorn*. NY: St. Martin's 1990.

Schapiro, Meyer. *Van Gogh*. NY: Abrams, 1983.

Sinclair, Upton. *The Jungle*. NY: Doubleday, 1906.
Slawenski, Kenneth. *J.D. Salinger*. NY: Random House, 2010.
Stanton, Edward. *Hemingway and Spain*. Seattle: University of Washington Press, 1989.
Stein, Gertrude. *The Autobiography of Alice B. Toklas*. NY: Modern Library, 1980.
——. *Lectures in America*. Boston: Beacon, 1957.
Stendhal. *The Charterhouse of Parma*. Trans. C. K. Scott-Moncrieff. NY: Doubleday, 1956.
Stevens, Wallace. *Collected Poems*. NY: Vintage, 1982.
Swedish Academy. "Report on the Nobel Prize," 1954.
Sweeny, Charles. *Moment of Truth: A Realistic Examination of the War Situation*. NY: Scribner's, 1943.
Toklas, Alice B. *Staying on Alone: Letters*. NY: Liveright, 1973.
Tolstoy, Leo. *War and Peace*. Trans. Constance Garnett. NY: Norton, 1966.
Van Gogh, Vincent. *Letters*. Ed. Mark Roskill. London: Fontana, 1972.
——. *Letters*. Ed. Ronald de Leeuw. London: Penguin, 1996.
Viertel, Peter. *White Hunter, Black Heart*. London: W. H. Allen, 1954.
Watts, Emily. *Ernest Hemingway and the Arts*. Urbana: University of Illinois Press, 1971.
Wilson, Edmund. *The Sixties*. NY: Farrar, Straus and Giroux, 1993.
——. *The Wound and the Bow*. Boston: Houghton Mifflin, 1941.
Woodhouse, C. M. *Modern Greece*. London: Faber, 1986.
Young, Philip. *Ernest Hemingway: A Reconsideration*. NY: Harcourt, Brace & World, 1953.

INDEX